Get the eBook FREE!

(PDF, ePub, Kindle, and liveBook all included)

We believe that once you buy a book from us, you should be able to read it in any format we have available. To get electronic versions of this book at no additional cost to you, purchase and then register this book at the Manning website.

Go to https://www.manning.com/freebook and follow the instructions to complete your pBook registration.

That's it!
Thanks from Manning!

T0100142

Architecture Modernization

Architecture Modernization

SOCIO-TECHNICAL ALIGNMENT OF SOFTWARE, STRATEGY, AND STRUCTURE

NICK TUNE
JEAN-GEORGES PERRIN
Forewords by MATTHEW SKELTON and XIN YAO

MANNING
SHELTER ISLAND

Manning Publications Co.
20 Baldwin Road
PO Box 761
Shelter Island, NY 11964

Development editor:	Doug Rudder
Technical editor:	Kamil Nicieja
Review editor:	Aleksandar Dragosavljević
Production editor:	Keri Hales
Copy editor:	Kristen Bettcher
Proofreader:	Jason Everett
Typesetter and cover designer:	Marija Tudor

ISBN 9781633438156
Printed in the United States of America

To Carole, Michel, Françoise,
Alain, and Delphine Reichenbach

brief contents

contents

forewords

Architecture serves a purpose. In the 1990s and early 2000s, the architecture of business and IT systems typically helped to automate previously paper-based processes. However, with the coming of automation and cloud technologies in 2008 and beyond, the architecture of organizations and software systems is now free to serve the needs of the user or customer through value streams. To achieve this, we need architecture modernization for fast flow.

In this book, Nick Tune brings together a vital collection of techniques and approaches that help to shape software and organizational architecture for fast flow. Informed by approaches including Team Topologies, domain-driven design (DDD), data mesh, and Wardley Mapping, Nick shows how to plan, start, and evolve a journey of architecture modernization using a good mix of concepts and practical techniques.

I particularly like the emphasis on the need to build capabilities to change architecture continuously: "Everything evolves," says Nick in chapter 5, and "Prepare for constant evolution" in chapter 9. This perspective is crucial for any organization working with any kind of software-enriched services today. Core Domain Charts (see chapter 10) are essential to designing for constant evolution, so it's good to see a comprehensive treatment of this topic in the book. (Nick was instrumental in devising and shaping the techniques around Core Domain Charts.)

The book includes a substantial discussion of how to think about teams and team boundaries, drawing on the books *Team Topologies* (IT Revolution Press, 2019) and *Dynamic Reteaming* (O'Reilly Media, 2020). The language and patterns from *Team Topologies* (TT) are now widespread as the go-to approach for organizing for fast flow. Nick connects the TT ideas well to the challenge of architecture modernization. I was pleased to see an explanation of independent service heuristics (ISH), a technique I developed and evolved with my coauthor Manuel Pais and the wider practitioner community. I use it in almost every customer engagement these days. ISH is proving particularly effective for bringing together people from across the organization to discuss and shape team and system boundaries for fast flow, a key aspect of architecture modernization.

Having had the good fortune to work directly with Nick on several customer engagements worldwide, I know from direct experience that the patterns and approaches in *Architecture Modernization* work well and lead to meaningful outcomes for organizations. I have seen the results firsthand! I highly recommend this book as a source of inspiration and guidance for modernizing your architecture for fast flow. I look forward to using this book to guide my customers on their architecture modernization journeys.

—MATTHEW SKELTON, COAUTHOR OF
TEAM TOPOLOGIES AND FOUNDER AT CONFLUX

When I first became an architect, software architecture was proudly practiced in a "big design upfront" fashion for creating new code from a clean slate—architecture as a blueprint was carried over as a metaphor from the building industry. Fast forward 15 years and older software is eating our new world. Humanity's well-being hinges on a web of interconnected software in banking, commerce, traffic control, food production and energy distribution, smartphones, homes, hospitals, and even our bodies.

Software of age not only needs to fight entropy accumulated over time but also needs to adapt to constant changes. In recent years, evolutionary architecture has gained much praise as an agile way to react to changes in requirements and technology. Hence, a book about architecture modernization may trigger the old fear of all that scrap and rework in a re-architecture event.

As software-intensive organizations mature in their business growth cycle, they inevitably face a rising level of socio-technical complexity. The technical complexity around existing and new software is compounded by the social complexity around teams working with other teams and the value exchange between the organization and its environment. Software decisions, product decisions, and business decisions are interconnected—it is hard to bring all players onto the same page and even harder to let people influence and negotiate decisions.

This book is groundbreaking. It brings us to the next leading edge of the architecture discipline. In the new socio-technical reality, we need to transition from thinking in conventional software and enterprise architecture to thinking in socio-technical architecture, bringing software, product, strategy, organization dynamics, and way of working in deep alignment. It is no mean feat, but it is necessary and can be done.

As my career evolved from being a software architect to a socio-technical architect, I've felt the need to renew the architecture drill in a deep and visceral way when facilitating complex change efforts in large organizations. The first step in making this transition is to upgrade our thinking tools to the multidisciplinary language of architecture modernization, which is well-articulated in this book.

As a writer, Nick Tune has a rare gift of making extremely complex topics digestible and immediately actionable in real-life contexts where the rubber meets the road. This book connects the many dots of domain-driven design, Team Topologies, DevOps, product development, strategy, architecture, and leadership. The dots are connected into an exceptionally coherent yet practically applicable synthesis of visual models, thinking and communication tools, and collaborative design methods.

The book pools insights from Nick's many blogs and conference talks into a readily usable companion for modernization journeys, full of accessible and communicable decision models. It is a hands-on guide to initiate, survive, and thrive in large-scale socio-technical transformation programs.

What makes this book truly remarkable is not just its ingenuity in meshing together methods and models as intellectual artifacts. It is also a treasure trove of numerous field experiences and captivating case studies. Nick has interviewed a large group of socio-technical leaders, architects, and designers. From these conversations, Nick distilled a vast amount of practical perspectives and tips about collective discovery, visual modeling, facilitating deep conversations, and delivering tangible value in modernization endeavors.

As a socio-technical architecture practitioner, Nick excels at walking the walk. Many of the experience reports shared in this book are based on Nick's consulting work for an extensive client base worldwide.

Using the advice from this book, your modernization investments will not be a one-off re-architecture event. You will activate the energy from within your product and engineering teams to jointly affect the problem and solution space. Engineers and designers can grow to become strategists, cocreating the future with formal leaders. The collaborative design, modeling, and strategizing skills are your insurance for sustaining the momentum in a continual process of experimentation and learning. In the long run, this is the true competitive advantage that helps companies seize the next opportunity for change, modernization, or renewal. This book will teach you how to do that or take your skills to the next level.

Happy modernizing!

—XIN YAO, INDEPENDENT DOMAIN-DRIVEN DESIGN
CONSULTANT AND SOCIO-TECHNICAL ARCHITECT

preface

Suddenly, we could no longer leave our homes or spend time with our loved ones. We were unable to meet up with friends, and cities became ghost towns as we could no longer work in person in our offices. It was beyond belief when, in 2020, just as the new decade was being ushered in, the COVID-19 pandemic burst out of nowhere and rewrote the script. As a consultant who traveled regularly to work with clients and attend industry events, the idea of being home 24/7 was a shock. It also presented me with a serious question: What will I do with all of my free time?

I was fortunate to continue working remotely even during the strictest lockdowns. There were some books that I wanted to catch up on, and I finally got to spend some quality time with my Playstation and my cherished Gran Turismo. Even so, I still had a lot of free time in the evenings and weekends that would normally be occupied with work-related travel and networking. So, I began to think about writing a book.

I had already coauthored a book with Scott Millett called *Patterns, Principles, and Practices of Domain-Driven Design* (Wrox, 2015). It was a great experience, and I always dreamed of writing another book. But I only wanted to write a book when I had built up enough knowledge and experience to write a book worth writing. I didn't want to write a book just for the vanity of saying I wrote a book. It had to be something that would be valuable to others.

In 2020, I didn't quite feel like I was at that point. However, I could see that many organizations still treated modernization as a technical exercise, lacking the domain, organizational, and strategic perspectives needed to exploit the full potential of modernization that some organizations were achieving. So, I decided to start writing a book on Leanpub as an experiment to see what I could put together, where the gaps were, and if I was the person who could write this book.

Over the next two years, I continued to iterate on the content, regularly making wholesale changes. Having a work in progress allowed me to incorporate all the new things I was learning from every client engagement. Gradually, I felt like the book was growing into a piece of work that did fit my original criteria of being valuable to others, especially as I began working with industry practitioners to include case studies that added a whole new depth to the book that my personal experiences alone could never reach.

In 2022, one thing that still stood out as missing was data mesh. This was becoming a topic that many organizations embarking on architecture modernization journeys wanted to hear about. I sought an expert on the topic to write a chapter about this innovation. Fatefully, renowned data mesh industry expert Jean-Georges Perrin agreed to write the chapter. In addition, he also posed a question: Why don't you contact Manning and publish the book with them? And here we are. Over the past 12 months working with Manning, I have heavily revised and improved every chapter of the book with the help of many people. It's a huge leap in quality from the Leanpub version.

Writing this book over the last three years has been an extremely valuable experience. But what matters to me more is that I hope my ultimate goal has been achieved—that this book is valuable to you.

acknowledgments

Firstly, I would like to acknowledge the huge contribution of Jean-Georges Perrin for not only writing the data mesh chapter (chapter 14), but also for being the person whose idea made this book possible. In addition, I would like to acknowledge the crucial support and feedback from the hundreds of Leanpub readers since the book's inception in mid-2020. Your support showed me that the topic is important and that I should continue working on the project.

Acknowledging all the people (and their organizations) who contributed industry examples is essential. Your experiences make the book far more valuable, and it was such a great time putting together the examples with you. Here is the list in the order that the examples appear in the book: Kacper Gunia, Orlando Perri, Xin Yao, Katy Armstrong, Dean Wanless, Javiera Laso, Ornela Vasiliauskaite, Maxime Sanglan-Charlier, Kenny Baas-Schwegler, Shannon Fuit, Chris van der Meer, Chris O'Dell, Antoine Craske, João Rosa, Scott Millett, David Gebhardt, Christoph Springer, Krisztina Hirth, Damian Bursztyn, Andrea Magnorsky, and Timber Kerkvliet. Thank you all.

At Manning, I'd like to thank Doug Rudder, the book's development editor, who played a big role in bringing this book to its current standard. We met for an hour every week, during which his feedback and support were crucial in improving every chapter. In addition, thanks to all the members of the production staff for their hard work in creating this book.

The contribution of all the people who provided feedback on the book is important to acknowledge. It had a huge effect on the content and quality of the book. From the reviewers at Manning to all the people I reached out to directly for feedback and help, thanks to Alessandro Campeis, Alex Saez, Andrew Taylor, Arjan van Eersel, Arun Saha, Bill Delong, Bruce Bergman, Christopher Forbes, Daut Morina, Dave Corun,

David Goldfarb, Devon Burriss, Enrico Mazzarella, Ernesto Cárdenas Cangahuala, Ganesh Swaminathan, Gilberto Taccari, Gregorio Piccoli, Harinath Kuntamukkala, Harinath Mallepally, Ian Lovell, Ivo Štimac, Jackson Murtha, James Liu, James Watson, Jonathan Blair, Juan Luis Barreda, Kevin Pelgrims, Lakshminarayanan AS, Leonardo Anastasia, Massimo Siani, Matteo Rossi, Maxime Boillot, Michal Těhník, Michele Adduci, Mladen Knežić, Mohammed Fazalullah Qudrath, Neeraj Gupta, Neil Croll, Nicolas Modrzyk, Peter Henstock, Peter Mahon, Pierre-Luc Gagné, Polina Kesel, Ramaa Vissa, Ramnath Nair, Roberto Lentini, Roger Meli, Shawn Lam, Simeon Leyzerzon, Stephan Pirnbaum, Sune Lomholt, Sushil Singh, Swaminathan Subramanian, Tibor Claassen, Tiziano Bezzi, Torje Lucian, Vojta Tuma, Warren Myers, and Yannick Martel.

about this book

Who should read this book

This book is written primarily for technology leaders responsible for overseeing modernization, people with job titles like CTO, VP engineering, and head of architecture. Much of the book's content is also relevant to technologists who play a more hands-on leadership role, people with job titles like principal engineer, staff engineer, and architect. Many parts of the book are relevant to people who work closely with technology and architecture, even if they aren't directly involved in architecture design and writing code, people with job titles like the head of product, product manager, service designer, and UX designer. Because this book doesn't contain any code or guidance on specific technologies, this book is not aimed at software engineers looking for lots of code samples and in-depth guidance on refactoring legacy software.

How this book is organized: A road map

This book is organized into 17 chapters, each addressing a particular aspect of modernization. Most chapters contain a mix of theoretical concepts, practical techniques, and real-world industry examples. The book has been structured so that the chapters can be read sequentially. It follows a narrative of identifying the reasons for modernization, designing a modernized architecture, and carrying out modernization. However, the lines between topics are fuzzy, and not all chapters fit neatly into this simplified narrative.

- *Chapter 1: What is architecture modernization?*—This chapter introduces the key concepts of modernization covered in the remaining chapters of the book.
- *Chapter 2: Preparing for the journey*—This chapter raises important topics and common challenges that should be considered before embarking on an architecture modernization journey.

- *Chapter 3: Business objectives*—This chapter looks at the type of business benefits architecture modernization can bring and how to identify product north stars to clarify your organization's strategic ambitions.
- *Chapter 4: Listening and mapping tours*—This chapter explains how to start your architecture modernization journey by meeting with people from across the organization to uncover their most important challenges and opportunities so that you can then determine how modernization can best help.
- *Chapter 5: Wardley Mapping*—This chapter introduces the strategy mapping technique Wardley Mapping, which can be used to visualize your organization's business landscape/industry and explore how it will evolve, giving you a deeper understanding of which capabilities will be most crucial to invest in.
- *Chapter 6: Product taxonomy*—This chapter covers the topic of creating building blocks to design your architecture using the example of a product taxonomy, which is a product-centric approach to defining business and technology architecture.
- *Chapter 7: Big picture EventStorming*—This chapter introduces the big picture EventStorming technique, a highly collaborative workshop format for mapping out business domains and a good starting point for identifying domain boundaries.
- *Chapter 8: Product and domain modernization*—This chapter looks at how to avoid the problem of treating modernization as a project to rebuild the old system with new technologies by showing how modernization should also be treated as an opportunity to improve the user experience, remove long-standing pain points, improve workflows, and develop new capabilities.
- *Chapter 9: Identifying domains and subdomains*—This chapter shows how to organize your business into domains and subdomains, which become the foundation for your modernized software architecture and organizational structure.
- *Chapter 10: Strategic IT portfolio*—This chapter introduces principles, tools, and patterns for mapping your architecture as a portfolio to determine the optimal level of investment in each area based on business value and complexity.
- *Chapter 11: Team Topologies*—This chapter covers the organizational aspects of architecture using principles and patterns from Team Topologies to help identify, validate, and refine your value streams.
- *Chapter 12: Loosely coupled software architecture*—This chapter covers principles and techniques for designing a loosely coupled, domain-aligned software architecture and migrating from a current to a target state for each subsystem.
- *Chapter 13: Internal developer platforms*—This chapter looks at the intricate relationships between architecture and the platforms they run on, focusing on designing platforms that provide a great developer experience so that the architecture can evolve more rapidly and reliably.
- *Chapter 14: Data mesh revolutionizing data engineering (written by Jean-Georges Perrin)*—In this chapter, you will learn how the need for data mesh came to

fruition, its four fundamental principles, and how they depend on one another. You will also learn about the tools needed to architect your own data mesh.

- *Chapter 15: Architecture modernization enabling teams*—This chapter introduces the AMET, a type of team that guides and supports modernization to maintain momentum throughout the journey without becoming a centralized team that makes all the decisions.
- *Chapter 16: Strategy and road maps*—This chapter looks at how to build a compelling narrative and sequence modernization work into a roadmap, focusing on continuous evolution and delivering value early and often rather than big upfront design and planning.
- *Chapter 17: Learning and upskilling*—The book's final chapter focuses on the crucial topic of growing talent and architecture capabilities within the organization to ensure the new architecture takes full advantage of modern thinking and approaches.

How to read this book

It is not strictly necessary to read the chapters in order. Many chapters contain standalone concepts and techniques, along with references to other chapters where concepts are related or have previously been introduced.

liveBook discussion forum

Purchase of *Architecture Modernization* includes free access to liveBook, Manning's online reading platform. Using liveBook's exclusive discussion features, you can attach comments to the book globally or to specific sections or paragraphs. It's a snap to make notes for yourself, ask and answer technical questions, and receive help from the author and other users. To access the forum, go to https://livebook.manning.com/book/architecture-modernization/discussion. You can also learn more about Manning's forums and the rules of conduct at https://livebook.manning.com/discussion.

Manning's commitment to our readers is to provide a venue where a meaningful dialogue between individual readers and between readers and the authors can take place. It is not a commitment to any specific amount of participation on the part of the author, whose contribution to the forum remains voluntary (and unpaid). We suggest you try asking the authors some challenging questions lest their interest stray! The forum and the archives of previous discussions will be accessible from the publisher's website as long as the book is in print.

about the authors

NICK TUNE is a principal consultant who helps organizations modernize their architectures and ways of working toward empowered product teams and continuous delivery. He works with clients in various sectors like travel, finance, e-commerce, and government. He is always trying to find the optimal balance of facilitator, coach, and consultant on every project.

JEAN-GEORGES "JGP" PERRIN is a technology consultant focusing on building innovative and modern data platforms, president of AIDA User Group, and author of *Spark in Action, 2nd edition* (Manning, 2020). He is passionate about software engineering and all things data. His latest endeavors bring him to more and more data engineering, data governance, industrialization of data science, and his favorite theme, data mesh. He is proud to have been recognized as a Lifetime IBM Champion. Jean-Georges shares over 25 years of experience in the IT industry as a presenter and participant at conferences and publishing articles in print and online media. Visit his blog at http://jgp.ai. He enjoys exploring upstate New York and New England with his wife and kids when not immersed in IT, which he loves.

about the cover illustration

The lady on the front cover is wearing a 19th-century costume from the Swiss region of Valais/Wallis. The image is taken from a collection of 19th-century drawings housed in the Mary Evans Picture Library.

In those days, it was easy to identify where people lived and what their trade or station in life was just by their dress. Manning celebrates the inventiveness and initiative of the computer business with book covers based on the rich diversity of regional culture centuries ago, brought back to life by pictures from collections such as this one.

What is architecture modernization?

Antiquated legacy architectures are a business risk and a competitive disadvantage. They are difficult and slow to change, more expensive to maintain, and prone to unreliability, handing the advantage to your competitors. Southwest Airlines demonstrated this during its 2022 scheduling crisis caused by a decades-old scheduling system. In one week, 14,500 flights were canceled, and its brand suffered stinging damage as it became a top international news headline for all the wrong reasons.

In contrast, carefully designed modern architecture is a powerful competitive advantage. Cazoo, a UK-based startup, built an online car dealership in just 90 days and became the UK's fastest-ever unicorn. A key factor in Cazoo's ability to innovate at speed was having no legacy to constrain them. As a result, it was able to use technologies like Serverless, which provided higher levels of productivity with leading-edge capabilities like elastic scalability as standard.

Even architectures that are well cared for will degrade over time due to various factors like changes in the business strategy, old features that are no longer used, quick fixes and hacks that were never cleaned up, and outdated technologies. So it may seem inevitable that as companies age, they inexorably regress from fast-moving startups to rigid old enterprises, weighed down by their legacy architecture. But companies like Netflix have proved that it is possible to reverse the trend and be an established market leader that innovates at speed.

In 2009, Netflix transitioned from a monolithic architecture to hundreds of cloud-based microservices to protect and grow its advantage in the online streaming market. Adrian Cockroft, Netflix CTO at the time, explains why: "There is an existential threat . . . . If you're doing quarterly releases and your competitor is doing daily releases and continuous delivery, you're going to fall so far behind in the user experience you're just going to suffer" (https://soundcloud.com/a16z/microservices).

Every leader should always be asking themselves questions like Netflix did: Are we at risk of falling behind the competition? Could we keep up if a fast-moving startup entered our market? Would our brand reputation be enough to retain market share against a superior product and, if so, for how long? Are mission-critical parts of our business held together by dated systems that could result in serious revenue loss or reputational damage?

Many organizations have successfully modernized, as Netflix did, converting their architectures from a liability into a competitive advantage. This book is a guide for business, technology, and product leaders who would like similar successes in their organizations. However, modernization isn't free. It means investing time and finances that would otherwise be spent on improving the product. Because of these short-term compromises, many leaders are reluctant, so work continues in the legacy systems. But as figure 1.1 shows, this creates a negative cycle in which system health

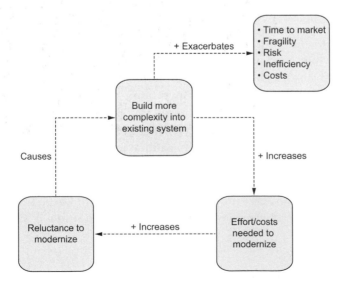

Figure 1.1   The negative cycle of declining architecture health

gets worse, the cost of modernization increases, and leaders become even more reluctant to invest in modernization.

Research by Adam Tornhill and Markus Borg shines a light on what happens when this cycle continues unchecked. In their paper "Code Red: The Business Impact of Code Quality—A Quantitative Study of 39 Proprietary Production Codebases," they found that up to 42% of developers' time may be wasted because of the levels of technical debt in a system (https://arxiv.org/abs/2203.04374v1).

With systems growing evermore complex as more of the world runs on software, the disadvantages of dated architecture and the advantages of modern architecture are likely to be magnified. The growing complexity of modern systems has many factors, such as increasing integration, data volumes, and user expectations. One indicator of the continued growth in complexity is the number of connected Internet of Things (IoT) devices, which is expected to rise from 8.6 billion in 2019 to almost 30 billion in 2030 (http://mng.bz/lWd8) (figure 1.2). Are you ready to break the negative cycle and convert your architecture from a liability into a competitive advantage?

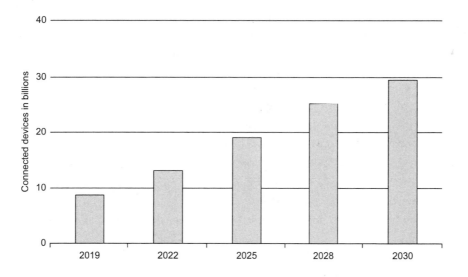

Figure 1.2 Increasing numbers of IoT devices is one indicator of architectures growing evermore complex. (Source: Statista)

NOTE This first chapter outlines the key aspects of an architecture modernization journey and how they fit together, which should help you understand what this book is about. Each topic is covered in greater detail in subsequent chapters, along with practical techniques and real industry examples from my career and experts who have contributed their stories to the book.

1.1 Architecture is more than technologies and patterns

On the surface, architecture modernization may seem like a purely technical endeavor. Take Netflix's transition to microservices, for example. Microservice architecture is commonly perceived as a pattern for designing software systems, often associated with an ecosystem of tooling to make building, deploying, and operating microservices easier.

But look closer and you'll see that microservices is a socio-technical architecture pattern. Their benefits are just as much organizational as technical. Sam Newman, author of *Building Microservices* (O'Reilly Media, 2021), explains this unequivocally: "The third reason [to adopt microservices] is really where you're looking to enable a higher degree of organizational autonomy. You're looking to push and distribute responsibility into teams; you want those teams to be able to make decisions, roll out software, and reduce the amount of coordination those teams need with other parts of your organization" (http://mng.bz/BmP8).

> **NOTE** Although this chapter uses the example of Netflix and its modernization journey, which involved microservices, this book does not promote microservices as the only valid architectural style, and the ideas in this book are not limited to microservices-based modernization initiatives.

To truly exploit the potential of modern architecture, leaders must look beyond technologies and patterns and view architecture more holistically. This begins by understanding the factors that enable a modern organization to be high performing and how architecture contributes. Jonathan Smart's *Better Value Sooner Safer Happier* (figure 1.3) provides the perfect model for thinking about the value modernization can bring. It's a model of five principal outcomes that contribute to organizational performance and long-term prosperity:

- *Better* represents improvements in quality that lead to improved efficiency and less time wasted on rework.
- *Value* represents business outcomes like improving revenue or customer retention.
- *Sooner* represents sooner time to learning and hence value, enabling genuine agility.

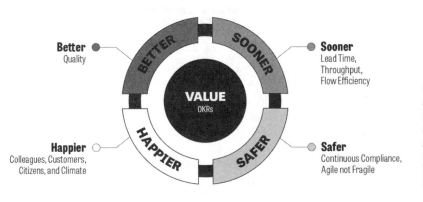

Figure 1.3   Better Value Sooner Safer Happier. (Source: Smart et al., *Sooner Safer Happier: Antipatterns and Patterns for Business Agility* [Portland, OR: IT Revolution 2020])

- *Safer* represents factors like governance, risk, security, and compliance.
- *Happier* represents an improvement to the lives of people involved, like making employees happier at work.

Better Value Sooner Safer Happier (BVSSH) is a model that we can employ at all times. For every decision we contemplate, we can ask how it affects each element of BVSSH. This encourages us to balance all stakeholders' needs, giving us a greater chance of getting their buy-in and support. Now that we have a model for describing the different outcomes that need to be optimized and balanced to build high-performing organizations, we can explore how architecture modernization can contribute to each outcome.

1.2 Independent value streams: The building blocks of modern architecture

To truly exploit the potential of architecture and maximize the return on your modernization investments, it is necessary to design architecture using building blocks optimized for BVSSH. This begins by understanding value streams.

A *value stream* is a sequence of activities that leads to the creation of new value. In a software development context, that means the sequence of activities a team performs, from discovering user needs and wants to building new features in software and then delivering them to users. Figure 1.4 shows a high-level overview of a software development value stream (a more detailed version would show more granular activities like starting a piece of work, reviewing code, and deploying to various environments).

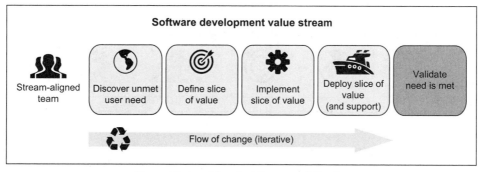

The goal is to achieve fast flow, e.g, delivering
small slices of value/learning every day.

Figure 1.4 A high-level overview of a value stream

NOTE Figure 1.4 doesn't convey all of the nuances of modern product development approaches. Product experts such as Melissa Perri, Marty Cagan, Teresa Torres, and Jon Cutler are advocates of approaches that fall under the umbrella of continuous discovery and delivery or dual-track agile. Architecture modernization is a good time to adopt modern product approaches.

This is touched on in chapter 8, along with my own experiences. If you're looking for a deep dive, check out the books and content of the previously mentioned product experts.

An *independent value stream* (IVS) is a value stream with the following key characteristics (also illustrated in figure 1.5):

- *Domain aligned*—It is set up to create value in a particular business subdomain (a specific area of the business low enough in complexity to be owned by a single team; e.g., pricing, ordering, search).
- *Outcome oriented*—The success of the value stream is determined by its contribution to business outcomes and product north stars (key metrics), such as revenue and engagement, rather than delivering predefined requirements (aka the *feature factory* antipattern).
- *Team empowered*—Each IVS is owned by a single team that has the autonomy to make product and technology decisions, deploy changes, and define their development processes.
- *Software decoupled*—The software for each IVS can be developed and deployed independently.

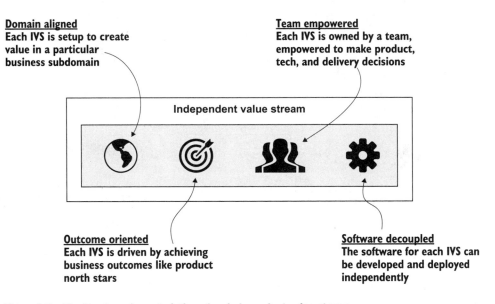

Figure 1.5   The four key characteristics of an independent value stream

NOTE   The concept of a value stream has existed for decades and has been adapted to various contexts during that period. In this book, *value stream* always refers to a software development value stream. The team that owns a value stream is known as a stream-aligned team (terminology taken from Team Topologies, which is covered in chapter 11).

The IVS characteristics are important because they enable BVSSH. Well-shaped domain boundaries reduce coupling in the business by grouping related domain concepts that change together when new product features are being developed. As a result, fewer dependencies exist in the software and between teams, meaning new product enhancements are delivered sooner due to fewer blockers and lower coordination.

An outcome-driven approach leads to better value in the form of better product and feature ideas. Rather than treating teams as feature factories (feeding them pre-defined solutions), giving them outcomes to achieve and the freedom to discover solutions in their subdomains unlocks more of their creative talents. As renowned product management expert and author Marty Cagan says, "If you're just using your engineers to code, you're only getting about half their value. . . . The best single source for innovation is your engineers" (www.svpg.com/the-most-important-thing/).

Better quality is achieved because teams are aligned to a domain and responsible for the software. Teams know that they will be responsible for any choices they make, so they will naturally want to keep their code healthy, evolvable, and easier to support in production. Similarly, safety is improved because teams can think about security rather than just focusing on delivering a fixed scope by a specific date. Both of these factors contribute to more reliable systems that are less likely to result in catastrophic brand damage.

In combination, the previously mentioned characteristics and benefits contribute to happier team members who are more motivated at work. Being accountable for business outcomes within a specific subdomain provides a strong sense of purpose and autonomy. Fewer dependencies further improve a team's autonomy while reducing the frustrations caused by dependencies such as being blocked. Ownership of technical artifacts and development processes enables teams to continuously improve how they work, creating the conditions for mastery. Working in a team where you are delivering value every day is an excellent feeling.

> **NOTE** Remember that this is an overview chapter, briefly introducing the fundamental topics of modernization and how they fit together. The remaining chapters discuss each concept in greater detail—supported by practical techniques, such as EventStorming and Wardley Mapping, and real industry examples.

1.2.1 Minimizing change coupling with well-defined domain boundaries

It must be stressed that even when teams own the software and are empowered to deploy to production multiple times per day, a value stream still may not be sufficiently independent. There may still be a high level of *change coupling*, where changes in one value stream require corresponding changes in others. For example, developing a new product feature requires three teams to each implement a part of the functionality, as shown in figure 1.6

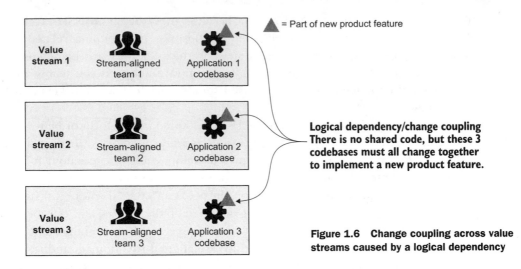

Figure 1.6   Change coupling across value streams caused by a logical dependency

Change coupling is problematic because it requires the teams responsible for each value stream to coordinate their work. Coordination is undesirable because it's easy for delays of days or weeks to occur due to shared rituals such as planning, having conflicting priorities among teams, needing to integrate and test various components, and a host of other reasons. This is why tools like CodeScene that visualize change coupling are becoming essential, especially for architecture modernization.

Well-defined domain boundaries are one of the crucial measures in minimizing change coupling. They should be defined carefully and not on a whim. Event-Storming is a great starting point for identifying loosely coupled domain boundaries. It's a collaborative technique that involves mapping out steps in business processes and journeys along a timeline. As shown in figure 1.7, different parts of the timeline can be grouped into domains and subdomains.

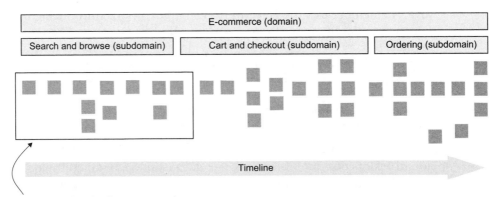

Figure 1.7   Using EventStorming to collaboratively identify domains and subdomains

Because of the involvement of a diverse group of participants—domain experts, software developers, product managers, UX specialists, and potentially anyone interested—the insights gained during EventStorming lead to higher-quality domain boundaries (as well as many other benefits that you'll see later in the book).

Collaborative techniques like EventStorming also surface another essential part of modernization: adopting modern practices. To unlock the full potential of modern architecture, a co-creation approach is necessary, bringing together people from various disciplines to codesign and coevolve the architecture. This is a monumental departure from traditional approaches that involved a centralized team of architects handing over designs to teams.

> **NOTE** Throughout the book, you'll see several examples of how organizations in different industries defined some of their domains and subdomains.

Although domain boundaries are vital to achieving truly independent value streams, they are only one part of the puzzle. This book provides a holistic approach, validating that domain boundaries are optimal from business, organizational, and technology perspectives before modernizing. Figure 1.8 provides an overview of the approach covered throughout the book.

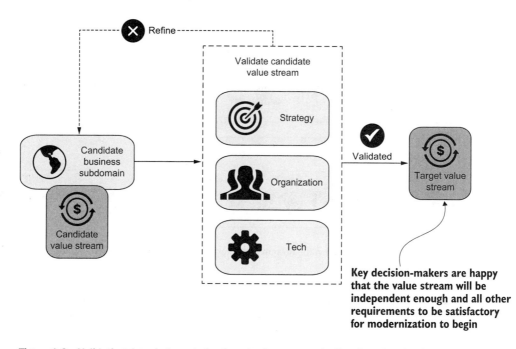

Figure 1.8   Validating domain boundaries from business, organizational, and technology aspects

> **NOTE** Internal developer platforms (IDPs) are another crucial component to achieving IVSs. IDPs reduce the friction of building, deploying, and

supporting code by providing an exceptional *developer experience* (DX) through the use of concepts like paved roads/golden paths. This allows stream-aligned teams to focus on business outcomes without being bogged down by extraneous infrastructure-related activities and development friction. IDPs are covered in chapter 13.

1.2.2 *Architecting at multiple scopes for global optimization*

IVSs are a foundational building block, but independent doesn't mean completely isolated. Well-designed IVSs reduce as much unnecessary coupling as possible, but some level of dependency among value streams will always exist. Many products are too large for a single team to build, requiring multiple teams to work together, each delivering a piece of the puzzle.

Focusing only on individual value streams can easily result in local optimizations, whereas effective modernization is about optimizing BVSSH globally. Therefore, it's better to think of organizations as networks of interconnected value streams. Teams owning related subdomains contributing toward shared business outcomes will need to collaborate. Understanding the domain relationships is crucial so that teams can be grouped into domain-aligned organizational units based on the cohesion of their subdomains, as the example in figure 1.9 shows.

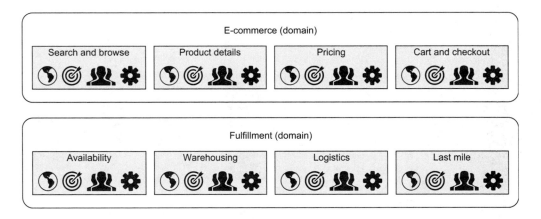

Figure 1.9   Grouping related value streams into domains based on the cohesion of their subdomains

As the complexity of an architecture increases, more layers tend to emerge. In larger organizations with thousands of employees, even higher-level domains come into play. It is, therefore, critical to have a deep awareness of architectural scopes when modernizing, especially as systems continue to grow in complexity.

Every modernization decision will need to be set at the most effective scope. For example, at what scope does a technology decision apply? Should every team get to choose its programming language, or should groups of teams working in the same domain be expected to use the same programming language? Or should it perhaps be an enterprise-wide decision?

Another common and often controversial example is reuse. For example, should each team decide if they want to use an internally developed shared service (like a notifications service), or is that a decision made at a level above, scoped across many teams?

This book provides a range of principles and practical techniques for designing architecture and making decisions at different scopes. However, one of the most critical factors is understanding what we are optimizing for—and that is ultimately a business decision. By using techniques like Wardley Mapping and Core Domain Charts, we can gain the strategic clarity and alignment we need to make informed architectural decisions that deliver maximum business impact.

1.3 Modernization as a portfolio-driven evolutionary journey

For many organizations, moving from aging to modernized architecture will take multiple years. No quick fix exists for systems that have declined over the course of years or decades. But this doesn't mean that it should take years for the modernization to start delivering value. Rather than treating modernization as a project where a full target-state architecture is defined upfront, an evolutionary approach is better. Value can start being delivered in the first three to six months, and continuous feedback will be harvested to continuously improve the architecture and roadmap.

An evolutionary approach works best with a portfolio mindset. Modernization isn't just rewriting the old system with new technologies. It's an opportunity to completely rethink the UX, product functionality, business processes, and domain model and remove unneeded complexity. But this level of effort won't be necessary in every subdomain. In fact, it will lead to much higher costs and delay delivery of the highest-value modernization opportunities.

This book shows how to use tools like the Modernization Strategy Selector, shown in figure 1.10, to identify the optimal modernization investment in each subdomain and the most effective sequencing of priorities. You'll learn all about this in chapter 12.

For organizations with a deeply ingrained traditional mindset, a fundamental hurdle that prevents an evolutionary mindset is a project-like mindset where modernization is seen as a sequence of phases: discover what is possible, design the target state, and then spend multiple years following a rigid plan to transition from the current to the target state.

Discovering opportunities, designing architecture, and delivering modernization are key aspects of modernization. But they are parallel streams of work rather than discrete phases. As figure 1.11 highlights, work can be ongoing in the different streams in parallel. Some parts of the architecture can be modernized before discovery and design have even begun in others.

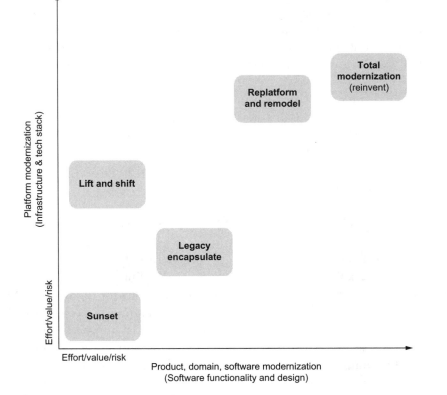

Figure 1.10   Identifying the optimal modernization return on investment per subdomain with the Modernization Strategy Selector

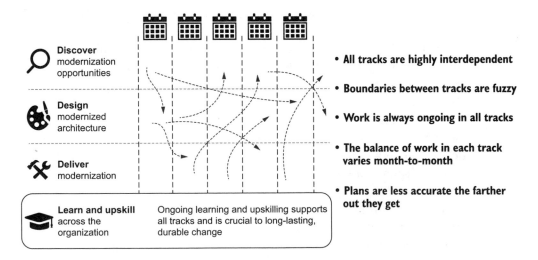

Figure 1.11   Architecture modernization is parallel streams of work (not phases) supported by continuous learning and upskilling.

The parallel ongoing work in each stream is the enabler of an evolutionary approach. Activity in each stream continuously influences the others: discovery in one quarter may influence what gets delivered in the next quarter; delivering a piece of modernization may surface unexpected consequences that feed back into the design of subsequent work; and so on.

The importance of ongoing learning and upskilling cannot be overstated. It is perhaps the most important part of architecture modernization. Figure 1.11 symbolizes how it is the foundation for modernization. If teams don't have the time and opportunity to learn and practice modern concepts, there is a serious risk that new architecture will be designed with the old ways of thinking, and many of its flaws will be carried across.

Another common challenge is modernization running out of steam or even struggling to get started. In chapter 15, you'll see how an architecture modernization enabling team (AMET) can be formed to address this problem and keep modernization momentum high. AMETs are not like traditional architecture teams that make decisions; they are facilitating teams that support other teams and focus on establishing sustainable improvements that continue even after modernization is over.

1.4 Topics not covered in this book

This book does not contain any technology-specific or vendor-specific concepts like how to implement a microservice in Java using AWS Lambda or how to build an IDP using Kubernetes and containers on Google Cloud Platform. Although technology choices and implementation details are important parts of modernization, it's best to consult books that provide in-depth coverage of your preferred technologies. All of the concepts in this book are technology agnostic.

This book is not tied to any specific business/enterprise/software architecture metamodels, proprietary frameworks, bodies of knowledge, or certifications. This book is a toolkit of principles and techniques that can be combined according to your organization's needs and are all free to use. Although this book does use some specific terminology like value streams and subdomains, you are not obliged to adopt them to get value from the book. You are welcome to translate between the terminology used in this book and the terminology used in your organization.

Summary

- Architecture modernization is about converting dated architecture, which is a business liability, into modern architecture that provides a competitive advantage.
- Modernization requires short-term compromises for long-term prosperity, which is why leaders are reluctant to commit, but this creates a negative spiral where the architecture becomes even more of a liability.
- As more of the world is run by software, systems will become more complex, and architecture will become even more important.

- Modern architecture is more than just technology and patterns; it is socio-technical architecture.
- Better Value Sooner Safer Happier (BVSSH) is a guide for understanding the value architecture can provide in modern high-performing organizations.
- Independent value streams are the building blocks of modern architecture; they connect business, domain, organizational, and technology concerns to enable BVSSH.
- Well-defined domain boundaries are crucial in establishing truly independent value streams and avoiding high levels of change coupling and coordination.
- Modern architecture practices such as EventStorming are highly collaborative and a big departure from traditional ivory-tower architecture mindsets.
- Architecture is multiple scopes depending on the size of the organization.
- Architectural scopes are used to design architecture at different levels of abstraction and identify the scope of architectural decisions.
- Modernization is an evolutionary journey driven by portfolio thinking; it's not about designing a target architecture upfront and following a rigid plan.

Preparing for the journey

2

This chapter covers
- Gauging organizational readiness
- Establishing a holistic view of architecture
- Preparing for a new architecture mindset
- Avoiding modernization silver bullets
- Nurturing modernization leaders

Before starting on a journey, it's a good idea to think about some of the challenges you may face and ensure you are adequately prepared. I live in the United Kingdom, so whenever I go on a journey, I always make sure I am prepared for rain, even if the sun is shining brightly and the skies are clear blue when I leave the house. The same is true for an architecture modernization journey. If key stakeholders aren't prepared to make difficult decisions and change how they think and work and the rest of the organization isn't ready, you are destined for disappointment.

This chapter covers some of the fundamental challenges that organizations face on a modernization journey—challenges that usually require a change in mindset and challenges that cause difficulties or even the complete downfall of modernization initiatives if not addressed. These challenges touch on diverse areas like business, product, technology, culture, mindset, ways of working, and organizational change because modernization inherently involves all these topics.

Every organization faces many obstacles and modernization challenges. It's completely normal. So you don't need a comprehensive solution to these challenges before starting the journey. But it is valuable to identify where you expect the biggest challenges to arise so you can get a head start addressing them, like identifying where new hires or external help will be needed.

Remember that few modernization problems can be solved purely with tools and techniques. Among successful leaders, one of the most distinguishing qualities I've observed is their ability to build relationships and have professional, empathetic conversations with people of all levels and disciplines.

2.1 Is leadership prepared?

If you're considering an architecture modernization journey, leadership support is crucial. The following questions are a good starting point for understanding if you are prepared to lead and how you can work with other leaders in your organization to better prepare them for the modernization journey.

2.1.1 Are business and product leaders truly ready to slow down the delivery of new features to allow modernization?

One of the most difficult challenges I've faced and observed during modernization initiatives is getting enough time to do modernization work. Despite many promises from leadership about putting business-as-usual work on hold and being serious about modernization, there are frequent exceptions and special cases that creep in and consume large amounts of time that were allotted for modernization.

I recommend that leadership teams have frank and clear conversations about the level of commitment and compromise needed. It's also important to build a compelling business case (covered in the next chapter), which articulates the benefits of architecture modernization in clear business terms so all leaders understand why they should invest and what they will get in return.

2.1.2 Do leaders understand that legacy systems and ways of working are complex and difficult to change?

There's a natural tendency to look for quick fixes. Even though legacy systems have been built up over years or decades, there is so often pressure for a quick solution. If it was that easy, the concept of legacy systems would not exist, and it wouldn't be one of the biggest problems technology companies face. The reality is that it's going to take time, usually years, to modernize technology and ways of working, so all stakeholders need to be fully aligned with realistic expectations.

2.1.3 How will leaders react when the unexpected occurs (which is inevitable) and there are major delays or increased costs?

Modernizing legacy systems and ways of working requires dealing with highly complex systems and fundamentally changing how people do their job. There is an unlimited number of technical and social things that could go wrong, and it's guaranteed that some will. A legacy system might be harder to split up than originally anticipated, or some team members might be in conflict about proposed changes. You have to be prepared for things to deviate from the optimal path, so it's good to talk with stakeholders and try to understand how they will react.

2.1.4 Are leaders ready to change how they work? Can you imagine leadership supporting changes to funding models, work prioritization, and development processes and empowering teams to make more decisions?

Modernization can touch every aspect of an organization's operating model—for instance, the funding model and the level of autonomy that teams have. These types of deep changes are difficult and require leadership to change how they work, especially in regards to giving up some of their control to allow teams to be more independent. It's a good idea to discuss these changes with key decision-makers and understand just how deeply they are prepared to change the organization.

2.1.5 Are leaders willing to invest sufficient time and funds into learning and training for all employees so that they can carry out modernization skillfully?

Modernization does not happen without learning new skills and acting differently. Leaders need to be aware that a significant investment is necessary for supporting every employee involved in modernization to ensure they have the required skills. If not, modernization may take far longer, or the new architecture may look just like the old one or even worse. Learning and upskilling (the topic of chapter 17) is not a one-time workshop or training course; it's an ongoing financial and time investment. Learning needs to be built into the organization's culture.

Learning and upskilling cannot be negated by hiring lots of people with the desired skills. Employees still need to learn the company's domain, systems, and culture, which can take months. Hiring too quickly in a short period can be detrimental to modernization.

2.1.6 Will technologists be able to articulate to business leaders and other stakeholders the business and organizational benefits of their ideas?

Sometimes the problem isn't that leaders aren't supportive; it's that they just don't understand what they are being asked to invest in and what the benefits are. "The developers all have OCD. They're always talking about technical debt and rewriting things." This quote is from a CEO I worked with. I don't agree with their opinion or tone, but the theme is a common one: when engineers aren't able to communicate the business benefits and justifications of their architectural proposals to leaders and other stakeholders, they are perceived as programmers who just want to rewrite systems and play with tech for the fun of it. Engineers should be exposed to the business domain and the business/product strategy so they can communicate the importance of their ideas in a common language to every audience.

2.2   *Prepare to embrace a new architecture mindset*

It's not just leaders who need to be engaged with a modern mindset toward architecture. It's everybody involved in building, designing, and deciding about architecture. The contrast between traditional and modern approaches is immense, but many people have been working with traditional approaches for so long that they aren't aware of modern approaches or they just aren't willing to let go of traditional approaches that they are so used to.

2.2.1   *Prepare to embrace Conway's law*

Everybody involved in architecture needs to be aware of Conway's law. Conway's law states that "organizations which design systems are constrained to produce designs which are copies of the communication structures of these organizations." In other words, the design of a system is heavily influenced by the communication patterns and organizational structure of the people that design and build it.

A range of problems can arise due to being naive or oblivious to the effects of Conway's law. Tightly coupled and overly complex software and high levels of dependencies between teams are some of the most common. To minimize the chance of these problems and other negative effects of Conway's law, it is essential to adopt a socio-technical mindset to architecture, where software architecture and organization design are jointly optimized rather than being designed in isolation by different groups of people.

Before starting on a modernization journey, ensure that the concept of Conway's law has been widely circulated throughout the organization. To make it more tangible, look for real examples inside your organization. You'll find them everywhere due to Conway's law being so pervasive. Look at the way your teams are organized and collaborate and look at the design of the architecture. For example, I worked with a client who had a very siloed organizational mentality. Teams all had their own objectives and worked independently wherever possible. As a result, changes made by one team would often cause things to break in other teams. Data was also siloed, causing frustration as people could not generate deep insights by combining all of the company's data. It also led to a fragmented user experience for internal and external users.

2.2.2   *Prepare to embrace collaborative architecture practices*

Conway's law emphasizes the importance of a socio-technical approach. Teams aligned to a loosely coupled software architecture can deliver work faster and more efficiently. But Conway's law doesn't say what teams and architecture should be aligned to. As figure 2.1 shows, loosely coupled architecture requires loosely coupled

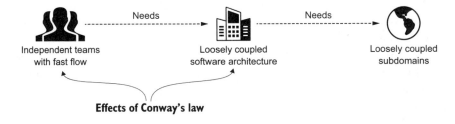

Independent teams   Loosely coupled   Loosely coupled
with fast flow   software architecture   subdomains

Effects of Conway's law

Figure 2.1   Fast flow requires loosely coupled software architecture, which requires loosely coupled domains.

domain boundaries. This means that when teams implement new features, they change concepts within a single business subdomain aligned to a single codebase. No coordination with other teams is needed.

In addition to embracing Conway's law, domain modeling needs to be embraced as a foundational concept of modern architecture. And further, the idea of collaborative approaches to domain modeling and architecture should be embraced because they lead to better designs. As mentioned in chapter 1, modern techniques like EventStorming are more collaborative and inclusive. They bring together people from all disciplines to combine domain knowledge and choose the best solutions. But I often find high levels of friction to this way of working because it is in strong contrast to traditional approaches.

The following quote from a conversation I had with a technology leader in 2023 is typical of what this mindset divergence looks like in practice:

> *We're a successful company with legacy systems that have built up over a couple of decades. Leadership has started to realize that the current architecture doesn't allow us to move fast enough and some things we'd like to do, like exposing internal data and capabilities externally, just aren't possible. But after attending this workshop and seeing techniques like EventStorming, I've realized that we're approaching modernization in completely the wrong way. Our architects, who have been here for 16 years, have gone away on their own and started by designing a monolithic database schema for the entire system.*

Later in the book, you'll see techniques and suggestions for adopting these kinds of techniques, but right now it's a good time to ask yourself how different this approach to architecture is compared to your current approach. When preparing for your architecture modernization journey, it's a good idea to start experimenting with collaborative workshops like EventStorming as soon as possible to understand how well they are received.

2.2.3 Prepare to connect architecture and strategy

"My CEO says I need to be more strategic!" This quote from a VP of engineering highlights another mindset shift needed to unlock the potential of modern architecture and approaches. It's not enough for architects and engineers to focus on the technology choices and fashionable architecture patterns; they need to be able to connect architecture modernization decisions to business outcomes and demonstrate how each decision is optimal for the desired business outcomes.

One of the best ways to achieve this is to involve everyone in strategy. Make your strategic processes more collaborative and inclusive. Chapter 5 shows how Wardley Mapping is an excellent technique for collaboratively connecting architecture and strategy. But the question to ask yourself now is, "What is the chance that business and technology experts would want to get together and explore strategy?" If strategy has traditionally been very top-down, you may want to test the waters of a collaborative approach as soon as possible by facilitating a Wardley Mapping session with a diverse group of attendees.

2.2.4   *Prepare to move beyond business and IT silos*

The traditional approach of treating business and IT as separate units rather than as integrated parts of a single organization limits innovation and hinders achieving common goals. It reduces flow due to the handovers between teams, and it also takes longer to implement features because IT people don't truly understand what they are being asked to build.

A fruitful architecture modernization journey requires seeing business and IT as two sides of the same coin. But in some organizations, this mindset can be tough to accept. IT is sometimes seen as a bunch of programmers who just take requirements and convert them into code. Adopting a modern, product-centric mindset in which teams are empowered to make product decisions and own their roadmap is a monumental shift and probably won't happen overnight.

But now is a good time to understand where you are and where you'd like to be and also to start thinking about how you can take small steps toward a more integrated operating model. One exercise I practice with organizations involves John Cutler's Journey to Product Team infographic, shown in figure 2.2. I ask everyone (including leaders and individual contributors) to place a dot where they are now and where they would like to arrive. We then discuss what is stopping them and how they can get there.

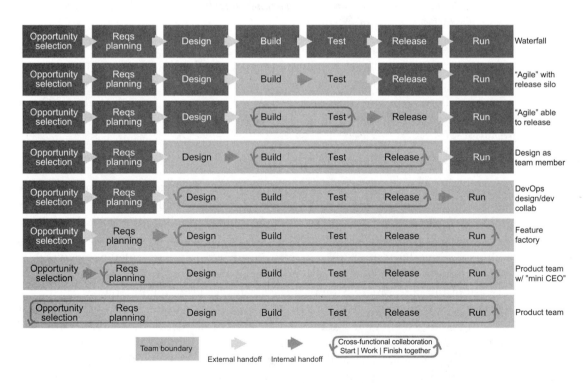

Figure 2.2   Product development approaches from waterfall to empowered product teams (Source: John Cutler, Amplitude, https://amplitude.com/blog/journey-to-product-teams-infographic)

This infographic is the perfect prop for these kinds of conversations. It gives people a model to think about the different ways of working and to put their current approach into context. Highly recommended.

2.3 Industry example: Hitting the right note—modernizing music royalty processing at ICE

> **NOTE** The following industry example was authored by Kacper Gunia, engineering manager and deputy VP of engineering at ICE (https://www.iceser vices.com/). I've known Kacper for many years; he is one of the first people I reach out to when I need advice on topics like domain-driven design (DDD) and architecture. Many of the concepts and techniques mentioned in this example are covered in subsequent chapters of the book. This example shows what is possible when organizations are willing to adopt a new architectural mindset and apply modern principles and practices. ICE Services achieved outstanding business and organizational outcomes as part of their portfolio-driven, evolutionary architecture modernization journey.

As a leading provider of copyright and royalty-processing services in the music industry, ICE (International Copyright Enterprise Services) faced obstacles with our IT systems and infrastructure. The rise of online music streaming caused a significant increase in volumes of data and resulted in slow processing speed. Additionally, our old architecture relied heavily on manual steps and actions, leading to higher complexity and a higher risk of errors. To further the problem, our method of working on new functionalities was centered on individual projects and change requests, making it hard to promote modern engineering practices and sustainable development. In light of these issues and to stay competitive in an ever-evolving industry, we initiated a modernisation effort in 2020. The goal was to enhance our IT systems' speed, accuracy, and scalability while shifting toward a product-centric approach.

In order to revamp the royalty processing IT infrastructure, we employed various strategic methods. We started by utilizing Domain-Driven Design (DDD) and Event Storming as a means of understanding our domain and its specific behaviors. During the Big Picture Event Storming sessions we focused on capturing the relationships and interactions between various stakeholders, systems and events happening in the royalty processing domain. The sessions included a broad audience to ensure a variety of perspectives and knowledge as we wanted to gain a comprehensive overview of the business domain.

Once the big picture was captured we then conducted deep dive sessions with smaller and more relevant groups of people. Each of these sessions focused on an individual subdomain which led to more in-depth discussion and brainstorming and at the end to a common understanding of the problem at hand. This approach enabled us to pinpoint the critical business events, their behaviors, and the business rules that keep the system running. With this rediscovered knowledge, we constructed a high-level process model that helped us understand the problem at hand and establish a shared language to communicate effectively with our stakeholders.

We then planned a gradual migration using the strangler pattern, which allowed us to prove the viability of this approach by prototyping on the first subdomain—Usage Ingestion. The prototype was used to demonstrate the new architecture's benefits and gain stakeholders' buy-in. We then worked on a business case that will deliver value incrementally instead of a big bang—this helped us to create a plan that would deliver value in smaller chunks that could be used to justify further funding of the ongoing migration. We started to ramp up the team and defined the product taxonomy, including domains, subdomains, and products, as well as the capabilities of these products and the teams responsible for them (see figure 2.3).

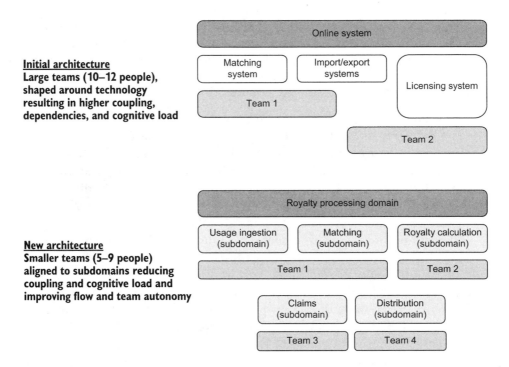

Figure 2.3   From a technology-driven organization to a domain-driven, socio-technical architecture

With the team in place, we started to implement new ways of working within the development teams. We set up continuous integration/continuous deployment and infrastructure as a code so that we could automatically build, test, and deploy code changes multiple times a day. Additionally, we started to adopt pair and mob programming, which helped to increase knowledge sharing and collaboration within the teams.

We also made sure that our development teams were working closely with the business teams and that the team members were empowered to own and understand their products. This allowed us to scale out the strategy and set up more teams and transform the organization into one that works with quarterly and yearly product roadmaps, delivering value frequently and in small increments.

The modernization effort resulted in several significant improvements. One of the most notable was a reduction in data ingestion processing time by 80%, which significantly improved the organization's ability to handle large volumes of data. Additionally, we were able to reduce the time of onboarding new service providers from months to weeks, which helped to increase the organization's agility and competitiveness. We also completely replaced and decommissioned old ingestion systems within 1.5 years, which significantly reduced the complexity of the organization's IT infrastructure.

Another key result was an improvement in the manual matching process, which allowed for more precise work prioritization and resulted in a 5x increase in productivity and increased match rates by 5 percentage points. Additionally, we introduced full audibility of the matching indexes, which helped to build trust with customers and explain why matches were made. Furthermore, the core part of the platform responsible for royalty calculation began to be modernized, which helps provide faster and more accurate royalty calculations. Overall, the modernization effort so far was a great success, as it delivered a wide range of benefits that improved the organization's performance and competitiveness.

In addition to these business aspects of the modernization effort, we also used cloud services to minimize operational overhead and optimize costs. By utilizing cloud services, we were able to take advantage of features such as autoscaling, which allowed us to dynamically allocate resources based on the current demand, thereby reducing costs and improving efficiency. Additionally, the cloud provided us with a scalable infrastructure that could easily accommodate the increased volumes of data caused by the rise of online music streaming. By employing cloud services, we were able to minimize operational overhead, optimize costs, and ensure that our IT systems and infrastructure could support our growing business needs.

The modernization provided valuable insights into the importance of understanding the domain and empowering teams to take ownership of it. By empowering the teams to understand the domain, we greatly reduced the feedback loops and improved the overall quality of the solution. Because the teams are self-organizing and cross-functional, they had full responsibility for designing, developing, testing, deploying, and running the application, which incentivized them to do the best possible job. Another key insight was the benefits of changing the funding model from project-centric to product-centric, which helped us focus on delivering value instead of creating estimates.

However, we also encountered challenges, particularly of a social nature, such as finding ways to integrate and cooperate with existing teams and making this cooperation productive. Trying to integrate product-centered teams and project-centered programs of work faces problems related to having very different feedback loops, resulting from different approaches to estimating, design, development, and testing. Based on our experience, I would recommend that organizations take care to address the social aspects of modernization efforts, as they can be just as important as the technical aspects.

Our job is far from over. While the modernization effort has been a great success, several subdomains still need to be modernized, and the effort will take another couple of years. Having a well-defined product taxonomy has been instrumental to our progress so far, and without it, we would not have been able to create autonomous teams that continuously deliver value. As we continue to modernize the organization, we plan to implement this model of aligning teams with subdomains and products across the entire organization. This will ensure that the benefits of the modernization effort are realized to their fullest and that ICE remains competitive in an ever-evolving industry.

2.4   Beware of modernization silver bullets

When leaders are told that modernization will take years, cost large sums of money, and require reduced delivery of product features in the short term, it's not the easiest thing to hear. Surely there must be a way to start innovating faster that doesn't cost as much and is less disruptive. Unfortunately, most of the time, there is no quick fix.

2.4.1   Beware of bolt-on modernization

One silver bullet–style solution I have frequently encountered is the attempt to modernize a system without addressing fundamental architectural challenges. This is what is referred to as a bolt-on, where easier parts of the system are changed to provide the appearance that a system has been modernized but is still coupled to legacy systems and databases on the inside. Effectively, it is bolted onto the legacy systems, like putting lipstick on a pig, as some say. While this approach can certainly be a valid transitional step, in many cases the fundamental legacy systems are never addressed and continue to impose stifling product and technology limitations.

When building a government service in the mid-2010s I encountered problems with bolt-on modernization firsthand. My teams were able to build new websites that provided a far better user experience than the legacy applications they were replacing, but we weren't able to provide the improvements users were asking for because we still had to integrate with legacy systems and databases that could not be changed. We couldn't add a new text box to a web page to capture information or provide additional information to users that weren't exposed by the legacy system's API.

A similar problem is when organizations believe that they can buy an off-the-shelf tool, like a rules engine, that will allow business people to rapidly make changes without needing programmers. There are many situations where rules engines and low-code solutions can be cost-effective and provide good-enough levels of quality. But buying these tools to avoid addressing technical debt is more like wishful thinking than due diligence.

When preparing for a modernization journey, it's important to understand if leaders are looking for bolt-on modernization or silver bullet tools. These signs are indicative of a more fundamental problem: leaders are looking for a quick fix and don't understand the level of investment needed to truly address some of the organization's core modernization challenges. If you suspect this is the case, then it's another situation where building relationships and having honest conversations up-front may be better than simply hoping that things will work out. It's good to have a picture of some of the most complex modernization challenges and talk through them with decision-makers so they understand the true investment that is necessary.

2.4.2 Beware of the structure and process fallacy

Some leaders hold a mechanical view of organizations. They like to use factory metaphors. This is problematic because it overlooks human factors, resulting in missed opportunities and unrealistic expectations. As a consultant, one manifestation of this mindset is when I'm asked by organizations to help them run a workshop so they can identify their optimal organization structure and then do a big reorganization that will solve all of their problems.

This antipattern is *the structure and process fallacy* (http://mng.bz/8rDW). The notion that a simple change in organizational structure or adoption of a new process (such as agile), without making deeper changes, will greatly enhance performance is misinformed. If it was that simple, every company would have already done it. Comprehensive changes like promoting teamwork, giving teams control over product decisions, breaking down business-IT barriers, altering funding models, and investing in technical quality are needed to boost development speed. While the organizational structure and development processes are crucial, these changes alone will only bring limited improvement. It's important to have these conversations early in your journey.

2.4.3 Prepare to invest in quality technical practices

Avoiding silver bullets that promote superficial changes is crucial. Instead, embracing the reality that deep changes are needed is necessary. In particular, quality technical practices keep a system healthy and prevent the need for big modernization efforts. Investing in technical practices is crucial for achieving this. Sustainable technical practices ensure that code remains well designed, easy to understand, easy to test, and therefore easy to change with lower maintenance costs over its lifetime. The start of a modernization journey is the perfect opportunity to introduce these new practices.

I've always been a fan of test-driven development (TDD) and pair/mob programming. These techniques focus on designing quality, well-tested software through studious design and continuous refactoring. These are important steps when searching for the simplest and most maintainable way to implement new functionality. From the outside, it may seem that these techniques take longer and increase costs, but when applied effectively, I've always found that they provide a great ROI in the short, medium, and especially the long term. As with most techniques, however, they can be highly divisive. Not all teams like TDD and mob programming, so find what best suits your organization. I don't advocate forcing things onto teams to which they do not consent (on the other hand, people need to try things outside their comfort zone occasionally).

If your organization lacks expertise in technical practices, addressing this problem is crucial before going too far with modernization. You don't want to start building a legacy from day one of your modernization journey. You'll need to provide training and upskilling opportunities for your teams, and you may want to bring in outside help. It's not a topic covered in this book, but if you're looking for a practical starting point, check out *Agile Technical Practices Distilled* (Packt Publishing, 2019).

2.5   *Prepare to support leaders at all levels*

Modernization is a long journey with many important decisions and challenging moments. Leadership and role models are needed at all levels, from the boardroom to the teams writing code.

Collectively, modernization leaders have many responsibilities, including

- Understanding and contributing to the business strategy
- Defining the modernization strategy
- Designing and evolving the architecture
- Setting up an organizational structure to develop the architecture
- Communicating vision and progress
- Build vs. buy vs. partner decisions
- Setting rewards and incentives that encourage the desired behaviors
- Continuing business as usual (BAU) while simultaneously delivering modernization
- Ensuring engineering teams are immersed in the business domain
- Shaping engineering culture
- Developing and managing people
- Introducing modern technical practices and coaching teams
- Continuously infusing new ways of thinking and working

With all of these responsibilities, modernization efforts cannot be led by a single superhero or even a small group of them. Before starting your modernization journey, it's a good idea to look at this list of modernization responsibilities and any others you expect to face and then identify which leaders can take on which responsibilities and whether there are gaps. In addition, you'll need to think about how these people will work together to collectively lead modernization initiatives across the business.

Depending on where your organization starts, you probably won't have all these people fully skilled from day one. That means you'll need a short-term solution and a longer-term plan for getting there. This is the purpose of the architecture modernization enabling team (AMET) covered in chapter 15.

Leaders at all levels

To get a sense of the implications of leadership at all levels, depending on the size and type of your organization, the following is a nonexhaustive list of people that may need to play a leading role in architecture modernization:

- CTO
- VP of engineering
- Director of engineering

- Chief architect
- Architect
- Principal engineer
- Staff engineer
- Engineering manager
- Platform architect
- Head of platform engineering
- Enterprise architect
- Data architect

In addition to these technology roles, it's also crucial to closely involve leaders from other disciplines, such as product, user experience (UX), customer support, finance, and marketing.

Summary

- Every organization faces a range of challenges during an architecture modernization journey; it's a good idea to identify upfront what the biggest challenges may be so you can get a head start addressing them.
- Financial commitments to modernization while putting other work on hold is a common challenge.
- Getting leadership onboard and aligned with the approach is vital.
- Modernization requires a new way of thinking about architecture that involves Conway's law, collaboration, and inclusion; it's a good idea to experiment with these approaches as soon as possible.
- Treating IT as a separate silo is a dated mindset; it's important to understand how deeply ingrained this mindset is in your organization before starting the modernization journey.
- Unfortunately, you probably won't find quick fixes to address your deep modernization needs, so beware of silver bullets like bolt-on modernization and the structure and process fallacy.
- Investing in technical practices to create deep change and avoiding rebuilding a new legacy is essential.
- Modernization requires leadership at all levels, so identify upfront how you will support leaders and where you need to bring in new faces to address skills gaps.

Business objectives

Modernization is a significant investment in systems and operating models. To get buy-in from stakeholders and maximize return on investment, you must have a solid understanding of the business outcomes you aim to achieve and clearly articulate how investing in architecture modernization will move the business toward its strategic priorities.

Identifying the optimal level of modernization is critical to avoid wasting time and money on things that don't move the business forward. It requires a view of the business and product strategy across multiple time horizons. By recognizing your growth strategy and how each product in your portfolio contributes to it, you can identify which areas of your architecture will truly benefit from modernization and how to modernize your architecture most effectively for your business needs.

To do this, you must ask: Which new capabilities need to be developed? Which parts of the system will require the most development? What is the current level of technical debt in each area of the system? Are you looking to create new products in new markets or increase market penetration by improving the quality of existing product offerings? Is it about the speed of innovation, reducing operating costs, or improving scalability to support the rapid growth of the user base? This chapter begins by looking broadly at the typical business reasons for investing in architecture modernization. Then it finishes by showing how you can identify your organization's most important business and product metrics—north stars.

3.1 Business justifications for architecture modernization

This section outlines common business scenarios where architecture modernization is beneficial. It's not an exhaustive list, so modernization may still be valuable if you find yourself in a different scenario.

Once you have identified business justifications, a good technique for quickly attaining feedback is to ask clarifying questions to different stakeholders. For example, "So it's fair to say you're not worried about losing ground to fast-moving competitors, and we should be 100% focused on reducing operating costs?" "What are the biggest threats you see from outside the organization, like faster-moving competitors or changes in consumer spending?" "How unique is our product? Do you think it could be recreated easily by other companies?"

3.1.1 Falling behind faster-moving competitors

According to Simon Wardley, "Success breeds inertia," and "Inertia increases the more successful the past model is." In essence, successful businesses lose their incentives to be innovative. At the same time, new players in the market have the opposite mindset; they have a big challenge to overcome established brands, and they need to be highly innovative and willing to take risks. In addition, new players can start from a blank canvas with the latest technologies and ways of working, while incumbents have years or decades of technology and organizational debt. These are the perfect conditions for disruption, a scenario many established businesses find themselves in as new competitors emerge in their industry or existing competitors invest in modernization and can innovate much faster.

One of the most worrying concerns for business and technology leaders is not realizing how far behind their development capabilities are until it's too late. Everybody knows stories of famous companies that were disrupted, like Blockbuster (http://mng.bz/EQMD), Netscape (https://airfocus.com/blog/why-did-netscape-fail/), and Nokia (https://www.bbc.co.uk/news/technology-23947212). Not every business realizes when it's too late. As the Netflix example in chapter 1 highlighted, some visionary leaders spot the warning signs early, giving them a greater chance of surviving and thriving.

I like to ask, "How long could you carry on without making any improvements until you are at risk from competitors?" One COO responded, "We have about 18 months until our competitors catch up and overtake us." In that situation, 18 months was a good number. It was close enough that the company was incentivized to start modernizing but far enough in the future that they had time to make sensible decisions and not rush into bad decisions. Keep in mind that the amount of time doesn't tell the full story. For example, if the organization was larger and had millions more lines of older code to modernize, 18 months may not have been comfortable.

Organizations at risk of falling behind faster-moving competitors need to make judicious modernization decisions about where to modernize. Wasting a year modernizing a legacy system that isn't going to evolve much in the future could be catastrophic.

Wardley Mapping (covered in chapter 5) focuses on the evolution of business landscapes and identifying where the future advantages will be and where there is potential for disruption to occur. It's an essential technique to employ in this scenario.

INDUSTRY EXAMPLE: FINANCIAL SERVICES MARKET LEADER LOSING GROUND

A financial services organization approached me to support the new CTO in establishing a multiyear modernization initiative. The context was fascinating and appealing. The company had been a market leader for over a decade and was always top of industry rankings, creating a mindset in the organization of optimizing for stability and security and avoiding risks. Thanks to its highly reputable brand, the company would remain the market leader as long as the system was online and customers could use it.

While the business results were good, internally, the organization was performing poorly. Factors like draconian security policies, highly restrictive development processes, little investment in addressing technical debt, and a top-down management style resulted in engineers constantly banging their heads against the wall trying to complete simple tasks. The relationship between Dev and Ops was notably bad.

Gradually, the industry started to change. Faster-moving competitors emerged with a better UX, and the client lost their place at the top of the industry rankings. Their product was falling behind, and intelligent people were frustrated and leaving. The executives knew that they could no longer avoid the warning signs. They had brought in the new CTO (along with other experienced business, product, and technology leaders), who had previously built high-performing organizations in the financial sector.

I was involved at the start, leading the first two teams designing and building modernized architecture and working in new ways. I also worked closely with operations teams to establish the development platform and architecture teams to establish the vision. I spent a lot of time evangelizing the ideas across many parts of the organization to various stakeholders and teams. It was such a completely different way of thinking that they needed time to learn, absorb, and decide if they wanted to be part of or leave the company.

Due to the competitive nature of the industry, leadership demanded to see major product improvements within six months as part of the modernization investment.

Unfortunately, with so much technology and organizational debt, it took a year to put a single line of modernized code in production, despite modernization having a high level of support from the executives, which caused a lot of stress. Teams were blaming each other for failing to deliver, even though each team was working to the best of their abilities within the constraints. The pressure caused teams to look for shortcuts and tactical solutions, such as building new applications on the old infrastructure.

If the organization had accepted it was falling behind sooner and realized the effort needed to modernize was much greater than first anticipated, it wouldn't have been in an unhealthy rush to modernize and would have been better able to deal with the many expected and unexpected challenges gradually. The next example shows what's possible when organizations spot the warning signs early and make sufficient modernization commitment and investment. Keep in mind, however, that the two companies are completely different, so this is not a direct comparison.

INDUSTRY EXAMPLE: OPENTABLE

In 2011, OpenTable was the market leader in restaurant bookings, with little competition. But things changed when competitors like Yelp entered the market. OpenTable had a lot of great ideas to maintain its market leadership, but engineering was the bottleneck. They couldn't develop product innovations as fast as their competitors. At that time, OpenTable had a monolithic, big ball of mud codebase, which all 100+ engineers were working on. Due to the high levels of coupling, making changes was slow and risky, and the chance of merge conflicts was always very high. The deployment cycle was 4 weeks and involved multiple days of manual QA testing.

> **NOTE** This industry example was coauthored with Orlando Perri, who worked at OpenTable from 2010–2015.

The team in London knew that productivity could be much higher. A decoupled, domain-aligned codebase would enable teams to work independently, and a highly automated continuous delivery infrastructure with a great developer experience would enable multiple deploys to production per day. Importantly, this would also enable them to improve product feedback cycles through A/B testing. Achieving this vision would put OpenTable well ahead of its competitors, but getting there and getting buy-in wouldn't be straightforward.

After multiple iterations of pitching a modernization vision that articulated the business benefits, the board eventually agreed to put all feature work on hold to allow a complete modernization of the existing systems. A new forward-thinking CTO joined the organization and endorsed the modernization vision, supported by hiring engineers with expertise in DevOps, continuous delivery, and domain-driven design.

This story is fairly unique because the senior leadership team agreed to stop all feature work to allow complete modernization. This decision was made because everybody wanted to ensure that modernization was completed as soon as possible and that everything got modernized with nothing left behind. One challenge with this was that the board wanted a timeline. The engineers made an educated guess at 6 months, but it took around 8 months until new product features could be added again and almost 12 to finish everything. The story ends positively, though. At the end of modernization, the vision had fully been realized. Highly autonomous teams were working independently and pushing code to production multiple times per day. OpenTable's development capabilities were a big step ahead of the competition.

Stopping all work and focusing on intensive modernization was a good decision for OpenTable. But for most organizations, this approach isn't sensible or even possible, so a more gradual approach will be necessary. Several key factors contributed to this being the right move for OpenTable—notably the quality of people they hired, the fact that stopping feature development for eight months was possible without severe business consequences, and a solid articulation of the business ROI of modernization.

3.1.2   Architecture stifling business growth

Even when new players or existing competitors pose little threat, architecture can still play a decisive role in preventing a business from maximizing its potential. Almost every company seeks growth. Sometimes slowly and gradually, sometimes in big, rapid increments. As a modernization leader, it's vital to understand your organization's growth ambitions and potential because this will help you to identify the extent that architecture is a limitation and blocker to business growth. Architecture modernization should support the company's growth ambitions, like addressing existing scaling weak points or optimizing for innovation speed in strategic domains.

There are four major growth strategies to be aware of: *market penetration*, *market development*, *product development*, and *diversification*. Any number of them could be in play across your organization at any time. Growth strategies and how they connect to modernization are addressed later in the chapter.

3.1.3   Pursuing an exit strategy

For some businesses, the key strategic objective is achieving an exit strategy, such as being acquired by another company or going public with an IPO (initial public offering). In early 2022, for example, the CEO of one of my clients explained to my team that his objective was to make the company attractive to buyers and be acquired within three years. When we discussed architecture modernization, he was only interested in discussing initiatives that would deliver a significant business value within that time frame. Any modernization that did not deliver short- to medium-term benefits would not be considered. The tech leads and engineers found this to be the case when the company wouldn't commit more time and resources to break apart the giant legacy database coupled with most parts of the system.

Ultimately, the owners of the company were seeking an exit. Therefore, limiting modernization to a three-year time horizon was their decision. But it's worth remembering that modernized architecture may help the organization look more attractive to investors and achieve its exit strategy. One architect involved in many M&A activities warned: "I can promise that a good architect will look at the prospect's code, architecture, design docs, test processes, etc. If you are aiming for an exit, you can't just present a pretty face and hope they won't notice. Anyone doing a good job at due diligence will toss out a company that is all shill and shell. An exit strategy needs to be *more* architected and modern than most."

Focusing on a two-to-three-year horizon may benefit companies not pursuing an exit strategy. It can help to focus on initiatives that will deliver an effect in the shorter term. It shouldn't take three years for modernization to deliver benefits. The key for most companies, however, is developing a portfolio of short, medium, and long-term modernization initiatives that deliver value regularly—and also putting in place a plan for addressing the highly complex fundamental architecture challenges that will take years to address fully. Common examples are giant monolithic databases and archaic COBOL systems.

As the CEO demonstrated, when an exit strategy is a goal, business leaders focus on making the company look as attractive as possible to potential buyers. Typically, this involves optimizing certain business and accounting metrics like gross margin, revenue growth, or net income (aka the bottom line). In some industries, leaders seek to optimize their EBITDA (earnings before interest, taxes, depreciation, and amortization) to make their business look efficient—an accounting metric that highlights the profitability of an organization and is often used to compare companies against each other. For companies seeking to entice investors, this is sometimes the key metric. However, it is important to understand that EBITDA, like any metric, doesn't tell the full story and can be misleading.

Understanding company performance beyond EBITDA is valuable for modernization leaders. Not only will you be able to prioritize modernization initiatives better, but you'll also be able to speak the language of the business better and improve your credibility. A good starting point is the book *Financial Intelligence* (http://mng.bz/N2lx).

3.1.4 Growth by acquisition

Mergers and acquisitions (M&A) are key for some businesses. They can help with all growth strategies, like acquiring existing competitors to increase market penetration and acquiring businesses in different markets to support a diversification strategy. A recent example is Salesforce's acquisition of Slack for a reported $27 billion (http://mng.bz/D4Xg) in 2021. Salesforce believes that acquiring Slack will allow it to offer a more complete package in the new era of remote working. Another example is Microsoft's acquisition of GitHub for $7 billion in 2018, which helped it develop innovations like GitHub Copilot, an AI-powered programming assistant.

Working as a principal engineer at Salesforce, I first understood the architecture modernization challenges inside a large organization with a big appetite for M&A. On the outside, customers just expected Salesforce's large portfolio of products to fit together seamlessly. On the inside, this was also the ambition of business and product leaders, but the picture was much different technology-wise. Each acquisition added even more sprawl to the technology landscape. They were legacy monoliths built in different eras and cultures, with different technology stacks running on different infrastructure stacks, all bought together under the roof of one company and expected to fit together.

As the company kicked off initiatives to create a more joined-up user experience by integrating systems, there were initiatives like a single, centralized identity solution. But with so many diverse teams and needs to consider, these initiatives moved very slowly. Some other challenges I noticed were teams losing their place in the bigger picture, silo boundaries forming, fragmented user experience, duplication of capabilities, lack of alignment on domain boundaries, and conflict over technology and infrastructure choices.

Not all companies with an M&A strategy will operate at the scale of Salesforce, but some or all of these challenges are likely to apply to some degree. As a result, a fundamental rethink of products, domains, software, and teams may be required to identify the optimal post-acquisition architecture.

> **NOTE**   For an excellent industry example that touches on the themes in this section, check out Ora Egozi Barzilai's talk from MuCon 2019 (http://mng.bz/lW6R). She recounts her experiences leading multiple iterations of architecture modernization at Taboola in 2016 following a key acquisition.

If your organization is actively seeking growth by acquisition, but the current architecture is not conducive to integrating the technologies of acquired companies, a crucial part of your modernization strategy will be outlining these challenges and justifying how modernization will accelerate the onboarding and ability to employ acquired systems.

3.1.5   *Poor UX holding the company back*

For some products, the UX can make or break the whole business model. And when the UX is lacking, a website redesign may not be sufficient to address the problem. Deeper architectural modernization may be necessary.

One way that architecture can be a fundamental factor in poor UX is through unreliability. My friend Dan Young had an unfortunate experience with this. In the autumn of 2021, he tried to hire a rental car but unintentionally hired three due to poor UX caused by architectural problems. The website told him to retry his payment because the backend returned an error, even though the backend had successfully created the booking. Initially, the company only offered to refund one of the bookings, causing much-unneeded stress for Dan. This interaction completely ruined any trust he had in the brand.

During the modernization of a system I worked on, a major user pain point was the inability to enter enough information about their case, resulting in additional hassles like phone calls and letters, which frustrated them. Unfortunately, the character limit was enforced by the XML schema, the database, and an intermediate database—all part of a fragile legacy system. So what appeared to be a simple UX problem couldn't be resolved due to architectural complexity multiple layers deep.

Leaders unfamiliar with technology constraints sometimes assume that UX problems can be fixed with a website redesign without understanding that deeper modernization is required. So it's important to help all stakeholders understand the deeper causes of UX problems and the limitations of not addressing those deeper causes. It's not just a new lick of paint.

3.1.6 Inefficient internal tooling and processes

The user experience of internal-facing products can be just as problematic, or even more so, for some organizations than the external-facing products. There seems to be a prevalent mindset that the user experience of tools used by employees is less important than that of external customers. This results in employees, like agents and case workers who depend on internal systems, struggling to get their work done as they wrestle with internal systems. As a result, operational costs and critical lead times can become significant concerns for organizations, especially over a long period, as the systems progressively degrade.

In one company, I worked with frustrated agents who had to use three different tools for a simple workflow. Each tool had a high learning curve and an outdated UX, which exacerbated the friction caused by constantly switching between the various tools. In addition, the lead times for processing cases were many times greater than they should have been, so the organization had to try and hire more agents to accommodate.

Three complex internal tools meant the costs, time, and effort to onboard new agents were also excessive. Over time, the problem had become a major bottleneck in the organization's plans to develop a new product because they couldn't scale their operational processes quickly or efficiently. They had reached the point where modernizing the UX and architecture of their internal systems was unavoidable.

3.1.7 Improving hiring and retention

The ability to hire and retain talented people can easily be overlooked, yet it can be a notable benefit of modernization. In 2018, I spent time with a large European aviation company struggling to hire and retain senior engineers. One of the prominent factors was their legacy C++ monolith with over ten thousand business rules. It was a dead-end career move that scared talented people away. As a result, they had a high reliance on junior engineers and graduates, which continued to deteriorate the architecture. I could feel the tension in my initial two day workshop. There was a desperation to turn things around and find short-term solutions quickly.

Talented people in the right environment are the key to creating better products, delivering innovations faster, and implementing sustainable long-term systems. Modern architecture, or a genuine commitment to architectural modernization, increases the chances of hiring talented people. They see the opportunity and potential to solve exciting problems rather than fighting legacy systems and constricting processes with no hope of improvement.

Hiring and retaining talent may not be the primary motivation for modernization, but it's worth calling out. And it might be more important than you realize.

3.2 Connecting modernization to growth strategies

This section looks at common business growth strategies and the types of architecture modernization challenges that can apply to them. These growth strategies are based on Ansoff's Matrix (figure 3.1), a 4 × 4 grid categorizing growth based on new and existing products and markets. Remember that multiple or all of these strategies could be at play within a single organization. It's also worth noting that there's no need to try and force everything into one of these four boxes. Instead, employ the matrix as a conversation starter.

Figure 3.1   Ansoff's Matrix

3.2.1 Growth strategy: Product development

A product development growth strategy focuses on building market share in existing markets by developing new products and services. A market in this context can be understood as the group or subset of people interested in or likely to purchase a certain type of product. Market segmentation, for example, involves grouping subsets of a market based on characteristics like age, profession, number of employees, industry, and revenue. For console video gaming, the market would be all the people who play console video games, and they could be further segmented by the games they like to play. Effectively, this means that a product development growth strategy is about building new products and services that target the same people as existing products.

With this type of growth strategy, the company will be developing new products likely to have some level of similarity to existing products because it's targeted at the same people. A few obvious architectural considerations include shared capabilities, product integration, and balancing investment between new and old.

Shared capabilities might be necessary where both products use similar business rules, calculations, or data, and it would be expensive to build them twice. It could be generic capabilities like identity systems or domain-specific capabilities. There are many risks and challenges associated with shared capabilities. Firstly, extracting a shared capability from an existing system designed to be a single product can be a significant amount of work, and it's not always clear to business stakeholders why something that already exists cannot easily be reused.

There are other challenges to consider, like determining the appropriate level of reuse and designing a domain model and interfaces that are not overly specific or overly generic. There is always the risk that the shared capability becomes a bottleneck and that the reuse level turns out to be less than anticipated. This topic gets much more coverage in later chapters about domain modeling, architecture design, and Team Topologies.

Customers will typically expect synergies and integration when they use multiple products from the same company. When I worked at Salesforce, customers found having multiple usernames and passwords for different products very frustrating. "This is all Salesforce. Why do I need to log in to five different products with different credentials?" Accordingly, the architecture must facilitate technical integrations with APIs and data feeds. As with shared capabilities, re-architecting legacy systems designed to be a single product to integrate with other products can require a significant modernization investment involving risky changes to core parts of the system and data.

Developing new products alongside existing products also raises challenges around mindset and prioritization. New products often have more potential, and the speed of experimentation and innovation will likely be faster, while existing products may have a large customer base and require more stability. It can be problematic when multiple teams are trying to move at different speeds and when people feel the other product is getting more investment than theirs.

INDUSTRY EXAMPLE: MARINE PRODUCT DEVELOPMENT

I was once fortunate to work with a company that built hardware and software for multiple marine markets—from luxury yachts to small fishing boats to commercial tankers. It was executing a major business model expansion with a product development growth strategy. Up to that point, it had been mainly in the game of hardware devices and embedded software. Still, it aspired to enhance its offering to existing customer segments by developing internet-connected experiences—for example, the ability to put a geofence around a boat and receive notifications when the boat moves outside the geofence and the ability to remotely monitor the sensors on a boat, like the engine speed and temperature. The company wanted to own the ecosystem of connected experiences. Talented people had signed up for the journey.

Technology-wise, however, catastrophic problems arose. The project had delivered little in two years. As a result, the CEO was feeling pressure from the board. The technology teams had tried to build the connected platform within their existing architecture: on-premises; SQL database; big ball of mud architecture; and home-rolled, event-driven capabilities were some of the major red flags. These constraints did not work for an IoT platform that needed to process thousands of telemetry events per second. When tested, the system could only handle around five connected devices concurrently. For reference, the business model was built around thousands of connected devices.

Architecture modernization was necessary to achieve the company's market development growth strategy. But gaining buy-in from senior leadership wasn't easy because they sometimes got lost in technical jargon like cloud-based services, polyglot persistence, microservice architecture, Azure, event-driven architecture, domain-driven design, and so on. However, they did eventually commit to modernization, and I believe the ability of technology leaders to continually connect modernization back to the business outcome of supporting thousands of concurrently connected boats was vital.

3.2.2   *Growth strategy: Market penetration*

A market penetration growth strategy focuses on building market share within existing markets by getting more out of existing products and services. High market penetration is a sign of a market leader. Not only does this mean increased revenues, but it also helps to build a strong brand. That brings other benefits like economies of scale and less reliance on marketing. Market penetration strategies can be implemented in various ways, including pricing changes, enhancing existing products, acquiring competitors, and sales and marketing initiatives.

The specific approach to increasing market penetration will determine the types of architecture modernization initiatives that are most applicable. Optimizations will likely need to be made to existing systems since no new products are being developed. This may involve making significant changes to existing parts of the system, which would necessitate modernizing those parts to enable a faster rate of innovation. Modernization may be a key part of reducing operating costs, such as automating manual processes or improving the user experience of internal tools and products to improve employee productivity.

Business and technology leaders need clarity on priorities regarding investing in new markets vs. increasing penetration in existing markets. There may be a desire to invest heavily in both, so it's vital to identify the level of modernization needed to support both strategies. It may be necessary to articulate that pursuing multiple approaches is not feasible and that reducing focus to fewer markets is required until sufficient progress with modernization has been achieved. This is, though, a good example of how to break down modernization and deliver value sooner by focusing on a single market: identify business opportunities in a single market (new or existing) and determine the modernization investment required to achieve those specific outcomes.

INDUSTRY EXAMPLE: LATIN AMERICAN CHALLENGER BANK MARKET PENETRATION

I worked with a Latin American challenger bank that had established itself in the market by moving quickly and having the best UX, as validated by its app store ratings. Getting more people to use it as their primary bank was essential to continue the bank's impressive trajectory, so customers needed to have their salaries paid directly into their accounts.

At that time, customers mostly used the bank for secondary accounts. The strategic north star was clear, but the business and product leads knew they needed a big investment to achieve their bold target of fully displacing the traditional banks. They were targeting another series of funding but had been advised that they needed to show a clear path to profitability to give investors sufficient confidence.

As a startup, the company had focused on gaining traction. It had built up lots of legacy very quickly and had operational processes that wouldn't scale to the future volumes necessary for the business model to succeed. A modernization initiative was needed to move the company toward becoming profitable and attractive to investors whose funds were required for them to make the next big step.

But a careful balance needed to be struck. The company couldn't afford to stop developing for a year while modernizing. It had to maintain its image as an innovative next-generation bank.

Customer support costs were identified by various stakeholders as a key area of focus in the journey to becoming profitable. Growing their customer base required linearly growing their customer support team due to inefficient and manual processes and buggy code that resulted in excessive support tickets. It was completely unsustainable, meaning there was a clear justification for modernizing architecture, ways of working, and operational processes.

3.2.3 Growth strategy: Market development

A market development growth strategy focuses on expanding into new markets with existing products and services. Usually, this starts with market research to identify new customer segments interested in the product. Uber is a classic example of market development. Initially, Uber focused on ride-sharing. After successfully penetrating that market, they began adapting their products and services for new markets like food delivery and freight delivery.

Understanding the needs of new customer segments and how these needs differ from and are similar to existing customers is crucial in identifying the level of investment needed to adapt the product to new markets. This can then be correlated with the areas of the system that will need to change, including the development of new capabilities. This is another scenario in which shared capabilities may need to be extracted, in this case, to support various market-specific services.

In general, shaping architecture and organizing teams can be challenging when a single product supports multiple markets. Should the architecture and teams remain general, focused on all market needs, or should specific parts of the socio-technical architecture be dedicated to specific markets? EventStorming is one technique that can be applied to collaboratively map out the current business workflows and user journeys in a high level of detail. Each granular step of the flow can be analyzed to identify the modernization required to support the new markets. Later in the book, you'll learn about EventStorming and how to use it for various purposes.

INDUSTRY EXAMPLE: TRAVEL COMPANY MARKET DEVELOPMENT DURING THE PANDEMIC

During the COVID-19 pandemic, we learned that massive, unexpected events don't just happen in the movies. We should be aware of areas of the architecture that don't scale. Even if there is no obvious scaling need, suddenly there could be.

A European travel company I worked with had small volumes of customer refunds pre-pandemic. It was a manual process using spreadsheets and other low-tech solutions. For years it had been just fine with no problems.

However, refunds increased by orders of magnitude during the pandemic, leaving the business in utter chaos. They couldn't process cases anywhere near quickly enough. Customers got mad, industry watchdogs got involved, and the brand reputation took a hammering across various forms of media.

Prepandemic, the company intended to pursue a market development growth strategy, adapting its existing capabilities to target new types of customers. However, the pandemic showed that they needed to fundamentally modernize their systems and ways of working before that would be possible. The architecture wouldn't enable their ambitious growth, so they built a business case outlining these challenges and a realistic path that would eventually allow the desired market development growth strategy.

3.2.4 *Growth strategy: Diversification*

A diversification growth strategy focuses on launching new products or services in a market(s) that the organization does not currently target. One organization that has consistently applied aggressive diversification to tremendous success is Amazon. Originally, a bookstore that grew into a retail giant, Amazon established its AWS cloud business, which generated over $60 billion in 2021 (http://mng.bz/Bmnl). Later, Amazon diversified into other markets, such as video streaming, music, groceries, smart homes, and video conferencing. As Ansoff's Matrix showed, diversification is the riskiest strategy that even Amazon gets wrong from time to time, evidenced by its difficulty breaking into the video games market.

Not every company has the deep resources and technical talent that Amazon has. For technology leaders, this means understanding how well the current architecture will support business diversification ambitions and the level of investment required. One positive thing to consider is that it may be possible to develop the new product completely standalone outside of existing systems and infrastructure. This is an opportunity to apply modern technology and ways of working from the start that can feed back into older parts of the organization. Unfortunately, this can also work in reverse, where the old system and ways of working infect the new systems and teams. That is something to prepare for from day one. Previously mentioned architecture modernization themes may also apply in a diversification strategy: shared capabilities, integration, diverse mindsets, general vs. market-specific domain models, and investment prioritization conflicts.

INDUSTRY EXAMPLE: REGULATED E-COMMERCE DIVERSIFICATION

After a decade as the market leader in a health-related, regulated, e-commerce vertical, growth had slowed for the organization. The company built its brand and gained high market penetration by being a first mover in establishing an online presence. But with near market saturation, year-on-year growth was in the low single digits.

New sources of growth were needed for more ambitious year-on-year growth. As a result, the company decided to employ a diversification strategy by moving into a new market with a new product.

The target market was still an offline experience, but the company wanted to be the first mover in providing an online experience. However, unlike their previous market, this physical product required a high level of customization and in-person specialist appointments. But, the landscape was evolving; emerging technologies would soon make it possible to go through the customization process remotely using a mobile application.

A high level of complexity was involved in establishing the new multimarket business model, and there was an urgent need for architecture modernization. However, there were some synergies between the new and the old market, particularly around operational and regulatory workflows. The leadership of the new product hoped to reuse some of the existing capabilities reducing their costs and time to market.

The existing architecture and ways of working had been completely designed around a single-vertical business model. In addition, it was running on-premises using dated technologies. As the market leader, the business faced no pressure to modernize until now. But now the need was urgent. The company wanted to be a first mover and become the early market leader as it had done in the previous market.

The head of enterprise architecture believed that architecture modernization could help in various ways, like improving time-to-market and reducing costs by reusing existing capabilities. I worked with him to validate the idea of extracting shared services using the techniques and ideas covered in the book's remaining chapters.

One challenge involved extracting a shared capability to support operational processes, which included not only extracting the software but also understanding how the caseworkers would operate in a multivertical world and how new UIs would need to be designed to support them. It also uncovered big challenges pertaining to shared dependencies like funding models. The company had never faced these challenges before, so it was impossible to plan too far into the future with much certainty.

3.3 Identifying north stars

North stars are a popular technique for identifying the most important business and product outcomes. Identifying the right north stars clarifies where and how to modernize your architecture best.

Sean Ellis, the coauthor of *Hacking Growth*, defines north stars as "the metric that best captures the core value that your product delivers to customers. Optimizing your efforts to grow this metric is key to driving sustainable growth across your full customer base" (http://mng.bz/d1B1).

North stars are a great approach to defining outcomes. However, they're not a shortcut for careful research and deep thinking. Choosing the right north star can take considerable effort, even for seasoned experts. For example, John Cutler's North Star Framework (http://mng.bz/rWpj) includes seventeen activities.

3.3.1 Choosing the right north star

Sean Ellis offers the following advice for identifying north stars: "You must understand the value your most loyal customers get from using your product. Then you should try to quantify this value in a single metric. There may be more than one metric that works, but try to boil it down to a single NSM."

North stars will vary according to factors such as industry, product type, and evolution stage (in the Wardley Mapping sense). For a software as a service company, north star metrics (NSMs) could be monthly recurring revenue (MRR), customer lifetime value (CLV), or net promoter score (NPS). In contrast, NSMs for an e-commerce product could be conversion rate, average order value (AOV), customer lifetime value (CLV), or customer acquisition cost (CAC).

There are also important caveats to be aware of with north stars. In particular, avoiding vanity metrics and carefully thinking through scenarios where the NSM could lead to the wrong behaviors like "if you made your NSM 'average monthly revenue per customer,' then the fastest way to grow this number would be to eliminate all customers that have a relatively low value" (http://mng.bz/V15x). Keeping north stars simple is also essential. "Remember that the point of the NSM is to align everyone on your team to work together to grow it. So it's important that it is simple enough for everyone to understand it and recall it." North stars can be defined at multiple levels, from individual products to product portfolios (chapter 6).

3.3.2   *Using a north star framework*

If you're new to the concept of north stars and want to avoid the previously mentioned caveats while identifying your optimal north stars, it makes sense to use a framework. Amplitude's north star framework (https://info.amplitude.com/north-star-playbook) is highly recommended. It provides a great visualization for thinking about north stars, as shown in figure 3.2.

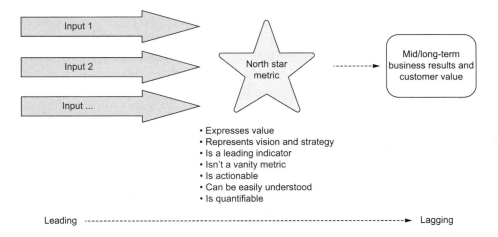

Figure 3.2   Amplitude's north star framework

Amplitude's framework begins with multiple input metrics that feed in from the work, defined by Amplitude as follows: "A North Star Metric and Inputs should be connected to the tasks of research, design, software development, refactoring, prototyping, testing, and such. We call this 'the work.'" Input metrics are leading indicators, meaning they help to predict future outcomes. The NSM

- Expresses value
- Represents vision and strategy

- Is a leading indicator
- Isn't a vanity metric
- Is actionable
- Can be easily understood
- Is quantifiable

The NSM should feed into mid/long-term business results and customer value. The full framework contains a lot of practical advice and is worth checking out.

3.3.3 Industry example: North stars at Danske

> **NOTE** The following industry example is provided by Xin Yao (https://www.linkedin.com/in/xinxin/). She's a leading voice in the world of architecture, strategy, and domain-driven design. This story shows the level of effort that goes into identifying great north stars, in addition to the benefits of using a structured framework and a highly collaborative approach.

Danske Bank is a multi-national bank with 21000+ employees from 10 countries. Danske has launched an ambitious transformation agenda to scale its agile practice and modernize its IT systems.

The North Star Framework (NSF) has been used to collaboratively kick off some complex change initiatives involving multiple systems, teams, and business domains. It's been effective in facilitating a shared, deeper understanding of the initiative's strategy (we call it the "Why"), before linking strategy to everyday work and team goals (we call it the "Way"). When many teams solve a big puzzle together, it's been beneficial to "Lead with the Why, not the Way."

The PSD2 example was originally launched as a compliance initiative. The bank uses credit decision models to automatically approve or reject credit applications. These models must comply with banking regulations to become fact-based and individualized, by utilizing the customer's actual account transaction history data. This is made possible by the Payment Service Directive 2 (PSD2), a European Union legislation obligating banks to provide APIs that allow account and payment information to be accessed by third parties when a consent has been given by the consumer. Prior to the PSD2 age, banks' credit decision models relied on manual customer data entry (which is cumbersome to validate) and demographically based statistical estimates (which is less precise).

It was soon evident that our PSD2 initiative required redesigning the product and customer experience. A key element in the customer journey is the design around data retrieval consent. To kick off the initiative, we used the NSF as a connecting thread in an adapted design sprint with cross-functional participation. The design sprint is facilitated by the initiative architect who leads product-, team- and domain-oriented collaborative design efforts. The North Star ideation phase has a strong human-centered design (HCD) flavor.

Among other workshop formats, we held empathy mapping sessions (see figure 3.3), where compliance requirements got reframed in the customer context. We asked

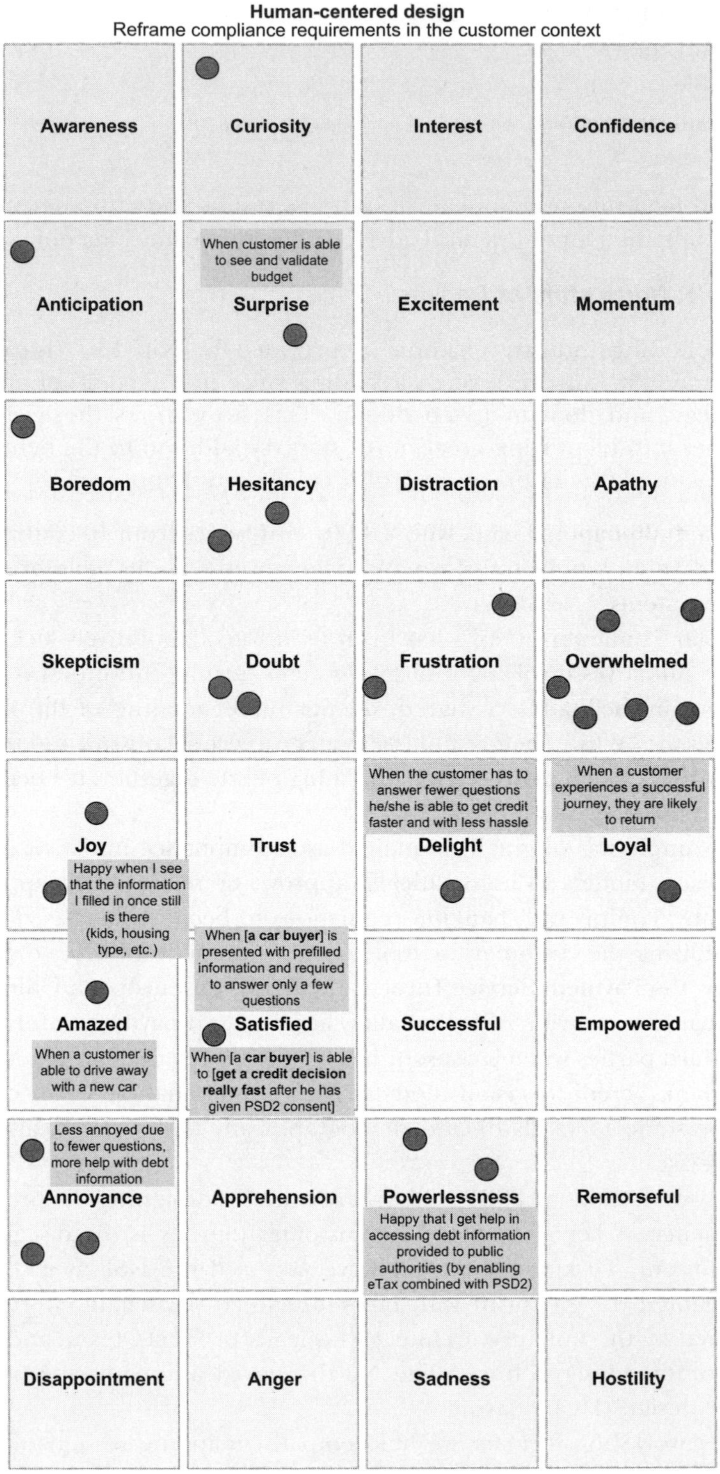

Human-centered design
Reframe compliance requirements in the customer context

Awareness	Curiosity	Interest	Confidence
Anticipation	When customer is able to see and validate budget Surprise	Excitement	Momentum
Boredom	Hesitancy	Distraction	Apathy
Skepticism	Doubt	Frustration	Overwhelmed
Joy Happy when I see that the information I filled in once still is there (kids, housing type, etc.)	Trust	When the customer has to answer fewer questions he/she is able to get credit faster and with less hassle Delight	When a customer experiences a successful journey, they are likely to return Loyal
Amazed When a customer is able to drive away with a new car	When [a car buyer] is presented with prefilled information and required to answer only a few questions Satisfied When [a car buyer] is able to [get a credit decision really fast after he has given PSD2 consent]	Successful	Empowered
Less annoyed due to fewer questions, more help with debt information Annoyance	Apprehension	Powerlessness Happy that I get help in accessing debt information provided to public authorities (by enabling eTax combined with PSD2)	Remorseful
Disappointment	Anger	Sadness	Hostility

Figure 3.3
PSD2 design sprint empathy mapping— charting the path through a customer's emotional journey

everyone, software engineers included, to chart a path through the customers' emotional journey in the current state, i.e., before intervention. We saw many red dots in the bottom two sections, which represent negative emotions, on the Empathy Mapping chart.

We then asked everyone to fast forward to the future, and imagine how a successfully deployed strategy could move the customers' emotions to the more positive side.

Similar sessions enabled us to collectively work on a shared language of the Why, forming a customer value exchange narrative. We saw really engaged software engineers and business participants alike in these experience discovery sessions. A shared sense of purpose emerged from framing the initiative as a story of "how what I do can make a difference in someone else's life." This would not have been possible if we had treated the initiative as a pure compliance exercise.

Eventually, we converged on the North Star of this initiative: fast credit decision using account transaction history. This statement is a synthesis from collaborative discovery, rather than the result of a top-down cascade of abstract goals. And since software engineers have first-hand experience empathizing with customer pains and wants, the NSF ideation process helped us paint a compelling big picture before assigning chunks of work to different teams. This way, we also avoided premature convergence and superficial understanding of high-level goals, which is a classic cause of rework or unmet user expectations.

The NSF also enabled us to work with different types of models, linking "value-related bets" (NS and NS inputs) to "work-related bets" (Opportunities and Interventions). The value-related bets are a more persistent model about how value is created and preserved for customers, users, and the business, in ways that contribute to mid-long-term sustainable, differentiated growth.

At the top level, the North Star is the guiding star, pointing at the difference we want to make in a customer's life with our unique strategy. Around the North Star, we have some small stars, just like Polaris is surrounded by constellations like the Great Bear or Little Bear. These small stars are called NS inputs. They are a small set of influential, complementary factors that together contribute to the North Star, and which we believe we can influence through our strategy.

Figure 3.4 shows the five North Star statements for value-related bets in our PSD2 initiative, like the Efficiency/speed input "Increase credit decision automation by using transaction data to cut down on manual rules as well as customer input questions."

After collaborative elicitation of the NS and NS input statements, we found good North Star Metrics. The heuristics that go into our PSD2 NS inputs and metrics are illustrated in figure 3.5 (the NS input metrics are omitted for brevity). For example, the Efficiency heuristic is "How fast can a customer succeed with her goal?"

Teams heavily debated the North Star Metric, the most important success indicator of our initiative. Are we essentially playing a transaction game or a productivity game? We arrived at a unified view of the NS being a primary productivity game, i.e., how efficient we are at supporting the job to be done (JTBD) for the customer through automated credit decisions.

PSD2 north star statements

Our ability to succeed in the mid/long term with our PSD2 strategy is a function of our ability to ...

Provide new and repeat PERSONAL customers **a** compliant, fast & trustworthy automatic credit decision requiring minimal manual input **through the use of** account HISTORY AND OTHER PUBLIC DATA SOURCES

... which is a function of our ability to:

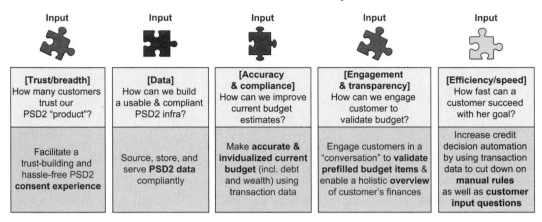

Input	Input	Input	Input	Input
[Trust/breadth] How many customers trust our PSD2 "product"?	**[Data]** How can we build a usable & compliant PSD2 infra?	**[Accuracy & compliance]** How can we improve current budget estimates?	**[Engagement & transparency]** How can we engage customer to validate budget?	**[Efficiency/speed]** How fast can a customer succeed with her goal?
Facilitate a trust-building and hassle-free PSD2 **consent experience**	Source, store, and serve **PSD2 data** compliantly	Make **accurate & invidualized current budget** (incl. debt and wealth) using transaction data	Engage customers in a "conversation" to **validate prefilled budget items** & enable a holistic **overview** of customer's finances	Increase credit decision automation by using transaction data to cut down on **manual rules** as well as **customer input questions**

Figure 3.4   PSD2 north star statements

Break down the north star into actionable input metrics

PSD2 value formula

f (Star) =	**Breadth**	x	**Data**	x	**Accuracy**	x	**Engagement**	x	**Efficiency**
	How many customers trust our PSD2 "product" & give consent?		How can we build a usable & compliant PSD2 infrastructure?		How can we improve current & future budget estimates?		How can we engage customers to validate prefilled budget?		How fast can a customer succeed with her goal?

Inputs are the handful of factors that, together, influence the north star.

Figure 3.5   PSD2 NS inputs heuristics and metrics

The NS metric was phrased as "avg # of changes to the budget made by advisors/customers per case after credit model assessment." Through nuanced discussions, we also reached the deeper insight that there are interdependencies between the five NS inputs. The NS inputs build upon each other over time, e.g., Breadth builds on Data, Accuracy depends on Breadth, and Efficiency is contingent on Data and Accuracy. We visualized the flywheel of NS input dependencies, reminding ourselves not to fall into the reductionistic "flat listing of parallel goals" trap (e.g., a bullet list of goals lacking cohesion, appearing somewhat arbitrary rather than collectively well thought out).

NS input elicitations were also a good time to review the existing team boundaries. If each NS input requires all teams to coordinate at every decision point to deliver outcomes, then perhaps it is time to rethink the team APIs. One benefit of letting software engineers be part of a collaborative NS elicitation process is better and deeper insight into business domains. Say a developer got the lucky Jira ticket "design the consent UX" or "author the consent text." Having been through this NSF ideation process, this developer would have had a much deeper understanding of the larger problem context about how his work relates to the North Star and contributes to making a difference in the customer's life. So the work eventually done will have better odds of actually targeting that "trust-building" and "hassle-free" consent experience (NS input).

Another benefit is when developers understand the linkage from strategy to everyday work, they can make better design decisions and ask better questions, like "why should we use time on doing this instead of that?" "Is there a better opportunity to influence the North Star input?" In this way, we can unlock the teams' potential of generating design variations, compared with the scenario when they just receive their Jira tickets as prescriptive work items (i.e., a feature factory).

Summary

- Architecture modernization should connect modernization initiatives to strategic business and organizational goals.
- Investing in modernization is expensive, so to maximize the return on investment, it is essential to identify which areas of architecture will benefit most from modernization and which areas will be a poor investment.
- One reason to invest in architecture modernization is to improve the ability to innovate at a faster pace, which is vital to organizations that have fallen behind faster-moving competitors and risk losing market share as a result.
- Organizations stand a much greater chance of competing with faster-moving competitors if they identify the need for modernization earlier. There is a tendency to look for quick fixes and silver bullets in organizations that have fallen behind competitors and have not realized early enough.
- Wardley Mapping is a technique that can be used to map out business ecosystems and anticipate evolution, helping to identify opportunities and threats while there is still time to react.
- Four broad types of business growth strategies are based on product and market strategy. Understanding which of these are in play is the basis for identifying where architecture modernization may be most effective:
  - A product development growth strategy involves building and developing products and services in new markets.
  - A market penetration strategy involves increasing market share in existing markets by improving existing products and services.

- – A market development growth strategy involves adapting existing products to target new markets.
- – A diversification growth strategy involves building new products for new markets.
- Some organizations are pursuing an exit strategy. Leadership may only be interested in investing in initiatives within a shorter time frame, like two or three years, so a vision that looks beyond these horizons may struggle to get the desired level of investment.
- A shorter-term outlook does have some advantages. It can help focus on delivering immediate value but also prevent fundamental problems from ever being addressed, like a monolithic legacy database coupled with everything.
- A portfolio-based approach usually makes the most sense, balancing short-term wins with a clear commitment to attacking fundamental, long-term challenges.

Listening and mapping tours

4

Starting a modernization journey is an exciting yet daunting experience. It will touch many people and could fail in many socio-technical ways. It may seem intuitive to begin by building a compelling vision and marketing the idea throughout the company, showing people the importance of modernization and your brilliant ideas for achieving it.

However, I recommend taking the opposite approach: start by *listening*; listen to a diverse group of people, from senior leaders to individual contributors, to understand what they're trying to achieve and the challenges they face on their journeys.

Listening to people is a great way to build up a picture of the true value of modernization. It's also an excellent opportunity to work on building relationships. Not only does listening to people's needs lead to better business outcomes, but it also increases your chances of getting support and buy-in. It's liberating in the sense that you can enjoy having conversations and not feel the pressure of needing to provide immediate solutions.

This chapter provides guidance for how to conduct listening and mapping tours, where modernization leaders spend time meeting various stakeholders, individually and in group settings. They are a mixture of listening and facilitation to identify the most valuable opportunities for modernization, which can then be used to build a compelling vision. As you talk to people across the organization, from the CEO to senior engineers, you'll hear many different perspectives about strategic priorities and architectural challenges.

Before starting on a listening and mapping tour, remember that the keyword is *listening*. Don't abuse this opportunity by pushing an agenda like trying to get buy-in for a preconceived solution.

4.1   *Who to meet*

It's tempting to say that it's best to speak to as many people as possible, but it could take hundreds of hours and be inefficient. But, getting broad and deep coverage is essential. So as you meet people, schedule follow-up sessions to explore specific topics in more detail where necessary. Therefore, you can start by speaking with a smaller group to understand how many more people you would like to talk to and how many follow-up sessions you tend to schedule.

When considering who to meet first, you'll need to assess scope: Do you already know that your modernization business case will be limited to a particular business area, or is the whole organization in scope? You may also want to narrow the focus of topics. For example, do you want to get a high level of clarity on the business strategy before mapping the technical landscape? As a sensible default, meeting a diverse mix of business- and technology-oriented stakeholders in the first step of the listening tour is wise. But if you want to avoid wasting time talking to the wrong people, gaining clarity on the strategy first might be the sensible option.

Questionnaires and surveys can be employed to gain insights from people you don't have time to speak with. Meeting multiple people together can also help make efficient use of time, but it can influence the information they feel comfortable sharing.

If you need help thinking of the first group of people to meet with on your listening tour, pick at least one role from each of the following categories, ideally with a mix of leaders and individual contributors, and arrange 1-hour sessions. The sessions will total around 10 to 15 hours, which you can spread out over 2 to 3 weeks for a comfortable immersion:

- *C-Suite*—CEO, COO, CMO, CD(digital)O, CFO, CP(product)O
- *Directors/VPs*—EVP, SVP, VP, senior director, director

- *Sales and Marketing*—Head of sales, head of marketing
- *Product*—Head of product, product manager, product owner
- *Engineering*—Head of engineering, senior engineering manager, principal engineer, senior engineer, head of testing, test engineer
- *Infrastructure*—Head of platform engineering/DevOps, platform architect, platform engineer
- *Architecture*—Head of enterprise architecture, head of security architecture, business architect
- *Data*—Data architect, data engineer, database administrator
- *Delivery*—Head of delivery, program manager, project manager
- *Support*—Head of customer support, customer support agent
- *Other*—Head of UX, ways of working lead, subject matter expert, customers

4.2   Who conducts the tour?

Another aspect of listening tours to consider is the people conducting the tour. This question could be a proxy for a more strategic question: Who will be leading the modernization initiative? One approach is to establish an architecture modernization enabling team (AMET). This group is responsible for starting a modernization initiative and maintaining momentum. An AMET can steer modernization in the right direction by facilitating a listening tour.

An AMET can include anybody well-equipped to lead and steer a modernization initiative. Usually, it's good to have a mixture of people from technical and product backgrounds, and it's ok to include external experts. The AMET is also free to involve others in the listening tour as necessary. Chapter 15 covers the topic of AMETs.

After establishing the group responsible for conducting the listening tour, they must organize themselves to carry out the tour. If the group is small, up to three people, then they can all attend each session. Otherwise, listening sessions may be divided among smaller groups or individuals. Individual groups must work closely and assimilate the insights from the various listening sessions to have a clear and consistent picture.

Recording the listening sessions so that all the insights are permanently recorded might be tempting. However, this will limit the amount and type of information people are willing to share. Therefore, I think it's better to focus on creating the safest environment for conversations and having another facilitator(s) take notes.

4.3   Conducting an effective tour

Conducting a listening tour might sound easy. It's just talking to people, right? Yet, I have seen great technologists struggle to lead listening tours. Asking the right questions; steering conversations in a useful direction; and being comfortable switching between high-level strategy conversations with the CEO, financial discussions with the CFO, and technical deep dives with a senior engineer requires some practice. This section covers important factors that will help you to have a successful listening tour.

NOTE   If you're yearning for more after this section, you may enjoy Indi Young's book *Time to Listen* (https://indiyoung.com/books-time-to -listen/).

4.3.1   *Create a safe space*

In the movie *Office Space*, the classic IT film from the '90s, the leadership team at Initech hires efficiency consultants to help downsize the company. The consultants commandeer a meeting room in the office and use it for interviewing each employee individually. It's an intimidating space. Two stern-faced consultants on one side of the table ask a series of intrusive questions to employees who hope it's not them who will be fired.

As you probably guessed, this is not the environment you want to create during a listening tour. You should aim to uncover what people genuinely believe are the most valuable strategic opportunities and significant impediments, which requires creating a safe space, not a threatening one.

In *Office Space*, there was a power imbalance. Two intimidating consultants on one side of the table interviewed a lone employee on the other side whose participation in the meeting was mandatory. These characteristics could resemble your listening tour, especially if consultants are involved. As a result, people may question your real intentions and worry that their job is at risk. Yet, if you're careful, it is possible to have an imbalance and still create a safe space. I always keep in mind the *Office Space* movie. It reminds me to try and lighten the mood and use softer language.

Setting can also affect how comfortable people are sharing their thoughts. For example, consider a coffee shop or a green space outside the office. Timing also plays a key role. I've had the unfortunate experience of leading a listening session with a head of product just after he came out of a very tense meeting. It was an uncomfortable situation; he revealed personal frustrations unintentionally. In these scenarios, it's best to stick to safer topics or reschedule the meeting.

The goal is always to create an environment where people feel safe to reveal their honest thoughts but also are in a state of mind where they share only what they are comfortable sharing. It takes a while to build a sufficient level of trust with many people, so you'll need to foster a healthy relationship and be patient, especially if you're a consultant and they know very little about you.

When receiving an unexpected email notifying you of a mandatory interview, it's easy to feel like an employee at Initech. Approaching the idea face-to-face or informally via chat is less intimidating. Before getting to the interview details, it's also helpful to provide them with context about the initiative and what you hope to achieve with the tour and reassure them of confidentiality. It is also vital to reiterate that you don't have solutions in mind at this stage and are not pitching ideas. You sincerely do just want to listen.

Finally, be careful with the word *architecture*. People will try to do some filtering for you and share only their problems and challenges that relate to what they perceive architecture to be. Therefore, at this stage, describe the initiative more vaguely without using the word *architecture* yet still conveying importance.

4.3.2   Harness a toolbox of techniques

Various techniques will be employed during a listening tour to build on the insights that emerge during the conversations. Some techniques can help dig deeper into specific topics, while others help to zoom out and see the bigger picture. A substantial benefit of many techniques is visualizing the concepts that emerged during the conversation and seeing how they connect. In addition to the techniques introduced in subsequent chapters, the following are short introductions to other tools and techniques that can provide value throughout a listening and mapping tour.

When you want to discern a particular stakeholder's top priorities and how they plan to achieve those objectives, Impact Mapping (https://www.impactmapping.org/) is an effective technique for structuring the conversation and visualizing how deliverables connect to business goals.

Figure 4.1 outlines the syntax of an Impact Map. On the left are business goals that connect to actors who may help to achieve those goals. One or more impacts are associated with each actor, often captured as improvements to specific metrics or changes in behavior. Finally, each impact connects to deliverables representing potential solutions for achieving the desired impact.

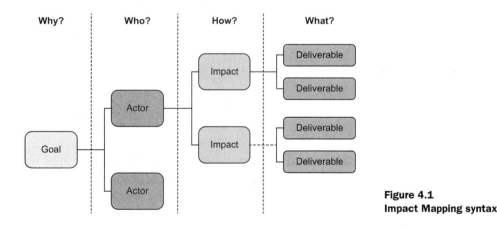

Figure 4.1
Impact Mapping syntax

Figure 4.2 shows an extract from an Impact Map produced during a listening tour in a session with a VP. One of their top-five business goals was to help increase revenue by $20 million in one business area. They had identified a subset of users representing 45% of all users and two potential impacts that could lead to more revenue from the group—one of the possible deliverables connected to both impacts, making it a high-leverage opportunity.

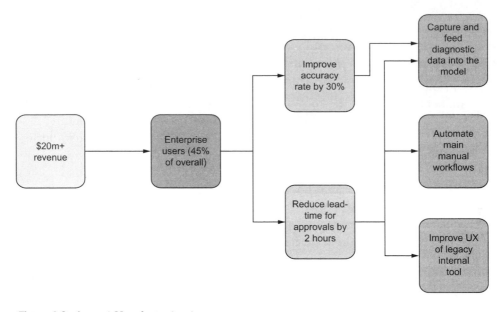

Figure 4.2   Impact Mapping extract

This starting point provided an ideal platform for further discussions. Notably, the deliverable of using data better needed to be more concrete. Further discovery was required to ascertain how to employ the data, such as producing better recommendations. This gave the team a lot to work with—a clear business goal, an opportunity to identify new impacts that might help achieve the goal, and a specific area to zoom in on and design deliverable solutions.

> **NOTE** You can find a list of the techniques covered in this chapter on the book's Miro board (http://mng.bz/wj2W), including links to useful resources to learn more and download artifacts.

The Business Model Canvas (BMC) (http://mng.bz/qj1E) is a tried and tested technique for visualizing the key aspects of a business model. During a listening tour, the BMC can be used to capture a particular stakeholder's perspective of the company's business model, allowing you to compare and identify where different stakeholders are aligned and not aligned. In addition, the BMC can be used at a more granular level to capture the business model in different areas of the business. The BMC is suitable for both current and future state business model exploration. Similarly, the Product Vision Board (http://mng.bz/7vYg), shown in figure 4.3, is another canvas-style technique used to outline the strategy for an individual product.

The Product Vision Board comprises five sections: Vision, Target Group, Needs, Product, and Business Goals. In the context of a listening tour, this tool is beneficial in understanding what the future looks like for each product. Your modernization vision

Product vision board

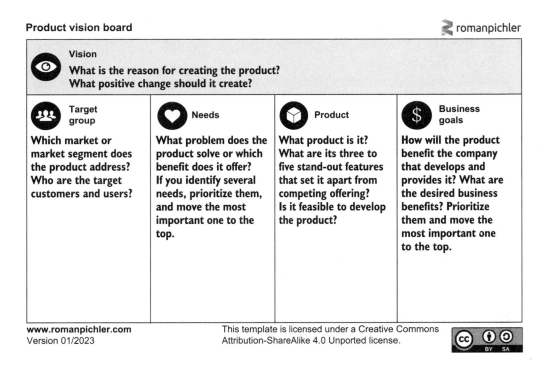

Figure 4.3   Roman Pichler's Product Vision Board

can then emphasize how it will support the specific future aspirations of each product and shared capabilities that will support multiple products.

Another useful technique is Risk Storming (https://riskstorming.com/). This technique identifies the most significant challenges and constraints within the existing architecture. It covers general risks, such as a monolithic legacy database coupled to almost everything, and risks pertaining to a particular aspect of the business strategy, like known hotspots that are ok at the moment but will not scale to support target business outcomes.

Architectural diagrams are a precursor to Risk Storming. The standard approach is to create C4 diagrams (https://c4model.com/), such as context and container diagrams. Risks are then overlaid onto the diagram with sticky notes by the people with the best knowledge of the parts of the architecture covered by the diagrams. Figure 4.4 shows a simplified container diagram for part of a holiday booking system that contains risks like business logic in stored procedures.

After storming for risks, the next step is to assess the impact and probability of each risk. A sensible default is to assign a probability score from 1 to 3 and impact score from 1 to 3 and then multiply the two scores. A score of 6 or above is color-coded red to indicate a major risk with high priority, while a score under 3 can be color-coded green with a low priority. Between red and green is amber, which indicates a medium priority in the context of the architecture modernization business case.

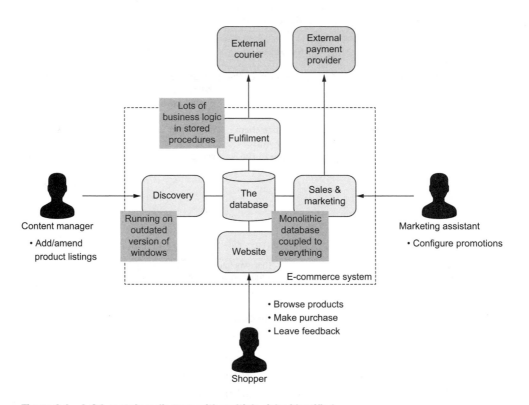

Figure 4.4   A C4 container diagram with multiple risks identified

These techniques cover many needs and will carry you a long way. During a listening and mapping tour, however, you can put to work any techniques that are relevant to the conversations you'd like to have. Good places to look for new techniques are the Miroverse (https://miro.com/miroverse/) and the book *Visual Collaboration Tools* (https://leanpub.com/visualcollaborationtools).

4.3.3   *Structured vs. unstructured discussions*

Listening tour sessions can range from entirely unstructured to structured with minute-level precision. Unstructured sessions can be advantageous because any insight may emerge, and the conversation can move in any direction based on what feels important.

Unstructured sessions can also feel more organic and authentic. It could be two people having a casual conversation in a cafe. But on the flip side, the conversation may not move in a beneficial direction and could end up with the interviewee expressing their frustrations about something at the front of their mind. Unstructured sessions are also daunting if you're uncomfortable conversing with various stakeholders in their language.

If unstructured conversations feel like too much of a risk, structured conversations are more suitable. You can start with a basic list of questions and then move into more unstructured discussions where you feel comfortable. However, jumping straight into canned questions like "What are your three top priorities for this year?" can feel forced and lose a sense of authenticity.

With structured conversations, you can create bespoke questions for each person or have a standard set of questions used for all interviews. The latter is practical when you need to compare responses across various conversations. For instance, you might want to compare people's feelings about using a given off-the-shelf tool.

The following list provides an example of the questions you can ask spontaneously in unstructured sessions or as part of a standardized format in structured sessions. Mostly these are different ways of asking people what they are trying to achieve and what problems they face:

- What are the top priorities on your roadmap for the next one/three/five years?
- What does a good year look like for you this year?
- How will you know that you have had a good year?
- What would happen if you fail to achieve your top objectives?
- What do you see as the biggest risks for achieving your objectives?
- What is your opinion on the level of innovation within the company?
- How satisfied are you with the speed at which new innovations get delivered?
- How well does this company use technology, and do you see opportunities to use it further?
- Can you tell me about the tools you (or your team) use to get your job done?
- What do you wish you had more time for in your job?
- What changes would help you to be happier at work?
- Is anything work-related keeping you up at night?
- Are there things that take up a lot of your (or your team's) time that you wish could be avoided?
- How would you (or your team) spend your working day in an ideal world?
- How well do you feel that people across this company are aligned on strategic objectives?
- If I asked a mid-level software developer to describe the strategic objectives, would their response match yours?
- How would you describe the effect of legacy debt on this company?
- If you could change any three things about the company, what would they be?

In addition to these generic questions, you can ask questions unique to your context, referring to particular products, systems, or ways of working. For example, "We recently switched from project-oriented teams to product-oriented teams. What has been your experience so far?" With all questions, and especially this type, it's easy to ask leading or biased questions like "How important is architecture to achieving your business goals?" So be very careful when asking questions and make every effort to not influence the interviewee's response.

EMPLOY A VARIETY OF QUESTION FORMATS

It's a natural tendency to ask questions in a direct and repetitive format. Yet learning to ask questions using various structures can lead to more engaging conversations and creates conditions for more interesting insights to emerge.

An easy question is, "What's the biggest problem you're working on right now?" It's not a bad question, but it's direct and something people will be used to, so it might only elicit a quick response without encouraging deeper reflection. Now consider a Complete the Sentence question on the same topic: "One thing about my work that makes me angry right now is _____."

People will replay this sentence in their mind as they fill in the blank, and it may trigger deeper and different thoughts that lead to further insights by tapping into alternative thought patterns and emotions. In any case, it's more fun.

The following are a variety of question formats that are worth learning and applying to verbal and written scenarios:

- *Complete the sentence*—As discussed previously, this format helps to elicit a different response than direct questions, potentially tapping into other emotions and deeper reflection.

- *Choose an emotion*—This type of question prompts people to look at an emotion/feelings wheel (https://imgur.com/tCWChf6) and pick an emotion that best describes their feelings about a certain topic. For example, "Which emotion stands out to you on the emotion wheel when you think about the speed at which new features are implemented?"

- *Pick an image*—A great way to encourage novel thinking and deeper reflection is to show people a selection of images and ask them to pick an image that reflects their feelings about a particular topic. A real example I've used is "Choose an image that describes how creative you feel in the current working environment." Prepare to be positive when you try this for the first time. It's an amazing technique. The Ethnographica Deck (http://mng.bz/mjEM) by Jennifer Mahony is a great collection of images. You simply lay them out in a grid so people can easily see all of the images, move between them, and have a space to connect with one (or more).

- *Worst possible*—These types of questions create the space for highly creative thinking by encouraging people to go in completely the opposite direction than expected. Imagine being encouraged to answer this question: "What is the worst possible business opportunity that this organization could go all in on?" It's a real license to think differently. Worst Possible questions serve a number of purposes like highlighting where the organization is actually doing the worst possible thing and identifying crazy ideas that can actually be refined into something with potential.

- *Just for fun*—This type of question is more about bringing a sense of fun into the process, which can help put people into a more relaxed and creative mindset, eliciting deeper responses to more important questions that follow. For example: "(Just for fun) If you could hire any celebrity to help us with modernization, who would it be and why?" Obviously, it's important to be careful with this type of question. Some organizations don't quite appreciate the importance of making things fun; sometimes, people might think you are not taking things seriously. Don't be put off, though. Try it in small doses and see what kind of response you get.

- *Devil's advocate*—These questions are an excuse to challenge people's beliefs constructively. For example, if someone believes investing in new products is key, you could ask, "So you are 100% convinced that reducing operating costs is the wrong focus and nothing would ever change your mind?" These questions need to be delivered skillfully, and it needs to be clear the intention is an exploration, not a direct challenge or an insult.

Some people think that these question formats are a gimmick. I used to be of that opinion, too. But I worked alongside people who used them and noticed that most people enjoyed them and their responses were more interesting, and it felt more playful.

USE QUESTIONNAIRES

Questionnaires and surveys are great for many aspects of modernization, including the listening tour. They can be used pre-, post-, and even during meetings and workshops to great effect using the question formats in the previous section.

In the context of a listening tour, an initial workshop or survey can be sent out to a large group. The survey results can be used to identify the key people to speak to and key themes and trends to discuss during the listening tour. A survey can also mitigate the problem of not having the time to speak to every person individually for the desired amount of time.

When putting together a questionnaire in the context of a listening tour, there are a few themes to touch on. Of course, problems and opportunities are the obvious candidates, but it's also useful to ask people about their level of interest and desired participation in the process, such as "How much would you like to be involved in designing and running workshops to explore these topics?" And it's always good to ask for feedback about the process, such as "What have you found interesting about the listening tour so far?" Be careful not to spam people with questionnaires too frequently.

ENCOURAGE EXPLORATION

When conducting a listening tour, anticipate that the people you meet may not have perfect clarity on their top priorities and challenges. They may have been so focused on delivering a certain project that they haven't recently reassessed the big picture or considered other potential priorities.

Your job is not simply to take what they say and treat it as their final and comprehensive thoughts. You also need to challenge them by thinking of alternative possibilities and asking devil's advocate questions like "If we were to meet again one year from now, how confident are you that we will still be talking about this as the top strategic priority?" or "Do you really feel that it's completely impossible that <other scenario> could happen?"

Try to recognize when someone isn't sure and they're in the process of reflecting on a topic and trying to understand how they feel. In this situation, you want to give them space and not push them too hard while in reflection mode.

On the other hand, when someone is convinced of their opinions, it may be better to push them harder to help them try to see those alternative realities outside of their tunnel vision. You may not trigger an instant change of mind, but you might plant some doubt that, over time, leads to a change of opinion.

As you can see, your role is also to coach people and help them to think about topics, not just get prebaked thoughts out of their heads. Try to keep this in mind and reflect on the type of questions you are asking. If you're co-interviewing, ask your partner(s) for feedback and encourage them to step in and guide the conversation when necessary.

GOING DEEPER

It's easy to stay high level and drift between various topics in a listening session, but sometimes it may be beneficial to focus on a single specific topic and go further into the details. The *5 Whys* (http://mng.bz/5o4D) approach is a very simple idea that can help with this if you're not sure how to steer the conversation in a more organic fashion. As the name implies, it simply involves asking "why" five times. For example, if someone raised the following concern, "It takes a long time to onboard agents," asking "why" might reveal, "Because we have to teach them how to use three internal tools, which are all difficult to use." Asking "why" again might reveal, "The developers built the user interfaces," and another "why" could reveal, "In this company, developers always build the user interface for internal tools because internal tools are not considered important enough for UX specialists."

As you can see, asking "why" five times can lead to deeper insights and trends that are highly relevant to modernization. However, you might want to explicitly state to the interviewee that you're about to use the technique; otherwise, it may seem impolite if you just keep asking "why."

HAVE A WING PERSON TO SCRIBE

I find that it's generally better to conduct listening tour sessions as a pair (keeping in mind the potential risks of the imbalance). While one facilitator is asking questions, the other can take notes. This allows maximum productivity from the limited time available and avoids one facilitator trying to speak and write at the same time, which can ruin the flow. If you don't have a wing person to scribe, you can record the session if the interviewee consents.

One technique that can lead to great conversations is reviewing the notes during the session. When playing the wing person role, I use Miro to capture notes as stickies. I connect and cluster them to pick out various themes and use colors to highlight concepts like business metrics, opportunities, and problems.

Figure 4.5 shows an extract taken from a real listening session. The actual text is obscured because it will be completely unique to each conversation, but the image does give an idea of what this activity can look like. As you can see, it's very messy, so if your boards look messy, don't worry; it's normal. Check out my blog if you'd like to learn more about this freestyle approach (http://mng.bz/6nO6).

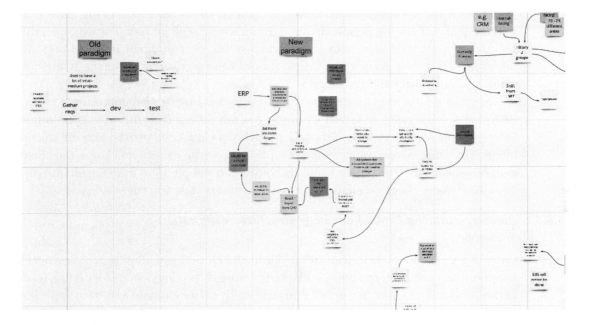

Figure 4.5 Capturing a remote listening session as sticky notes

REPEAT BACK TO VERIFY

During a listening tour, you'll be meeting people who do different jobs and work in different domains with different processes. It will take time to immerse yourself in their world and grasp the concepts they mention. You won't fully understand everything they are saying immediately, and you don't need to. But it's definitely an advantage if you can understand and absorb more of the information they share. One way to do this is to repeat back what you have understood and ask them to verify. Very often you'll have misunderstood, and this gives them a chance to correct you.

You can use these techniques on an ad-hoc basis during conversations as necessary. I also like to use this when I'm playing the scribe role. When the main facilitator invites me into the conversation to ask questions or share observations, I will share my screen and talk through all the visual notes I captured on the Miro board. This can take the conversation in interesting directions, like the interviewee wanting to go back and explain a certain topic in more detail, or they realize that they haven't mentioned a key theme or topic, or they might explain that a note isn't quite accurate and needs to be re-explained.

4.4   Bringing groups together

Typically, a listening tour starts with a divergent mindset, seeking to uncover the conflicting opinions of all stakeholders. However, convergence around priorities is essential when pitching a modernization business case. The solution is to bring people together for group sessions, creating a space for them to discuss themes that emerged from individual sessions.

These types of workshops are more ad hoc, tailored to the topics being addressed and the dynamics of the people involved. But it's not 100% ad hoc. For example, the techniques presented previously in this chapter can be combined in novel ways. In addition, Liberating Structures (https://www.liberatingstructures.com/) is a goldmine of useful advice and techniques.

Liberating Structures allows people to have a meaningful dialogue using a variety of formats. For example, Troika Consulting is one of my favorites. It's a technique where people work in groups of three, and each person takes a turn to play the role of client. First, they have a short amount of time to describe a problem. Then, the client remains silent and turns away while the other two people play the consultant role. They discuss the client's scenarios and provide advice while the client is listening.

4.4.1   Industry example: Clinical oncology structured exploration workshop

One of my clients, an American nonprofit in the clinical oncology space, contacted me about a broad modernization initiative covering technology, ways of working, leadership, and other factors. We decided to start slowly in one domain and then apply lessons learned to other domains across the business. The initial step was to build a business case together, identifying the modernization possibilities within the domain. One of the client's modernization ambitions was to improve collaboration across parts of the organization and empower everybody to contribute to continuous organizational improvements. We used the actual process of building a business case to begin role modeling and introduce these desired behaviors.

Initially, we spoke to people individually and then sent out a questionnaire asking people for thoughts, opinions, and ideas about the specified domain. We gained a number of insights that allowed us to design the first workshop. Attendance of the first workshop was optional. Anybody working in the domain or interested in being part of the journey was welcome to attend. We structured the workshop into three parts, sandwiched by loosely connected check-in and check-out questions. The first part of the workshop focused on a meta level, giving participants the opportunity to think about what a modernization journey might look like so they could decide on the process they wanted to adopt. We presented them with eight journey metaphors, including a waterfall, the double diamond (http://mng.bz/or4v), and the design squiggle (https://thedesignsquiggle.com/). The workshop contained over 40 attendees split into eight breakout sessions. None of them selected rigid processes like a waterfall, and the majority selected the double diamond or the squiggle.

The design squiggle, shown in figure 4.6, represents the chaotic and unpredictable nature of design. In the beginning, the future is highly uncertain. It's not even clear which problem needs to be solved, and there is lots of back and forth, diverging and converging, trying to figure it out.

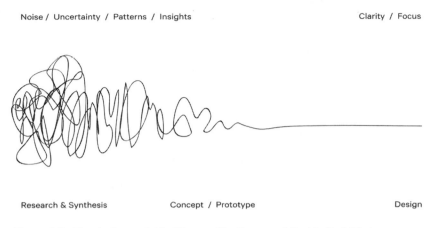

Noise / Uncertainty / Patterns / Insights   Clarity / Focus

Research & Synthesis   Concept / Prototype   Design

Figure 4.6   The design squiggle (Source: The Process of Design Squiggle by Damien Newman, thedesignsquiggle.com)

The double diamond design process, shown in figure 4.7, also involves problem identification with diverging discovery, which converses toward a problem definition. It's then followed by a diverging solution design converging toward a clear solution. This

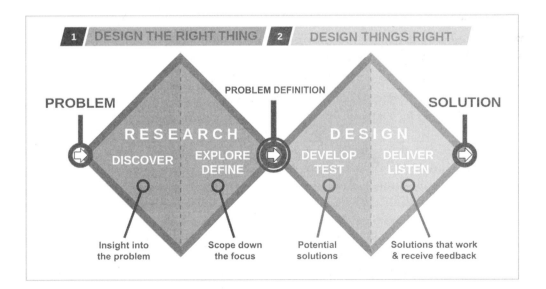

Figure 4.7   The double diamond design process

model was useful because the group recognized they had to define the problem first, which was a departure from their regular feature factory approach where they were given requirements to implement. The model was also useful because it emphasized the need for multiple divergence and convergence phases. But the double diamond is not perfect and does have its critics. In this context, it was simply used as a way for people to think about different metaphors to empower them to be in control of their journey.

In the second part of the workshop, the group was asked to define the domain. We simply gave them a space with two circles slightly overlapping, representing inside the domain, outside the domain, and somewhere in between. We were intentionally vague, adding the least amount of structure possible to avoid overconstraining the group's thoughts. It was great to see some groups modifying our structure to better express their understanding of the domain, such as by showing concentric circles.

The third part of the workshop was about identifying the next steps. Working in breakouts, each group was challenged to address the question, "What are the most important questions this group needs to answer next?" The responses from all groups were combined, and then each person had three votes to identify the questions they wanted to answer next.

Effectively, the approach taken with this client was to crowdsource building the business case for modernization in a particular domain. In this scenario, structured group workshops and questionnaires, using a range of question formats, were key techniques that allowed the modernization leaders to facilitate group discussions and empower the group to drive the process. This approach may not be realistic in your context. For one, it can take much longer. However, the key takeaway is to think about how you want to conduct your tour and choose structured versus unstructured sessions and individual versus group sessions accordingly.

4.4.2 *Industry example: Kickstarting modernization in a large Scandinavian enterprise*

A modernization Kickstarter workshop is one type of workshop that can be highly effective for transitioning from listening and mapping to delivering modernization. This type of workshop aims to bring people together to decide, design, and start planning the first steps of modernization. There is no set format, but a default starting point is a three day, in-person gathering, which follows some remote listening and mapping sessions and preparation workshops (which can be remote).

This example outlines the approach Eduardo da Silva (https://www.linkedin.com/in/emgsilva/) and I took with a large Scandinavian company seeking to move from a tightly coupled monolith to a loosely coupled architecture and teams as part of leadership's ambition to double the company's revenue within five years.

To begin the initiative, we spoke to various stakeholders, including product owners, engineers, leaders, and support staff. We followed up with some product overview and strategy sessions where we watched them using their own product and discussed where the user pain points were and the opportunities for future improvements.

Following these sessions, we designed group workshops to capture the mission's north stars/key objectives. One of the techniques we used was Impact Mapping to capture the top-level business goals and how they connected back to initiatives and deliverables, which touched on capabilities within the monolith. We then started designing a three-day workshop to be held in person at the client's offices, with around 15 product and engineering people. Our high-level agenda for the workshop was

- Business and product vision
- Mapping out the current monolith's capabilities and purposes
- Exploring the domain
- Selecting a first slice of modernization
- Designing the architecture for the first slice
- Planning the delivery of the first slice

The workshop was kicked off by product leads and the head of IT, who perfectly articulated the medium- and long-term business vision. This framing was vital because it provided a reference point for all of the architectural discussions that followed—how did each idea or proposal fit with the business and product objectives?

We then moved on to mapping out the current monolith. Attendees worked in small groups of three or four, and it was interesting to see how each group had a different understanding of the capabilities within the monolith. There was some convergence but much divergence around boundaries and naming at multiple architectural scopes. A crucial part of this workshop phase was each group identifying what they considered to be the key business metrics to which the monolith contributed.

On day two, we spent the morning mapping out the domain with process modeling–style EventStorming. We modeled the case of a real customer end-to-end journey led by the product owners, who were happy to embrace role play, which made the activity fun and engaging. There were many questions and clarifications; it was a great learning opportunity for the engineers.

After much deliberation and seeming deadlock, the group unanimously agreed on which part of the monolith to break out first (thanks to the modernization Core Domain Chart covered in chapter 16). It was a subdomain that would provide immediate business value and was reasonably complex, so it gave an idea of what to expect when modernizing other parts.

Day three was all about designing the future-state architecture for the first slice and starting to sketch out what the group would do in the next six months, again working in groups. By the end, there were still outstanding questions, but the group could see where it wanted to go and the challenges on which it needed to focus.

After the first day of the workshop, the whole group had dinner together in the evening. Everybody felt good and agreed that the first day had been positive. This opportunity to socialize also contributed to higher engagement and energy during the remaining two days. This touches on why a three-day, in-person experience is ideal for the Kickstarter and was a big change for the team. Getting together in person was a great way to start things on the right foot by building momentum and creating social connections.

Not every group member was equally excited and believed in the initiative. Some were skeptical that it wouldn't lead anywhere after past disappointments. So at the end of the three days, the head of IT invited the CTO to close the workshop and convey the magnitude of this journey. His speech was inspiring and exactly what needed to be said in that moment. He explained the seriousness of modernization due to the changing business landscape. He pledged to the engineers that this would receive his full support.

Of course, a three-day Kickstarter alone doesn't change much. It's a great way to build excitement and momentum and establish the first step of a journey, but it's effortless to lose the momentum and fall back into the regular pattern. That's why we recommend establishing an AMET.

NOTE An excellent resource for anyone designing a workshop is The Design Aspects (https://www.whenandhowstudios.com/design-aspects), created by Dan Young and Mike Rozinsky. It covers all key considerations for structuring a workshop, like The Basic Environment, The Art of Questions, Growing Relatedness, Framing, Individual and Collective Thought, Inviting Dissent, and more.

That's now the end of this chapter covering the first steps of a modernization journey, identifying the business and organizational rationales for your modernization initiative, and beginning the process of building a compelling vision. In general, the ideas from this chapter can be used at any point during the modernization journey. The next chapter focuses on a single technique known as Wardley Mapping, which is also useful during a listening tour and at many points throughout a modernization journey. It's used to map out business and technology landscapes with the goal of making better strategic choices, a crucial skill for modernization leaders.

Summary

- A good way to start is by listening before designing solutions.
- A listening and mapping tour involves meeting various stakeholders to understand what they are trying to achieve and the challenges they are facing.
- A solid modernization vision that has strong support and buy-in can be built from the insights gained during a tour.
- It's good to meet a whole variety of stakeholders from all different parts of the business, with different roles, and a mix of managers and individual contributors.
- The tour should be conducted by people who will lead or guide modernization, like an architecture modernization enabling team (AMET).
- The most important part of a listening tour is listening and not pushing a preconceived agenda or biasing the discussions.
- Listening sessions can be structured or unstructured according to your goals, preferences, and level of experience.

- You can use any technique to map out what's important. It's good to have a diverse toolbox with techniques like Impact Mapping, the Product Vision Board, and Risk Storming.
- Asking great questions in various formats can make sessions more varied and interesting, leading to deeper insights using techniques like the Ethnographica Deck.
- Bringing groups together after individual sessions can be useful for spreading awareness of themes that emerged and gaining alignment and agreement on what's important.
- Kickstarter workshops are a technique for moving from conversations to creating a plan of action and building excitement and momentum for the modernization journey.
- A good format for Kickstarter workshops is three days in person together, starting from the business and product vision and ending with a short- to medium-term plan for getting started.
- It's easy to lose momentum after a Kickstarter and fall back into normal work patterns, so it's a good idea to establish a group of people who will keep momentum going, like an architecture modernization enabling team.

Wardley Mapping

Wardley Mapping is essential for business and technology leaders, especially during an architecture modernization journey. It has emerged as a popular and highly effective tool. It moves beyond simple 2 × 2 grids and gut instinct to a model that involves mapping out businesses using value chains and their evolution. It is the enabler for richer and more nuanced discussions about strategy. Even better, Wardley Mapping makes strategy more collaborative, allowing diverse groups, including technical and business experts, to explore their landscape and connect the business and technological aspects of value chains.

Not only is Wardley Mapping a technique, but it is also a large community that continues to grow. It is becoming mainstream, and the terminology used in

Wardley Mapping is becoming the de-facto strategy language in business and technology environments. Therefore, it's essential to learn Wardley Mapping to know the terminology and its nuances. Another reason to learn Wardley Mapping is that it is often combined with many other techniques in this book, like Team Topologies.

In this chapter, you'll see the steps involved in creating a Wardley Map and some of the principles and patterns closely connected to the technique. Wardley Mapping is a big topic that takes a long time to master, so this chapter aims to help you get started and provide valuable links and resources to help you continue your journey.

As you work through the chapter, remember that Wardley Mapping has broad applicability. While it is a great technique to help you build and demonstrate a business case, it's also a tool that can help you to understand the landscape better and communicate ideas to others. You can apply it throughout a modernization journey at every architectural scope.

Also, remember that there isn't a linear flow between the activities in this book. For example, after putting together a Wardley Map, you may need to dig into the domain with EventStorming (covered in chapter 7) to understand the domain better or explore possible solutions, allowing you to iterate on your Wardley Maps.

One final thing to remember: practicing is the best way to learn Wardley Mapping. After finishing this chapter, why not create your first Wardley Map for the industry you work in? Or at least put an hour in your calendar sometime in the next 2 weeks.

5.1 *The Strategy Cycle*

When practicing strategy, especially with Wardley Mapping, it helps to have a strategic process model that outlines the steps involved, how they fit together, and when to perform each step. This helps to answer basic questions like: "Where do we start?" "What should we do next?" and "Are we doing this completely wrong?" Simon Wardley, the creator of Wardley Mapping, is also the creator of the Strategy Cycle, shown in figure 5.1,

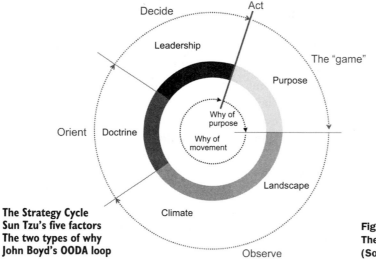

The Strategy Cycle
Sun Tzu's five factors
The two types of why
John Boyd's OODA loop

Figure 5.1
The Strategy Cycle
(Source: Simon Wardley)

which outlines an iterative approach to strategy with five steps: purpose, landscape, climate, doctrine, and leadership. It's based on Sun Tzu's Five Factors (http://mng.bz/n1E4) and John Boyd's OODA Loop (http://mng.bz/vPOr).

Starting out on an iteration of the Strategy Cycle begins with defining your purpose. In essence, this is something resembling a mission statement. It describes the motivation for an organization to exist and its ultimate ambitions. Here are a couple of publicly available examples:

- "[Flatiron Health's purpose is] to improve and extend lives by learning from the experience of every person with cancer."
- "Hargreaves Lansdown empowers people to save and invest with confidence. Offering a service that supports them in building their financial resilience and achieving the right outcomes."
- "Carbon Re will remove Gigatonnes of CO_2-equivalent from humanity's emissions each year. Our focus is on the biggest opportunities and challenges in sectors such as cement, steel and glass production. We know that for a 50% chance of keeping below 1.5 degrees global warming by 2050, we need to leave 90% of known coal reserves and 60% of known oil & gas reserves in the ground."

As you conduct a listening tour, you can ask each stakeholder to describe in their words the purpose of the organization. Then you can assess the level of divergence and convergence across the range of responses.

Moving to the second step of the cycle involves mapping out the landscape. This means understanding what products, services, capabilities, and other relevant things affect the strategy and identifying relationships between them. Landscape takes the perspective of the whole competitive business landscape, including competitors, not just your organization. Keep in mind that this step isn't about defining a strategy or identifying solutions; it's simply about understanding the current situation, which can then be used as the basis for strategic exploration. With Wardley Mapping, a Wardley Map visualizes a landscape using value chains (covered later in the chapter with examples).

After mapping the landscape, the next step is to consider the climate your business operates in (not Earth's climate). This is about identifying changes outside your control that will or could affect your business landscape. Every landscape is constantly evolving due to various climatic forces. Even if a business stood still and did nothing, the landscape would still be evolving, and a variety of forces like competitor actions, world events like a pandemic, and the introduction of new laws and regulations would affect the business. Blockbuster, for example, tried to continue with their brick-and-mortar DVD rental service without acknowledging the climatic signals that online streaming was about to change the landscape dramatically.

Identifying potential climatic changes could be the difference between strategic success and complete disaster. A Wardley Map can be used to visualize the effect of climatic changes, and there are climatic patterns to guide you. This allows modernization leaders to anticipate their journey based on future possibilities rather than just the current hot topics.

   Doctrine follows climate in the cycle. Doctrine is less about how the map will evolve and more about how your organization will operate to achieve the desired purpose. The Wardley Mapping framework provides a collection of doctrine principles (https://learnwardleymapping.com/doctrine/), like use a common language, strategy is iterative, and optimize flow. These touch on nearly all aspects of the company's operating model and are addressed throughout the book. Doctrine is an often-overlooked aspect of strategy; without an effective operating model, it's harder to be successful, even with a genius strategy.

   Lastly, the cycle moves into the leadership section. This represents intentional, strategic actions businesses could or will take, like expanding into new markets or developing new capabilities to improve existing products and drive market penetration. A Wardley Map, with a mapped-out landscape and climatic forces represented, is the foundation for deeper strategic conversations and informed leadership decisions. Several gameplay patterns exist within the Wardley Mapping ecosystem, like Market Plays, which are covered later in the chapter.

   As you can discern from figure 5.1 and its name, the Strategy Cycle uses a cycle metaphor to accentuate the iterative nature of strategy. As you build a modernization vision and begin delivering architecture modernization, the landscape will always be evolving, so you should continue regularly iterating on the strategy with Wardley Mapping to keep modernization on the optimal path. As Simon Wardley emphasizes, even your business's purpose can change: "The Climate may affect your purpose, the environment may affect your strategy, and your actions may affect all . . . Your purpose isn't fixed, it changes as your landscape changes and as you act. There is no 'core,' it's all transitional."

5.2   Creating a Wardley Map

The process of creating a Wardley Map can be broken down into six basic steps covering parts 1 and 2 of the Strategy Cycle—purpose and landscape:

   1 Define the map's purpose.
   2 Set the scope.
   3 Identify users.
   4 Add user needs for each user.
   5 Create value chains using components.
   6 Map components along the evolution axis.

After creating a few Wardley Maps, the process becomes automatic, and you won't need to think about these steps, but it's helpful when getting started. Ben Mosior's Wardley Mapping Canvas (http://mng.bz/46vv) is an excellent visual tool for guiding beginners through the process. The following section shows how to build your first Wardley Map using the canvas.

Using Ben's canvas, we will create a Wardley Map for an online food delivery company for this example. It implements a multisided marketplace business model that brings together restaurants and customers. Accordingly, their purpose includes the needs of each group: "To connect hungry people with the best and widest variety of local takeaway food" and "To enable all restaurants to offer an efficient takeaway service." These details are directly entered into the first step of the canvas, as shown in figure 5.2.

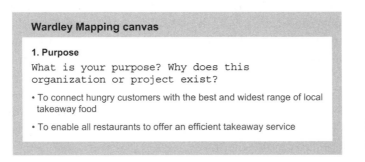

Figure 5.2
Purpose—step 1 of the
Wardley Mapping Canvas

Step two of the canvas sets the scope of the map. Maps can be at any level, from a macro level covering an entire business to a micro level covering an individual product or capability. The scope of the map will determine the granularity of the components created and shape the type of conversations that are likely to occur. In this example, the scope is set to a macro-level overview, as shown in figure 5.3. This is a sensible default choice if you're starting a modernization journey and haven't yet set any boundaries or priorities about where to focus.

The next step is to describe the users who benefit from what is being mapped. This can include users from inside and outside the organization, like customers, employees, and partners. In our food delivery example, the organization has three broad user types at a macro level: *customers*, *restaurants*, and *riders*, which are added to part 3 of the canvas, as shown in figure 5.4

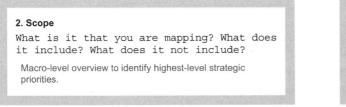

Figure 5.3   Scope—step 2 of the Wardley Mapping Canvas

Figure 5.4   Users—step 3 of the Wardley Mapping Canvas

The fourth step of the canvas involves associating user needs with each user. Figure 5.5 shows customers who want to enjoy great food without cooking, restaurants who wish to grow their business, and riders who want to earn money. It's possible to show multiple needs associated with a single user and some needs that multiple users may share. It's also possible to break users down more granularly, such as "regular customer" and "occasional customer." The purpose and scope of the map will drive these choices.

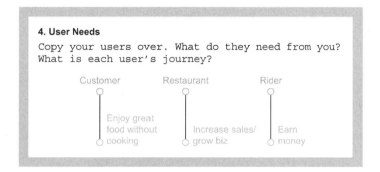

Figure 5.5   User needs—step 4 of the Wardley Mapping Canvas

After step 4, things start getting more interesting and complicated in step 5, which requires value chains to be created from components. At this point, it's worth emphasizing that the precise definition of "component" can be distracting, especially if you have experience with other techniques that use precisely defined meta-models. Working back from a user need, what are the things/capabilities needed to satisfy the user needs? A component can be practically anything that seems useful to map, like activities, data, practices, and knowledge. One thing to avoid when mapping is getting sucked into circular debates about the precise definition of a component and whether something is or isn't a component. It's better to pick what feels most beneficial for the map you are creating.

Figure 5.6 shows the first steps of creating the food delivery value chains, starting with the *customer* and *restaurant* perspectives. The *customer* uses the *customer mobile app*, the restaurant uses the *restaurant management web app* for managing their restaurant, and the kitchen staff uses the *kitchen iPad app*. One function of the restaurant management app is to build the *menu* while the *customer* uses the mobile app to browse the *menu*. Therefore, both apps depend on the *menu* component. The kitchen staff uses the iPad app to process incoming orders, while customers place orders using the mobile app, so both apps depend on the *ordering* component. At the bottom of the diagram is the *cloud platform* component. The company uses this internal platform to build and run server-side software, so all components that run on a server depend on this component.

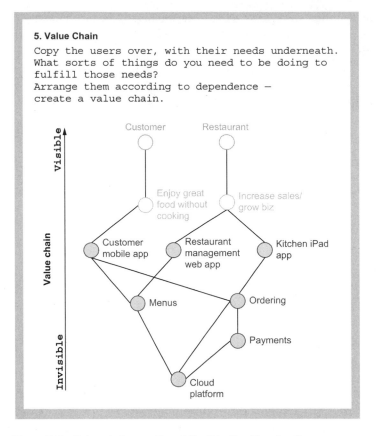

5. Value Chain

Copy the users over, with their needs underneath.
What sorts of things do you need to be doing to
fulfill those needs?
Arrange them according to dependence –
create a value chain.

Figure 5.6   Value chains section of the Wardley Mapping Canvas

You'll notice in figure 5.6 that the vertical axis is labeled as *Visible* at the top and *Invisible* at the bottom. This signifies that items higher up are more visible to the user while items further down are not visible to the user; the user might not be aware that they exist. In this example, the *customer* sees and interacts with the *customer mobile app*, so it's highly visible to the user, yet the *customer* sees nothing of the company's *cloud platform*.

Finally, step 6 of the canvas is where a Wardley Map is actually created. The *value chains* are copied across from step 5, and each component is moved to one of four evolution stages: *genesis, custom built, product,* or *commodity*. *Genesis* represents new and novel concepts that may have much unproven potential. On the opposite end, *commodity* is for concepts that are highly standardized—that is, all organizations in the industry have very similar versions—meaning there is no opportunity for differentiation.

As shown in figure 5.7, the cloud platform is considered a commodity because it is an established concept similar to competitors. Some bits are built in-house, but it's mostly delegated to a cloud provider. There is minimal opportunity to differentiate with these components. Meanwhile, *ordering* is considered more of a product because there is still believed to be some opportunity to differentiate from competitors, although not a great deal. The four stages of evolution are covered in more detail in section 5.3.

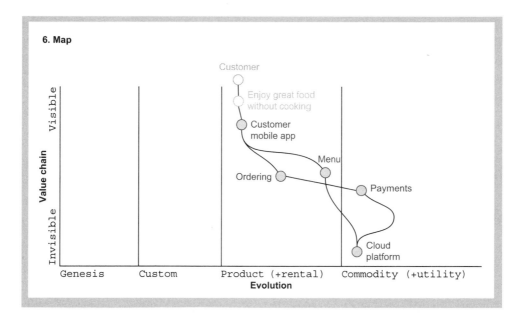

Figure 5.7   Step 6 of the Wardley Mapping Canvas, a Wardley Map

Figure 5.7 shows only the customer value chains to help accentuate examples of evolution. Still, on a real map, you can show multiple users, their needs, and the relevant value chains.

Things get even more interesting now that you've put a map together. You can start discussing the patterns that stand out to you. I always ask one facilitation question: "If you removed all the text from this diagram, what would it tell you?" As an example, figure 5.8 shows a Wardley Map with no text next to the components, but we can still identify a few potential themes that might be worth digging further into.

Firstly, there are no components in genesis or custom built, which is a warning sign that the company has no innovations in the pipeline. That may be the case, or it might simply be that they aren't shown on the map, but it's an obvious topic to explore, potentially requiring additional workshops and techniques to verify.

Secondly, many components are a commodity, yet the company doesn't use any off-the-shelf tools. The warning sign is that the company is investing a lot of resources into building things that can be purchased easily (admittedly, to identify this pattern required a bit of context knowing that the organization doesn't use off-the-shelf tools, but this is still reflective of a real situation).

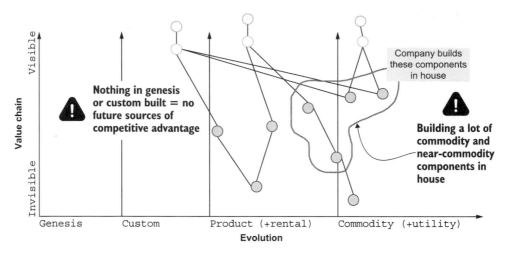

Figure 5.8   Identifying strategic themes on a Wardley Map

As you can see, just by visualizing the landscape, you can already start to understand where modernization might be most needed or where you want to zoom in and dig deeper.

5.3   Grasping evolution

A common challenge newcomers face to Wardley Mapping is fully grasping the intricacies of determining a component's correct stage of evolution. *Genesis, custom built, product*, and *commodity* are fairly common words. However, they have more intricate definitions in Wardley Mapping, with specific assessment criteria.

A contextual understanding of the stages of evolution is paramount to learning Wardley Mapping and getting value from the technique faster. In this section, you'll learn about the key characteristics and learn a short exercise to help you and your team quickly get up to speed.

5.3.1   Evolution characteristics

One of the great things about Wardley Mapping is that Simon Wardley himself and the community around Wardley Mapping have put together so many resources that support creating and using maps. For assessing evolution, the community recommends three characteristics and twelve properties (https://learnwardleymapping .com/landscape/). These are referred to as weak signals; some may be more appropriate to certain components than others. Unfortunately, it's not as easy as following a flow chart for each component and producing a precise assessment. There's an element of subjectivity and industry expertise required, along with skill from practice.

The three characteristics, ubiquity, certainty, and publication types, are shown in table 5.1. Each characteristic is presented with criteria for determining what stage a component belongs to according to that particular characteristic. If a component is rare, meaning very few or no other companies possess this capability, it matches in the *genesis* phase of evolution for the *ubiquity* characteristic.

Alternatively, if something is widespread and every company has it, it would fit into *commodity* for the *ubiquity* characteristic. *Certainty* is a characteristic that represents how well the use of a component is understood. According to this characteristic, components are in *genesis* if players in the landscape are just starting to explore how to apply the concept. Components would instead fit into *commodity* for the *certainty* characteristics if components have fully evolved and there is nothing more to learn about using the component.

Table 5.1 The three evolution characteristics

	Genesis	Custom built	Product	Commodity
Ubiquity	Rare	Slowly increasing consumption	Rapidly increasing consumption	Widespread and stabilizing
Certainty	Poorly understood	Rapid increases in learning	Rapid increases in use/fit for purpose	Commonly understood (in terms of use)
Publication types	Normally describe the wonder of the thing	Build/construct/ awareness and learning	Maintenance/oper-ations/installation/ features	Focused on use

In the online food delivery example, the concept of a *menu* is both widespread and commonly understood. Every competitor's product provides menu capabilities, and everybody knows how to use a menu. Menu, therefore, looks to be a *commodity* or very close.

Now consider another capability, *restaurant optimization,* that one or two organizations have started to develop. It's about helping restaurants to grow their business through advice and recommendations. This is a new concept, and industry players are still figuring out how to develop this capability and are constantly experimenting with new features and ideas. It's not being used by many restaurants, although there are signs of increasing adoption. Therefore, it would appear to match more closely with *slowly increasing consumption* and *rapid increases in learning,* seemingly fitting into *custom built.* Of course, we should ensure we have various perspectives from domain experts in this area. We don't want to make the wrong impression that this is of high strategic value when we might be missing key insights.

In table 5.2, you can see a sample of the *general properties,* which also help to identify the most relevant stage of evolution. The *market* property represents market maturity. Effectively, how established are the people who will consume the component? In *genesis,* there is no market yet, whereas in *commodity,* the market is mature and no longer growing.

User perception is a property that captures the expectations of users. If a component is unusual, confusing, exciting, or surprising, it belongs in *genesis.* At the other extreme, if a certain component is a table-stakes expectation, it fits in *commodity.* A restaurant menu capability has both a mature market and is a standard capability in the industry, again fitting into *commodity*. *Restaurant optimization,* on the other hand, could be exciting if restaurant owners are shocked to see the potential or perhaps even confused if they don't understand how to leverage it.

The market would also appear uncertain—can this apply to all restaurants or just certain types of restaurants? So this time, *restaurant optimization* appears to sit somewhere between *genesis* and *custom built* based on the current level of understanding.

Table 5.2   A sample of the general properties

	Genesis	**Custom built**	**Product**	**Commodity**
Market	Undefined market	Slowly increasing consumption	Growing market	Mature market
User perception	Different/confusing/exciting/surprising	Leading edge/emerging	Common/disappointed if not used or available	Standard/expected
Perception in industry	Competitive advantage/unpredictable/unknown	Competitive advantage/ROI/case examples	Advantage through implementation/features	Cost of doing business/accepted
Focus of value	High future worth	Seeking profit/ROI?	High profitability	High volume/reducing margin

What is competitive advantage?

Investopedia says, "Competitive advantage refers to factors that allow a company to produce goods or services better or more cheaply than its rivals. These factors allow the productive entity to generate more sales or superior margins compared to its market rivals" (http://mng.bz/QRgQ). Further, competitive advantage can be broken down into comparative advantage and differential advantage.

Comparative advantage is an advantage derived from being able to extract greater profits while delivering a similar product or service. A differential advantage, on the other hand, is about offering products and services that are superior in some way, like more features or better usability.

Perception in industry and *focus of value* are related properties that focus on the possible level of competitive advantage gained through a component and will therefore be valuable indicators of strategic priorities. A restaurant menu is largely a cost of doing business, a table-stakes feature (http://mng.bz/XqAp). It's also not an area where organizations want to invest more resources than necessary to keep it running. As table 5.2 shows, both of these signs are more evidence that *menu* is a *commodity* and is not of high strategic importance.

Restaurant optimization, however, *is* considered a source of competitive advantage. If you can help restaurants to be more profitable, they are more likely to partner with you, bringing customers along with them. *Restaurant optimization* may even have a net negative effect on company finances, because the effort invested is more than the value it generates. But the company is still excited due to its high future potential. These two signs also indicate that *restaurant optimization* is somewhere between *genesis* and *custom built.*

It could be argued that, for some restaurants, designing a menu is a competitive advantage by offering different and unique recipes. It would be better to model this as a separate component, like *menu R&D,* to distinguish it from the capability of administering and browsing menus. There's also a deeper question: Is this a capability that the food delivery company considers part of the landscape? Even if it's not, it could still be worth mapping because it represents a potential growth opportunity.

5.3.2 *Rapid learning exercise: Grasping evolution*

When teaching Wardley Mapping or mapping with first-time mappers, I facilitate a short preparation activity to help them grasp evolution. The activity takes only 20 to 30 minutes and immediately gets people to a level where they need to be for a productive first mapping session. The activity can be performed as a group or in small breakouts. To prepare the activity, you only need two things: an example component (or multiple) to map and the lists of characteristics and properties. Then, work through each individual criterion and determine which stage of evolution it best fits (like you saw in section 5.3.1 but with all 15 criteria). Finally, identify which criteria are most relevant to the component and assess which stage it belongs to. If working in breakout groups, you can review the results of each group as a large-group exercise and notice where there is divergence and convergence.

You will learn from this activity that components do not always neatly fit into a single phase of evolution. Some criteria may match on *product* while others match on *commodity,* for example, so an overall assessment needs to be made about which feels best. This helps to convey another key principle of Wardley Mapping: there is no objectively correct answer for where a component should go. There is usually an element of subjectivity because different people have different mental models of the value chains. Surfacing this divergence is good because it's a learning opportunity, allowing the group to improve their shared understanding.

The main thing is to have productive conversations discussing why a component could fit in multiple places. This is one way to challenge the map.

On the book's Miro board (http://mng.bz/wj2W) you can find a template all set up for this activity. There's also an example scenario if you want to practice on a fictitious example before trying this exercise on components from your business. Why not give it a try right now?

5.4 *Climatic forces*

Evolution is the defining characteristic of Wardley Mapping. By focusing on how each component is evolving, you are naturally drawn into looking ahead to possible future scenarios. This is a big advantage for overcoming biases, like the *recency bias* (a cognitive bias that gives greater significance to more recent events), which can cause us to remain overfocused on current opportunities and constraints. In Wardley Mapping, the *climate* refers to changes that are happening to the landscape outside of your control, like competitor innovations and major world events. The better you identify climatic signals, the better you can anticipate changes and incorporate them into your strategic thinking.

You can apply climatic forces to your map by working through each of your components individually and thinking about the possible scenarios outside of your control that could cause it to change. In addition, you can think about new components that may appear in the landscape. You may not have all the information to answer these questions, so further research is needed, but that's normal. Wardley Mapping isn't a one-shot activity. Before applying climatic forces to your first map, it's good to learn about the climatic patterns (https://learnwardleymapping.com/climate/) provided by the community. These will help you understand the principles underlying climatic forces and what to consider when looking for climatic signals in your landscape. The following sections introduce some of the most common climatic patterns to help you get started.

5.4.1   *Everything evolves*

The first and most fundamental climatic pattern to grasp is that all components evolve. It's not always clear how quickly or when they will evolve, but according to the principles of Wardley Mapping, all components will evolve from left to right or could die at any point during evolution.

Take a moment to think about some of the systems you have worked on and the products you use. How have they evolved, and how do you anticipate they might evolve in the future? On my desk, I see my iPhone. In the late 1990s, mobile phones had no cameras and only elementary games like Snake. Today, smartphone cameras have evolved from an amazing and exciting idea to a table-stakes expectation, albeit still with some room for differentiation.

Table 5.3 highlights some characteristics (https://learnwardleymapping.com/climate/) and how they appear at each end of the evolution spectrum. *Genesis* is considered uncharted territory, treading a new path that hasn't existed before. As such, it's a highly chaotic, uncertain, and unpredictable phase in pursuit of future sources of competitive advantage. Meanwhile, *commodity* is considered to be *industrialized*. It's ordered, known, and measured. Competitive advantage has come and gone, and now the focus is on stability and efficiency, a cost of doing business rather than a source of competitive advantage.

Table 5.3   Some characteristics that change with evolution

Uncharted	Industrialized
Chaotic	Ordered
Uncertain	Known
Unpredictable	Measured

Table 5.3 Some characteristics that change with evolution *(continued)*

Uncharted	Industrialized
Changing	Stable
Future worth	Low margin
Exciting	Obvious
Competitive advantage	Cost of doing business

An interesting question to ponder is, "Why does everything evolve (or die)?" The answer in Wardley Mapping is *supply and demand competition.* The more demand for a component to evolve, the more likely it is to evolve because of incentives. When assessing potential climatic changes, this is a great question: "How much demand is there for this component to evolve?"

5.4.2 *Components coevolve*

As you've seen, a Wardley Map is constructed from *value chains,* which are effectively components and their dependencies. Dependencies signify that a change in one component may affect connected components. Often, components of different types will evolve together. Examples of this are all around us and are present throughout history.

Earlier today, I went to the supermarket to purchase my regulars, bread and milk. I used a self-scanning checkout. A few years ago, all checkouts required a staff member to scan each item and take the payment. With self-scanning checkouts, it's now possible for one employee to oversee multiple checkouts. And the activity has changed, too. This person is now responsible for fixing problems when customers cannot scan items and pay themselves.

In the business world, a good example has been the coevolution of components in the remote working space. With the increasing pervasiveness of the internet and a new generation of remote collaboration tools like Zoom, Slack, and Google Drive, the conditions were created that allowed the practice of working remotely to evolve rapidly.

HIGHER-ORDER SYSTEMS CREATE NEW SOURCES OF VALUE

One important coevolution pattern is called *higher order systems create new sources of value.* As shown in figure 5.9, this pattern is characterized by the creation of new *genesis* components, enabled by the evolution of other components toward becoming more commoditized. As electricity became more of a widespread commodity, it allowed the creation of many new types of products. As online payment services evolved, more businesses were able to operate online. Likewise, as the internet developed and became more widespread, it became the source of many types of recreational and commercial sources of value. This is always a pattern to consider when applying climatic thinking to your own maps. You can ask questions like "As this component evolves, what becomes possible? What new *genesis* components could come into existence?"

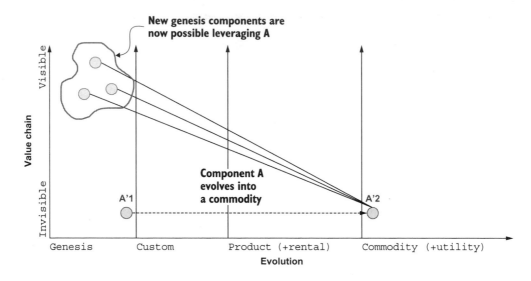

Figure 5.9   Higher-order systems create new sources of value

EFFICIENCY ENABLES INNOVATION

The evolution of one component may not lead to the creation of new sources of value—that is, new *genesis* components. Instead, it may lead to the evolution of existing components. Amazon Web Services is a classic example of this. As Amazon evolved its e-commerce capabilities, its business grew immensely. As a result, Amazon became an expert at managing infrastructure for high-scale internet traffic. It then split this out into a separate cloud computing business, moving IT infrastructure toward becoming a commodity. Whenever exploring the evolution of a component on your map, it's healthy to explore how other components might also be able to evolve as a result of a changing landscape with new or different constraints.

5.4.3   *Past success breeds inertia*

As the old saying goes, "Why change something if it isn't broken?" When a business establishes itself as a market leader and all of its key metrics, like revenue, continue to look healthy, why risk changing? But because the climate is always changing, this can turn out to be a false sense of security as companies like Kodak found out (http://mng.bz/yZ2y). Chapter 3 also gave examples of internal manifestations of inertia, like legacy systems and inefficient ways of working not being modernized through complacency. Inertia is always something to look for on a Wardley Map, especially in the *product* phase, where concepts are most profitable but also most likely to become industrialized and lose value. It's good to ask probing questions like "Is this really still a product, or is it becoming a commodity?" "Are we too focused on current revenue streams and blind to changes that are happening to this component?" or "Is it possible new entrants could disrupt us here?"

Inertia is something you can highlight on your map, using a filled-in rectangle shape, as shown in figure 5.10, which demonstrates a component evolving from product to commodity, but the organization is unwilling to accept or does not recognize this and, therefore, has inertia.

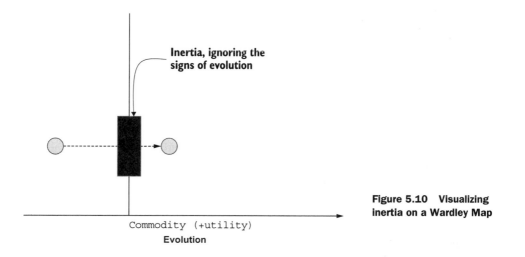

Inertia, ignoring the signs of evolution

Commodity (+utility)
Evolution

Figure 5.10   Visualizing inertia on a Wardley Map

Two other closely related inertia patterns are *inertia increases the more successful the past model is* and *inertia can kill an organization.* You can operationalize the principles behind these patterns by trying to understand just how successful your business is regarding certain components and how attached stakeholders might be to those components. Questions such as the following can help open up these conversations: "How much would you say <component> contributes to the success of this organization?" "What if we were disrupted and <component> was no longer relevant?" "It looks to me like <component> will soon be widespread. Should we move on from this and invest in something more differentiating?"

These questions are intentionally provocative to try and see how much conviction people have in current/past successes. I find turning up the heat a little bit in small doses helps people challenge their own beliefs; just be careful not to go over the top.

5.4.4   Change is not always linear

A Wardley Map might give the impression that each component follows a predictable path of evolution from *genesis* to *commodity.* The truth is evolution is a complex topic. How, why, when, and how fast evolution happens are all things that can vary significantly. Some industries may be slow-moving, but a sudden change, like new technology, can rapidly speed up innovation. A number of industries experienced this with the pandemic, notably Miro, the online collaboration platform. In-person work was no longer possible, and we all switched to Miro (or similar products) for workshops, meetings, conferences, and any other collaboration that would typically have been in person.

84 CHAPTER 5 *Wardley Mapping*

According to a case study on the AWS website (http://mng.bz/M9Wo), Miro grew steadily in the years before the pandemic. But during COVID times, Miro grew 500% in just two years to reach 30 million users by January 2022, including 99% of the Fortune 100. It's staggering, considering that Miro scaled so quickly and was able to provide a highly reliable product. Companies all around the world in every time zone rely on Miro to be up and running. If Miro had not been able to scale its business, technology, and organization when the rate of change in its landscape increased enormously, Miro would have missed out on a market-defining opportunity.

As you work through the components on your Wardley Maps, keep the story of Miro in the back of your mind (or a story that's more relevant to you and doesn't involve pandemics). Don't just look at how likely components are to evolve in the future; look at how quickly they evolved in the past. This might help you to see signals that the pace is about to change or alert you to where you aren't prepared for a change. It could very well be that parts of your architecture would be the bottleneck if your landscape entered a market-defining era where the pace of change suddenly intensified. This doesn't mean building an infinitely scalable system, it's all about assessing the probabilities and making conscious decisions about which risks and opportunities you want to invest in and be most prepared for.

5.4.5 Assessing the effect of climatic changes

After applying potential climatic forces to your map, it's good to zoom out and look at global themes similarly to when the map was initially created. For example, as shown in figure 5.11, it might be that all of your components are moving to the right of the

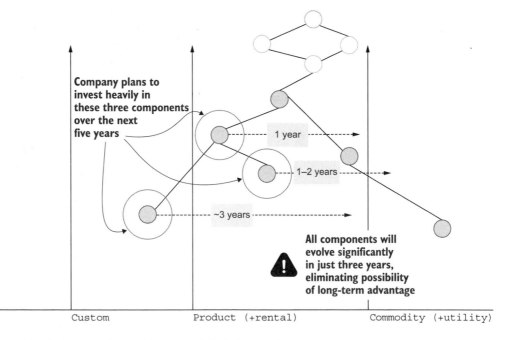

Figure 5.11 Climatic changes indicating a lack of future differentiators

map, and your organization has no source of future competitive advantage. It could also be the case that a lot of your components are going to become a commodity within one to two years. That could be a significant warning if your current strategy involves major investment in those areas because they will no longer offer a chance to differentiate. It would most likely be a big waste of resources for a component that will soon be available off the shelf.

A UK-based company I spent some time with had built an in-house CRM about a decade previously when such a decision was justifiable. When I worked with them, they were very keen to get to a modern CRM like Salesforce, which was much cheaper to operate and had way more advanced capabilities. The problem, however, was that the CRM was part of the same codebase as some of their more bespoke capabilities. It was highly coupled at the code and database levels. Essentially, the costs of moving to a commodity service were very high. This is the type of insight that technologists can bring to Wardley Mapping sessions: thinking ahead to potential future build-vs-buy decisions and identifying the architectural costs that would be associated. Even better is to identify things that might evolve into a commodity earlier and not couple them to other parts of the system in the first place.

During a Wardley Mapping session with a North American company in the property management space, I asked people for their observations. As we got to the head of product, he remarked, "Everything in our industry evolves so quickly! From left to right in just a year!" This was because competitors were easily able to copy each other, so there was no way to create a lasting advantage in any area, which was a big lightbulb moment for some of the group, especially those with less of a business and product mindset. They understood that a constant source of new innovations was necessary.

5.5 *Making strategic decisions*

When reaching part five of the Strategy Cycle, it's time to start thinking about choices. How do you actively want to change the landscape? Which components do you want to evolve, how will you prioritize investments, and how much is right to invest in each area? Answering these questions on a business level will enable modernization leaders to focus on building a compelling modernization vision around identifying the highest leverage modernization opportunities.

It must be stressed that making decisions doesn't have to happen in the same workshop where the Wardley Map is created. It's normal to have multiple sessions with different people and groups. And it might be necessary to get deeper into the landscape, using techniques like EventStorming, to create more refined maps before going too deep into decision-making. Of course, it's ok to explore possible strategic choices from the first session and continue to refine them over time. The main risk is staying high level and getting attached to early ideas that are not validated with more rigorous analysis.

As with other stages of the Strategy Cycle, Wardley Mapping also provides principles and patterns for the Leadership step. These patterns are considered advanced. It's much more important to master climatic patterns and doctrine before attempting a Hollywood-style strategy. You need to have the right culture, thinking, and ability to execute in place first. Nevertheless, the gameplay patterns are fascinating and worth learning if you keep the caveats in mind. The community has put together more than sixty gameplay patterns (http://mng.bz/am4o). The next section introduces a selection of the patterns to help begin your journey into the topic.

5.5.1 *Accelerators to evolution*

One option for purposely attempting to evolve the landscape is to apply *accelerators*. These actions accelerate the evolution of one or more components to your perceived advantage. For each component on your map, think about how you may gain an advantage from the component evolving, and then explore the list of accelerators to identify the best option. Accelerators are visualized on a Wardley Map using fat arrows, as shown in figure 5.12.

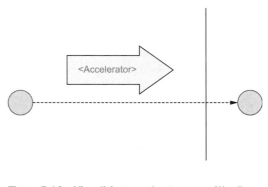

Figure 5.12   Visualizing accelerators on a Wardley Map

OPEN APPROACHES

Open approaches, like open sourcing, are a common *accelerator.* By open-sourcing a component, the component becomes more widespread, and anybody interested in the component can contribute to developing it. Big Tech relies heavily on open source. Google, Amazon, and Microsoft all rely on open source to varying degrees. Microsoft, for example, open-sourced the entire .NET Framework. Open source is an enabler of community-driven innovation in various fields and academia. TensorFlow (https://github.com/tensorflow/tensorflow) is an open-source machine learning platform with over three thousand contributors on GitHub. It started life as an internal capability used by the Google Brain team. But rather than keeping it private and gaining some advantage, the team decided to use *open source* as an *accelerator.*

Open-sourcing a component means giving away any advantage you may have since now all your competitors can use it. It makes more sense when looked at from the other perspective. If your competitor gains an advantage over you through a certain component, open-sourcing your version of the component can remove its advantage by allowing a large community to contribute and out-develop competitor versions. In addition, you will gain the brand reputation boost because you gave it to the open-source community.

Many leaders are reluctant even to discuss the idea of open-sourcing a component to which their competitors could have access, but it's important to explore the possibilities, particularly keeping in mind that a competitor could use *open source* against you.

NETWORK EFFECTS

In the same way that open-sourcing a component accelerates evolution by opening up the possibility for entire communities to contribute, *network effects* accelerate evolution by allowing a wider group of people to contribute. *Network effects* are particularly noticeable in social networks. The more people that join the platform—particularly high-value content creators that draw in crowds—the faster the ecosystem grows and develops. Is it possible that network effects could accelerate the evolution of your landscape?

A good example to keep in mind is Slack, the enterprise chat tool. Slack used network effects as an accelerator by opening up Slack to allow developers to create custom Slack applications. Slack integrations are a prominent feature of how most enterprises use the tool, evidenced by the 2400 applications in Slack's marketplace. This catalog of custom applications helped evolve the ecosystem much more rapidly than if Slack had to build all those custom applications in-house (which would be impractical, if not impossible).

COOPERATION

Cooperation is another accelerator to consider when seeking to accelerate the evolution of a component. Partnering with another company can provide access to necessary capabilities much faster and more cost-effectively than building them yourself. We saw this in 2019 when Apple and Goldman Sachs joined forces to launch a new credit card, Apple Card. Apple wanted to offer physical credit cards to accelerate its Apple Pay service. But Apple didn't have the capabilities to launch a credit card on its own, and cooperation was much more cost-effective and faster than developing the necessary capability itself.

5.5.2 De-accelerators to evolution

In contrast to *accelerators*, *de-accelerators* can be applied to slow down evolution. Whenever you identify a component from which you derive an advantage, you will naturally want to lock in or extend the duration of your advantage by slowing down evolution as the component moves toward *commodity*. The following are examples of *de-accelerators* you should consider applying to your components. As with accelerators, de-accelerators are visualized with a fat arrow facing from right to left, as shown in figure 5.13.

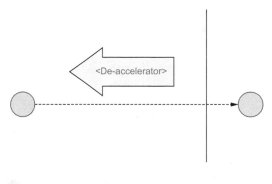

Figure 5.13   Visualizing De-accelerators on a Wardley Map

INTELLECTUAL PROPERTY RIGHTS

Intellectual property (IP) rights are deployed to protect competitive advantage in some industries. They act as *de-accelerators* by preventing competitors from employing certain capabilities that you invented. One of the biggest IP lawsuits in recent years was the Apple vs Samsung case (https://www.bbc.co.uk/news/business-44248404). Samsung was ordered to pay Apple $539 million by a South Korean court after being found to be in violation of multiple Apple patents. Apple claimed that Samsung had illegally copied aspects of the iPhone design that were protected by its patents. Apple's iPhone was revolutionary, so it made sense that it wanted to protect its advantage as strongly as possible and make competitors work harder to build smartphones as good as the iPhone.

FEAR, UNCERTAINTY, AND DOUBT

Another way to de-accelerate evolution is to alter the perception of users negatively, reducing their demand for a more evolved component. Effectively, it's a propaganda technique that creates false narratives or overhypes small risks into major showstoppers. The last few years have seen *fear, uncertainty, and doubt* (FUD) used as a technique to scare customers away from serverless technologies. Notably, vendor lock-in is pushed as a reason to avoid serverless—for instance, "Don't use AWS, you are giving Amazon access to all your data" was long used as a fear tactic to scare businesses from using the cloud. Examples of FUD can also be found outside tech. In 1877, the *New York Times* wrote an article attacking Bell's invention (http://mng.bz/g7Yx)—the telephone. The narrative caused fear among readers by stirring up privacy concerns.

When looking at your own maps, you may notice signs where FUD could be employed. Perhaps a disruptive new entrant has joined your industry and is moving much faster than you can. If you're unable to compete through innovation, then employing FUD as a marketing technique may be your only choice. There are obvious ethical and moral problems concerning FUD.

5.5.3   *Market plays*

Market plays is a category of gameplay patterns that involve taking actions that change some aspect of a market, like product development, perception change, and pricing policy. This section provides a brief introduction to two common market plays that are relevant in a wide range of industries.

DIFFERENTIATION

One obvious approach is to differentiate your products by addressing user needs better than your competitors. When looking for opportunities to differentiate each of your components, the following list of product attributes is a good starting point: better customer service/after-sales service, more variety, faster or cheaper shipping, location, aesthetics, usability, exclusive features, and customization. The story of Airbnb's early history provides a good example of product attribute differentiation. Airbnb improved its listings by adding professional-quality images. This was seen as a critical moment that led to huge growth for the company (http://mng.bz/eERP). Zalando's 100-day return policy (http://mng.bz/p1E2) is an example of customer service being a differentiating attribute, and T-Mobile USA differentiates on exclusive features by allowing tourists to purchase an eSIM before they arrive in the country.

HARVESTING

Sometimes data is the key asset to gaining an advantage in an industry. By having access to data that reveals market trends and unmet user needs, a company has the powerful ability to identify new opportunities. *Harvesting* is achieved by building a platform or creating a marketplace, allowing others to build on your offerings. Having other businesses, including competitors, profiting from your capabilities sounds risky. You're giving away your advantage to help competitors who could use it to take away market share. But by having all of their interactions on your platform, you will have the most insights about consumer behaviors and unmet needs.

One organization building a market-specific IoT platform faced just this dilemma. They could either create a platform with capabilities like geofencing, remote monitoring, and fleet management exclusively for their customers or open up the platform and allow their competitors to use the platform as well. Ultimately, their vision was to own the whole ecosystem and have access to all of the data, even from their competitors, so opening up their platform to everybody was the obvious decision.

NOTE I highly recommend two excellent books for going deeper into the world of Wardley Mapping and complementary techniques: *Adaptive Systems With Domain-Driven Design, Wardley Mapping, and Team Topologies* by Susanne Kaiser (http://mng.bz/OPAo) and *The Value Flywheel Effect* by David Anderson (http://mng.bz/YROK).

Summary

- Wardley Mapping is becoming the de-facto strategy tool in business and technology communities. It's a collaborative technique that involves mapping business landscapes as value chains with evolving components. It's a valuable technique when building the business case for architecture modernization.
- The terminology from Wardley Mapping is also becoming widespread.
- Wardley Mapping can be used at many points in a modernization journey rather than a tool just used for a few workshops at the beginning.
- An iterative approach to strategy is best, combining the strengths of other techniques like Event Storming to get deeper insights about the business, which can help to create better maps.
- The Strategy Cycle is a visual tool for thinking about the strategy process and guiding you through the process. It comprises five parts: purpose, landscape, climate, doctrine, and leadership.
  - *Purpose* is the ultimate ambition of an organization, such as reducing carbon emissions.
  - *Landscape* is all of the things that are strategically relevant, like products, capabilities, and practices.
  - *Climate* is the forces outside your organization that cause a change in the landscape.
  - *Doctrine* is about ensuring your organization is set up to achieve the strategy effectively.
  - *Leadership* is making decisions, deciding how you want to affect the landscape to gain an advantage.
- When creating your first map, Ben Mosior's canvas guides you through the process in six steps:

- *Step 1*—Define the purpose
- *Step 2*—Set the scope of the map
- *Step 3*—Identify relevant users
- *Step 4*—Articulate the needs of each user
- *Step 5*—Construct value chains of components for each user need
- *Step 6*—Move the value chains onto a map, and move each component to the stage of evolution that seems correct

- After constructing the map, it's already possible to identify strategic risks and opportunities like not having any future differentiators or investing too heavily in components where no advantage can be gained.

- There are four stages of evolution: genesis, custom built, product, and commodity.

- Grasping the nuances of evolution can be tricky, so the community has provided characteristics and properties for determining the correct stage of evolution for a given component.

- Ubiquity and certainty are two of the characteristics for assessing evolution. Ubiquity represents how common a component is. A rare component would fit in genesis, while a widespread component would fit into a commodity. For certainty, a poorly understood component would fit into genesis, while a commonly understood component would fit into commodity.

- Some of the general properties used to determine evolution are market, user perception, perception in industry, and focus of value.

- There are two types of competitive advantage. Comparative advantage refers to an advantage gained by extracted greater margins through similar products or services to competitors, while a differential advantage is an advantage through better products and services.

- After building a map, it's important to consider climatic forces like competitor actions and world events (like a pandemic). You don't want to build a strategy around current constraints that may be about to change.

- There are several climatic patterns provided by the community, including everything evolves, components coevolve, and higher-order systems create new sources of value.

- Inertia is a climatic pattern that is common to many successful organizations. The more successful they become, the more complacent and risk-averse they become. This creates an opportunity for competitors.

- Patterns exist to help with making strategic decisions. Some examples are as follows:
  - Accelerators are actions that aim to intentionally speed up evolution of components like open source and cooperation.
  - De-accelerators are actions that aim to intentionally slow down acceleration to protect an advantage like IP rights and FUD.

- A Wardley Map can be used to highlight architectural options and decisions like codebase boundaries, team organization, and platforms.

Product taxonomy

This chapter covers

- Defining building blocks to describe your architecture
- Guiding principles for designing a product taxonomy
- Mapping modernization opportunities and challenges in each business area

An important part of architecture modernization is building a vision of the modernized architecture. This enables you to identify the opportunities and challenges in each area and plan your journey from the current state to the future vision. To do this, you'll need a language—a set of building blocks—for describing your architecture, from a top-level macro view to individual software applications.

There is no universally accepted language for describing architecture. So you'll need to choose—or invent—one that works for your business. In this chapter, I'll show you one possible approach, called a product taxonomy. It's a set of building blocks for describing architecture driven by a company's products and the business and customer outcomes they enable.

I recommend a product-centric approach because it helps you to design an architecture and organization structure for empowered product teams with sustainable fast flow optimized for key business outcomes. But you don't have to use the building blocks presented in this chapter to benefit from the ideas in the book. It's just one possible approach (although a good, sensible default). You can translate to your preferred building blocks accordingly.

Keep in mind that this chapter focuses on defining a language to describe your architecture. It doesn't cover using the building blocks to design an architecture, which is covered in later chapters.

6.1   Defining the building blocks

Defining the building blocks is the first step toward building and using a product taxonomy. You will use these concepts to model your architecture and the language used to describe your business. You're welcome to define building blocks that make the most sense for your organization.

This section provides example building blocks you can use as a starting point. It doesn't try to cover every possible scenario for every organization. You should adapt, extend, or completely replace as necessary. For example, not all products and capabilities will be digital. Therefore, you could show non-digital concepts to keep the complete picture in mind when making design decisions. While reading this section, remember that the following chapters cover each concept in greater detail.

6.1.1   Independent value streams

Independent value streams are a crucial building block because identifying independent value streams is key to achieving fast flow. In this book, value streams refer to development value streams; the sequence of activities a team goes through from identifying unmet user needs to delivering a solution and validating that it addresses those needs (shown in figure 6.1), like adding new features to a product. Typically, this will involve many activities, such as product discovery sessions, defining requirements, planning, coding, reviewing, testing, and deploying.

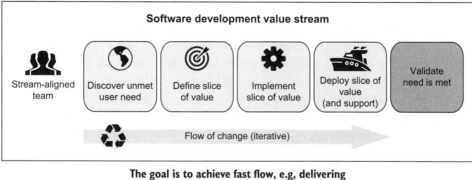

**The goal is to achieve fast flow, e.g, delivering
small slices of value/learning every day.**

Figure 6.1   The high-level activities in an independent value stream

The nature of value streams can vary. Some examples include a price calculation service exposed by an API, a search service with an API and UI widget, and a mobile application (if small enough to be owned by a single team).

As shown in figure 6.2, there are four crucial characteristics to establishing an independent value stream with fast flow:

- Being aligned to a loosely coupled business subdomain (or other part of the product like a frontend)
- Being driven by purposeful business outcomes
- Being owned by an autonomous stream-aligned team
- Having decoupled software architecture aligned to the business subdomain, which the team is empowered to change and deploy

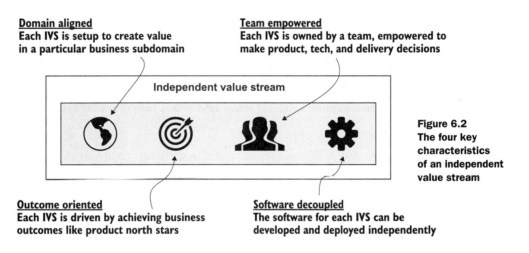

Domain aligned
Each IVS is setup to create value in a particular business subdomain

Team empowered
Each IVS is owned by a team, empowered to make product, tech, and delivery decisions

Independent value stream

Figure 6.2
The four key characteristics of an independent value stream

Outcome oriented
Each IVS is driven by achieving business outcomes like product north stars

Software decoupled
The software for each IVS can be developed and deployed independently

When these aspects are in place and value streams are highly independent, teams will be motivated to achieve a business outcome and empowered to design, implement, and deliver solutions with minimal dependencies on people outside the team. These aspects are covered in more detail throughout this and the following chapters.

6.1.2 Domains

Value streams will never be 100% independent. The power of organizations is that the work of many teams together produces higher-level capabilities that no single team alone could deliver. Therefore, it's necessary to identify value streams that contribute to the same higher-level business outcomes and group them so that the relevant teams stay aligned, share knowledge, and cooperate as effectively as possible to achieve end-to-end fast flow, not just within a single value stream.

Domains are the building blocks that represent a group of related subdomains that involve similar domain concepts and contribute to the same higher-level purposes. Therefore, value streams are organized into domains based on the relationship between their subdomains and business outcomes.

Figure 6.3 shows the example of two domains. One is a *fulfillment* domain composed of four subdomains: *availability*, *last mile*, *warehousing*, and *logistics*. A dedicated value stream has been established for each subdomain.

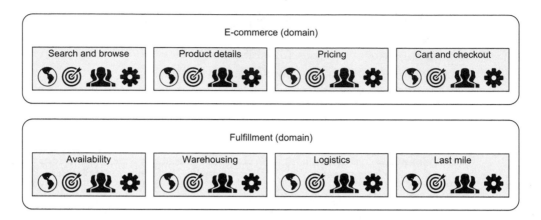

Figure 6.3   A fulfillment domain composed of four subdomains, each with a dedicated value stream

In larger organizations, domains may be defined hierarchically at different scopes to align related groups and establish higher-level lines of accountability. Figure 6.4 illustrates this concept, as based on Ruth Malan and Dana Bredemeyer's Architectural Levels of Scope (http://mng.bz/yZ1o):

- *Architecture scope 1/scope 1 domain*—A single subdomain/value stream or small cluster owned by the same team
- *Architecture scope 2/scope 2 domain*—A group of related scope 1 domains with complexity that requires multiple teams
- *Architecture scope 3/scope 3 domain*—A group of scope 2 domains that requires multiple groups of teams to handle the levels of complexity

The number of scopes will depend on the size of the organization and complexity of the domain. Some organizations have more than three scopes, as the Salesforce example later in the chapter shows. And some organizations have fewer.

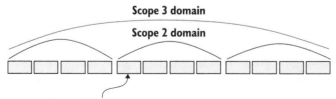

**Figure 6.4
Architecture scopes 1 to 3**

Not all domains at a given scope will be the same size and complexity. Figure 6.4 is a simplification to express the general concept, not an aspirational one-size-fits-all.

6.1.3 Products

Identifying the optimal value streams and domains hinges on an important question: What business outcomes do you want to optimize for? Many inputs are required to answer this question (including listening and Wardley Mapping sessions). One important step is identifying the organization's products and ascertaining the business and customer value they provide. This is critical to understanding how to shape domain boundaries and how they all fit together to enable strategic business outcomes.

A successful product creates value for both customers and the business. Products should be desirable to the customer, feasible for the company to build, and strategically viable. It's essential to keep these in mind when determining each product's outcomes. Improved productivity and increased sales are examples of customer value, while money and data are examples of business value. Some products will be internal. The value they provide will include improved productivity or reduced operating costs. Identifying and choosing the right outcomes using north stars was covered in chapter 3.

Products can vary widely in size and complexity. It's natural for them to start small and continue to grow in complexity over time as new features are added. Some are small enough that they can be owned by just one or a few teams, whereas others require dozens or more teams. Therefore, there is not a 1:1 mapping between products and scopes. A single product could be fully satisfied by the value streams within a single scope 2 domain or could span multiple scope 3 domains as shown in Figure 6.5.

Small product

Larger, more complex product

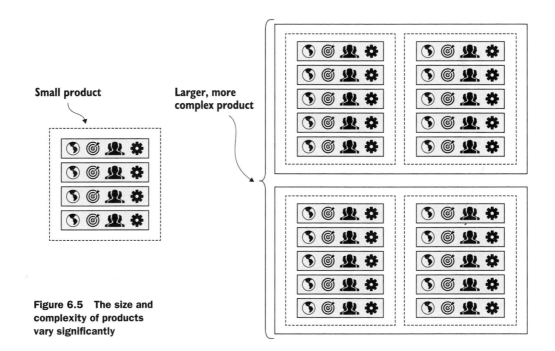

Figure 6.5 The size and complexity of products vary significantly

The word product is highly ambiguous. If it's a word that you're struggling to define, a suggested definition is provided at the end of the chapter.

6.1.4   *Platforms*

Organizations with multiple products often have to consider reuse and economies of scale. When multiple products all use the same or similar capabilities, platforms can be created to centralize the shared capabilities.

Platforms are always a delicate challenge to balance. On the one hand, they're cost-efficient and provide economies of scale because capabilities are built once and reused many times rather than duplicating the work in each team. On the other hand, platforms very easily become bottlenecks when they cannot keep up with all consumers' needs or provide the capabilities in an easy-to-consume way.

Broadly, there are two types of platforms, as shown in figure 6.6 (both of them go by various names in the industry):

- *Domain platforms/horizontals* provide capabilities relevant to the business domain, like a shared booking system.
- *Internal development platforms (IDP)/internal technology platforms (ITPs)* provide capabilities to help teams build and support their products.

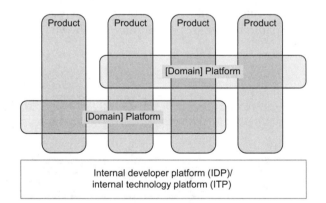

Figure 6.6   Platforms provide reuse across multiple products

Both types of platforms are crucial to architecture modernization. The following two industry examples clarify what these terms mean and what they look like in practice.

The scope of platforms is variable. Some are limited to a small set of products, while others can be enterprise-wide, supporting all or many of a company's products, like a centralized identity platform.

INDUSTRY EXAMPLE: UBER'S TRIP FULFILLMENT PLATFORM

Uber's trip fulfillment platform (http://mng.bz/M9xD) (aka fulfillment platform) is an excellent example of a high-value *horizontal* that supports multiple *verticals* (e.g., products, services, markets), as shown in figure 6.7. Uber refers to this as a foundational Uber capability and describes its purpose, "Fulfillment is the 'act or process of delivering a product or service to a customer.' The fulfillment organization at Uber develops *platforms* to orchestrate and manage the lifecycle of ongoing orders and user sessions with millions of active participants."

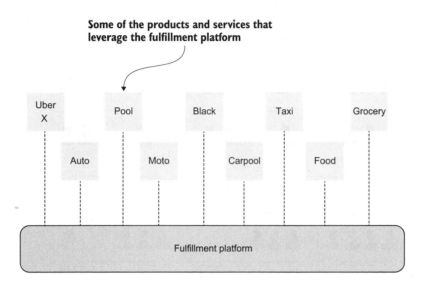

Figure 6.7   Uber's products and services that use Uber's fulfillment platform

When Uber started expanding from a single- to a multi-product company, it didn't need to build completely new fulfillment capabilities for each new *vertical*. It extracted fulfillment into an enterprise-wide *platform* that all verticals could directly use to reduce costs, improve time to market, and increase retention of customers and drivers. As a result, Uber's fulfillment platform has a very high level of reuse, which is not always the case for all *platforms*. It's common to see platforms that have become organizational bottlenecks due to the unique feature requests of each team that consumes the *platform*. Reuse is always a double-edged sword that should be applied carefully by considering domain, technical, and social criteria.

INDUSTRY EXAMPLE: NAV'S INTERNAL TECHNOLOGY PLATFORM

NAV (Norwegian Labour and Welfare Administration) is the largest public agency in Norway. Its mission is to assist people in work and provide a series of benefits related to pensions, disease, unemployment, and others. NAV normally provides services to around 2.5 million citizens every year. Internally, they have over 100 teams working on their digital operations. To help these teams build and operate products more effectively, NAV developed an *IDP* that they refer to as their internal technology platform (http://mng.bz/am79), as shown in figure 6.8. The *platform* is itself composed of multiple *sub-platforms* as opposed to being considered a single monolithic entity. Examples include an infrastructure platform (https://nais.io/), a data platform (https://docs.knada.io/), and a design system.

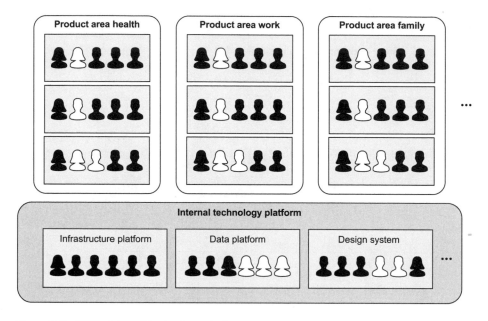

Figure 6.8   NAV's internal technology platform

Decomposing a large platform into sub-platforms is a common pattern in organizations where platforms reach a certain maturity and scale. It's a key step in preventing platforms from becoming bottlenecks, as it allows individual teams to be responsible for individual parts of the platform rather than requiring every team member to know about every part of the platform, an approach that does not scale and can lead to employee burnout.

A key takeaway from NAV's platform story is that, while the *platform* is large and varied in nature, it was developed on an as-needed basis. It wasn't fully specified upfront and delivered as a big three-year project. Those kinds of big-bang platform projects are notoriously risky and unsuccessful. Another key highlight from NAV's platform approach is that they treat IDPs with the same mindset as their other products. They think of internal employees as the customer and try to make the platform as attractive as possible by reducing the cognitive load, freeing them up to perform their work more effectively. This is a crucial aspect of building platforms, referred to as platform-as-a-product (http://mng.bz/g7N8), that enables fast flow. It is covered in more detail later in the book.

6.1.5 Product groups and portfolios

For large and very large organizations with tens of thousands of employees, there is even greater complexity at higher levels of scale. In their product taxonomy, Ross Clanton et al. (http://mng.bz/eEdG) propose the terms *product group* and *product portfolio* for these higher levels. A product group is a collection of products that contribute to related outcomes or have delivery dependencies, and a product portfolio is a collection of product groups that share some relationship. Platform group and platform portfolio are the corresponding macro structures for platforms. While modernization may not always result in changes at the product group and portfolio levels, it's good to have a clear understanding of them and how lower-level modernization decisions fit into the bigger picture.

6.1.6 Industry example: Salesforce product taxonomy (2017)

Salesforce is a good example of a large organization with multiple *product portfolios*. In 2017, I worked as a principal engineer in the Salesforce marketing cloud. At that time, there were around thirty thousand employees globally, although Salesforce was continually growing organically and through regular acquisitions. As a result, Salesforce had a large, heterogenous IT estate and various organizational cultures across multiple international regions. At the top level, Salesforce was architected into more than ten *product portfolios*, referred to as clouds. Examples include sales cloud, service cloud, marketing cloud, and commerce cloud.

Marketing cloud was a product portfolio that by itself attained revenues of $933 million in 2017 (http://mng.bz/p1gR). It had its own dedicated CTO and CEO who reported to the global CTO and CEO, respectively. The marketing cloud was composed of multiple *product groups*, which were often, but not always, referred to as studios—for example, social studio, mobile studio, email studio, and advertising studio (as shown in figure 6.9).

The advertising studio *product group* comprised three *products*: advertising campaigns for building and running campaigns on social networks like Facebook and LinkedIn, advertising audiences for creating lookalike audiences based on existing customers, and lead capture for connecting leads from social networks to a customer's Salesforce account. Each of these was a product that customers could purchase separately and had its own codebase and teams building it. However, these products were architected as a *product group* for multiple reasons. Commercially, they were targeted at the same customers, and the company tried to package them up into B2B contracts. Additionally, the domain knowledge for the three products was very similar, so it made sense for the people involved to work closely together.

Individually, each *product* was composed of multiple software parts owned by multiple teams. Advertising campaigns, for example, had a variety of components, including a customer UI, an application for creating campaigns, an application for running and tracking campaigns, and an application for configuring campaign rules based on triggers and conditions.

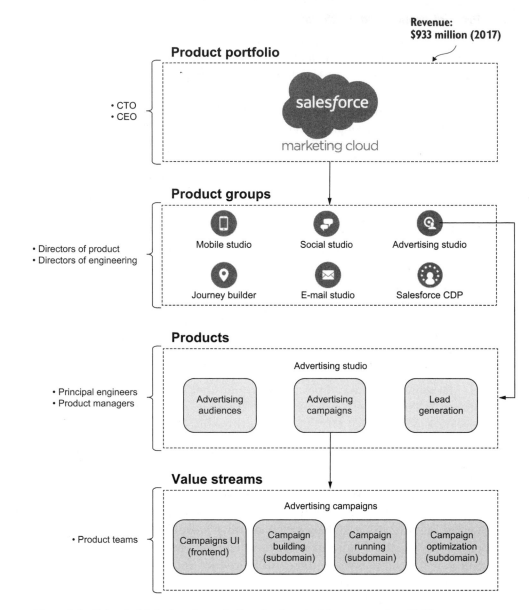

Figure 6.9   Extract of Salesforce's marketing cloud product taxonomy, circa 2017

6.1.7   *Building blocks cheat sheet*

Several concepts have been introduced in the section, and it may take a while to become familiar with them and how they fit together. Figure 6.10 is a cheat sheet to which you can quickly refer. You can also find an interactive version on this book's Miro board (http://mng.bz/OP2j).

Remember, these are just example building blocks you are free to adapt or use as a source of inspiration, or you can use your own completely different building blocks. This model does not try to account for every possible scenario. For example, you may need to add building blocks for non-software products and capabilities.

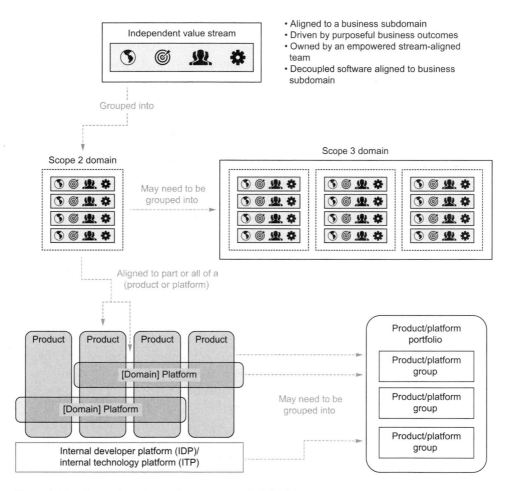

Figure 6.10 Cheat sheet for product taxonomy building blocks

NOTE There are many models for describing architectural concepts and their relationships at different levels of scope and in varying levels of granularity. Examples include Intersection's EDGY (https://intersection.group/tools/edgy/); Evan Bottcher's teams, domains, and verticals model (http://mng.bz/YRPj); Ruth Malan's architectural levels of scope (http://mng.bz/G9WA); BVSSH's value stream network (http://mng.bz/z0M6); and The Open Group's ArchiMate modeling language (http://mng.bz/orN2).

6.2 Designing a product taxonomy

Having established the building blocks of your product taxonomy, you can then use them to design your architecture as a product taxonomy. Many aspects of designing a taxonomy are covered in the remaining chapters of the book, and every organization's journey will be unique. However, this section highlights a few general principles that are worth keeping in mind before you start.

6.2.1 Start with the easier parts

Getting started can sometimes be the hardest part, so I recommend starting with the easier parts—things that are less subjective and less contentious. One example is individual products and services marketed and sold to customers as cohesive offerings. Reviewing a company's website and marketing materials is a good source of insight.

Another technique is looking at the organization chart. Reporting structures can indicate which parts of the business are considered independent from each other. Caution is required, however, because sometimes the existing organizational structure will require major changes to enable modernization. But you may still be able to use some of the current organization chart as a starting point to challenge and evolve.

After establishing individual products, you'll need to zoom in and explore how each particular product could be decomposed into value streams and identify where shared capabilities used by multiple products could be extracted into platforms. These decisions will usually be much more subjective and require deeper analysis using appropriate techniques.

6.2.2 Use appropriate techniques

One of the first questions people ask when designing a taxonomy is how to do it. The simple answer is that you can use whatever techniques with which you are comfortable or you feel are relevant. The techniques in this book, like EventStorming and Wardley Mapping, are tried and tested. However, if you feel that other techniques are needed, or you are more comfortable with them, that is totally fine.

One recommendation I always offer, regardless of the techniques used, is to avoid making critical taxonomy decisions based on a superficial high-level understanding. It's easy to fool yourself into thinking you have made good choices by staying at a high level. Some techniques are specifically designed to allow you to see the big picture but lack the level of detail needed to make more granular architecture decisions. So you will need to zoom into each area using techniques that surface more complexity. For example, if you use a technique that maps out a large part of your business in just ten sticky notes, it's likely to be missing a lot of key information needed to make more granular architecture decisions.

6.2.3 Expect constant evolution

Landscapes are constantly changing due to supply-and-demand competition, as Wardley Mapping teaches us. And it's easy to make the wrong decision when you know the least: perhaps an area turns out to be more complex than originally intended and needs to be split up, or perhaps unexpected dependencies have arisen that require excessive coordination, necessitating a rethink of the architecture. Therefore, there is no end-state. The product taxonomy will need to evolve, and this thinking should be baked into your approach from day one.

If you're ever in a situation where you have to get a decision correct up front because there will not be a chance to change it later, it's an alarm bell. Where is the pressure coming from to make such high-stakes decisions? What is the blocker to course correction in the future? This may be an indication of deeper cultural concerns that should be addressed. Of course, some decisions are more complicated to reverse than others, so it makes sense to spend more time planning up front where decisions will be more expensive to reverse later.

It's a good idea to publish an updated taxonomy regularly, like once per quarter. It signals that change is normal. The teams themselves will frequently discover the need for changes as they are closest to many triggers for evolution, like excessive collaboration with other teams or unclear priorities. So they must be encouraged to raise concerns when they feel evolution is necessary and not live with the misconception that the design is fixed.

6.2.4 *Distribute design responsibility*

One of the key reasons to define a taxonomy is to establish who is responsible for making decisions in each portfolio area, both during modernization and after. What are the responsibilities, and how will you assign them?

When designing the taxonomy, it is essential to avoid the antipattern of a centralized architecture team that designs the system and hands over the designs to the teams. In a product-led organization, responsibility is more decentralized, and the flow of changes is too high for a centralized team to oversee everything. As a result, the process of designing a taxonomy is more decentralized. It's a good idea for an AMET to facilitate and oversee the process, at least at the start of the journey.

Deciding where to allow autonomy and standardization is always a delicate balance. More autonomy can result in problems like tech sprawl, where each team uses different technologies, making collaboration harder as engineers cannot understand or contribute to work in other teams or rotate between teams. On the other hand, too much standardization can be overly constraining, adding friction to a team's workflow and impeding their flow.

In the Salesforce example earlier in the chapter, the marketing cloud was a highly autonomous product portfolio. Within the marketing cloud, product groups had a high level of autonomy to design and evolve their part of the taxonomy. Each taxonomy level had dedicated product and technology leaders who worked as a unit to discourage silos from forming.

> **NOTE** An easy trap to fall into is spending too much time up front designing the taxonomy when you could have instead been delivering value. But the opposite problem is also common, jumping straight to delivery without considering alternative options that might have been superior. Chapter 16 provides some guidance and suggestions for finding the optimal balance.

6.3   *Mapping modernization opportunities, risks, and challenges*

Designing a product taxonomy is about creating a vision to guide your journey. The difficult part is carrying out organizational and technology change initiatives to move from the current to the desired structure. It's not as easy as just doing a big overnight reorganization. The modernization work will likely need to be prioritized and carried out gradually over multiple years.

Planning and prioritizing is, therefore, a crucial and challenging activity. The better you understand the value, costs, and risks of modernizing each area, the better you can prioritize the highest-value modernization options. This section touches on some common themes to capture when mapping out the taxonomy. They will feed into identifying the level of effort needed to transition from the current to the new structure in each area of the taxonomy and help begin preparation. The topics of prioritization and roadmaps are covered in chapter 16.

6.3.1   *Dependencies and misaligned boundaries*

Expect some, if not most, parts of your taxonomy vision to not align with your current software and team boundaries. While people can easily reorganize into different teams (although forming an effective high-performing team is not simple), reshaping software is far more complex, especially in tightly coupled legacy systems that are extremely risky to change.

Figure 6.11 shows a common scenario where an organization has identified target subdomains for which it would like to establish independent value streams, each owned by a different team. However, the current software architecture would mean all three teams working in all three codebases and needing to coordinate their work and deployments, affecting their flow.

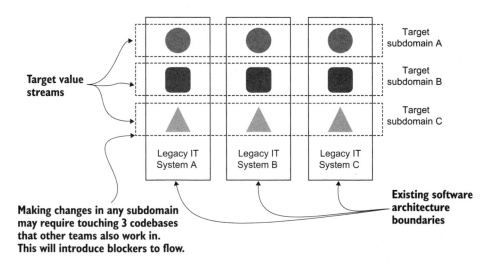

Figure 6.11   Current architecture does not align with target value stream boundaries.

When misaligned boundaries are identified to the extent in figure 6.11, the first thing to recognize is that there is likely to be a high level of uncertainty and risk. Depending on the amount of coupling and technical debt, this probably isn't a simple three month modernization and is unlikely to be a good first slice unless, for example, one of the subdomains is easy to extract or can easily be rewritten without requiring changes to the legacy.

Planning other work around a modernization initiative like this could be risky. So many unexpected delays could arise, like legacy code that takes far longer to decouple than anticipated, hidden infrastructure complexity, and a lack of knowledge about certain parts of the system because nobody currently working at the company understands them.

In one financial services organization, the first slice of modernization was delayed by months due to unknown compliance problems being discovered just when the team was ready to deploy. The most important thing is to get a rough idea of the level of misalignment in each area of the taxonomy and a list of the key challenges involved in moving to the proposed design.

6.3.2 *Unclear or lacking ownership*

Before modernizing an area of the taxonomy, a staffing plan for teams that will be responsible for the relevant value streams should be in place. It may be that existing teams will be moved across, or it might also be that the area is currently not owned by any team, and it's unclear which team will own it. In this scenario, a plan for forming the team will need to be established, which could involve bringing in existing employees, hiring new employees, using contractors, or some combination of the three.

Keep in mind that forming new teams takes time. If it takes four to eight weeks to hire the team, and they each have to work a notice period of four weeks with their current employer, it could easily be three months (or even longer) before a team is in place to start work on a given modernization initiative. Highlighting this challenge before important prioritization decisions are made is essential.

I've been in situations where senior leadership has given the green light on a particular project and expected work to start immediately, ignoring that no team is in place yet. Then there is a rush to hire people quickly, which puts everyone under pressure and doesn't allow adequate time to hire the right kind of people or cultivate the culture needed for modernization.

6.3.3 *Skills gaps*

Even when there is a team lined up to be responsible for a certain area, the team may lack the necessary skills to carry out the desired modernization. Training and upskilling may be required, and additional expertise or outside help may need to be hired. The bigger the gap between how the team currently works and how they are expected to work, the more time that will need to be built into the roadmap to allow them to upskill. Chapter 17 covers this topic in more detail.

6.3.4   *Product and domain modernization*

Architecture modernization is not just about rewriting the old system with new technologies or even moving to new patterns and structures; it's equally about modernizing the product and domain to create new value through improvements, such as

- Redesigning the UX
- Automating business process steps
- Redesigning colleague workflows
- Clarifying ambiguous domain terminology to help speak a common language
- Removing unneeded features/complexity

These activities may involve a large amount of discovery—for instance, user research sessions, discovery workshops, and lots of prototyping. Identifying which parts of the taxonomy will most benefit from product and domain modernization is useful to ensure there is enough time to prepare and carry out effective discovery, especially if there is potential for a high ROI. If collaborative product discovery is a new concept to your organization, highlighting these opportunities is even more important because you will need more time to adapt to this approach. Chapter 8 covers these topics in more detail.

6.3.5   *Complexity and cognitive load*

Not all parts of a system will be equally complex. Some areas will involve more complex business rules and workflows or higher scalability challenges or may be written in very old technologies that require a higher modernization investment. Establishing this is important because it highlights where risks and challenges may arise. It's also important because it helps to ensure that a single team will not be responsible for multiple domains that are highly complex, which would exceed their cognitive load. Assessing complexity and using it to prioritize modernization initiatives is touched on in later chapters.

6.3.6   *Macrolevel constraints and challenges*

Macrolevel refers to the large-scale structure of an organization, scope 3 and above. Changes at those levels potentially affect thousands of people, making them both expensive and risky. Decisions at this level are usually made by senior leadership for major strategic reasons, like in 2015 when Google split into a collection of separate companies owned by a new holding company called Alphabet (https://hbr.org/2015/08/why-google-became-alphabet).

While decisions at higher scopes may be outside of the scope of modernization, there is still value in understanding the bigger picture and how it may constrain modernization. You may even discover opportunities that nobody realized were possible.

One macrolevel theme to be aware of is reuse. When a large company has many products and is active in many markets, debate about what to centralize and what to let each area build always arises. Imagine a global fast-food chain organized around regional markets (*verticals*)—for example, the United States, United Kingdom, Sweden, and Japan—and the company is active in over 100 countries. Figure 6.12 highlights a key macrolevel business architecture decision: Should each vertical be free to develop its own capabilities like Loyalty and CRM, or should they be centralized into a horizontal that is shared by all verticals?

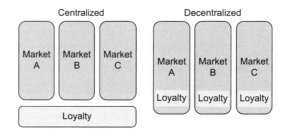

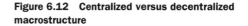

Figure 6.12 Centralized versus decentralized macrostructure

Determining how to shape verticals and horizontals is a ubiquitous and complex problem with many trade-offs to consider. It's a contentious topic in some companies. Some of the key considerations are

- *User experience*—Is it common for users to be active in multiple verticals? If so, how will you balance the need for a consistent UX across all verticals with an optimized UX within each vertical?
- *Prioritization*—How will work in horizontals be prioritized when there are multiple verticals that are all requesting new features and improvements? How specific will the needs of each vertical be? How much concurrent demand is there likely to be?
- *Funding*—How will funding be determined for horizontals that do not directly generate revenue and are considered cost centers?
- *Dependencies and complexity*—Does the number of dependencies and level of domain knowledge required cause teams to have an excessive cognitive load or introduce excessive coordination across teams? This was a key factor in Docker's large-scale modernization (http://mng.bz/n1Qe).
- *Efficiency versus time-to-market*—Does allowing each vertical to implement similar functionality reduce time-to-market? Do the costs of that duplication outweigh the benefits?

In addition to the above, Wardley Mapping is always a good idea for getting a picture of the whole landscape and anticipating future opportunities rather than being too focused on the current pains.

INDUSTRY EXAMPLE: STRIPE TREASURY

There are various possibilities between the two extremes of complete duplication within each vertical and full reuse as an enterprise-wide horizontal. At Craft Conference 2022 in Budapest, Prajakta Kalekar (http://mng.bz/vPN1) provided insight into how products are built at Stripe.

Prajakta started the talk by framing Stripe's journey from a payments company to an economic infrastructure company. She then talked about the story of a new vertical that Stripe built called Stripe Treasury (https://stripe.com/treasury), a banking-as-a-service platform.

The talk contained many interesting insights, including Stripe's approach to platforms and reuse. Early in the vertical's lifecycle, the teams duplicated some of Stripe's core payments infrastructure to optimize for "short-term efficiency." Effectively, this was about enabling the new vertical to validate ideas as quickly as possible and reduce time-to-market at the cost of duplication.

Later in the vertical's lifecycle, Stripe decided to migrate the treasury vertical onto Stripe's existing core-payments infrastructure. They wanted to "avoid rebuilding Stripe inside Stripe" and instead strive for "longer-term efficiency."

6.4   What is a product?

The word *product* is used extensively throughout this chapter, yet it's a highly ambiguous word with many clashing definitions throughout the industry. This final section of the chapter provides a recommended definition of the word *product* and related concepts. There will not be consensus on the word, so this isn't positioned as the single correct definition. However, if you're struggling to define the concept in your organization, it's a good definition to use. If you already have a clear definition in your organization, then feel free to skip this section.

6.4.1   Products vs. features vs. components

Melissa Perri is a leading voice in the world of product management. She's a consultant, author, and senior lecturer at Harvard Business School. She spoke in her opening keynote at the Agile 2022 conference in Nashville (http://mng.bz/46OD) about her definition of *product*.

Melissa's definition centers around products being a complete offering: "A repeatable solution that can be offered to a market that solves a want or need (job to be done)." She then provided credit cards as an example. The physical card alone is not a product; it's only a part. By itself, it does not solve a want or a need.

Roman Pichler shares a similar opinion and clearly distinguishes between products, features, and components. In my experience, many people use the word *product* to refer to what Roman calls a feature or component (http://mng.bz/QRQR). Roman uses the example of search and checkout used by e-commerce companies like Amazon. Some people would consider search and checkout to be products because separate teams own them and have separate product managers. But that doesn't fit with Roman's or Melissa's definition.

Roman argues that search and checkout are features. His rationale is that they do not provide value to customers independently. Roman also uses the concept of a component, which he also refers to as architectural building blocks. These are things like UI layers and backend APIs but are also not considered independent enough to be products.

Figure 6.13 provides a visualization of Melissa Perri's product overview. In this model, five key aspects help to ensure you focus on a complete product: customer/user research, market data and research, financial data and implication on sales, user data, and technology implications. If you're unfamiliar with any of these concepts, check out Melissa's keynote or her book *Escaping the Build Trap* (http://mng.bz/Xqg1).

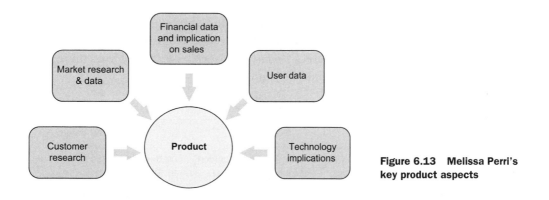

Figure 6.13   Melissa Perri's key product aspects

6.4.2   *Products vs. variants vs. journeys*

Multiple versions of the same product are known as *product variants* according to Roman Pichler. For example, many products have a web app, an Android app, and an iPhone app. Each of these applications provides the same or similar functionality as part of the same business model. So really, they are variations of the same product rather than being stand-alone products themselves.

A *user journey* may involve interacting with multiple *products* and *product variants* and could also include actions that don't involve interacting with products. Therefore, a *user journey* is not a part of the *product*; it is the steps the user is taking as part of their *experience*. A *user journey* can be further broken down into *user tasks* (as shown in figure 6.14).

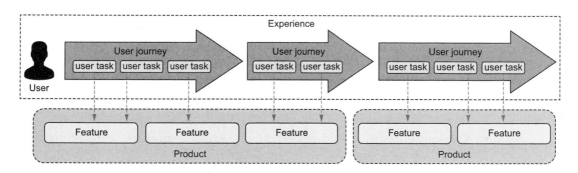

Figure 6.14   A user journey is part of the experience of using products.

6.4.3   *Product mode*

While platforms, features, components, and product variants are not products, they can still be treated similarly to actual products. Sriram Narayan has coined this *product mode* (http://mng.bz/am7o). Table 6.1 highlights some of the key comparison points between *product mode* and traditional development approaches that employed a project-centric or feature factory–like operating model. In brief, traditional project-centric approaches have focused on delivering a fixed scope on time and on budget with short-lived teams, whereas *product mode* focuses on long-term continuous product enhancements owned by durable teams.

Table 6.1   Key characteristics of project versus product mode

	Projects	**Product mode**
Funding model	Building a predefined solution or outstanding scope	The team is funded to build, run, iterate, and pivot if necessary.
Team responsibilities	Separate teams for ideation, development, deployment, and ongoing maintenance	Each team is responsible for discovering, building, and running capabilities.
Team lifespan	For the duration of a project, and then disbanded—usually less than a year	Usually multiple years, as long as their reason to exist remains
Definition of success	The fixed scope is delivered on time and within budget.	Improvement of business-related metrics connected to north stars

Product mode outlines what empowered product teams look like in practice: how they are incentivized, how much ownership they have from ideation to ongoing maintenance, and how they are funded. Transitioning to these behaviors from completely different, deeply ingrained ways of working is hard and won't happen overnight. But it's necessary to fully exploit the potential of a well-designed product taxonomy and modern architecture.

Summary

- Transitioning to a product-centric operating model requires a deep change to the structure, culture, and ways of working in an organization.
- A *product taxonomy* is a tool for designing an organization's business architecture based on continuous improvements of products and customer experiences. It is used to define areas of team accountability and ownership and shape the software architecture accordingly.
- A *product taxonomy* should not be designed by a centralized architecture team who hands over the plans for teams to build.
- Taxonomy updates should be published regularly.
- You can define your own building blocks for your taxonomy.

- A value stream (or, more specifically, a software development value stream) is the sequence of activities a team goes through in a particular domain to discover and deliver product enhancements.
- Products can be internal, used by employees of the organization, or external, used by those outside the organization.
- Platforms are internal capabilities employed by multiple products.
- Development platforms help teams to build and support products.
- Domains are a hierarchical concept. A larger domain may be composed of multiple subdomains, which may be composed of more granular subdomains. There are many naming conventions used to describe these levels; this book uses scope 1, 2, 3, and so on.
- A product taxonomy should only be designed in sufficient detail to support the current objectives, such as defining an initial slice of modernization that can be delivered within three to six months. It's not necessary or encouraged to fully define a product taxonomy before any modernization work begins.
- A product taxonomy is always in a constant state of evolution.
- North stars are key product metrics that help to clarify the value and cohesiveness of a part of the taxonomy.
- One of the common macro challenges is the choice of decentralizing capabilities so that each vertical is free to develop its own version versus centralizing into a single shared platform used by all verticals. There are many factors to consider, like consistency of user experience and funding models.
- Transitioning to a future-state product taxonomy usually takes multiple years and is done gradually. Identifying the risks and challenges in each area can help with planning, preparation, and prioritization.
- Some of the common transitional challenges to identify in each area are misaligned boundaries, lack of ownership, skills gaps, level of product and domain modernization required, and the general complexity and cognitive load.
- *Product* is a highly ambiguous word. This book represents a complete offering that provides value to a customer. A *product* comprises *features* and *components* (architectural building blocks), but they themselves aren't *products*.
- Even though *platforms* and *components* are not *products*, they can still be delivered in a similar fashion to *products*. This is referred to as *product mode*.

Big picture EventStorming

7

This chapter covers

- Mapping out your business with EventStorming
- Beginning the process of identifying domains and subdomains
- Understanding the principles behind EventStorming
- Planning and running EventStorming workshops
- Identifying business problems and opportunities with EventStorming
- Facilitating EventStorming workshops

Modernization leaders must steer clear of making crucial architectural choices based solely on a limited, shallow grasp of the landscape. It's easy to fool yourself into thinking a bad design is good when you are too disconnected from the details. When I was coaching a chief product officer at a client in the property sector, he identified three high-level domains as the basis for the new company structure. He was very confident it was the right approach. But when we put the idea in front of various employees, they found multiple reasons why the proposed architecture wouldn't work. They had a much deeper understanding of domain intricacies, which he lacked. He was intelligent and humble enough to seek and accept feedback, but others choose the Ivory Tower Architect path (http://mng.bz/g7Nx) and enforce their naive ideas.

One technique that modernization leaders can use to prevent ivory tower thinking from creeping into a project is big picture EventStorming. The workshop format lets you get into a domain's details and ensure any hidden complexity or nuance is not missed when making important modernization decisions. It's a flexible technique that will come in handy throughout a modernization journey, from the first step of building a vision to identifying the domains and subdomains that shape the product taxonomy. And it's effective for organizations in many types of industries. I've used it with clients in various sectors like finance, travel, and real estate. It's one of the most important tools in my toolbox.

EventStorming is designed around the idea of maximizing attendee participation and diversity. Bringing together people from across the business with different skills and roles makes it possible to build a true reflection of how the business works. There is no limit to who can attend and be productive in an EventStorming workshop: product people, software developers, subject matter experts, quality engineers, UX designers, accountants, and just about anyone involved in contributing to the company's business model. This is possible because EventStorming has been intentionally designed with a simple notation that allows anybody who attends a workshop to easily share their knowledge of the domain and combine it with everyone else's knowledge. The notation is called *domain events*, defined simply as "events that happen in the domain," which are formed into a timeline running from left to right, as shown in figure 7.1. Note that this is a tiny sample; a large wall space of 8 to 20 meters will be covered with orange sticky notes in a real session.

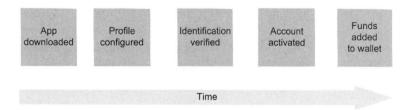

Figure 7.1 **Using domain events to map out a business on a timeline from left to right**

In this chapter, you'll learn about the principles behind EventStorming and get the practical guidance needed to plan and facilitate your first big picture EventStorming workshop. You can also find links to interactive EventStorming exercises on the book's Miro board (http://mng.bz/5oNZ) along with other useful resources like notation cheat sheets covering the different formats and flavors of EventStorming.

NOTE EventStorming was invented by Alberto Brandolini in the mid-2010s and has grown hugely popular with an active global community. This chapter discusses big picture EventStorming, but two other formats (process modeling and software design) are introduced in later chapters. If you want to learn more about EventStorming and connect with other practitioners, Mariusz Gil's Awesome EventStorming (https://github.com/mariuszgil/awesome -eventstorming) resource is an excellent starting point, with references to blogs, videos, and online communities.

7.1   Understanding EventStorming

EventStorming is intentionally designed to be a simple technique that eschews barriers to entry, like complicated notation and strict roles and rules. Understanding the basics is mostly about understanding the mindset of EventStorming, how it is optimized for maximum collaboration and participation, and how it differs from techniques optimized for other things you may be familiar with, like precision.

You're free to use other techniques when mapping your business and building a product taxonomy. EventStorming isn't positioned as a silver bullet that makes other techniques redundant. But when you do apply EventStorming, it's important to embrace its philosophy to get maximum value from your sessions.

7.1.1   Notation

The basic premise of EventStorming is to build a timeline that runs from left to right using *domain events*, expressed through orange sticky notes. While some techniques, like Service Blueprints and Customer Journey Maps, are highly structured, EventStorming is more flexible. You'll notice that in figure 7.2, there are various branches

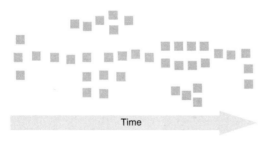

Time

and random-looking clusters rather than a single line of events running from left to right. This is because EventStorming focuses on getting all of the useful information onto the wall and representing the unique complexity of your domain in whatever shapes emerge by chance or purposefully. Capturing all of the detail is more important than tidiness.

Figure 7.2   An EventStorm runs from left to right but does not need to be neatly and precisely laid out.

DOMAIN EVENTS

A *domain event* is loosely defined as "something that happens in the domain." This definition has little precision to avoid excluding anyone who may have something valuable to contribute. Anything that seems relevant to your business can be represented on the timeline. The following lists types of events followed by an example of each.

- *User interacting with a product*—e.g, Review Added, where a user interacts with a product like using a mobile app

- *Actions in the user's life*—e.g, Thought About Moving Home, where a user does something that does not involve interacting with a product but is still interesting to the business
- *Actions within the organization*—e.g, Claim Approved, where an employee within the organization performs an action or makes a decision
- *Actions managed by software*—e.g, Driver Selected, where automated business rules and algorithms perform some action, like calculating a value or making a decision

You'll notice from all these examples that *domain events* are phrased in the past tense. This is one of the only rules in EventStorming that should be adhered to wherever possible. If everybody uses the past tense, the timeline will be consistent and easier to understand. Further, using the past tense makes it possible to refer to a precise point in time. For example, a Review Published event would refer to the exact moment a review was published and visible on the website, which makes it easier to refer to specific points on the timeline and to unambiguously articulate what comes before and after.

It's common to see beginners using more vague names like User Registration. The problem with this type of naming is that it's unclear where it starts and stops and what is included. There is a lot of nuance behind that one sticky, which could be important to unpack.

EventStorming is not overly specific about the granularity of events. However, there are a few basic principles to keep in mind. On the one hand, staying too high level means that important details and complexity of the domain will be hidden. For example, it's important not just to explore happy paths but also various other scenarios and edge cases. On the other hand, events that are too detailed might obscure the true business narrative with unnecessary detail, like User Clicked Form and Item Saved to Database. Sometimes the mechanics are useful, but usually, it's better to focus on the domain: What was the user's intention when they clicked the form (for example, Membership Requested)? And what item was saved to the database (for example, Membership Application Received)?

PEOPLE, SYSTEMS, AND HOT SPOTS

In addition to orange *domain events*, other notation can be used in a big picture Event-Storming session, as shown in Figure 7.3. Small yellow stickies are used to represent

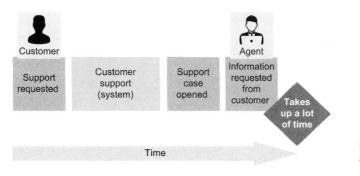

Figure 7.3   People, systems, and hot spots

roles or *personas* in the domain, like a *customer, rider,* or *agent.* Large light-pink stickies are used to represent *systems* like an order management system *(OMS)* or an external third-party payment platform. Rotated dark pink (fuchsia) stickies are used to represent *hot spots.* A *hot spot* is used as a placeholder to represent something important, like a problem or an area of disagreement. Generally, these notations are gradually introduced to keep the learning curve low.

Keep it simple with notation

At the start of a workshop, domain events on orange sticky notes are perfect. The idea is to keep the learning curve low and engagement high. Additional notation adds more complexity and can confuse people, so it's best to add it once momentum has been built and people feel comfortable. But even then, it's best to use these notations sparingly. For example, there's no need to show a yellow role next to every orange event. It can get messy and distracting, making it harder to move things around.

The goal isn't to be precise; it's to share knowledge and uncover insights. More notation does not necessarily mean more knowledge and insights. It can be counterproductive.

EDGE CASES, PARALLEL FLOWS, AND LOOPS

In any complex domain, many branches will represent various possible scenarios and edge cases. There are often processes happening in parallel, too. Unlike other techniques, EventStorming doesn't have a specialized notation to illustrate these concepts. Yet they can still easily be represented. The most straightforward approach to visualizing multiple possible scenarios is to maintain a happy path on the main flow and show edge cases as horizontal flows below the primary flow, as shown in figure 7.4.

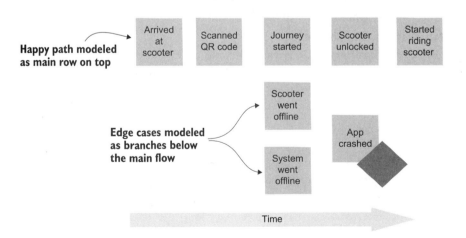

Figure 7.4   Modeling edge cases as branches below the main timeline

You'll notice in figure 7.4 that the hot spot is left blank, whereas other figures have explanations written on them. My general rule is that when the problem is already clear, I'll save time and leave the hot spot blank. In this example, it's obvious that the app crashing is a problem. Where there isn't a single happy path, annotations can be added at the start of each flow describing the name of the scenario, as shown in figure 7.5

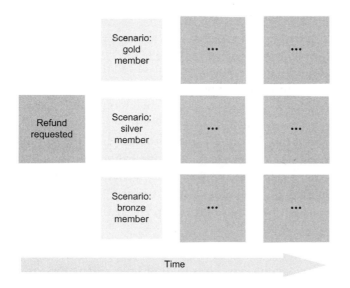

Figure 7.5   Modeling multiple scenarios as branches with labels

Parallel flows can be visualized by splitting the main flow into multiple branches, as shown in figure 7.6. If it's not easy to discern whether a particular branch runs in parallel or is an alternative scenario, additional notes can be added. The example in

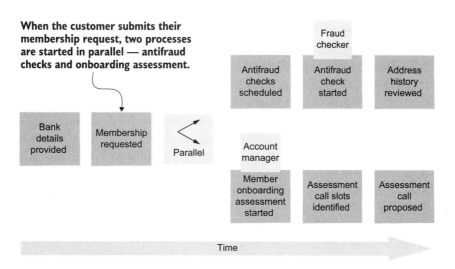

Figure 7.6   Splitting the main flow into multiple branches for parallel flows

figure 7.6 uses a yellow sticky note with the word parallel on it. In addition to these techniques, it's also possible to use various sorting strategies, covered later in the chapter, like creating swim lanes to accentuate the nature of a domain and the different flows.

Representing loops is a more intricate question than just deciding how to visualize them. We must ask, "Do we really need a loop here, or is there a better approach?" We can't go back in time in real life, and that's generally the case with the timeline in EventStorming.

Take the example of a late payment to an ISP (internet service provider). If a customer does not make a payment on time, the ISP sends them a reminder letter. Another letter is sent if the customer still does not pay after 30 days. This may seem like a loop, but is it? Does it continue forever, and is each loop iteration the same? For example, if a customer ignores the first message, they receive another message with stronger language and threats to disconnect the customer's internet. If the customer still does not pay, the third iteration would be a phone call rather than a letter. And then, finally, if the customer still does not pay, their services are canceled, and the debt collection process begins. So whenever you feel the urge to use special loop notation, first try mapping out a few iterations of the loop and try to identify what is different with each iteration.

LINES AND ARROWS

A common desire in EventStorming sessions is to draw lines and arrows, as with other techniques. Lines and arrows cannot easily be moved around as sticky notes can, and this is highly problematic because *domain events* are moved around a lot in a typical session. Conceptually, lines and arrows don't make sense anyway because it's impossible to travel backward and forward in time. It might seem hard as you fight against your instincts, but you will quickly get used to not needing lines and arrows.

7.1.2   *Chaotic exploration*

In addition to a wall covered in orange sticky notes, the other defining characteristic of big picture EventStorming is *chaotic exploration*. Most techniques for mapping out user journeys and business processes have a structured step-by-step approach. EventStorming, on the other hand, starts with the whole group adding lots of *domain events* and putting them on the wall in parallel. This looks very messy, and participating in an EventStorming session for the first time can seem a little uncomfortable. However, the chaotic phase of EventStorming is a key part of the philosophy. It enables every participant to surface what they know about the domain and what is important to them, getting as many ideas and insights as possible onto the wall with the fewest biases and prefiltering possible. In essence, individual brainstorming aims to allow the most important themes to emerge. The mess is easily tidied up and sorted out later.

Chaotic exploration is also an enabler of *emergent structure*. This concept is about allowing domain boundaries to emerge from the mess and chaos rather than defining any structure upfront. Adding some structure up front, like existing domain or organizational boundaries, will bias the structures defined during the workshop. At the same time, allowing structures to emerge using techniques like *pivotal events* (covered later in the chapter) is more likely to surface ideal domain boundaries that are not influenced by incorrect assumptions.

In some situations, chaotic exploration is not the right approach. Remote sessions are one example. Chaotic exploration and parallel conversations are hard to recreate remotely, so a single-threaded mode can be used where only one person is putting the events on the timeline and other attendees are guiding them. I sometimes use single-threaded mode for in-person workshops when the energy is low or I want to control the direction of the workshop.

7.1.3   *Optimized for learning and collaboration*

For many people, the ideas presented in this section can make it hard to understand EventStorming. For example, the lack of notation and precision often results in comments like "This is a mess; it's not consistent. Some events are very high level, and in other parts of the timeline, there is much more detail." Getting over these stumbling blocks requires accepting that EventStorming is a technique optimized for collaboration and learning. The timeline on the wall is a way for people to collaboratively map out what they individually know into a picture of their collective knowledge as the basis for conversations.

If some parts of the timeline are more detailed, it may be because people decided it was more valuable to zoom into certain areas and not others. It could also reflect that some people who understand the less well-defined areas were missing from the workshop. The sticky notes on the wall are just a prop for having great conversations, sharing knowledge, and identifying opportunities for improvement. Don't get too obsessed with the artifact or reuse value after the session. But feel free to take pictures and distill any important learnings into other formats after the session.

7.1.4   *When to use EventStorming*

Having EventStorming in your toolbox means being equipped to deal with a wide range of scenarios. When building a vision for architecture modernization, it's useful for exploring parts of the domain to identify opportunities for modernization or validate an existing proposal to modernize a particular area of the business.

At one e-commerce client, we were looking for an area of the business suitable for an initial slice of modernization. We had identified four candidate areas that seemed like they could be a good fit based on delivering business outcomes and learning opportunities. Still, we needed more information to help us make the final choice. So we decided to run EventStorming sessions. After running an EventStorming session in one area, we quickly ruled it out. As we got into the details of the domain, we could see a large number of dependencies between the different subdomains. Modernizing that area would have involved five teams and touching five code bases. It was too challenging and risky for an initial slice.

One of the fundamental themes of an architecture modernization effort is designing software and organizational boundaries, which domain boundaries should drive. For me, EventStorming is an essential tool in this process and often acts as the starting point because the EventStorm can be partitioned into domains and subdomains, as figure 7.7 shows.

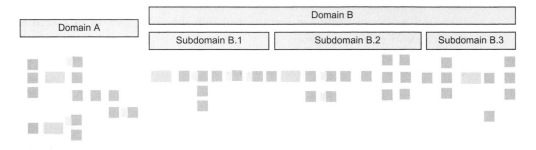

Figure 7.7   Partitioning an EventStorm in domains and subdomains

What's great about using EventStorming to define domains and subdomains is that the EventStorm represents the collective domain knowledge of diverse perspectives. This gives us a very high level of confidence that we are shaping domain boundaries based on all of the key details of the domain, and we aren't missing vital assumptions (as long as we ensure all of the key people are in the workshop).

Later chapters demonstrate using an EventStorm to identify domains and subdomains (chapter 9), including a range of principles and heuristics. Other techniques, like Domain Message Flow Modeling (chapter 12) and Team Topologies (chapter 11), can then be applied to assess and refine the boundaries identified with EventStorming. Collectively, these tools help to challenge the design from many perspectives, giving a high level of confidence that all of the important factors have been considered and the design is optimized for the desired modernization outcomes.

This chapter focuses on big picture, while later chapters touch on process modeling (chapter 8) and software design EventStorming (chapter 12). Big picture is optimized for chaotic exploration and group learning across a large area. Process modeling can be used to map out smaller areas of the domain in higher granularity using more structure and notation. It's great for mapping out the current state and designing new or improved processes. Software design EventStorming (aka design-level EventStorming) adds even more structure and detail and is used as a stepping stone to map between the domain and software that is highly aligned to the domain.

INDUSTRY EXAMPLE: EVENTSTORMING AT A COMPANY GET-TOGETHER

In 2021, I was contacted by an organization planning to meet in person for the first time since the pandemic's start. They were having a company get-together on a farm in Germany, and they wanted an external person to run a workshop. My colleague and I agreed to do an EventStorming session.

On that day, we had many attendees spread across five teams in addition to customer success people and even someone from accounting. The session was full of talking points. I noticed a lot of conversations around topics that affected multiple teams. People were connecting dots and seeing new opportunities that weren't obvious when they were all working in their teams and not thinking about the big picture. During the session, we also began exploring domain boundaries and started conversations about how the company should be organized as it entered a period of growth.

One of the workshop's most fascinating moments occurred as we talked through the timeline as a group. As a facilitator, I was asking general facilitation questions to try and uncover insights. I pointed to one event that was part of an edge case representing a bug. I asked a developer, "How often does this happen?" He intimated that it wasn't a prevalent problem and wasn't something we needed to spend time on. At that moment, a member of the customer success team joined the conversation and explained to the whole room that it was quite a common error. She had spoken to two users that morning who had reported that type of problem.

This is typical of what happens in an EventStorming session. In our day-to-day work, we carry around many incorrect assumptions and misunderstandings about how the business works, like the developer who thought that a bug in his team's code wasn't that big of a problem. In an EventStorming session, when we bring a diverse group together, we create a space where we can learn and correct our misunderstandings and make better decisions during our day-to-day work.

At the end of the workshop, we had a compelling presentation. We walked along the EventStorm, describing how the business works and how different products fit together. People would step in and out of the conversation to clarify points and add extra details. At one point, a team mentioned that they would build an API to fix a problem that had been raised. But then another team explained that they already had an API that does what is needed. That evening those two teams were sitting together at dinner, and they implemented the code to call the API and resolve the problem raised during the day.

When everybody went back to work, there were probably more improvements like this. Everybody now had a much better understanding of the big picture, and whenever they were doing work in their team, they were better aware of how it might affect other teams and where they might get help.

One thing to take away from this story is that EventStorming is a technique that creates a space where valuable conversations and learning take place. If multiple teams work in the same business area or as part of a larger initiative, just bringing them together for an EventStorming session could lead to many positive outcomes even without a clear purpose up front. That's discovery—we don't know what we will discover. It's hard to put a return on investment on a discovery workshop, but if you don't invest time in discovery, you may never know what important learning opportunities you're missing.

7.2 *Running an EventStorming session*

While EventStorming is based on a simple notation that allows a large group with diverse skills and expertise to collaborate easily, I must admit that planning and running an EventStorming is a bit more challenging. Finding a time that works for everybody, preparing a room with a lot of modeling space, and especially managing the dynamics of a mixed group of personalities can be tricky. Fortunately, it does get easier after the first few workshops. Like most skills, practice and perseverance is the key. This section is to help prepare you for your first workshop by providing guidance for each step of the process.

7.2.1 *Planning a session*

Scope and purpose are the first elements to consider when planning a big picture EventStorming session. If you set the scope too narrow, you may miss important connections between different parts of the domain that are crucial to the area on which you are focusing. Yet if you set the scope too broad, you'll have to invite too many people, and it may become impossible to facilitate such a large group. I usually work to the constraint of around 15 attendees for a big picture EventStorming session, with an upper limit of around 22, possibly more if the attendees are experienced and there are multiple facilitators. I find this number to be a sweet spot for many diverse insights and perspectives without the number of people becoming overwhelming. With this human constraint in mind, it's then a question of how wide you can set the scope while including all the people that need to be in the session.

To build an accurate picture of how the business works, attendees should represent as much of the business as possible: UX designers, product people, subject matter experts, engineers, testers, support people, and so on. Let's say you are building a proposal for the first slice of modernization and have identified a particular domain (scope 2) that could be a good starting point. The domain contains five subdomains, each owned by a separate team, with approximately 30 software engineers working in the domain. The minimum attendee list would look something like this:

- 5 software developers (at least one from each team)
- 1 principal engineer/architect/engineering manager (responsible for the whole domain)
- 2 product managers (collectively responsible for the whole domain)
- 1 UX designer (works across the whole domain)
- 1 subject matter expert
- 1 customer support agent
- 1 ops/platform engineer
- 1 tester

Choosing a single scope-2 domain assumes that the boundaries at that level have already been established. But what if they haven't, and the purpose of your workshop is to define them? In this scenario, it would make sense to have a series of workshops first defining the scope-2 boundaries and then having deeper-dive sessions into each of them. EventStorming workshops that cover multiple scope-2 domains could span across 15 teams or more, so at that level, it may not be possible to have an engineer from every team. It may be just the tech lead of each domain that joins.

> **NOTE** Architectural scopes 1 to 3 were introduced in chapter 6. They are an essential mechanism for analyzing, designing, and making decisions about architecture at different levels of abstraction.

Inviting the participants and helping them to see the importance of attending the session can sometimes require effort and patience. There is usually a desire for clearly defined outputs and an agenda for the session. Since EventStorming involves a large amount of discovery, providing a list of specific outputs and a minute-by-minute agenda up front is not possible.

In the context of modernization, I find that connecting back to the purpose of the initiative is usually sufficient with a description like "We are looking to modernize this area of the business, and this workshop is going to involve mapping out the current state and exploring future states," or "We are looking to define the domains and subdomains in this area, and we will be using a technique called EventStorming as the starting point."

Duration is also an important consideration. For a basic EventStorming session with a little time to explore problems and opportunities, I suggest 3 hours as a minimum. Alternatively, if you plan to map out a domain, explore multiple problems and opportunities that arise, and identify subdomains, then I recommend setting aside 3 full days as a starting point.

7.2.2 Preparing the space

The available space and layout of the room can greatly influence how well the session goes, so preparing the modeling space is essential. At a minimum, you should aim for 8 meters of wall space, like in figure 7.8, where participants can easily gather and move around. It's best to put paper on the wall using a roll of paper because it's too risky to rely on the wall surface being suitable for stickies (unless you have used the wall and are confident it will be OK). A small table for all the stickies, pens, and other workshop stationery is also needed. Apart from that, removing all other tables from the room is best to minimize outside distractions like people using their laptops. A typical session lasts between 3 hours and a whole day, so it's unreasonable to forbid chairs completely, but you might want to take them away for the first hour or two when you want energy and engagement to be high. One benefit of virtual sessions using tools like Miro is that you don't need to worry about these things and get unlimited modeling space.

Figure 7.8   A room prepared for an EventStorming session

7.2.3   *Kicking off the session*

I like to start workshops with a quick overview of the purpose, followed by a social check-in question with some connection to the workshop theme. In addition to the usual introduction covering the person's role in the company and their hopes for the workshop, this question also creates a space for people to reveal something about themselves and bring some fun into the session. Some examples I've used include the following: "What was your first job?" "What was your favorite TV show when you were a child?" and "Who would you most like to meet (any person living or has lived) and why?"

There are multiple possibilities for beginning to map out the domain. Some people like to dive straight into EventStorming and build the timeline (covered in the next section), while others like to begin with other activities. EventStorming is intentionally chaotic at first; it can be a while before people start seeing the value. Therefore, I like to start with an activity that gets people warmed up thinking about the domain and delivers enough value that people have confidence that the rest of the workshop will also deliver value. The technique I use is mapping out roles and personas in the domain.

By listing all the people in the domain and describing their purpose, jobs to be done, and other helpful information about them, you start to touch on different areas of the domain and have valuable conversations. You're already starting to build the big picture and form connections, which is ideal preparation for a big picture Event-Storming session. Product and UX people may have already done this, but I recommend starting from a blank canvas. The purpose is to get warmed up for the session and get everybody thinking. Then, preexisting personas can be brought in afterward as a comparison.

In figure 7.9, you can see an example of mapping out roles and personas in a domain. This is based on a workshop with a client in the real estate sector (the content is not real). Just by listing out the roles and responsibilities, people began partitioning them into *demand side* and *supply side* and defining key terminology. We also highlighted where the same person could play multiple roles, like a single person is often a buyer and seller simultaneously.

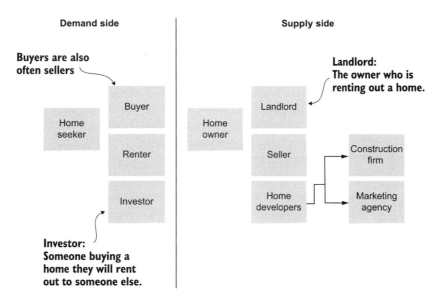

Figure 7.9   Mapping out roles and personas before kicking off an EventStorming session

7.2.4   *Building the timeline*

When you are ready to begin EventStorming, the first step is to build the timeline. Each person is given some orange stickies and a pen. Then everybody is told to start adding domain events along the timeline, placing them wherever feels right. A short explanation of domain events is required first, and then people can start adding stickies anywhere they like.

I typically explain domain events as something that can happen in the business process or the user's world, phrased in the past tense. And I provide some general examples like Order Placed, Menu Published, Incident Reported, and Device Activated. It's also important to explain that things can be imperfect. I emphasize to attendees that the first part is a messy brainstorming phase, and then we'll tidy everything up.

A more controlled technique for beginning the session is facilitating the initial few events. As the facilitator, ask an attendee to give an example of an event and place it on the timeline. Then ask another attendee for a different one. In this mode, I get attendees to think of events happening at other parts of the timeline, as shown in figure 7.10. This way, people think about the whole process and fill up the entire timeline on the wall. The whitespace between the events indicates that I expect attendees to fill in the gaps and get into the details of the domain rather than staying at a high level. After four or five seed events are added, and people know what a good domain event is, the session switches to chaotic exploration.

Time

Figure 7.10   An EventStorm seeded with initial events and a lot of whitespace

The first few moments when building the timeline can be a confusing period. People still aren't exactly sure what to do and what a domain event is. As a facilitator, the best thing to do is keep reminding people not to worry because the timeline will be tidied up and sorted out later. At first, the goal is to get as many events on the wall as possible wherever they seem to fit. However, you will need to step in and correct people if they go too far off the tracks. For example, if you notice someone not putting events in the past tense, you can gently correct them. After 5 minutes, some people may not have put on any events, so you can ask them if you can do anything to help. You may want to encourage them by asking them to describe their work and then start modeling it for them, but then politely step back and let them know that they should continue.

I don't mind if people are talking during the first phase as long as they continue adding events and discussing the events on the wall. If it seems they are talking too much, I recommend politely encouraging people to keep brainstorming events and letting them know we'll discuss them later. As a rough guide, I like to see at least 25 minutes of solid activity and a wall that is well-covered with orange stickies before allowing long conversations. When the energy dips, you can announce to the group that it's time for a break, and when we rejoin after the break, you'll tidy up the mess and make sense of it.

7.2.5   *Sorting the timeline*

This phase involves tidying up the messy timeline using one of the multiple sorting techniques. The most straightforward approach is to ask the group to review all of the events and put them in what seems the correct order. Not all events will naturally fit in a single place, so you can let attendees know they can either pick one place or duplicate the events for now. This is often a good point for the group to use the roles/personas and external systems notation.

Just asking a group to sort the timeline out is a bit optimistic, so a more structured approach can be helpful. The most common approach is called *pivotal events*, which involves slicing the timeline into sections using special events as the point of delineation between different areas, using yellow strips of tape to highlight them. I also make the pivotal events larger and black when working remotely, as shown in figure 7.11.

Choosing *pivotal events* is not an exact science, yet people often seek precision and perfection when identifying them. The most important thing is to split the timeline into roughly 5 to 10 smaller sections so the events can be sorted more easily. My

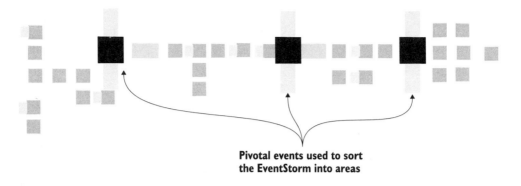

**Pivotal events used to sort
the EventStorm into areas**

Figure 7.11 Using pivotal events to sort the timeline

simple explanation for identifying pivotal events is to look for a transition point, like the start or end of a process or subprocess. Some examples include Membership Requested, Support Ticket Raised, Account Deactivated, and Article Published. One way to check if you have suitable pivotal events is to ask: Do the pivotal events alone tell the high-level story of the domain?

It's also possible to sort an EventStorm using horizontal swim lanes. However, this isn't an approach I often use because it can be too constricting, but it can be a good choice when the domain involves intricate back-and-forth interactions between multiple actors.

As shown in figure 7.12, temporal milestones is another approach where the timeline is partitioned based on specific moments. For example, I ran an EventStorming session for an airline technology company that builds software to help airlines plan and manage flights. We added temporal milestones like the day of the flight, the day before the flight, one week before the flight, one month before the flight, and so on based on milestones that had the most significance to domain experts.

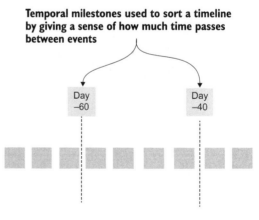

**Temporal milestones used to sort a timeline
by giving a sense of how much time passes
between events**

Day
−60

Day
−40

Figure 7.12 Using temporal milestones to sort a timeline

7.2.6   *Timeline walk-through*

After the timeline has been reasonably sorted, the whole group comes together and walks through the timeline. This is when people will start to see the big picture and how different parts of the business may influence each other. It's a time when people learn a lot about parts of the company with which they aren't familiar. As the facilitator, I ask an attendee to volunteer to walk the timeline. When they do this, they read out the events on the timeline like a story as they walk from left to right along the timeline. Questions are allowed from attendees and the facilitator at any time.

When walking through the timeline, the intention is not to stop and discuss every problem or opportunity. The intention is first to tell the end-to-end story so that everybody can see the big picture and second to identify all possible interesting conversations. Therefore, at this stage, you can use *hot spots* as a placeholder, as shown in figure 7.13 (hot spots can be placeholders for anything you want to return to, like problems, complex parts, disagreements, etc.). Whenever a conversation about a specific area of the timeline lasts for more than 2 minutes, let the group know that you're placing a hot spot and will continue moving along the timeline.

Figure 7.13   A group walking the timeline, adding hot spots and domain boundaries

As you're walking the timeline and telling the story of the business, you may want to add and refine events or continue adding additional notation, such as systems and roles. It's also good practice to define important or confusing industry terminology, as demonstrated in figure 7.14. For in-person sessions, you can use large yellow sticky notes or small sheets of paper for terminology definitions.

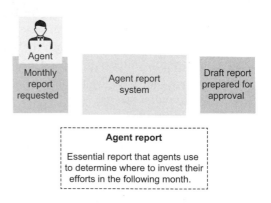

Figure 7.14   Adding roles, systems, and clarifying terminology

7.3 Surfacing problems and opportunities

For modernization leaders, it's essential to understand more than just how the current system operates. Identifying the problems and opportunities present within the landscape is important to ensure that modernization delivers more than just rewriting the old system with new technologies. Having built and sorted the timeline with many key people in the room, this is the perfect opportunity to surface these insights. There will already be some hot spots on the timeline from the walk-through. Still, before voting on which of them to dig into, it's good to give participants 5 to 10 minutes to add their problems and opportunities using the same hot spot notation for problems and green stickies for opportunities.

One thing I always appreciate about this part of the workshop is that everybody has great ideas. People we might label as technical, such as developers, testers, and architects, often have some of the best business and product ideas. Accordingly, as a facilitator, it's vital to encourage everyone to share their ideas regardless of their role. The whole team is responsible for discovery and delivery when moving toward a product-centric operating model. So this type of moment is a perfect opportunity to encourage and role model these desired cultural behaviors.

7.3.1 Problems

There's no real limit on the type of problem that can surface in an EventStorming session. Anything negatively affecting the customer, employees, product, internal processes, company culture, system reliability, or job satisfaction might be worth highlighting. This section touches on some common examples to give you an idea of what to expect.

USERS DROPPING OUT OF A FLOW OR FUNNEL

Users dropping out of a flow is something I always look for because this is often a place where something about the product is not optimized, and the business is missing out on potential revenue. Events like Shopping Basket Expired, Customer Switched to Competitor, and Monthly Plan Canceled shown in Figure 7.15 are all examples of a customer dropping out of some pipeline or funnel where it might be valuable to dig deeper and understand why these events are happening and how they can be prevented.

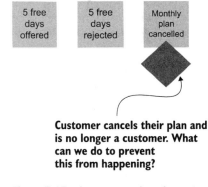

Customer cancels their plan and is no longer a customer. What can we do to prevent this from happening?

Figure 7.15 A customer dropping out of the funnel, resulting in lost revenue

USER FRUSTRATION

User frustration, in general, is something to always look for. Which parts of their experience interacting with your products and organization cause them the most stress, disappointment, and anger? Maybe the product forces them to jump through too many hoops to get a simple job done, or the customer support workflow bounces between multiple agents, giving them contradictory information. Multiple people who understand users' needs, like product managers, UX researchers, and support agents, are essential in uncovering true user frustration. When building internal products, you should invite the users themselves into the workshops to get their first-hand experiences.

There are usually multiple perspectives to consider when looking at ways to address user frustration. On one side, how can you prevent the problem from happening? And on the other side, if it cannot be fully prevented, how can you mitigate the problem when it does occur? One company devised the idea of incentivizing users to flag incorrect data. This helped prevent future problems and helped deal with them by showing users that they were trying to address the problem.

UNRELIABLE TECHNOLOGY

In some domains, technology is a major source of problems, from unreliable systems that contribute to poor user experience to IoT systems where devices can suddenly go offline or start behaving erratically. When I worked with a travel company, one of the employees responsible for configuring holidays explained how she had to create records in a mainframe system and then copy the ID generated by the mainframe system into another system so she could configure other aspects like the price. As you can probably guess, a range of problems resulted from an unintentional human error to systems that failed to synchronize correctly. This shows why getting into the details of different systems is important. Adding some of the big pink stickies to the timeline may unlock valuable conversations about key technology modernization opportunities.

MISSING AND DISPUTED KNOWLEDGE

Knowledge—both missing and disputed—is another major source of problems. In one EventStorming session I ran in 2019, nobody understood how the product worked beyond the UI because all the developers who worked on that part of the system had left. Normally, it's not this extreme, but a lack of knowledge is common and worth highlighting.

Disputed knowledge can be even more interesting when different people disagree on the facts. In 2017, I was running a workshop for a company in the financial advice industry, and I asked, "How is this metric calculated?" A developer jumped in to explain the algorithm, but then the head of marketing overruled them. The developer opened his laptop to verify how the code worked, and the marketing manager was shocked to realize why their reports had not been making sense. They had been carrying that misconception around and making decisions based on it for a while.

PROCESS INEFFICIENCIES AND BOTTLENECKS

Lead times are always useful information to look for in an EventStorming session. How long does a customer have to wait to receive an order? How long does it take for a new restaurant to be onboarded? How many refund requests are being processed per day? When processes like these are inefficient, revenue, customer experience, and operating costs can all be negatively affected. This is why it's important to invite people to the workshop who are responsible for carrying out these processes and to ask questions about how long things take and how long the duration can vary. A very simple facilitator question is, "What is the range of durations between these two events?" Even though an EventStorm is represented as a timeline, the durations aren't always clear, so it's worth making them explicit.

7.3.2 Opportunities

Every problem can lead to opportunities, but many types of opportunities can be found even when things are working well or as expected. For example, during an EventStorming session, one good question that can help find improvements is to ask, "How could we benefit from this happening earlier?" In the domain of eScooters, a company could have marketing campaigns at train stations so that when people get off the train, they see the ads and pick up a scooter. Thinking about how this could be done earlier, you might decide to run advertising campaigns on the train so that people are thinking about scooters even before they get off.

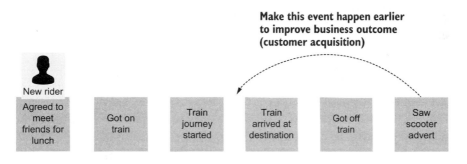

Figure 7.16   Does making an event happen earlier in the process improve business outcomes like customer acquisition?

TARGETING NEW CUSTOMER SEGMENTS

Modernization is an investment that positions the company to grow and innovate. One type of opportunity to look for is expanding the TAM (total addressable market) of your products and services. As you walk through the EventStorm, ask, "Which customers that we don't currently attract might be interested in this?" or "How much would we have to adapt this part of the system to make it appealing to different types of customers?" For example, if the product is B2C, could it be adapted for B2B as well? Think back to the Uber example from the last chapter, where the fulfillment platform supports more than 10 verticals. An EventStorming session would provide a great backdrop for discussing other potential scenarios in which their fulfillment capabilities could help target new customer segments.

USING DATA BETTER

A common theme you'll encounter in EventStorming sessions is data. You'll hear comments like "If we were able to capture more of this information, we could use it to do

<thing> much better," or "We capture so much data, and there is so much more we could be doing with it." As a facilitator, you can bring awareness to these topics and ask people to add opportunities along the timeline where they think more useful data could be captured or applied. In one session with a health organization, we were discussing how some doctors were problematic partners because of their unresponsiveness. One of the engineers raised the point that the organization already has tons of information and could very easily start measuring the performance of doctors and advising customers accordingly much earlier in the process about the most responsive doctors in their region. The problem was that the data was fragmented across various legacy systems and databases.

INCREASING ENGAGEMENT

In some domains, exploring opportunities to increase customer engagement can be valuable. When I worked with one travel company, they explained that seasonality was a big problem. People book a holiday once per year, and for the rest of the year, there is little or no continued engagement. The travel company was looking for ways to increase year-round engagement with the customer, like writing useful content to build stronger connections and loyalty with their customer base. EventStorming, with its timeline-based approach, provides a good backdrop for these conversations. For example, in-between each customer interaction, you can ask the question, "Are there ways we could engage with the customer in this gap?"

USING NEW TECHNOLOGIES

As we saw in the Wardley Mapping chapter, landscapes are continuously evolving. During an EventStorming session, it's important to consider how the landscape has evolved recently and what new opportunities may be available. This could be in the form of new technological advancements or new software-as-a-service (SaaS) products that have entered the market. It's always worth challenging each part of the timeline and asking, "Has the landscape around this event changed? Are there any new possibilities that weren't available when this part of the system was originally designed?"

7.3.3   *Addressing problems and opportunities*

In most cases, you will uncover a large number of problems and opportunities. You won't have time to address all of them during the session, so you will need to work as a group to decide the best use of your time together. The default approach is dot voting, where each person gets a set number of votes to put next to the discussion points they think are the most important. In some cases, a single key stakeholder may determine where to focus when the workshop has a specific purpose and the stakeholder has the greatest understanding of the matters that need to be covered.

For any matters that cannot be addressed during the session, there are a number of follow-up possibilities available, including

- Organizing further big picture workshops scoped to a particular area.

- Spending time with users to fully grasp their experience. EventStorming is great, but sometimes the best way to learn about the domain and its opportunities is to spend time with the people working in it.
- Scheduling process modeling EventStorming sessions to design new and future state processes.
- Scheduling workshops to validate domain boundaries (using techniques covered in the following chapters).

Having discussed the format of workshops and how an EventStorm is a great foundation for uncovering problems and opportunities, it's important to facilitate workshops effectively to unlock the potential of these concepts, which is the theme of the next section.

7.4 Facilitator tips and challenges

Slapping stickies on the wall in an approximate timeline sounds quite simple, yet the more you practice EventStorming, the more you learn to extract benefits from each session. The learning curve for attendees is intentionally small, but as a facilitator, the learning curve is nearly infinite. Nothing beats practice, but the following tips and tricks will help you to accelerate your learning curve and avoid common beginner problems.

7.4.1 Modeling heuristics

The quality of the events placed on the timeline can greatly affect the insights gained and the problems and opportunities uncovered. Good events prompt people to ask interesting questions and allow the knowledge of different people to be connected to a collective vision of how the business works.

As touched on throughout the chapter, there aren't strict rules, processes, or flow charts to help you determine what a good event is. And it probably wouldn't be useful anyway because the idea is to maximize the number of ideas shared and then filter out what is not useful rather than risking important information not being shared because people are worried about breaking the rules. Yet some heuristics can guide you in the right direction without harming participation, and they are the focus of this section. Just remember not to apply them too eagerly at the start of a workshop to ensure that you don't make people uncomfortable and put them off while they are acclimatizing to this new technique.

BE WARY OF OVERABSTRACTION

When domain events abstract away too much information, they keep important domain nuances hidden. Figure 7.17 shows a sequence of events that seems like good domain events. They're on orange sticky notes, they're phrased in the past tense, and they explain what is happening in the domain rather than being too technical, like button clicks and database transactions. However, a large amount of complexity is represented by just four events. There's little to be learned at this level of detail. How can we identify opportunities to improve the processes of signing up, subscribing, or creating campaigns if they are each covered by a single sticky note?

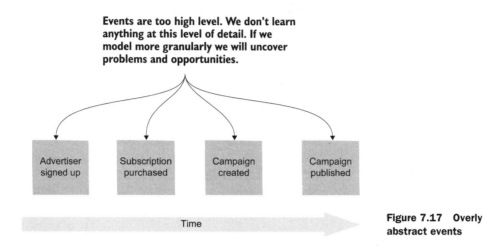

Figure 7.17   Overly abstract events

The scope of the workshop will have an effect on what is considered too high level and what is reasonable, and it's likely not possible to get deep into the details in every part of the domain. Deciding where the group should and should not focus is one of the most important skills as a facilitator and, unfortunately, one of the hardest to master.

DON'T MODEL; TELL A STORY

To compensate for overly abstract events, a good heuristic to keep in mind is "Don't model; tell a story." This little cliche means embracing the details and the specifics and not trying to create abstract models that cover all use cases. Applying this heuristic to the example in figure 7.17 would mean telling a story about a real advertiser. We might define a persona and describe more specifically what they are seeing and doing at a granular level of detail. We can then start to tell the story of another advertiser and see how their experience is different, as shown in figure 7.18, where the sign-up process varies based on the size of the company for which the advertiser works.

For engineers and architects who enjoy modeling, this may feel unnatural. But it's an important ability to be able to switch between specifics and abstract models at appropriate times.

REPEATING DIVERGENCE

When you identify divergence in the domain based on some characteristic, it's a good idea to look for similar divergence throughout the timeline. In figure 7.18, the timeline initially diverges based on whether the advertiser works for a startup or an enterprise. After the sign-up phase, the timeline may converge and the experience could be similar in some places, but the type of advertiser may be a reason for subsequent divergences later in the flow.

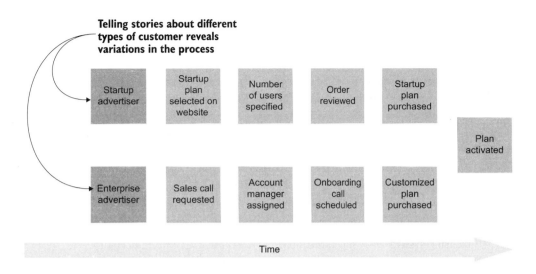

Figure 7.18   Tell stories for different customer segments or personas.

The example in figure 7.19 shows an event, Advert Received No Engagement, where an advert is performing poorly. This can happen to both types of advertisers, but what happens next varies. The startup plan only includes free generic advice to help improve the performance of the advert, whereas the customized plan includes help from an expert.

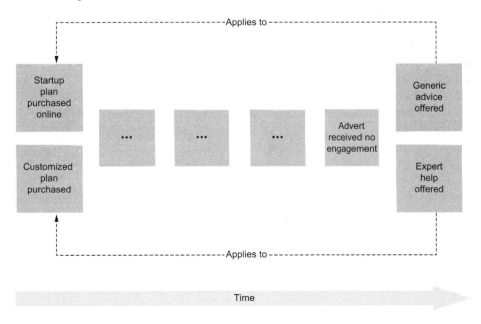

Figure 7.19   A timeline that converges and then diverges at some point later based on the same characteristic

Note that the arrows in figure 7.19 showing the relationship between events are annotations used to clarify the visualization. You wouldn't draw those arrows in a real workshop.

BE CURIOUS OF UNINTRODUCED CONCEPTS

When a new concept suddenly appears on the timeline, it may be a sign that parts of the domain have not been represented. In Figure 7.19, for example, the domain role of an expert appears in the event Expert Help Offered. If this is the first time the concept appears on the timeline, it's good to ask some probing questions like "How does an expert come to be available at this moment?" or "Could you describe the story of an expert?" By adding the story of the expert to the timeline, it may reveal new insights and opportunities that people thought were irrelevant. Discovery is all about exploring new avenues and challenging assumptions.

QUALIFY EVENTS WITH THE SAME NAME

Sometimes there are events that appear in multiple places in the timeline. At first, it might seem like the same event, but there is a danger that a subtle difference exists between the events that is hidden. A good facilitation question is, "Can the same things happen after each event?" In the airline example mentioned previously, what appeared to be a single event had different effects according to the temporal milestone (e.g., one day before the flight vs. six months before the flight) so unique event names were created to make the nuance explicit. It may seem pedantic or academic, but clarifying and cleaning up domain terminology to create a common language makes collaboration much easier.

KEEP SIMILAR EVENTS THAT LOOK THE SAME

Sometimes it might appear there are multiple events representing the same thing, and you might be tempted to keep one and throw the other away. However, before doing so, it's worth digging deeper. It might be that the two events represent slightly different things or the same event from different people's perspectives. Two events that appear to be the same might even be an indication of domain boundaries. Take, for example, the events Message Sent and Message Received. It may seem like they happen at the same exact time and represent two perspectives of the same thing. However, they could represent each side of the boundary between two subdomains like Message Composition and Message Viewing. This is an example of a more general heuristic, Make Conflict Visible. You don't always need to rush to find a solution; sometimes, it's good to visualize conflicting opinions and let them stand for a while.

USE EMPTY SPACE PURPOSEFULLY

As a facilitator, you can use whitespace to encourage participants to proceed deeper into the details. If you feel that the events are high-level and overly abstract, you can take two events together, spread them out, and let the group know that you would like them to fill the gap with more events at a more granular level. This is the heuristic from figure 7.10, which uses whitespace to set the expectation that you want them to fill the whole wall with stickies. You can do this at any point during the workshop.

COMBINING EXAMPLE MAPPING AND EVENTSTORMING

Example Mapping (https://cucumber.io/docs/bdd/example-mapping/) is a collaborative technique used for uncovering different scenarios and edge cases. When combined with EventStorming, it is a great way to zoom in on particular areas of the domain and search for hidden insights and complexity at a higher level of granularity. It's like taking a magnifying glass to a small area of the domain.

EventStorming-flavored Example Mapping starts by picking an event on the timeline and then specifying an action, using a blue sticky note, that triggers the event. For example, the Order Canceled event may be triggered by the Cancel Order action. Then, the goal is to think of other scenarios that can apply when the action is performed. For example, if a customer requests a refund for an order that has already left the warehouse, then a Cancelation Denied happens instead. As figure 7.20 shows, the scenarios are inserted as green stickies between the action and the event that occurs in the given scenario.

Figure 7.20   EventStorming-flavored Example Mapping

When switching to Example Mapping mode, I always try to encourage participants to think of as many scenarios as possible and to be creative, thinking outside of the box. As you uncover more scenarios, you may realize that it makes sense to split them and make certain concepts more explicit. In figure 7.20, for example, it may be better to split out the voucher scenario into a separate action that focuses on all the scenarios relating specifically to vouchers. Keep in mind that it's unlikely you will have time to apply Example Mapping to every single event on your timeline, and you don't want to introduce the technique too early in case you prematurely zoom into an area at the expense of making bigger-picture discoveries.

7.4.2   Common challenges

Facilitating EventStorming sessions can be challenging. From getting people into the right mindset to dealing with difficult people who refuse to collaborate, most challenges are people related. This section outlines some of the common challenges you are likely to face and some tips on dealing with them effectively.

GETTING ATTENDEES INTO THE DISCOVERY MINDSET

Something often overlooked when planning EventStorming and other discovery workshops is the need to create an environment where attendees can embrace the creative discovery mindset needed. When people are under pressure to deliver, particularly with urgent deadlines, it's a big challenge for them to put that to the back of their mind and spend hours or days mapping out business processes when it feels like no immediate progress is being made on short-term goals.

For an effective session, leaders must ensure that discovery work is prioritized accordingly and is not just an extra commitment that people are expected to do in addition to all of their other commitments. It doesn't hurt to reach out to workshop attendees ahead of time to ensure that they aren't already overcommitted. Otherwise, when they attend the workshop, their mind will be too focused on their other priorities, and they will probably be multitasking as well. For an EventStorming session to be effective, you really want everyone to be fully engaged and excited to be sharing their knowledge of the business and learning from others.

AVOIDING BIKESHEDDING

Bikeshedding (http://mng.bz/6njZ) refers to the phenomenon of spending lots of time debating details that don't really matter in the grand scheme of things. This was the cause of one of my biggest EventStorming failures, where an angry manager shouted at me in front of his team. We started walking the timeline, and the group spent a long time debating the registration process. I thought things were going great because there was lots of discussion. But I understand why the manager got angry: the registration process wasn't really that important. In a workshop where everybody was together (flown in from different countries) for just a few days to discuss bigger problems, there were more important things to focus on in the limited time.

To minimize your chances of repeating my mistake, don't let any conversations last for more than a few minutes when you are walking the timeline. Try to reach the end of the timeline before you dive too deep into one area. If it's truly the most important thing to talk about, the group will choose via voting to come back to it once they've reached the end of the timeline.

WE'VE ALREADY GOT DIAGRAMS OF THIS

Some people resist the idea of EventStorming because they think it is redundant. They've already created diagrams in some other format like UML or BPMN. In one workshop, a process engineer said, "I've got diagrams of all these processes; I don't see the point in this workshop" and continued to labor the point throughout the workshop. One of the employees who worked in the area for which the diagrams were created said, "Well, where are they then? We've never seen them." The process engineer then conceded that the diagrams were outdated compared to what we had so far discovered in the workshop.

Sometimes a clash of cultures occurs where people think EventStorming is not as good as their existing tooling. I try to speak rationally with these people and invite them to the workshops, but if their behavior during the workshop becomes a problem, they should be removed. Sometimes, however, the problem runs deeper, and people think that they are expected to be the expert in the company's processes. An EventStorming session is a concern because it may reveal things that the expert doesn't know, or the expert likes to hoard knowledge to protect their status in the company. This is a much more complex social situation; how you approach it will depend on your relationship with the people involved and your company culture.

CAN'T SOLVE EVERYTHING IN A TWO-DAY WORKSHOP

Sometimes people are disappointed that they haven't redesigned their entire system and designed new Team Topologies by the end of a two-day workshop. These are unrealistic expectations, so it's important not to overpromise or overhype what is possible with EventStorming. Ensure realistic expectations are set in the invite and reinforced when kicking off the session.

IN-PERSON VERSUS REMOTE

When the pandemic took off in 2020, many EventStorming practitioners desperately sought ways to run remote EventStorming sessions. The focus was firmly on recreating that in-person experience as closely as possible in virtual environments. Many were disappointed because the remote experience was so different and lacked many of the benefits of in-person, such as parallel conversations and the ability to read body language. Meanwhile, others in the community set about looking for ways to optimize the online EventStorming experience, and they exceeded all expectations, not by recreating what worked in person but instead by playing to the strengths of virtual environments.

In-person EventStorming sessions require everybody to be in the same physical space. In many organizations, that takes a large amount of coordination, and in some organizations, it's almost impossible. The constraint of being in the same physical space also means that a whole series of workshops needs to be crammed into a short space of time when everyone is together. Remotely, these constraints don't exist (although it's still difficult to find a suitable time when everyone is available). It's possible to run many shorter sessions over a longer period of time. For example, I often run 2- to 4-hour sessions when running remote sessions. These can be spread over weeks or months, and after each session, we have opportunities to reevaluate the next steps and who to invite.

Remote sessions also benefit from not being constrained by physical sticky notes. In fact, virtual whiteboard tools like Miro allow you to be far more expressive, with a wider variety of shapes, colors, images, and emojis to express domain concepts and people's emotions. And another big advantage when running virtual sessions is the ability to copy and paste. This allows you to copy an entire EventStorm and break out into small group exercises where each group gets a copy of the EventStorm to explore and shape into domain boundaries.

These are a few of my favorite examples of optimizing the workshop experience for the given format. I encourage you to continuously think about ways to optimize each of your workshops for the format you will deliver them in.

You've now reached the end of this chapter about big picture EventStorming. It's a great technique for mapping out domains, aligning groups of people, and increasing the potential of modernization. In subsequent chapters, you'll also see how it's an excellent starting point for identifying domains and subdomains. Keep in mind that EventStorming alone won't cover all of your needs. For example, it's also a good idea to spend time with real users—a theme of the next chapter that goes deeper into modernizing the product and domain.

Summary

- Important modernization decisions should not be made based on superficial, high-level domain knowledge. It's important to uncover the real complexity and nuances in a domain with techniques like EventStorming.
- EventStorming is a flexible tool that provides value all through a modernization initiative, from building an initial vision to identifying domains and subdomains, which are the foundation for team organization and software architecture for large parts of an organization.
- The core philosophy of EventStorming is to maximize inclusiveness and optimize for collaboration. As a result, anybody involved in building products can participate in an EventStorming session without needing training or learning any specialized notation.
- EventStorming uses a simple notation, domain events, to map out businesses as a timeline from left to right.
- Domain events represent specific points in time that happen in a domain and are phrased in the past tense, like Order Placed and Customer Refunded.
- Orange sticky notes are used for representing domain events on the timeline.
- A productive EventStorming session requires 8 to 20 meters of wall space where the walls are covered with paper and distractions like chairs and tables have been removed.
- EventStorming isn't positioned as a silver bullet. You are free to use other techniques like Customer Journey Mapping and Service Blueprints, as desired.
- Domain events are a very general concept; they can refer to anything that happens in the domain, such as a user interacting with a product, things that happen to a person in their life away from the product, activities inside an organization, and rules or calculations performed by software.
- Event granularity is highly subjective. Some parts of an EventStorm may be represented in more detail than others, depending on the people in the session and where the group feels it's most valuable to spend their time.
- Domain events should not get into the mechanics and lose sight of the domain intention. Submit Button Clicked and Item Saved to Database are examples that don't reveal what is actually happening in the domain.
- Additional notation can be added to the timeline alongside domain events. Roles/personas are represented with small yellow stickies, external systems are represented with large pink stickies, and hot spots are represented with dark pink stickies turned into a diamond shape.
- Hot spots are used to denote problems or placeholders that the group may return to for deeper conversations.
- Different scenarios and parallel flows can be represented by branching from the main timeline. There is no special notation.
- It is best to avoid loops, lines, and arrows with EventStorming.

- Planning an EventStorming session requires clarifying the scope and purpose of the workshop and identifying the most suitable participants, up to a maximum of around 22 unless the group is mature and there are multiple experienced facilitators.
- Participants can include any role involved in building the product, like engineers, testers, product managers, UX designers, customer support, etc.
- To kick off the workshop, it's good to start with a social check-in exercise and overview of the session's purpose. It's also possible to start with a warm-up activity like mapping out roles or personas and their jobs to be done.
- The first phase of EventStorming is called chaotic exploration. Each participant has a pen and some orange stickies, and they add all of the domain events they can think of along the timeline.
- After 30 to 60 minutes, the timeline is sorted using a technique like pivotal events or temporal milestones.
- The timeline walk-through phase involves telling the story that has been mapped out along the timeline by walking from left to right and describing the events.
- After the timeline walk-through, participants are invited to add their problems and opportunities to the timeline.
- There is no strict limit on what is considered a problem or an opportunity. Examples include lost revenue opportunities, poor customer experiences, and process bottlenecks.
- In general, newcomers to EventStorming tend to stay high-level with events. This is a problem because many insights only emerge when getting deeper into the complexity and nuances of the domain.
- "Don't model; tell a story" is a useful heuristic to keep in mind when EventStorming. Think about real people performing concrete actions rather than creating a general model that covers all use cases.
- Sometimes people will have a lot on their mind, and it's hard to switch into the creative mindset needed for exploration and discovery. Try to schedule EventStorming workshops at a convenient time.
- Don't waste too much time on conversations that seem engaging but relate to unimportant parts of the timeline.
- It's common for people to question the value of EventStorming because they already have existing documentation. Documentation is usually flawed and does not offer the same learning potential as bringing a diverse group together and combining all of their knowledge.
- EventStorming can be combined with other techniques like Example Mapping, which is used to zoom in and flesh out details at a higher level of granularity.
- EventStorming can be done remotely, but the dynamics are different and need to be facilitated accordingly. It may be better to avoid the chaotic aspects and have more structured sessions with specific roles that limit who can place events on the timeline.

Product and domain modernization

A comprehensive approach is required to exploit the full potential of modernization. Modernization is often perceived as technological change, but the benefits extend far beyond that. It's also an opportunity to revamp the user experience, improve the value provided by your products, address those frustrating problems that have existed for years, and remove unneeded complexity.

It's common to see employees left with barely usable solutions involving green screen mainframes or 1990s-style UIs, often part of complex manual processes. These types of inefficiencies can grow into huge problems as organizations scale or as more complexity is bolted on top. Understanding what users really need will also highlight what is no longer required and can be deleted rather than modernized, saving valuable time and costs.

As Figure 8.1 shows, a full-stack approach involves improving the UX to make users happier and more productive, improving the software to use better tech and better align with the domain and creating a better conceptual domain model so people are more aligned and have a shared language that fosters better collaboration and innovation. And it's also crucial for opportunities to modernize the domain by identifying new capabilities that can bring new types of business and customer value.

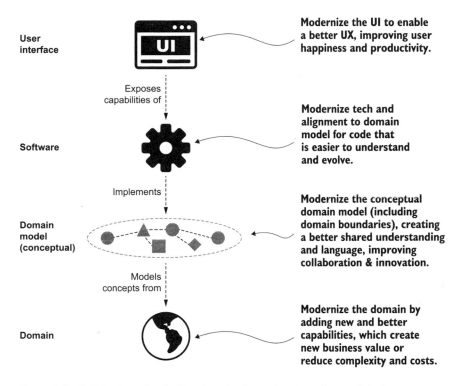

Figure 8.1 Full-stack modernization, from business domain up to user interface

This chapter helps you avoid the mistake of rebuilding the old system, with all its flaws, using new technologies and frameworks. The chapter begins with tips and guidance for eliciting better requirements and understanding what is no longer needed and finishes with two techniques to help you better identify the business and user needs that modernization will deliver by designing future states of the domain: process modeling EventStorming and Domain Storytelling.

8.1   *Industry example: Business property tax modernization*

This industry example is an experience of mine. I began the chapter with this story because I wanted to emphasize how modernization applies to much more than just technology. In this example, the user experience, business rules, and even government policies that had existed for decades were being completely rethought. I wanted to emphasize the enormous value of a diverse team with UX and other specialists and getting the whole team (especially developers) deeply involved in discovery, like user research. This story also alludes to how modernization can be successfully performed at a government scale, with principles and platforms rather than rigid frameworks.

I was once involved in modernizing a government tax service. It was part of a much more significant change, led by Government Digital Service (GDS), happening across the entire UK government to modernize the development of government digital services. Previously, UK government IT was known for terrible UX, big outsourcing contracts, infrequent big-bang deployments, and even for one of the biggest IT failures ever seen, costing around £10 billion (http://mng.bz/W1al). GDS began modernization by advocating for user-centric design, continuous delivery, developing code in the open (https://www.youtube.com/watch?v=h8vlLRZxedg), and other modern practices.

The project was highly complex—technically, organizationally, and politically. Everything was being modernized, including the domain where new government policies and processes needed to be defined. Some of the old ones had been in place for decades, if not more than a hundred years. The existing IT systems had a high level of technical debt and were owned by big consultancies. A significant investment was necessary due to the current approach involving excessive manual work that was too expensive and unsustainable.

Many of my experiences were positive. I learned a lot about product discovery and the UX aspects of modernization, thanks largely to GDS's principles and the culture they nurtured. Developing the new system involved a major amount of discovery, internal- and external-facing. Following the GDS service manual (https://www.gov.uk/service-manual/service-standard) helped us to do this well.

The service manual was not a framework, development process, or Jira workflow that teams were forced to follow. Instead, it was principles supported by guidance. Examples included Understand User Needs, Do Ongoing User Research, Make the Experience Consistent With Gov.uk, Have a Mutli-disciplinary Team, and Iterate and Improve the Service Frequently. An example of guidance was the range of skills needed in a team. The teams I worked with involved all the roles needed for modernization, like User Researcher, UX Designer, Content Specialist, Subject Matter Expert, Business Analyst, Product Manager, Developer, and Tester.

There were three teams, each responsible for one or more subdomains. They worked closely together. The developers sat next to each other in the same office, and the UX specialists needed to design an optimized end-to-end journey collaboratively. Every week the user researchers would interview real citizens that would be using the new service. They asked about their experiences with current IT services and got feedback about prototypes the team had built. A GDS guideline was that the whole team should be involved in user research. Our teams loved to. Even developers would attend research sessions in the lab. We also had regular group show-and-tells where research highlights were a core topic.

As we were developing the applications, we constantly had the user research front of mind. We got feedback for our changes from real users within two weeks. For example, when we added just a single extra textbox to one of the pages, there was a lot of pushback. Users complained the page contained too many unrelated questions, which increased cognitive load and anxiety.

Having all team members immersed in user research empowered the whole team to contribute new product and domain improvements. Even the apprentice software developers would discuss user research findings as we coded. I remember thinking, "This is exactly how teams should develop software." One apprentice (recently out of university) even went to London as the sole technical representative to talk to users to identify their requirements. Normally, that was the tech lead's job.

User research brought other advantages, too. One time, a senior stakeholder told the team to build a particular feature in a certain way. The team thought it was a bad idea but had little say. However, when we put the new UI in front of real users, it received negative feedback. From that moment on, after seeing the feedback, the stakeholder stepped back and left the team to work autonomously.

It's good to know all the skills and specialist roles that could help your modernization journey. For example, user research showed that citizens did not understand complex government jargon. Sometimes it was even a concern, like when people were warned they could be fined or go to prison for providing incorrect information, even if it was a mistake. So it was a privilege to have dedicated content specialists handling this challenging task.

In contrast to autonomy, the themes of scale and standardization were also central. For example, we had to honor the GDS principle *Make the Experience Consistent With Gov.uk*. Hundreds of teams were working across the government. GDS addressed this by providing open-source libraries and templates (https://github.com/alphagov/govuk-design-system) that contained most of the UI styling and UI widgets teams needed. Being open source, all teams could contribute changes for their own benefit with the positive side-effect of helping teams across the government. Platforms were also an important topic relating to scale. There's an example in chapter 13.

8.2   *Identifying product requirements*

It's easy to think that modernizing an individual product or application means that all existing functionality should remain intact with a fresh lick of paint on the UI. However, this is likely to be a big mistake. For one, some features may no longer be useful, while others may have never been useful. Identifying features that are no longer needed can save months or even years of effort and result in a modernized architecture that is much simpler.

Even features that are being used may not have achieved their full potential. Users may have been left with barely usable solutions that require hacks and workarounds to get the job done. Then there are all the opportunities to improve the product, which may not have previously been possible due to the existing architecture's design or complexity. Uncovering these opportunities early is key to maximizing the value of modernization and designing an architecture that will be adaptive to future needs.

This section provides guidance on uncovering better product requirements for your modernization. Remember that requirements gathering is not a phase that happens before development; requirements can and should evolve as modernization progresses. Chapter 16 looks at how to build evolutionary roadmaps using various techniques such as metrics to track success. Chapter 3 also showed the importance of defining product and portfolio north stars and inputs that are essential to determining product requirements.

8.2.1   *Involve the right people*

To prevent UX from being an afterthought in a technology-centric modernization, start by ensuring there are people with the right variety of skills and experience involved. This includes internal-facing applications where it's not uncommon to see developers being expected to design UIs because UX is considered to be less important for employees than external users. It doesn't cost much to put a bit of effort into internal-facing products, and the benefits can be high. For instance, employee satisfaction and productivity are often directly related to the quality of their tools.

To move away from this mindset and generally to ensure your modernization delivers the maximum value for users and customers, include some or all of the following roles in your modernization:

- *User researcher*—An expert who understands how to work effectively with real users to gather their feedback and translate it into useful insights for the team.
- *Product designer*—An expert who makes products compelling and easy to use by designing UIs and other customer touch points.
- *Interaction designer*—An expert who focuses on the moments when people interact with products, covering both physical and emotional dimensions.
- *Content designer*—An expert who is skilled in writing and rewriting content so that it is easily understood by the target audience of the product or service.
- *Service designer*—An expert who is able to see the big picture and design end-to-end journeys balancing user needs and business outcomes.
- *Subject matter expert*—An expert in a particular topic. Typically someone who has worked in or studied the domain.

As with job titles in general, some people may have experience in multiple roles, and the definitions of these roles can vary in different organizations. It's better to consider the qualities that each of these roles brings to a team and identify where you may have important gaps. With all of these roles, it's recommended that there is close integration with the whole team rather than a person working independently who hands designs and requirements over for others to build. You may not need all of these roles, but equally, you may need more than you think. In any case, I recommend that you have some product and UX people involved from day one who can help shape the process and advise on what additional skills are needed.

8.2.2 Identify the costs of not modernizing

One of the ways to help identify the value of investing in modernizing the UX is to consider the costs of not modernizing it. A company that understands this well is Citibank, one of the biggest and oldest banks in the United States. In 2020, employees at the bank made an error that cost the bank $500 million. The employees weren't to blame, however. The antiquated 1990s-style user interface, shown in figure 8.2, was the cause of the problem.

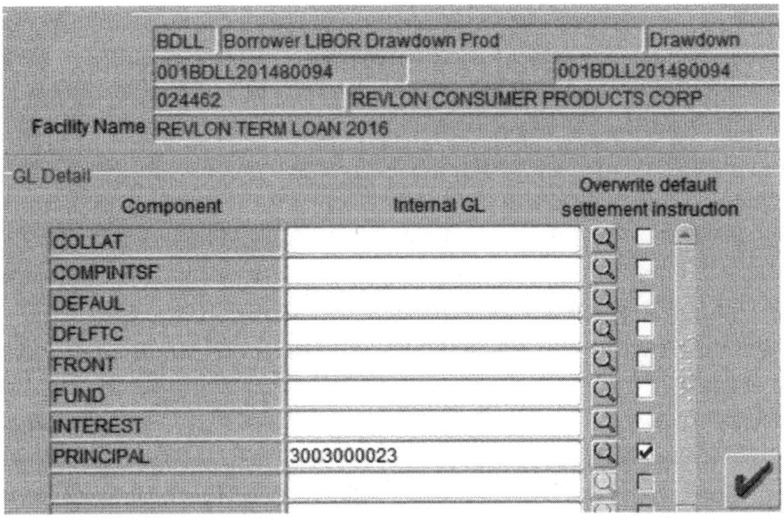

Figure 8.2   The user interface that Citibank employees used to pay interest to lenders (Source: United States District Court Southern District of New York, http://mng.bz/84J5)

When attempting to pay interest on a $1.8 billion loan to Revlon, the bank accidentally paid off the full outstanding amount of $900 million rather than just the $7.8 million interest payment. Many lenders paid back the erroneous payments, but some did not. Citibank tried to get the money back but lost in court, costing them $500 million and the title of "biggest banking blunder in history" (http://mng.bz/E9eX). The problem occurred despite three system users believing that they had correctly administered the transaction with one override—the *principal* field in figure 8.2. This was incorrect. They didn't consult the instruction manual, which explained that three overrides were required. In the end, Citibank was extremely lucky; they did manage to get all of their money back through a follow-up court case in September 2022 (http://mng.bz/NVAv), but this story still acts as a strong warning of the dangers of not taking UX seriously for internal products.

After reading the story of Citibank, how do you feel about the UX of your products and tools? Are your employees still using 1990s-style gray desktop applications with a poor user experience? Are they expected to remember certain special rules and combinations or consult instruction manuals? Do you have an idea of the costs and risks of not sufficiently modernizing the UX?

A simple starting question I like to ask people (especially during a listening tour) is, "What is likely to happen if nothing changes and things continue as they are?" Check out Jabe Bloom's Ideal Present Canvas (http://mng.bz/D9VA) if you'd like something more structured and visual to explore this topic.

8.2.3   *Don't mindlessly reverse-engineer the code*

To determine the requirements for modernization, it can seem logical to reverse-engineer the current system. This can be dangerous, however, for multiple reasons. Firstly, there are likely to be many features that are no longer needed in the existing system. They may have been useful in the past but now serve no purpose; they may have been superseded by other features or even disabled in the user interface because they turned out to be less useful than intended. We should also keep in mind that most new features are experiments. It's unclear how useful they will actually be until people use them. With that in mind, the current system likely contains some or many features that were never actually useful. Why waste time and effort carrying these across to the new system and trying to modernize them?

A second reason to avoid mindlessly reverse-engineering a current system is that even when features provide some value, they may be far from optimal. We've all experienced end users who have had to improvise or devise strange workarounds to perform their jobs. One client I worked with had employees processing customer applications by using two different tools. Those tools didn't talk to each other, so the users had to copy the information manually.

I've seen a few variations on the problems of integrating tools, like when email inboxes or spreadsheets are used as work management queues. At first, the problems might not be so bad, but as more workarounds get layered on top of each other and the number of employees using the system grows, the costs can be overwhelming. Fixing these problems in the old system may have been costly, but now that you are modernizing the systems, fixing some of these old hacks may be feasible, providing a win for the users.

8.2.4   *Analyze system information*

While completely reverse-engineering legacy systems is a bad idea, taking time to understand how they are used is a good idea. For example, identifying which features are no longer being used helps to pinpoint parts of the architecture that are dead and do not need to be modernized. One car manufacturer I worked with had millions of lines of business logic in stored procedures. Fortunately, it was possible to determine that around 30% was no longer being used and didn't need to be modernized.

Unfortunately, legacy systems don't always have analytics, meaning it's much harder to ascertain what's no longer being used. The fastest solution may be to add some form of observability. You can also use operational tools like logging and monitoring. Any information the system produces could reveal useful insights about usage and value. As a precaution, validating any insights derived from analytics with stakeholders and real users is sensible.

8.2.5 *Spend time with real users*

When facilitating workshops to help organizations start their modernization journey, I always ask engineers and architects, "How much time do you spend with real users?" I want to understand how much effort people put into thinking about the product and UX, in addition to the technical aspects like breaking up a monolith into microservices. The answer I often hear is something resembling "Not very often," which is a major concern.

Firstly, it results in a product with a worse UX and lacking valuable features. Secondly, it indicates that the problem of engineers not understanding their users' needs will persist. And thirdly, it sometimes results in stalled modernization efforts. Engineers have many possible ways to modernize the system and many choices about where to start, but they don't understand what is truly valuable to users. They get stuck in analysis and design paralysis.

Sometimes, engineers don't talk to users because of cultural perspectives. For instance, their only value is perceived as sitting at their desks coding. I've worked with clients where engineers built internal products that other company employees use. Even though they work for the same organization and one group is adding features to products the other group uses, they barely talk to each other. If you spot this behavior in your organization, I recommend addressing the problem early in your modernization journey. I would be worried about engineers making important modernization decisions without empathy for their users.

Some companies go beyond asking their teams to spend time with users. They also ask them to spend time in customer support resolving customer problems. Some even ask teams to spend time doing the job of their users. Where possible, both of these ideas are recommended for building a deeper level of empathy. A good example is provided by the German company Bettermile. As a last-mile logistics company, they build software to help drivers deliver parcels effectively. To help their teams build better products by empathizing with their users (drivers and consignees), employees get the opportunity to play the role of drivers by delivering real parcels using the company's products (http://mng.bz/lVpd).

If your users are internal employees, establish a regular habit by ensuring the two groups speak at least fortnightly. If possible, allow them to sit together. Ensure the communication pathways are always open so the two groups can easily contact each other when needed. Having product and UX specialists on the team who can facilitate these connections is helpful.

The idea that engineers shouldn't be spending time with users and are only valuable when producing code is an outdated way of thinking that must also be modernized. My friend Kacper Gunia (https://www.linkedin.com/in/cakper/) has the right mindset. He looks at the database access that has been given to employees to understand where tools are not meeting their needs. Whenever he identifies an unmet need or a new person asks for SQL access so they can query the production database, he spends time with them, understanding what they are trying to achieve and how tools can help them rather than giving them production database access (which is a bad idea for many reasons).

8.2.6   *Continuous discovery*

Spending time with users is most effective when done frequently rather than being a one-off phase at the start of a project. It helps everyone keep users' needs in mind and gets rapid feedback on new ideas. As mentioned in my government example, seeing this in practice was a big learning moment in my career. There was also the example of the senior stakeholder who pressured the team into building a new feature in a certain way but then reversed their decision after real user feedback was negative. This shows just how effective this approach can be.

Continuous discovery is a practice you can use during the modernization journey, and then your empowered product teams can continue to practice it indefinitely. This is what product expert Teresa Torres advocates in her book *Continuous Discovery Habits* (http://mng.bz/BADw). Part of her definition of continuous discovery directly addresses the two key points: "Weekly touchpoints with customers, by the team building the product." Continuous discovery means talking to customers weekly; teams should be empowered to do this themselves.

Teresa also makes another important distinction of which teams should be aware: a validation mindset and a co-creation mindset. A validation mindset is characterized by teams that put ideas in front of customers at the last minute when the feature is completed. It's about answering, "Did we get it right?" A co-creation mindset is about getting feedback much earlier in the process, so there is more time to act on the feedback and less resistance to changing direction. In practice, this might mean just talking about an idea with customers or a simple sketch before even mock-ups have been created.

Keep in mind that it's not enough that teams are just doing continuous discovery. They must also be empowered to act on the insights gained and make decisions about the part of the product for which they are responsible. Teresa proposes a trio-based approach to decision-making to give confidence in the decision-making process. In effect, each important decision should involve a product, design, and technology representative from the team. It doesn't mean the whole team must be involved in every decision; that would be too slow. It just means that each area of expertise is represented.

After my experiences working in the UK government, I have continued to see the rise of empowered product teams with a continuous discovery habit. It's an approach driven just as much, if not more so, by people like Teresa in the product management community. It's not software engineers demanding more responsibility. It seems to be the natural progression for building better products, like how we've moved from yearly to daily deployments. I encourage you to take this topic seriously, starting with Teresa's book, which includes all the insights and practical techniques you need to get started. I would also highly recommend attending a product management conference, like Mind the Product (https://www.mindtheproduct.com/conferences/).

8.2.7   What have people given up asking for?

During their keynote presentation at Domain-Driven Design Europe 2022 in Amsterdam (https://www.youtube.com/watch?v=olulGJDdpGQ), Olivia Cheng and Indu Alagarsamy from the *New York Times* shared a simple but effective technique they found useful during their modernization journey. They interviewed various users and stakeholders and discovered a powerful question: "What have you given up asking for?"

Often, people have given up pointing out certain problems and asking for changes to the current system. They have learned to live with the existing inefficiencies by using workarounds. When you talk to them, they may even be reluctant to raise these concerns due to their bad experiences, or they may just assume that the previous constraints still apply. For reasons like this, it should be clear that users won't just tell you the perfect requirements if you talk to them. There is a lot of skill involved in identifying true user needs, and you will need to work intelligently to identify the most valuable modernization requirements. This is another example of the value that UX specialists can bring to your modernization journey.

8.2.8   We've always done it that way

The opposite of people giving up asking for improvements is people not asking for improvements because they are satisfied with the current approach. They may be using green-screen mainframes or 1990s-style desktop applications or email inboxes as work queues and yet feel perfectly content with the approach. It's what they know and are comfortable with, even if the process is inefficient and error-prone.

From a business perspective, modernization may still be the right approach, even if the employees disagree. There could be deeper motivations as well. The employees may have a lot of power and job security because using the existing systems is difficult and requires lots of experience, making it hard to replace them. Or there may be a similar but less political reason; the users may be scared of change because there are big unknowns. Situations like this require a lot of empathy. It's important to listen to users' needs before talking about new solutions and changes. It can also be helpful to reassure them that their job is safe and that the goal is to improve their productivity and job satisfaction. Again, this takes skill, so it might be better to involve experts rather than letting developers, who have no experience with this, deal with the situation.

8.2.9   Finding shadow IT

In their book *Domain Storytelling* (http://mng.bz/ddPg), Stefan Hofer and Henning Schwentner highlight the importance of looking for shadow IT when mapping out existing processes with the intention of modernization. Shadow IT systems are those that non-IT people use without permission or the knowledge of the IT people who govern what is permitted. Examples include work management tools, collaboration tools, and analytics SaaS tools. Sometimes, shadow IT is the only way for people to be productive when internal IT doesn't help them to meet their goals, so it's important not to be critical. However, it is still important to discover shadow IT because it can help you to be aware of and better address the needs of people throughout the organization. This is another situation where empathy and building trust with users is key to creating a space where important insights, like shadow IT, can emerge.

8.2.10 *Industry example: Department for Levelling up, Housing, and Communities*

If you've never worked in an environment with a continuous discovery approach to product development, this industry example shows how you can introduce these ways of working while modernizing a system to find better requirements and deliver better results. Katy Armstrong and Dean Wanless show how they put different forms of user research into practice and how they took a data- and feedback-driven evolutionary approach.

Katy Armstrong (http://mng.bz/rjBx) is the deputy director for digital services at the UK government's Department for Levelling Up, Housing, and Communities. In 2018, she encouraged the department to make an important decision. The contract was ending with a large external supplier for Energy Performance of Buildings Register (http://mng.bz/VRqN), which is a government digital service to help people access energy certificates that they need for selling or leasing a property.

The consensus at the time was to draw up another long-term contract with a supplier, but Katy saw an opportunity to improve outcomes for UK citizens and make big cost savings. She aimed to improve the department's capability by developing the service in-house with a user-centric and continuous delivery approach. During the contract period, the cost of change was very high. As a result, there had been little improvement in the service during the previous 10 years. This meant that it was difficult to access the data inside the service for internal and external users, who could have learned considerable insight into key policy areas around reaching net-zero.

Two years later, the situation had transformed dramatically. The new service was live (https://www.gov.uk/find-energy-certificate). Dean Wanless (https://www.linked in.com/in/dean-wanless-25bb7b5/) had been appointed as the service owner, and a full internal team was in place. The team responsible for the service is now continuously improving the service with multiple deployments to production per day. Satisfaction from both UK citizens and government civil servants who used the service was substantially better. The costs had also halved, substantially reducing industry fees for sending new certificates to the register.

Impressively, the service began to deliver well beyond the requirements set for it. The original goal of the service had been to meet the EU requirement to have a register of energy efficiency, but the team discovered that there was a considerable scope to improve the service offering. For example, they built a data warehouse, which speedily aggregates data so that policy questions that would have taken weeks to answer with the old supplier can now be answered in a matter of minutes.

I asked Katy and Dean if they could highlight some key factors that contributed to this successful modernization effort. Katy said winning the hearts and minds of "the business" was key in terms of agile, user-centered ways of working. "We did this by demonstrating regular delivery and by embedding the team in the policy area, so they'd feel ownership of decisions and see progress."

Dean said that user research and continuous discovery were essential. It was the ongoing user research that allowed the team to go above and beyond the basic requirements that were expected. For example, very early into the journey, the team started to get a sense of just how much potential there was to improve the service based on feedback they received from users, such as the following quote: "This certificate is full of things that no one should care about." Dean said this feedback "pointed to the scale of the task that we had ahead of us!" The challenge was "how can we make an energy performance certificate that users understand and care about so that they improve their energy efficiency?"

They experimented with several designs, which were regularly tested with real users, removing unhelpful content and putting information that was important to users clearly at the top. The team retained control of the certificate so that unhelpful information wasn't added back in. Iteration of the design of the certificate continues as the policy matures.

The team found two forms of user research invaluable: contextual inquiry and usability testing. According to the Government Digital Service (GDS), contextual inquiry is "Similar to ethnographic studies. Contextual inquiry investigates how your potential users interact with their natural environment rather than just focusing on your digital product. It helps to identify what is possible. Contextual inquiry involves in-depth granular exploration of a small sample of people." The team used this form of research to answer questions like "Who are our current and potential users?" "What are they using our data for?" and "What opportunities exist to serve insights in a more user-centered way?" When doing this kind of research, the team collectively summarized the transcripts from lots of interviews and used Affinity Sorting (http://mng.bz/RmGR) to identify themes. For example, the team identified personas like "frequent forecaster" and relevant information about them, such as their motivations, wishes, and hopes and their data journey.

Using their research findings, the team identified key pain points and KPIs. This laid the foundations for a big breakthrough. The team was already publishing open data, but they realized they could provide more value by developing two new products for the public—Numbers on a Page, a simple service for the general public that will quickly answer top questions about energy efficiency, and APIs to give access to up-to-date data at the property level for data analysts. This is a great example of the difference between a feature factory mindset, where teams are told what to build, and an empowered product team mindset, where teams have the autonomy to discover new types of value.

Usability testing is a technique focused on solutions and validating ideas. The team uses this technique regularly and continuously as part of their continuous discovery. They put new ideas in front of users before they have even been built and validate them afterward. This is what they did when developing the new certificate, for example.

Katy highlighted another benefit of user research: "At the moment, we are continuously improving the service, and we have dedicated teams working on it. But we are always asked if this is still a good investment and whether the government money should be spent on something else instead. Our user research helps us to answer the question. By continuously talking to UK citizens about the service and their needs, we will know when there is no benefit to continued investment. However, for now, we're still uncovering many valuable opportunities through our ongoing user research."

There was another crucial factor in the success of this initiative that Katy wanted to emphasize: "It wasn't just designing better UIs that made our internal users happy; it was the fact that they had a team they could easily talk to and get changes implemented quickly." This is a good example of what it looks like when organizations move away from "the business" and "IT" as separate things. All people working on a particular capability work closely together, whether they are users carrying out operational processes or engineers building the systems to support those processes. The result is happier and more productive employees and better business outcomes.

> **NOTE** If you'd like to learn more about this example, check out the service's live assessment (http://mng.bz/ZRZN), DLUHC Digital's blogs about the energy performance of buildings register (http://mng.bz/27Jo), and Katy's blog (http://mng.bz/1JwQ).

8.3   *Modernizing the domain model*

There's a dimension to systems that is sometimes overlooked. It affects the value provided by products, the speed at which products are developed, and how well people communicate. This element is the domain model. More specifically, the conceptual model that people use to talk about the business concepts relevant to their products and services. Think about examples in your career where people have misunderstood each other and wasted time and effort going in the wrong direction or argued over what certain words and phrases mean.

When I worked with a North American client in the Smart Cities space, I remember clearly a meeting where a quality engineer and a solution architect seemed destined for a brawl, all due to the word *activated*. The quality engineer insisted that devices should be activated in the warehouse to connect to the server and identify problems before the devices were installed on the streets. Finding problems after a device had been installed meant an expensive truck roll, where an engineer had to go out and uninstall the device, load it onto a truck, and then bring it back to the warehouse for repair.

The solution architect, on the other hand, said that devices should be activated after they have been installed on the street because their physical location determines how they will be configured. The argument lasted almost 30 minutes (and had been brewing for weeks). Nobody else could break them apart or even get a word in, even though we all knew they were talking about two different steps in the process. It was possible for the extra checks to be done in the warehouse and additional configuration to occur following physical installation. We just needed a shared conceptual model that used two phrases to precisely describe each step, as illustrated in figure 8.3.

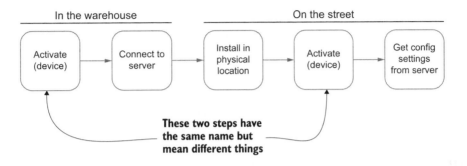

Figure 8.3   Problems arise when the same phrase is used to describe different domain concepts.

This example was about just a single word. In most organizations, many examples of confusing and ambiguous terminology exist. The resulting collaboration inefficiencies and productivity losses can quickly add up to substantial costs. Yet this doesn't seem to be an area that many organizations put much effort into consciously improving. Modernization is a good chance to reset that mindset and establish good practices around using language more effectively through intentional conceptual domain models.

Another reason why a focus on language is a good investment is that an ambiguous conceptual model is more likely to result in overly complex software for the domain concepts it represents. It frequently gets to the point where the language used by business and domain experts has little resemblance to the code. Consequently, translating a new feature idea into requirements and implementing it in code can be slow, expensive, and error-prone.

Creating a good domain model that aligns business and technology experts and results in simpler software doesn't need to be a costly or academic exercise. You've already seen big picture EventStorming, which creates a space for conversations about the domain. In the final part of this chapter, you'll see two more techniques that help you to consciously shape the future of the domain and design an intentional model. As you use these and other techniques, take the opportunity to clarify terminology and suggest improvements. It's not nitpicking or trivial to debate subtleties in language; it's a great habit to develop in yourself and encourage in others.

8.3.1   *Industry example: Royalties domain modeling*

Rebecca Wirfs-Brock and Mathias Verraes are two of the leading voices in the world of domain modeling. Their work in this area continues to move the field forward and inspire new generations of domain modelers from many disciplines, such as product management, UX, and software engineering. One of their most valuable contributions is an essay titled "Models and Metaphors" (https://verraes.net/2021/12/models -and-metaphors/). This is based on Mathias's experiences working with a client that acted as a broker for paying copyright holders for the use of their content. In a nutshell, this involved identifying the copyright holder for a piece of work, tracking usage claims, figuring out how much is to be paid, and managing the payments. The organization ended up with a very complex system that people struggled to understand and needed help regaining control of to add further innovations.

A key responsibility of the system was data matching, which is the process of reconciling data from multiple sources to determine the owner of a given piece of content and who needed to be paid. A major source of the complexity was the diversity of the various data sources, including research the company had done itself, publicly available data, private sources the company paid for, and agencies representing copyright holders. The data was messy, incomplete, inconsistent, in constant flux, and potentially susceptible to fraud.

The key to this example is that the organization originally perceived data matching as an engineering problem. People who worked in other business areas and weren't involved in writing code could not explain how data matching worked. Their ability to collaborate with engineers and improve their products was extremely limited. Mathias helped the organization resolve this problem by developing a shared conceptual domain model. Instead of using a generic, technical phrase like *data matching*, they built a language and a model around the concept of trust, which was reflected precisely in the code.

As Mathias facilitated whiteboard domain modeling sessions, he asked the team to describe all of their data-matching rules. As they did this, Mathias then encouraged the group to focus on what the rules were trying to achieve. Mathias noticed the group using words like *reliable* and *trust*, and through further conversations and whiteboard modeling, *trust* became the center of focus. For example, if a certain data source was considered more reliable, it should be trusted more.

To explore the concept of trust further, Mathias worked with the engineers to experiment with how trust might be modeled in code. The engineers created a trust code object that measured trust on a scale of –5 to 5, which had implications, like when a claim could be granted. For the group, this was a key turning point, and it's also an important lesson for you to keep in mind: when looking to create a better conceptual model and language in a particular domain, try to see how the model would look as code. This helps you to be more precise and to validate that the model will work as code.

As the team began using the trust-based model in their conversations and code, they continued validating the ideas with domain experts. In fact, they noticed that domain experts became interested in the topic and started to get more involved in the conversations. They felt much more engaged by the idea of talking about their domain using the model of trust compared to a generic data-matching technical algorithm. The business loved the idea of assigning and evolving trust, so much so that the new model became a shared conceptual model used throughout the business. As a result, engineers and domain experts were able to have much richer conversations about adding new features in the domain and more easily turn those ideas into working software because the model they used for communication aligned closely with the model they used in the software.

> **NOTE** You can read Rebecca and Mathias's essay in full, along with their other essays, in their book *Design and Reality* (https://leanpub.com/design -and-reality). The remaining sections of this chapter discuss two collaborative techniques for discovering new domain innovations and designing better models.

8.4 Process modeling EventStorming

When you've decided to modernize a product or a process, or you're interested in seeing what might be possible, EventStorming is an effective tool in this space. Whereas the last chapter introduced big picture EventStorming, which is built around chaotic exploration and understanding how the domain currently works, this section introduces process modeling EventStorming, which is less chaotic, more structured, and well suited to designing future states. The additional structure and detail take this technique closer to the implementation, yet it doesn't introduce any software-specific concepts, so it is still accessible and relevant for all types of stakeholders. The creator of EventStorming, Alberto Brandolini, even advocates that process modeling Event-Storming works well when turned into a collaborative game.

8.4.1 Notation

Process modeling EventStorming builds on the notation used in big picture Event-Storming. This flavor of the technique adds new concepts alongside syntax, restricting when each notation element can be used. For example, an orange *domain event* can only be used directly after a pink *system*. The following is the full list of notation and syntax. There is also a visual representation in figure 8.4 (and an interactive version on the book's Miro board at http://mng.bz/PRO8).

- *Actor/role*—Small yellow stickies are used to represent people in the domain or, more abstractly, the roles they fulfill.
- *Action/command*—Blue square stickies are used to represent instructions or triggers performed by a user or a policy trying to perform a task on a system.
- *System*—Large pink stickies represent software systems or applications that may be in-house or external.
- *Domain event*—Orange square stickies represent events that are produced by systems after a command has been invoked on them. These events represent the result of the command that was applied.

- *Policy*—Purple square stickies represent policies that are activated by domain events. They are like business rules or steps in a workflow.
- *Information*—Green square stickies represent information that people use to make a decision.
- *Hot spots*—These are notes or placeholders to come back and revisit. They are sometimes represented using diamond-shape fuchsia or red square stickies.

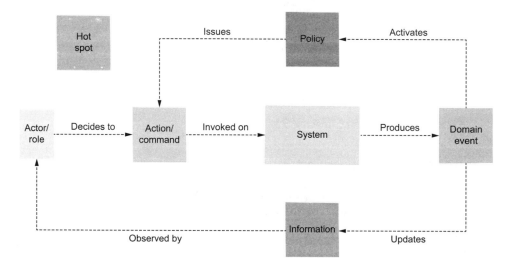

Figure 8.4   Process modeling EventStorming notation and syntax

Figure 8.5 shows the example of an EventStorm used to model a small part of the contract-approval workflow. The process begins with a salesperson who requests approval for a contract in the contracts system. A domain event, Contract Approval Requested, is then raised by the system, which triggers a business policy necessitating that the contract is legally approved. This policy is acted upon automatically via software by instructing the approvals system to request legal approval of the contract.

After legal approval has been requested, the outstanding approval is added to the list of new approvals, all of which are waiting to be approved by the legal team. In practice, this information is a screen on a website that the legal team looks at to see what work they need to do. After looking at the contract and being satisfied with the content, the legal team will approve the contract

Figure 8.5   A small part of a contract-approval workflow

So far, the example contains a single row, effectively the happy path. But with process modeling, it's also important to consider other scenarios and edge cases as well. Figure 8.6 shows an example of modeling additional scenarios. In this instance, the legal team may or may not approve the contract. If the contract is not approved, the legal team may request further changes, which sends the contract back to the salesperson and the contracts system for additional refinement. This flow is modeled as a row below because the general preference with process modeling EventStorming is to keep the top row as the common or happy path where possible.

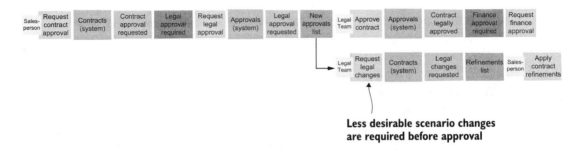

Less desirable scenario changes
are required before approval

Figure 8.6 Handling branches in process modeling EventStorming

NOTE On the book's Miro board (http://mng.bz/PRO8), you can find full-color cheat sheets covering the notation for each EventStorming format.

8.4.2 Planning a workshop

Planning a process modeling EventStorming workshop shares many similarities with a big picture EventStorming session. If you're running the session in person, you'll need a large amount of wall space, and regardless of format, you'll want a diverse group of attendees that represent all of the key perspectives, like product, engineering, UX, and domain experts. What's different with process modeling EventStorming is that the scope is usually much narrower to allow for finer granularity. Therefore, the number of representatives from different teams and areas of the business will be lower. Another aspect that's a little easier with this format is that it's easier to clarify the desired outcomes since the scope is narrower and more specific.

8.4.3 Facilitating a workshop

Facilitating process modeling sessions is a bit easier because there is no chaotic exploration at the start. Generally, the group works together with a single conversation happening at any given point. On the flip side, however, this can get tricky when the whole group tries to speak at the same time, so you will need some facilitation tricks to help get the group under control. My approach is to set some ground rules at the start of the workshop, explaining that we can't all speak at the same time and that we should show a basic level of courtesy if we want to have an effective session.

After the session has started, I find two techniques to be quite effective for keeping things under control: gently reminding people and using placeholders to park certain conversations. I also find periodic retrospectives useful, where the group can reflect on their behavior. For example, after a couple of hours, you can tell the group, "Let's do a quick retrospective. We'll go around in a circle, and each person has to answer two questions: What's one thing you've learned during this session? And what's one thing you would like to change in the next session?"

STARTING THE SESSION

The simple way to start a process modeling EventStorming workshop is to start with what seems to be the first step in the process and then gradually build up the timeline step-by-step with the whole group working together. If the group is new to the technique, it's good to designate a single person who can place the sticky notes and rotate the person every 15 to 30 minutes. For disciplined groups, it may not be necessary to define roles; instead, everyone is allowed to add and move stickies.

It's also helpful, but not necessary, to explicitly define the preconditions and the success, as shown in figure 8.7. The goal of this session is then to get from the start to the end. I do find that having a clearly defined start and end can help people to focus by giving a sense of how much progress is being made and how far there is still to go.

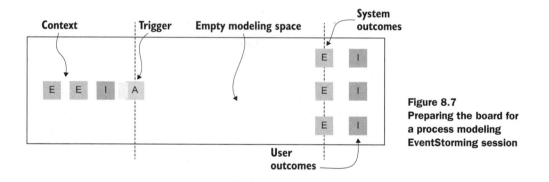

**Figure 8.7
Preparing the board for
a process modeling
EventStorming session**

EventStorming as a collaborative game

Alberto Brandolini, the inventor of EventStorming, is a big fan of gamifying process modeling EventStorming. His rationale for gamification is that process modeling EventStorming (when used to design future states) is about converging on solutions that require agreement. As you're probably aware, this is not easy to achieve when various stakeholders all have their own interests and opinions. Turning process modeling into a collaborative game removes the competitive nature and creates an environment where people need to work together.

Alberto defines four key rules in his process modeling game: all process paths are completed, the color grammar (shown in figure 8.4) is preserved with no holes or gaps, every possible hot spot is addressed, and all stakeholders are reasonably happy. To learn more about gamifying EventStorming, I highly recommend Alberto's talk Software Design as a Cooperative Game (https://www.youtube.com/watch?v =awyMC9PZNfc).

ASKING GOOD QUESTIONS

Asking good questions is an important facilitation skill. Good questions can unlock insights that rule out certain approaches or open the group to new possibilities. One thing to remember is that asking questions is about bringing knowledge into the whole group or challenging the group to think differently, which in turn allows the group to have better conversations and better understand the situation. Don't just view questions as a way for you personally to get the information you need to make a decision. This distinction is vital for thinking and acting like a good facilitator. This section provides generic facilitation questions you can use in almost any workshop.

"How many people will assume this role (or play this role, or be able to do this job)?" This question is about understanding the scale of the opportunity. Is there a small team of five people who share a responsibility or a call center with five thousand people? For example, automating the job of five people might not even justify the costs of building and maintaining the software, but if there are five thousand people, the equation is much different.

A related question is, "How many roles can a single person play?" This question can unlock conversations around making individuals more productive, like in the case where a person plays three roles but their expertise is only necessary for one of those roles, meaning time spent performing the other two roles is a waste of that person's talent. This is shown in figure 8.8, which applies these questions to roles in a prescription validation process. The new process can then be designed to optimize the value of each person involved.

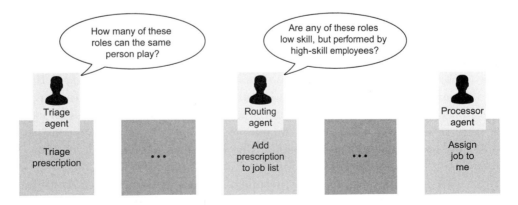

Figure 8.8   Asking questions about people in the domain to unlock valuable conversations

When there are multiple triggers or entry points to a process, a good question is "What's the likelihood of each scenario?" or "Which is the most common?" You can even apply a percentage split, as shown in figure 8.9. By making this information explicit, you have a better understanding of where valuable opportunities may lie. On the one hand, a large percentage of cases all flowing through a single trigger means more users will benefit from optimizations in that scenario. On the other hand, a low percentage of cases flowing through a particular trigger might also be a reason for greater effort in that area. One example I've seen is where only a small percentage of users seek help via an automated chatbot and instead prefer to talk to a real person. This way of entering the process has a higher cost to the business due to the manual work, so investing in greater modernization of this flow can result in more customers choosing this flow with the net result of lower operating costs.

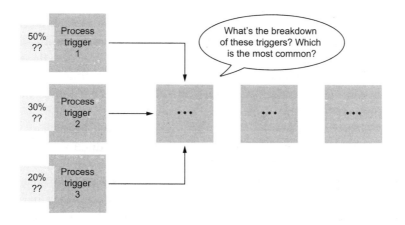

Figure 8.9   Explicitly marking the percentage breakdown of each flow through the domain

One of the most important questions is, "Does this always happen?" If you ask this question about every event and policy on the timeline, you are guaranteed to discover hidden edge cases and business rules. For example, consider a policy that states legal approval is required following an approval request for sales contracts. If we ask, "Is legal approval always required when the sales team requests contract approval?" we may get answers like "Actually not always. If the salesperson reuses an existing template with an approved client, then no legal approval is necessary." Similarly, you can ask the opposite question, "Should X never happen under any circumstances?" or "Is it 100% impossible that you would ever allow X to happen?"

As process modeling EventStorming is more solution-oriented, it doesn't hurt to have one eye in the future thinking about requirements that will need to be implemented. Thinking about service level agreements (SLAs) and general tolerance levels is a good starting point for asking these kinds of questions. For example "What would be the maximum possible amount of time you could allow between a contract approval being requested and a response from the legal team?" You don't need to nail down concrete requirements covering every scenario.

8.5 *Domain Storytelling*

Having a variety of workshop techniques in your toolbox is always a good thing. Different environments, domains, and people can all be factors in determining which technique is likely to be most effective in a given situation. You can also apply multiple techniques to the same challenge to see if different perspectives lead to different insights and opinions. For these reasons, Domain Storytelling (https://domainstory telling.org/) is a great technique to have in your toolbox alongside the various flavors of EventStorming.

The philosophy of Domain Storytelling is centered around the idea of telling stories. Stories are engaging and specific and revolve around people in the domain. These characteristics lead to a deeper immersion in the domain. Domain stories are generally modeled and told using a step-by-step approach with a single thread of conversation. It's not a technique where people must stand up and move around a lot while different subgroups form, with multiple conversations happening in parallel. It's a reasonably calm process, although, as with many collaborative techniques, facilitation skills are needed to prevent the group from all trying to talk at the same time and going down rabbit holes.

8.5.1 *Notation*

Domain Storytelling contains a few basic notation elements optimized for telling stories about the domain through interactions between people, systems, and other entities.

- *Actor*—People, software systems, or other entities that play a role in a domain story.
- *Work item*—A domain concept with which actors use and communicate.
- *Activity*—An actor doing something with a work item, often involving another actor.
- *Sequence number*—Indicates the order in which each activity happens.
- *Annotation*—Text used to articulate anything that cannot easily be expressed with other notation, such as the reason or motivation for a decision.
- *Group*—A group is used to show a relation between parts of the story, like a domain boundary.

Figure 8.10 shows the generic modeling icons used to represent each of these concepts. However, it's also possible to bring stories to life by using icons that are more representative of concepts in the domain being modeled. As an example, if you were designing the process for judiciary systems, you may use the icon of a judge to represent the judge actor rather than the generic actor icon.

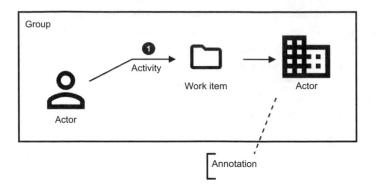

Figure 8.10   The five basic notation elements of the Domain Storytelling pictographic language

In figure 8.11, a desired future-state process of automatically validating prescriptions has been designed using the Domain Storytelling notation. The story begins with a customer who places an order for medication on the orders area of the company website. This is represented by the *customer* icon followed by the activity *places*, which is an arrow with the sequence number *01*. The arrow points to the *order for medication* work item and is followed by a second arrow that points to the *orders* system/capability. This reads as "The customer places an order for medication on the orders system." The

Prescription validation: future state

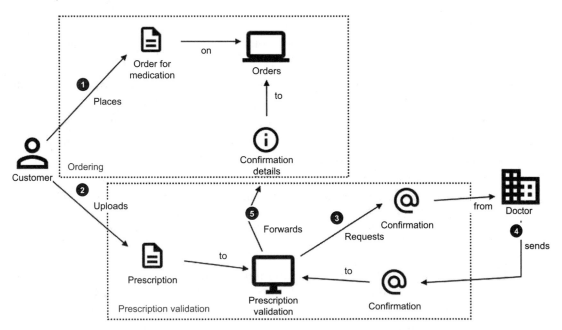

Figure 8.11   Designing a future-state prescription validation process with Domain Storytelling

next step is identified with the next sequence number, which is *02*. In this example, this step is where the same customer performs the activity of uploading a prescription to the prescription validation area of the website. The prescription validation service then goes off to the doctor to get confirmation that the prescription is valid via email, and once the email is received, it confirms the details with the orders system so that the order can be accepted and fulfilled.

8.5.2   *Planning and facilitating a workshop*

You may have observed in the previous example that, unlike EventStorming, there is only a single flow. There are no alternative scenarios or edge cases. This is by design and touches on another aspect of the Domain Storytelling philosophy, which is often expressed via a cliché that Stefan and Henning (the authors of *Domain Storytelling*, http://mng.bz/Jdzz) like to use: "A good example is better than a bad abstraction." They also quote Cyrille Martraire, who says, "One diagram, one story" in his book *Living Documentation* (http://mng.bz/wjlB). As a result, Domain Storytelling workshops are more structured and focused and require a bit more up-front planning. This section touches on the key aspects of planning and facilitating a Domain Storytelling workshop.

SETTING THE SCOPE

As Domain Storytelling involves telling precise stories with a single flow and no conditionals, we should clarify the scope up-front. Stefan and Henning propose three scope factors to consider when planning your workshop: *granularity*, *point in time*, and *domain purity*. Granularity refers to the level of detail and is defined as one of three broad levels: coarse-grained, medium-grained, or fine-grained. Coarse-grained refers to the highest level of granularity. Typically, this will cover large parts of the business involving multiple domains and teams, whereas a fine-grained story will be much more detailed, perhaps taking just one activity from a coarse-grained diagram and breaking it down into 10 or more steps. It's recommended that each domain story is modeled strictly at a single level of granularity rather than combining multiple levels.

Point in time is about determining whether the story will be based on the current realities or desired future improvements that have not been implemented. These two options are referred to as *as-is* and *to-be*, respectively. Establishing the point in time is a good idea because it clarifies the session's outcomes and prevents people from constantly switching between the two points during the workshop, which can cause a group to go off track and disengage. When modeling *to-be*, it's a good idea to manage expectations. This isn't just about mapping the current knowledge; it's about exploring possible future states and making decisions. There is likely to be less output, and people might feel like less progress is being made, so it's important to emphasize that converging on ideas and making decisions is valuable. That's not an excuse to go in circles debating ideas, so as always, it's important to step in and facilitate when time is not being spent productively.

Domain purity, the third scope factor, refers to whether the story should include software systems. A story with software systems has the domain purity of *digitalized*, whereas a story without software systems is considered to be *pure*. Choosing a pure domain story is a good idea when you want to focus on the domain concepts and not let software systems clutter the picture. Sometimes, however, understanding the role software systems play is crucial in understanding constraints and limitations, so it's a good idea to show them.

INVITING THE RIGHT PEOPLE

As with EventStorming and any technique for designing new domain capabilities, having the right people available is key to the quality of the ideas produced and the speed at which the group moves. Equally, the more people that are in a workshop, the harder it can be to keep things under control and make progress. The dynamics of Domain Storytelling don't really affect who should be invited to the workshop; the recommendations are the same as with EventStorming. The first step is to identify the questions you would like to answer during the workshop, and the next step is to think about who would be most valuable in the workshop to help answer those questions. When designing future state processes, that will mean people who understand the vision of the new system and the needs of users alongside those who will be designing and implementing the software. In addition, you may want to invite people who want to listen to the stories and learn without getting involved. Domain Storytelling is a good format for this.

PREPARING THE SPACE

Domain Storytelling is fairly flexible with regard to the modeling space. You don't need meters of wall space; in fact, you might not need any wall space. I've been part of Domain Storytelling sessions where a large whiteboard was sufficient or even a large screen where we used digital modeling tools for an in-person workshop. One thing I learned when attending a training workshop facilitated by Stefan and Henning is that they prefer a seat layout called the Stonehenge setup, shown in figure 8.12, where seats are in an almost complete circle or horseshoe shape focused on the modeling whiteboard or screen. I find this format to be cozy and engaging, and I really enjoy it. It taught me that you don't need to be standing up and moving around to have a great modeling session.

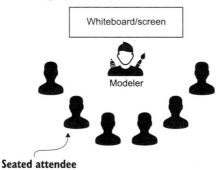

Figure 8.12   The Stonehenge room setup

If you're doing an in-person workshop and prefer to use physical rather than digital tools, a couple of options are available. Whenever I bump into Stefan and Henning at conferences, they actually have the Domain Storytelling icons printed out to stick on whiteboards and flipcharts. The alternative is to use sticky notes, but I think using the real icons looks better. I also find it enjoyable to use digital tools, even when in person. The two digital tools I recommend are Miro and The Domain Storytelling Modeler (https://egon.io/), which is an open-source tool that can be used online for free.

WORKSHOP ROLES

It's not necessary to introduce roles into a Domain Storytelling workshop; however, it can help ensure conversations stay on topic and get parked if they are going down a rabbit hole. Roles can also help to ensure that everybody gets an opportunity to speak instead of a few loud voices dominating. I've found that even with a group of experienced modelers, roles can still be advantageous, and I personally enjoy the structure that they bring. The following are roles to consider adding to your workshop:

- *Host*—This role is responsible for organizing the meeting and inviting participants before the workshop and has ultimate responsibility during the workshop for deciding how the time is spent (e.g., what scenarios are modeled).
- *Modeler*—This role is responsible for building up the story by adding notation onto the modeling space; usually, there is just a single person with this role.
- *Moderator*—This role is responsible for managing the space and the conversation to ensure the group has productive, on-topic conversations and everybody gets a fair chance to speak up and get involved.
- *Storyteller*—This role is responsible for sharing knowledge that the modeler will depict as a domain story.
- *Listener*—This role is for people attending the workshop to learn. They are welcome to ask questions and speak; they aren't forced to be silent listeners.

It's possible to combine some of these roles. For example, the same person could be the modeler and moderator. Where possible, I think it's best for separate people to play each of these roles; however, modeling and moderating both require a lot of attention and focus to do well. The roles of storyteller and listener can also be combined, especially when designing future-state processes where a combination of domain and technology expertise is required to design a solution.

KEEPING STORIES COMPREHENSIBLE

One of the big challenges with Domain Storytelling is keeping diagrams legible. It's easy to keep adding steps to a process and reach a point where there are so many lines, arrows, and icons that it's hard to understand what is happening. At the point you begin to notice the diagram starts to become a bit overwhelming, it's a good idea to stop reorganizing. One option is to end the story and start a new one from where the previous one finished. This works when there is a reasonably clean transition point, like the steps leading up to an order being placed and the steps after an order is placed.

Another strategy is to employ multiple levels of granularity. First, create a higher-level, coarse-grained diagram and then zoom into the areas where more detail is needed. It's hard to pinpoint when to stop, but I wouldn't recommend going too far past 20. Some modeling spaces, like a whiteboard, may not even allow you to construct stories that large anyway. As a facilitator, I often like to stop the group periodically and start from the beginning to recap our progress so far. During these moments, it can be obvious when the diagram is a bit too big or when we've mixed multiple levels of granularity.

8.5.3 *Replaying stories*

At Domain-Driven Design Europe 2022, Stefan Hofer joined my training workshop (https://dddeurope.academy/domain-driven-analysis-indu/) for an hour in the afternoon of day one. This was preplanned and was actually the idea of Indu Alagarsamy (https://www.linkedin.com/in/indualagarsamy/), with whom I was running the workshop. Stefan did a live modeling session, playing the roles of modeler and moderator. One of the workshop attendees played the role of the key stakeholder in the new process. After mapping out the first 9 or 10 steps of the process using the modeling tool (https://github.com/WPS/domain-story-modeler), Stefan put the tool into replay mode. This mode replays the story step-by-step on the screen. Attendees in the workshop gasped, and the stakeholder raised his eyebrows and said, "That's nice!" This captures one of the selling points of Domain Storytelling when using the purpose-built digital tool: the ability to tell the story step-by-step is very compelling and cool!

8.5.4 *When to use Domain Storytelling*

As you can see, the notation and philosophy of Domain Storytelling are quite a departure from EventStorming. EventStorming is fundamentally a timeline-based format reading from left to right with few or no arrows. Domain Storytelling does not have a timeline and allows flexibility in laying out the notation, relying on sequence numbers to show how the process unfolds over time. Another thing to compare is scope. EventStorming craves a large modeling space, capturing end-to-end flows and a variety of edge cases, all in the same model. Domain Storytelling scales in a different way by creating multiple stories for various scenarios at different levels of detail. However, both techniques work in a step-by-step fashion to build the process, so there are also some similarities in workshop dynamics.

If you like the idea of standing up, being active, and capturing everything in a single modeling space, including all variations, EventStorming is your best bet. More so if you don't want to worry about laying out the elements and drawing lines. On the other hand, if you prefer to use a purpose-built digital tool, you want to keep an electronic copy of the stories, you can evolve over time, and you like the ability to replay the stories, then Domain Storytelling will probably suit you more. It's hard to draw an exact line and decide when to use each technique, and personal preference will play a large role in the decision. You might think that EventStorming is more suited to in-person and Domain Storytelling for remote, but that isn't a pattern observed in reality. Both techniques are used in both modes.

EventStorming or Domain Storytelling for process modeling? You'll have to try both techniques and decide for yourself. And further still, you should learn about other techniques not covered in this book, like Service Blueprints (https://service

designtools.org/tools/service-blueprint) and Customer Journey Mapping (https://servicedesigntools.org/tools/journey-map).

Summary

- Modernization is often perceived to be about technology and software, which means stakeholders might risk missing out on opportunities to modernize the UX, product, domain, and domain model at great cost to users and the business.

- Identifying requirements for applications that will be modernized is not about copying across all existing functionality and reverse-engineering the current codebase.

- Involving experts who understand UX is vital to ensure that modernization delivers the maximum possible value.

- Consider the costs of not modernizing the UX. As your company plans to grow, will the current user interfaces act as a hurdle for growth or introduce risks?

- It's essential to spend time with real users to determine the requirements for modernization: some of the existing features may not be needed; some may be usable but very inefficient, requiring lots of manual workarounds; and some may be completely unusable.

- For optimal results, corroborate knowledge from the system, like current features, logs, and metrics, with the insights gained during conversations with users.

- A continuous approach to discovery is recommended, which means that the team of people building the product should be talking to their users weekly, both to get feedback on potential new improvements and on features that have just been implemented.

- Investing in a better conceptual domain model means improving how people talk about the domain—improving collaboration, simplifying the code, and removing expensive and error-prone translations between business speak and IT speak.

- Techniques like EventStorming, where business and software experts spend time discussing the domain together, are the perfect opportunity to focus on language and establish common terminology.

- Process modeling EventStorming is a technique that can be used to design future states of the domain, the user experience, and the domain model. It's an excellent technique for identifying modernization requirements before making technology-related decisions.

- As with every discovery and modeling technique, asking great questions like "How many roles can a single person play?" will help to uncover insights and clarify requirements for applications to be modernized.

- Domain Storytelling is another technique that can be used to explore future states of the domain and establish the most valuable requirements for modernization along with a better conceptual domain model.

- Domain Storytelling is based on telling stories using pictographic language and modeling individual scenarios up to around 20 steps in length, as opposed to EventStorming, which models end-to-end flows with many branches as a single timeline.
- You may want to introduce roles into your workshops to manage the group dynamics and maximize the usage of the available time.
- Choosing between process modeling EventStorming and Domain Storytelling is about personal preference and the constraints of the situation. It's best to try both techniques and decide which feels best for you and your colleagues.

Identifying domains and subdomains

9

This chapter covers

- Understanding the principles for identifying domains and subdomains
- Exploring possible domain boundaries with heuristics
- Identifying domains and subdomains with EventStorming
- Grouping subdomains into domains
- Assessing and refining domain boundaries

Whatever ambitious outcomes you hope to achieve with modernization, structuring teams effectively and designing a loosely coupled architecture will play an important role. Well-defined boundaries reduce dependencies in an organization and in software, empowering teams to deliver changes rapidly with fewer blockages. The benefits of good boundaries also extend into value discovery. Teams empowered to grow their expertise in a particular business area can contribute far more than just writing code. They can combine their domain knowledge and technical expertise to propose new product innovations. Good boundaries empower teams and help unlock their full potential.

So what is the secret to architecting loosely coupled organizations and software? If a primary objective is to reduce dependencies, then the key to answering this question is understanding where dependencies are unavoidable and where they can be avoided. Almost any dependency can be avoided if you are willing to pay a high-enough cost. A more valid question is: Which dependencies can be avoided without incurring high costs, and where must we accept dependencies because the cost of removing them is too high? This second framing is also better in that it conveys the fundamental nature of the challenge: how we architect systems is within our control. There isn't a single perfect solution that we need to find by following the steps in a flowchart. Every organization is a unique system with many factors affecting the optimal design, and the landscape is constantly evolving, which means the target is always moving.

The key to getting as close as possible to the optimal boundaries and dependency trade-offs is to start by analyzing the business—more specifically, the relationships between business domain concepts. When implementing new features, for example, which domain concepts are likely to change together? By organizing the business into cohesive groupings of concepts that change together, called *business domains* (used interchangeably with *domain* in this book), teams and software can be aligned with domains, resulting in lower coupling and faster flow.

This chapter shows how to identify domains and subdomains, starting with a few fundamentals and then a range of heuristics. The chapter also shows how to apply the principles and practices using EventStorming to identify domain boundaries.

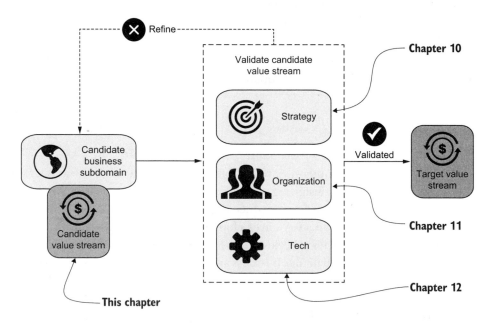

Figure 9.1 Potential business subdomains are candidate value streams that need to be validated from diverse perspectives.

Effectively, this chapter covers the first step in identifying independent value streams (see figure 9.1). Each subdomain is a candidate area for establishing a value stream. Before modernization, however, it needs to be validated from strategic, organizational, and technical perspectives. Then it can be considered a target value stream, meaning you are confident enough to begin.

9.1 The value of good domain boundaries

Good domain boundaries contribute to many organizational and technical improvements. As shown in figure 9.2, looser coupling results in fewer dependencies and faster flow—and, from personal experience, much happier teams. Cohesive boundaries that group related concepts lead to a clearer sense of purpose, aligning and motivating teams and incentivizing sustainable practices. Cohesion also makes it easier to learn the domain, in turn helping teams go beyond coding to contributing product and domain innovations.

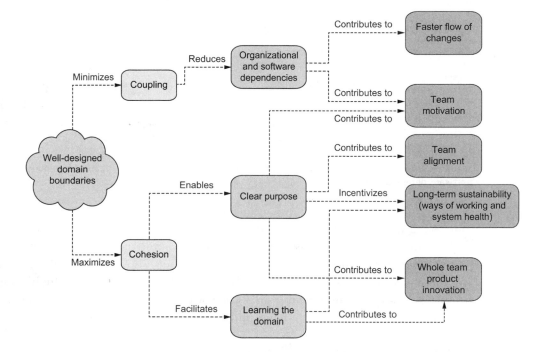

Figure 9.2 Well-designed domain boundaries maximize cohesion and minimize coupling, contributing to higher-performing teams and better products.

Consider the example of a travel company that offers loyalty points for each trip. They want to introduce a new loyalty levels feature that gives customers better rewards based on spending habits. It requires changes to the concepts *loyalty account*, *loyalty points*, and *rewards*. If those concepts were not modeled as part of the same subdomain, three subdomains would need to change along with three codebases and three teams needing to coordinate their work.

Alternatively, as per figure 9.3, when these cohesive domain concepts are modeled as a single conceptual domain, implementing the *loyalty levels* feature requires changes to only a single codebase by a single team. Fewer dependencies result in a faster flow of changes.

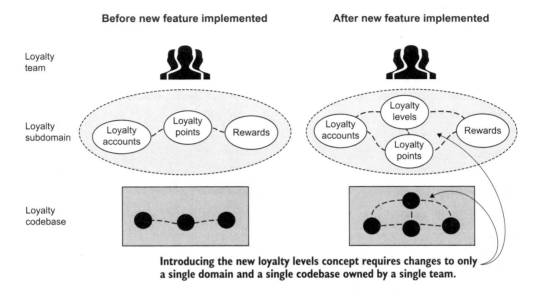

Figure 9.3   Identifying domains based on business concepts that change together to reduce team and software dependencies

Due to high cohesion, it's possible to define a clear long-term purpose with customer and business value: reward customers for their loyalty and increase their lifetime value (LTV). The team is motivated to continually seek new ways to achieve the goal, making them want to keep their code healthy and evolvable. The team is highly aligned around the purpose and able to work closely with the relevant domain experts, helping improve their domain knowledge and better reflect domain concepts in code.

9.2   *Domain identification principles*

Following good principles is the key to identifying effective domains and subdomains. This section introduces fundamental principles that will lead you toward a good design while avoiding common pitfalls.

9.2.1   *Domain boundaries depend on your goals*

The most fundamental principle to keep in mind when defining domain boundaries is that they are there to serve a purpose for your organization. There is no intrinsic, universally correct way to model boundaries in a domain. The optimal boundaries depend on the outcomes you aspire to achieve; therefore, you must decide what is best in your unique circumstances. Many factors can influence your decision, like academic research, topical books, industry standards, and other companies, but in most cases, there is no obligation to copy them. While it may be wise to follow existing conventions, it's still your decision based on well-informed rationales derived from a diligent process.

9.2.2   *Concepts can be coupled by multiple characteristics*

To grasp why there is no perfect solution and why it is important to arrive at your own decisions, refer to figure 9.4. There are shapes of different sizes and colors that represent domain concepts. These concepts can be organized into subdomains in various ways based on different characteristics: there could be a *green* subdomain for all green concepts or a *circle* subdomain for all concepts with a circle shape.

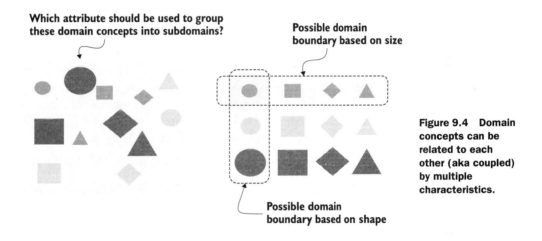

Figure 9.4   Domain concepts can be related to each other (aka coupled) by multiple characteristics.

The optimal characteristic for grouping the concepts in figure 9.4 may not even be apparent from this perspective. It could be weight, texture, or material, underlining the importance of deeper domain immersion.

Even individual domain concepts are highly subjective, as Rebecca and Mathias's case study in chapter 8 showed. They decided to introduce the concept of *trust* into their domain as a metaphor for corroborating competing sources of information when determining royalties. Suppose you spoke to competitor organizations in the same industry, trying to solve the same problems. They may see the domain differently and use a different language and concepts to describe it, even if their products offer similar functionality.

Choosing the appropriate boundaries is usually about understanding how you expect the system to evolve and reducing the effort it takes to make those types of changes. To demonstrate with the abstract shapes and colors, if your product strategy requires new features and business rules that change concepts based on their shape, the shape would be the most important criterion. However, if you choose boundaries based on shape, and you need to implement new business rules that require changing all of the red concepts, there will be high coupling in the form of changes to multiple subdomains. This extra coupling most often means that the costs to implement the change will be higher and it will take longer.

9.2.3   *Not all dependencies are equally costly*

While a primary objective when shaping domain boundaries is to minimize coupling between subdomains; it's important to recognize that not all coupling has the same costs. There will always be some coupling between domains, so it's essential to discern the implications on a case-by-case basis rather than just seeing all coupling as bad and to be avoided. When working with one client, I facilitated a workshop to help multiple teams collaborate more effectively. We presented several solutions to the CEO and asked which he thought best optimized for the product strategy. His response was: "I don't like any of these options. You should redesign the domain boundaries so there aren't any dependencies." It's a sentiment I see occasionally, yet it's unrealistic. It's important to accept that some dependencies will exist and to be comfortable with the nuance of coupling.

For a more realistic approach to coupling and to reduce some of the subjectivity in determining which coupling is more problematic, I recommend a formula proposed by Vlad Khononov: *Pain = Strength * Volatility * Distance* (http://mng.bz/n1ve). *Pain* is used as a measure of the costs of a given instance of coupling between two concepts. The higher the score, the more costly the coupling between the two concepts, the less desirable the coupling is, and the more justification for investing in alternative solutions that remove the coupling. *Strength* refers to the type of coupling between two concepts. This is measured based on how they are implemented in software like shared databases versus event-driven architecture. This will be discussed in more detail in chapter 12.

Volatility refers to how often two concepts change together. If two concepts rarely change together, for example, once per year, then *pain* will be low even if the other variables are high. There are a few important nuances to volatility. The first is that the volatility between two concepts can change based on the strategy and type of functionality being implemented. Historically, it may have been low, for example, but it could be much higher in the future based on a change in product direction. The second nuance is the current versus desired volatility. Existing constraints may limit how often two components change together (like legacy code), but a business may desire to develop innovations requiring them to co-change more frequently.

Distance refers to how far apart two concepts are. This has both organizational and technical implications. From an organizational perspective, the distance will be low if two subdomains that are coupled are owned by teams that sit closely together and report to the same manager. The teams should be able to coordinate their work easily. But if those two teams work in totally different departments, report to different managers, and are based on opposite sides of the world, the organizational distance will most likely be far higher. The technical implications of *distance* will be covered in chapter 12.

9.2.4 *Explore multiple models*

It might seem obvious, but it's worth being explicit: identifying good domain boundaries necessitates collaboratively exploring multiple possibilities. Because domain concepts are connected through various characteristics, exploring multiple models and assessing their trade-offs is essential when identifying the optimal domains and subdomains for your organization. Some options may promote autonomy and optimization of individual products at the expense of duplication and a lack of consistency in the UX across multiple products. In contrast, other options may employ higher levels of reuse at the risk of creating more dependencies. Before getting too attached to the first plausible option, it's advisable to put multiple options on the table. Then you can compare and decide which design best fits the outcomes you are trying to achieve. Using multiple heuristics and multiple techniques is the key to uncovering multiple models.

9.2.5 *Industry example: The British Broadcasting Corporation*

BBC is the world's oldest and the UK's largest national TV broadcaster, having existed since the 1920s. Nowadays, it runs one of the world's most-viewed news websites, with around 1.5 billion monthly page views and 61 million monthly video views (http://mng.bz/vPl1). Yet, the BBC website is much more than a news hub. It provides a range of services like TV streaming, radio streaming, sports, weather, and education. When BBC began a significant modernization initiative called WebCore, its high-level domain boundaries were aligned with these services (http://mng.bz/46eD), as shown in figure 9.5.

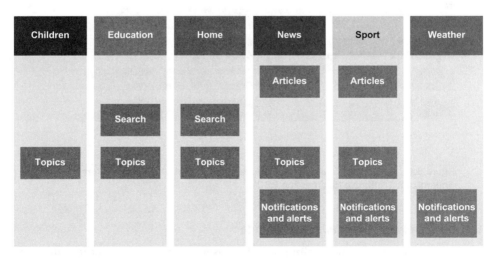

Figure 9.5   **The BBC's high-level domain boundaries prior to the WebCore modernization initiative**

Graeme Lindsay, an engineering manager for BBC at the time, explains: "Each is a major service in its own right—with millions of visits every week—and they have grown independently of one another over several years. This was reflected in the way the organization was shaped—with separate departments owning each digital service." These higher-level domains defined department boundaries composed of multiple individual teams.

As you may have noticed, in figure 9.5, there are commonalities across verticals, like the concepts of Topics and Articles. This resulted in individual products that were highly optimized but with some higher-level consequences as Graeme Lindsay explains: "The user experience across multiple services wasn't as seamless and consistent as it could have been" and "Lots of features, despite being conceptually similar, were implemented multiple times—with the total cost of maintenance also paid multiple times. Cross-cutting capabilities—for example, personalization and analytics—were major tasks that each product development team had to tackle themselves." As part of their modernization initiative, BBC wanted to address these problems by creating a single website for all services, building shared horizontal services, and allowing teams to share commodity components.

The outcomes BBC wanted to achieve were to leverage technology better and build more innovative features for the audience. As a result, BBC reenvisioned its domain boundaries to include horizontal domains like Articles, Search, and Topics, as shown in figure 9.6, and began transitioning its socio-technical architecture to align with them. Teams responsible for audience-facing verticals like news could then leverage these horizontals.

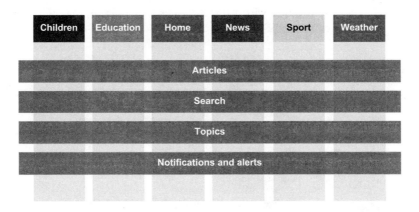

Figure 9.6   Horizontal domains that were identified as part of BBC's WebCore modernization initiative (Source: The BBC)

9.2.6   *Don't rely on superficial knowledge*

One of the most common mistakes I see is when important architectural decisions are made based on a shallow understanding of the domain. Some domain boundaries look like a good fit from a high level, but when you get deeper into the details and uncover more complexity, it changes your perspective completely. So, even when you are confident about a possible domain boundary, digging deeper into the details still makes sense by running more focused workshops and using various techniques that provide different perspectives.

9.2.7 *Good boundaries are not a panacea*

It has been mentioned in the book already, but it's worth repeating here because it is especially relevant when identifying domains and subdomains: even if you were to identify the perfect domain boundaries and use them to shape your teams and software architecture, there is still no guarantee that you will achieve your modernization ambitions. As the structure and process fallacy (http://mng.bz/QR0R) warns, structure alone is insufficient to create high-performing organizations. Other needs are essential, too, like prioritizing the right initiatives, incentivizing sustainable practices, and creating a learning environment.

9.2.8 *Prepare for constant evolution*

Identifying domain boundaries is not a one-shot activity; it's a continuous challenge. There can be many reasons for domain boundaries to evolve. One scenario you're likely to encounter is a subdomain growing too large for a single team due to the addition of many new features. Another is when initial assumptions lack key insights. After transitioning to the new domain boundaries, more complexity and dependencies emerge, and the costs are high.

In my experience, it's doubtful that your domain boundaries will be right at the first attempt, so you should assume that domain boundaries will change and ensure you have the flexibility to adapt. When asked to help define domain boundaries as a one-off activity, I explain that it's not a good idea. If you are in a similar situation, I would advise you never to commit to putting yourself in a position where you have to get the design right the first time. The more important matter to address is the source of these expectations. Understanding triggers for evolution is key to knowing when and how to evolve domain, team, and software boundaries, which is covered in chapter 11.

9.3 *Domain boundary heuristics*

There is no flow chart for identifying the optimal domain boundaries. This is because, as discussed in the first part of this chapter, domain concepts can be organized into domains and subdomains using multiple competing criteria. But that doesn't mean that identifying good domain boundaries is down to luck or is an innate skill. This is where heuristics are important. Heuristics suggest a possible course of action like "Take the train to work" if your goal is to get to work as quickly as possible. Learning about heuristics for domain boundaries can help you identify various design options and assess the trade-offs.

One thing about heuristics is that they don't guarantee you will arrive at the optimal solution by following them. For example, taking the train to work would not result in getting to work as quickly as possible on days when there is a train strike or major train delays. Another thing about heuristics is that sometimes they compete with each other. For example, "Cycle to work" is incompatible with "Take the train to work." Here, you can only choose one (although you could combine them into a new heuristic). Heuristics aren't quite a flow chart; they give clues about the direction to move, but you still have to do additional work.

Even though heuristics do not lead to the perfect answer, when you combine them with multiple techniques like EventStorming and Domain Message Flow Modeling, you will be well on the path to defining good domain boundaries. In this section, you'll learn about various heuristics for identifying domain boundaries, and then in the next part of this chapter, you'll see how to apply these heuristics in a practical setting with EventStorming.

9.3.1   *The five guiding domain-boundary heuristics*

There are many heuristics for identifying domain boundaries. As a starting point, I recommend five major heuristics that represent five top-level concerns when identifying and assessing domain boundaries:

- *Business heuristic*—Define domain boundaries based on business importance.
- *Domain heuristic*—Define domain boundaries based on relationships between domain concepts.
- *Organization heuristic*—Define domain boundaries to optimize for team motivation and productivity.
- *Technical heuristic*—Define domain boundaries that take into consideration software and technology constraints and opportunities.
- *User experience heuristic*—Define domain boundaries for the best user experience.

The *business heuristic* encourages choosing domain boundaries by separating strategically important domain concepts from less strategically important domain concepts. Depending on your target business outcomes, this could be faster innovation in subdomains of higher strategic importance, improved efficiencies through higher reuse, or optimized build versus buy versus partner decisions. Decoupling high-value from low-value concepts enables faster innovation in key areas because every extra concept adds cognitive load and increases the costs of changing the corresponding code. Anything of lower value that can be removed will result in a lower cost of change. In the BBC example, reducing duplication costs and enabling new innovation types were two key business outcomes. Identifying the most strategically important subdomains is the topic of the next chapter.

The *domain heuristic* encourages choosing domain boundaries based on the domain's inherent nature, such as relationships between domain concepts, like an *order* and *order items* or a *recipe* and *ingredients*. In essence, this is about looking for domain coupling and cohesion and uncovering the true complexity of the domain. These benefits are critically important for minimizing the coupling and complexity in the corresponding software. In the BBC example, the relationship between concepts like *topics* that appeared in multiple domains was strong enough to consolidate them into a single horizontal domain.

The *organizational heuristic* encourages choosing domain boundaries that optimize for the needs of the people building the system, like purpose, autonomy, and mastery. For example, a subdomain that is too complex for a single team can lead to many problems like burnout, unmaintainable code, and unreliability. This topic is covered in more detail in chapter 11.

The *technical heuristic* encourages choosing domain boundaries for technical reasons, like the constraints of legacy systems. You may have been surprised to see this heuristic. After all, shouldn't the software architecture be based on the domain and not vice versa? In an ideal world, that's correct, but realistically it's tough to change existing legacy systems, and the cost of adapting them to the desired boundaries may not be feasible in the short to medium term. Accordingly, you may need to define domain boundaries that are achievable in the shorter term, although it's still ok to have longer-term aspirations. To summarize, software shouldn't be the primary factor when driving domain boundaries, but it's important to understand technical concerns and constraints so that your choice is actually viable.

The *user experience heuristic* encourages choosing domain boundaries that offer the best possible user experience. This was one of the key reasons for the re-architecting of BBC's domain boundaries. The current domains resulted in a silo effect where each product had been fairly well optimized, but the consistent experience across all of BBC's product and services had suffered as a result. Domain boundaries might not be the most important factor in optimizing the UX, but they shouldn't be ignored.

Sometimes, these heuristics will all pull in the same general direction, which is nice, but often they will pull in different directions, and you'll have to decide which takes precedence. There is no natural precedence or simple answer. After comparing the options, you'll need to spend more time building a business case. Remember that boundaries need to evolve, and you are unlikely to get them perfect the first time regardless, so it may be better to pick the option that feels most right and make sure you have a buffer to evolve the design as you learn more.

These heuristics will guide you in the right general direction by ensuring you include all key considerations and balance competing forces. But they're very high level and still leave a lot to the imagination when defining specific domain boundaries. This is why they are most effective when combined with more granular heuristics for identifying individual subdomains, which are covered next.

NOTE You can find cheat sheets for all the heuristics presented in this chapter on the book's Miro board at http://mng.bz/PRO8.

9.3.2 *Subdomain boundary heuristics*

The heuristics in this subsection are used for defining the boundaries of individual subdomains. They are effectively the boundaries of individual teams (a single team may also be responsible for multiple lower-complexity subdomains) and parts of the software architecture. None of these heuristics is a rule, so in most cases, you'll need to consider all of them and choose the most appropriate. You should also look for novel heuristics that may be relevant to your context.

ALIGN SUBDOMAINS WITH PROCESS AND JOURNEY STEPS

One of the easiest ways to start identifying subdomains is to break up a process or user journey into a sequence of steps or subprocesses, each becoming a candidate subdomain to be owned by a separate team. For example, in an e-commerce setting, the Placing an Order user journey may be broken down into the steps and subdomains as shown in figure 9.7: Search and Browse, Product Details, Cart and Checkout, and Reviews.

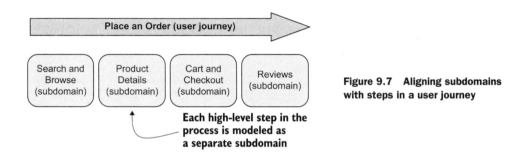

Figure 9.7   **Aligning subdomains with steps in a user journey**

This heuristic is a great starting point because everybody is familiar with techniques for mapping out processes and journeys, and it's only a small effort from there to then break it down into smaller parts. It is effective at finding boundaries when steps in a process are largely self-contained and share few overlapping concepts. The Reviews subdomains would fulfill this criteria if it needed to know very little about other subdomains like the ID of a product and the ID of the customer that had purchased the product. It could then allow customers to add reviews and ratings while being highly immune to any change affecting Customer and Order concepts in other subdomains.

One drawback of a process-based decomposition approach is that, very often, certain capabilities and concepts appear in multiple steps or journeys, and duplication costs may be too high. The next heuristic addresses this concern.

CENTRALIZE CONCEPTS THAT APPEAR IN MULTIPLE PROCESSES OR STEPS

If you start by mapping out processes and chunking them into steps, the next step is to look for commonality across steps and processes that should be extracted into dedicated subdomains, as shown in figure 9.8. Centralizing domain concepts into a single subdomain has several benefits, including grouping related concepts that change together and reducing the complexity within other subdomains. This was the case in the BBC example where Topics, Search, and Notifications and Alerts were centralized.

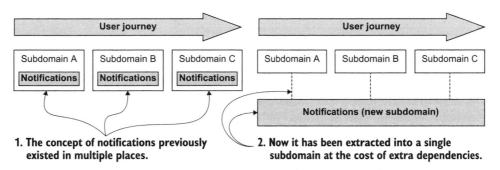

Figure 9.8 Centralizing concepts that appear in multiple subdomains into a single subdomain

It's important to be careful with this heuristic. When applied based on a superficial understanding of the domain, it is easy to create bottlenecks in the system and other problems. I often observe architects who have a strong desire for reuse and centralization without fully understanding the costs. This was the case when I worked with a client in the travel industry who had offerings tailored to both the mass and luxury markets. The mass market is generally about high volumes and low margins. A profit is made at the time of booking.

Luxury is the opposite: lower volumes of customers but a much higher profit margin on each customer. Architects saw that both domains had the concept of package building, which involves configuring the options on a booking like daily excursions, and wanted to centralize within a single Package Building subdomain used by all user journeys. The luxury team knew this was a bad idea. For them, package building was a highly customizable and tailored process that helped increase the value sold to each customer. As a centralized service owned by another team in a different country, it would drastically limit their ability to improve this part of their product continually. Fortunately, the luxury team convinced the architects that it wasn't a good idea.

The following is a list of questions you can ask to decide if following this heuristic and creating a shared subdomain makes sense in your modernization scenario:

- Will consumers (of the shared subdomain) lose any capabilities?
- Will consumers gain new capabilities?
- Will consumers have more time to focus on their core mission?
- Will consumers be slowed down by the new dependencies?
- Will it be possible for the team owning the centralized subdomain to be responsive to the needs of all their consumers?
- Could the number of consumers grow to be problematic over time?
- Will the cost for consumers to migrate be high?
- Will consumers have the option not to migrate to the shared capability?

With the responses to these questions, you can then answer a more fundamental question: What are the business and organizational outcomes you hope to achieve, and how confident are you that they will be achieved? In addition to these questions, the next heuristic is also crucial in deciding when certain concepts should and should not be consolidated into a single subdomain.

ALIGN SUBDOMAINS WITH ESTABLISHED SEMANTIC BOUNDARIES

Determining whether two concepts are essentially the same and should subsequently be considered part of a single subdomain often requires digging into the nuances of domain language. One clear pattern to look for is when the same concept is referred to by different names at different times. Imagine you worked in an organization where the terms *Lead, Rider*, and *Reporter* could all be used to refer to the same customer. Each is used in different scenarios with different semantics, which are candidate subdomains as shown in figure 9.9, where *Lead* is a term used in the Marketing subdomain, *Rider* is a term used in the Journeys subdomains, and *Reporter* (a person who reports a problem) is a term used in the Maintenance subdomain that maintains the fleet of vehicles.

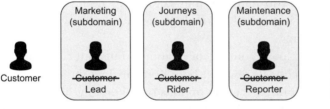

Figure 9.9   Aligning subdomains with established semantic boundaries

Another pattern to look for is when the same word or phrase has different semantics in different scenarios, like a tomato. In the Botanical domain, a tomato is considered to be a Fruit because it develops from the fertilized ovary of a flower. Meanwhile, in the Culinary domain, a tomato is considered to be a Vegetable because it is used in savory dishes (http://mng.bz/Xqp1). To disambiguate, the more precise terms *Botanical Fruit* and *Culinary Vegetable* are sometimes used. As this tomato example points out, aligning subdomains with established semantic boundaries is a good heuristic for domain boundaries because it is driven by identifying boundaries around a specific purpose, like making good food.

When looking for semantic boundaries, it helps to understand a few basic linguistic concepts. Try to find example words and phrases for each of the following linguistic concepts in your business domains:

- *Homophone*—Same pronunciation but different meaning, for example, seller versus cellar.
- *Homograph*—Same spelling but different meaning, for example, saw (to cut) and saw (to have seen).

- *Homonym*—Same spelling but different sound and meaning, for example, live (to be alive) versus live (happening right now).
- *Synonym*—Same meaning, yet either spelling or sound may be different, for example, drink versus beverage.
- *Synecdoche*—Where a part is used to describe the whole, for example, "All hands to the pumps," meaning everybody is needed to help out, not just their hands.
- *Metaphor*—Where a concept is used as a figure of speech but not literally, for example, "low hanging fruit" implies something that is easier to achieve than alternative options. In the previous chapter, Rebecca and Mathias's example demonstrated the Trust metaphor being introduced as a domain concept.

Etymology is another crucial linguistic concept that is essential to keep in mind. This pertains to how the meanings of words change over time, which is something that happens in many business domains. This concept implies that we must continuously be aware of evolving semantics and ensure that the software evolves in parallel. Take a moment to try and think of three phrases in your business domains that have different meanings now compared to a few years ago.

The general concept of semantic boundaries exists within different fields. In linguistics, there's a concept called a *semantic domain* (https://www.semdom.org/description), and in domain-driven design, there is a similar concept called a *bounded context* (https://martinfowler.com/bliki/BoundedContext.html).

DEFINE PURPOSEFUL SEMANTICS

The previous heuristic was about analyzing the current state of a domain to identify established semantic boundaries. That implies a one-way relationship, which isn't the case. It's within your control to define purposeful semantic boundaries, to determine where the same concept may have different meanings. A failure to define semantic boundaries will likely result in highly complex and coupled software. Take the example of a Customer. You could put everything about the Customer concept into a single subdomain called Customer. This would include anything that seems related to a customer, like their profile, order history, payment details, shipping preferences, loyalty, etc. The results are monolithic, tightly coupled systems that are hard to reason about. Defining purposeful semantics, even when there aren't existing semantics to follow, helps to avoid this problem.

To define purposeful semantic boundaries, we can determine that the clue is the name of the heuristic: start by identifying different purposes in the domain and then work backward to identify what value a particular concept brings concerning that specific purpose. Define the semantics based on the value provided relative to that purpose and then strip away anything from the definition that is unrelated. For instance, if your product allows customers to see their order history, then the semantics of a customer relative to this purpose is something that has placed historical orders. No business rules or logic related to this purpose require understanding the customer's loyalty points, support tickets, or notification preferences. They are not part of the

Customer semantics in relation to this purpose. With this in mind, Order History could be considered a separate subdomain aligned with these semantics, as shown in figure 9.10.

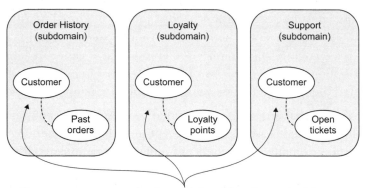

Figure 9.10 **Aligning subdomains with purposely defined semantics**

The customer concept exists in multiple subdomains, each with unique semantics related to the subdomain's specific purpose.

DECOUPLE SUBDOMAINS BY THE RATE OF CHANGE

As a general guideline, the larger a subdomain is, the more expensive the cost-of-change and lower the speed-of-change are likely to be. This is because when the domain concepts are implemented as code, more code is likely to result in some or all of the following negative effects: harder to learn the codebase, harder to understand the code, harder to change the code, and more time-consuming to test and deploy the code.

All of these negative effects increase the costs and time needed to change code. Therefore, by removing code that doesn't change very often, the cost-of-change for the code that does change often will be lower. Accordingly, the main intention of the *decouple subdomains by rate of change* heuristic is to define domain boundaries that allow a faster rate of change where it is most needed. Bear in mind that this is an oversimplification. A whole variety of other factors, like the quality of code and the skill of the team, also affect cost-of-change.

Another way to look at this heuristic is from the perspective of Vlad's coupling formula. If the coupling *volatility* between two concepts is low or even zero, the *pain* of the coupling will be low or zero. Ergo, even if the cost-of-change between two concepts is high, it's not a problem if it barely ever happens. The risk here is accurately determining the rate of change. It's effectively a bet on the future, so you can't be 100% certain. It's not pure guesswork, though. Firstly, you can look at the historical rate of change, and then you can look at the product strategy and roadmap to understand which areas are of the most strategic importance. They will likely receive a higher investment and change more often.

This heuristic is one I use often, especially in the context of modernizing tightly coupled legacy monoliths. There is often someone who will say something like, "Everything is connected to everything; it's impossible to break down this domain into subdomains." Spoiler: this has so far never turned out to be correct. I'll typically start exploring potential domain boundaries by asking people to draw what they consider to be all the individual parts that are tightly connected. Then, working through each relationship step-by-step, I'll ask questions like "How often does this change?" "How often do you implement new features here?" "How often do you implement new functionality that requires these two parts to change together?" It's normal to hear responses along the lines of "That part doesn't change very often" or "We might make one small change every few months to add a new type of <thing>." In these cases, you have identified a low or zero value for *volatility;* therefore, the two parts can be decoupled with high confidence because at least one of them changes very rarely.

One final point to add to this topic is the differentiation between the current rate of change and ideal rate of change. The current system may constrain how quickly changes can be implemented or may limit certain types of change altogether. The goal of modernization is to enable the ideal rate of change in each subdomain. Keep this in mind when calculating *pain*.

DECOUPLE BY SUBDOMAIN ROLE

One heuristic that is effective in many different types of domain is the *delineate by subdomain role* heuristic. This is about looking at the mechanics of each subdomain and the type of purpose it has. Figure 9.11 demonstrates three common roles that subdomains can assume. The first is the Specification role. This means the subdomain's purpose is to create a specification or description of something that must happen.

A specification itself usually doesn't provide value but rather describes something that would be valuable. In figure 9.11, the Campaign Building subdomain has this role because its purpose is to collect all of the information needed to run an Advertising Campaign. It then hands over the specification to the Campaign Running subdomain, which will execute some process or instructions based on the provided specification. Therefore, Campaign Running has the Execution role. The third subdomain is Campaign Optimization. It has the Analysis role because it receives data from multiple sources and produces insights about improving the Advertising Campaign's performance.

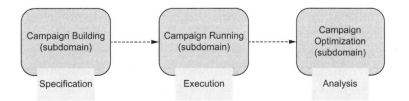

Figure 9.11   Three subdomain roles: Specification, Execution, and Analysis

As with all heuristics, this heuristic does not have a 100% success rate. Sometimes, it may be better to have a single subdomain with multiple roles like Specification and Execution. This is often the case when the complexity of one role does not justify being a separate subdomain, like when the steps to build a specification may only involve collecting a few pieces of information. It does pay to think longer-term, however. When the subdomain grows and becomes too large for a single team, splitting based on role might be the ideal approach, so it's wise to prepare for that by keeping the specification-related and execution-related concepts loosely coupled in the code.

SPLIT SUBDOMAINS ON KEY TRANSITION POINTS

A change of purpose is often punctuated by a defining moment where the transition takes place. A good way to apply this heuristic is by asking, "What is the exact moment when . . . ?" like "What is the exact moment when a person becomes an adult?" From a legal perspective in the United Kingdom, the answer would be "A person becomes an adult on their 18th birthday." This is the transition point: Before the day has started, a person is defined as a *Minor*, and after the day has started, the person is defined as an *Adult*. I find that the question format, "What is the exact moment when . . . ?" can sometimes uncover really profound insights, so I highly recommend using it in your workshops.

Another sign of a key transition point is where one process or subprocess stops and another starts, often accompanied by some type of handover from one person or role to another. An example of this is in a restaurant kitchen: after a Party of Customers seated at a Table has placed an Order, a Member of the Waiting Staff will Generate the Order. This will then trigger the processes Prepare the Starter, which is handled by the Starter Chef. The Prepare the Main Course process, handled by the Main Chef, is triggered by the Waiting Staff after they have Cleared the Starters from the Table.

9.3.3 *Subdomain grouping heuristics*

No matter how you slice domain boundaries at the subdomain level to create loosely coupled software and independent teams, some dependencies are always going to exist between them. Good domain boundaries minimize unnecessary coupling but they can't eliminate it altogether. When implementing new features or delivering certain types of work, co-change across multiple subdomains, and accordingly multiple codebases and teams will sometimes happen. A number of factors contribute to addressing this problem, and one of them is structure. By identifying subdomains that share a close relationship and grouping them into scope 2 domains (architectural scopes were defined in chapter 6), the costs of coupling can be reduced.

The benefit of grouping subdomains into higher-level domains is that the subdomains that change together will be owned by teams that work together, reporting into the same leadership structure and working towards the same business outcomes. Their communication will naturally be higher, and the barriers to collaboration will be lower. From the perspective of Vlad's coupling formula, this is a deliberate action that can be taken to reduce the distance between subdomains that share a high volatility.

The heuristics in this section are focused on identifying scope 2 domain boundaries by looking at the various ways subdomains can be grouped to maximize synergies and reduce the costs of dependencies. As with the subdomain heuristics, the five guiding heuristics also apply at this level. Business, domain, organizational, technological, and UX are all factors that need to be considered. And the same caveats apply too: no heuristic is right in every case so you need to make decisions on a case-by-case basis and understand which outcomes you want to optimize for.

Another benefit of well-defined scope 2 domains is the ability to evolve subdomain boundaries. If the boundaries of multiple subdomains turn out to be less optimal than expected, but they are part of the same scope 2 domain, the distance will be lower, and it should be easier to collectively evolve the boundaries. This is important to keep in mind when shaping scope 2 domain boundaries.

GROUP SUBDOMAINS INTO PRODUCT- OR SERVICE-FOCUSED DOMAINS

A *product-focused domain* or *service-focused domain* is a domain composed of subdomains that are all dedicated to providing capabilities for a single product or service. This heuristic typically encourages a faster flow of changes within a single product because all of the teams involved in building a product are closer together and more aligned. One of the drawbacks of following this heuristic is that the experience across multiple products may be neglected and the level of duplication may be very high. These were two key symptoms highlighted in the BBC example, where they started with service-focused domains and later introduced some horizontal domains.

It may not be possible to apply this heuristic in organizations with extremely large and complex products that have scope 3–level complexity. In these scenarios, a scope 2 domain can be considered a *product capability-focused domain*. These are scope 2 domains composed of subdomains that are dedicated to providing capabilities for a single part of a single large product.

GROUP SUBDOMAINS INTO HORIZONTAL DOMAINS

A *horizontal domain* is a domain composed of subdomains that provide capabilities to a platform consumed by multiple other domains. When used appropriately, this heuristic can lead to domain boundaries that reduce costs and complexity and reduce time-to-market for all of the platform's consumers and sizable value for the organization overall. You saw an example of this in chapter 6 with Uber's fulfillment platform, which handles over a million concurrent users and a billion trips per year while supporting more than 10 products and services like UberX, Food, Groceries, Taxi, and Package.

There are numerous potential downsides to following this heuristic. Most commonly, horizontals tend to become bottlenecks as all of their customers request enhancements and the teams cannot satisfy all their demands within the desired timeframe. Another risk is a poorly designed interface between the horizontals and consumers and poor reliability in horizontals that causes downtime for consumers. Uber invested a huge amount of effort in getting these aspects right: "We spent six months carefully auditing every product in the stack, gathering 200+ pages of requirements from stakeholder teams, extensively debating architectural options with tens of evaluation criteria, benchmarking database choices, and prototyping application frameworks options" (http://mng.bz/yZzo). You don't need to follow Uber's exact approach, but you do need to take the design and evolution of horizontals seriously and treat internal teams as well as you treat external customers because the cost of a bad decision affects many teams.

GROUP SUBDOMAINS INTO PROCESS- OR JOURNEY-FOCUSED DOMAINS

A *process-focused* or *journey-focused domain* comprises subdomains dedicated to providing all the capabilities needed to fulfill an end-to-end process or journey. This heuristic typically encourages a fast flow of changes across teams aligned to a key business outcome and jointly responsible for creating an optimized user experience from start to finish. This was the case in my business property tax example from the previous chapter.

Business Property Tax was considered a scope 2 domain. Within it, multiple teams each owned a step in the process, like Review, Resubmit, and Renegotiate (these weren't the real terms used but do not affect takeaways). The teams sat together, shared rituals, and had user researchers who worked together. It was just a natural day-to-day occurrence to always think about the end-to-end process, even if you only worked on a single part. Remember to pay close attention to things that are common across multiple user journeys.

GROUP SUBDOMAINS INTO CUSTOMER- OR USER-FOCUSED DOMAINS

A *customer-* or *user-focused domain* is a domain composed of subdomains dedicated to providing capabilities to a single type of customer or user. This heuristic encourages groups of teams to be fully devoted to serving the needs of a particular type of customer or user. This was the case during OpenTable's modernization in the early 2010s. The Customers domain covered all the teams who focused on people who wanted to reserve a table at restaurants, and the Restaurants domain covered all the teams who focused on the people working at restaurants.

One drawback of this heuristic is that it is usually not possible to categorize every subdomain as relevant to one type of user. Many processes and transactions affect multiple different types of users. Orlando Perri explains that this was the case at Open-Table: "A lot of things were touching both sides like reviews and availability. So we just had to decide which side was the most appropriate for each subdomain and be very aware of the dependencies."

GROUP SUBDOMAINS BY GEOGRAPHY

Geography-focused domains comprise subdomains dedicated to providing capabilities that apply only within a given geographical region. This heuristic is useful, therefore, in scenarios where you want a faster flow of changes and more freedom to do things differently in different regions. These benefits can be important if your customers in different parts of the world have diverse needs and expectations or laws, societal conventions, and regulations differ across international borders. On the flip side, the costs of greater autonomy within a geographical area must be balanced with the costs of duplication and the lack of consistency that customers active in multiple regions may notice.

9.3.4   *Industry example: Airline domain decomposition*

In 2015, a large airline started a modernization journey driven by four primary business outcomes: differentiated customer experiences, accelerated innovation and delivery velocity, untapped revenue opportunities, and improved operational performances with reduced costs. Their architecture was a major blocker, a big-ball-of-mud monolith that was complicated and risky to change. When making changes, the whole system had to be deployed. One thousand servers kept the system running in production, yet it was still unreliable on the three cyber days per year (peak traffic days). The lack of logging, monitoring, and general observability compounded these problems.

The airline had reached a point where the current approach was untenable, and the business case for modernization was evident. The real question was how to modernize the system and where to start tackling such a huge problem. Javiera Laso and her colleague used EventStorming sessions to learn about the current state and explore future opportunities and domain boundaries.

The group identified target domains and subdomains, including an Offer/Ordering domain, a Redemption and Loyalty domain, a Check-in & Boarding domain, and a Trip Management domain. Each domain was comprised of multiple subdomains, as shown in figure 9.12.

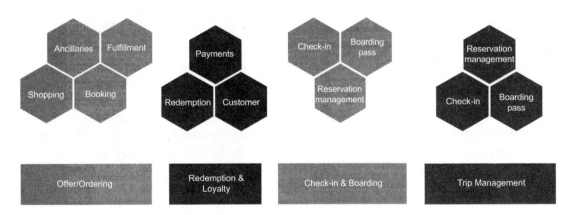

Figure 9.12   Domains and subdomains identified at the airline (Source: Javiera Laso)

One thing to note in this example is the naming. Everything is named according to domain terminology. All of these names had been defined collaboratively with input from many stakeholders, including subject matter experts. Good naming helps to see that the subdomains in each domain are cohesive. For example, the Offer/Ordering domain aims to provide offers that customers can purchase and handle the booking and fulfillment process. Each of these concerns was modeled out as a separate subdomain because it was believed that the level of coupling between them was not too high. Individual teams would be able to own each of the subdomains and work largely independently. Yet, there was some coupling of concepts. Some features touched multiple subdomains, so it made sense to consider them collectively as a single domain and organize the teams accordingly.

You may have noticed that the Check-in & Boarding and the Trip Management domains contain subdomains with identical names. For many architects, this is at odds with principles like reuse and standardization. However, based on the insights that emerged during EventStorming and other sessions, Javeria and colleagues identified distinct semantics tied to different purposes. Separate models were better because establishing unified models would have increased coupling and complexity for little gain.

With domains and subdomains identified, the airline had a portfolio of modernization opportunities. The costs and benefits of modernizing each subdomain were used to make value-based prioritization decisions. For example, Javiera explains that "the booking domain was chosen as the first slice of modernization because it is a crucial part of the business flow, where we can secure payments, but being so coupled, it was very difficult to scale and create new business rules." After modernizing, the system's stability improved, leading to increased profits at times of high user flow. In the past, the page was often down for many hours.

Javiera also articulated the necessity of an evolutionary approach to domain modeling and modernization. After the airline had modernized the first parts of the system, they continued to discover features, functionality, and edge cases in the old monolithic system of which they weren't even aware. As a result, there was more unplanned work to move them across. At times, it challenged their understanding of the domain and their proposed domain boundaries. This is typical of modernization. It is rarely a linear sequence of steps from A to B due to the complexity of legacy systems.

9.4 *Identifying domains and subdomains with EventStorming*

So far, this chapter has looked at principles and heuristics for identifying domains and subdomains. But how do you go from reading about these conceptual ideas to applying them in practice so that you can modernize your organization's architecture? There is not a single right way to do this; in fact, a whole variety of techniques can be used in identifying domains and subdomains. It's never a good idea to rely solely on one technique, yet I do recommend EventStorming as a great starting point in most cases. It's probably the technique I use most often because it allows diverse participation and surfaces a lot of vital information that is relevant to identifying domains and subdomains.

What's more, the different flavors of EventStorming are all complementary. Big picture is great for identifying higher-level, fuzzy boundaries, and process modeling and software design are perfect for getting deeper into the details, resulting in a very high level of confidence in the proposed domain boundaries. Software design EventStorming hasn't been covered in the book yet, but it will soon be introduced in chapter 12.

9.4.1 Pivotal events

Before slicing your EventStorm up into domains and subdomains, a nice preparation step involves identifying *pivotal events.* Pivotal events are the most important domain events that give clues about where the ideal boundaries might be. They are an example of how to apply the heuristic *split subdomains on key transition points* from the last section. Because pivotal events are just markers for important events, they should not be assumed to be domain boundaries. They're more of a way to uncover insights in areas where there might be a domain boundary. This is helpful because as soon as domain boundaries are drawn, people can get attached to ideas quickly. Starting with pivotal events helps to stay in exploration mode and uncover more possibilities for shaping boundaries.

To answer the question "What are the most important events?" there isn't a simple flow chart to follow or something obvious to look for. It's very subjective, meaning the criteria for determining what is important will vary from domain to domain and from person to person. This might sound problematic, but it's not really a big deal. Pivotal events aren't something to care about after the workshop. They don't need to be officially recorded or documented. It's better to consider them a stepping stone to identifying boundaries during the workshop. Simply asking people to identify their most important events can lead to great conversations that surface clues about how to shape boundaries. If a particular group needs more guidance, I'll refine the task to "What are the key transition points or milestones in the domain, like the moment when a lead becomes a customer?"

Figure 9.13 shows the example of a pivotal event called Applied for Membership, which is part of the application process for a financial institution. A Non-member installs the app and then provides their personal and bank details. They are then able to apply for membership. After applying for membership, two things need to happen. The Fraud Checker needs to run some security checks and an Account Manager needs to conduct an Onboarding Assessment. Do you think this is a useful pivotal event, and do you think it is an indicator of a domain boundary?

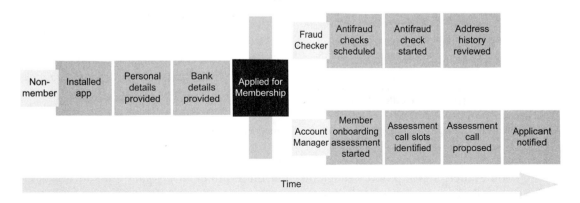

Figure 9.13 An Applied for Membership pivotal event and surrounding domain events

There are a number of reasons why the Applied for Membership pivotal event is a useful pivotal event and is also a good indicator of a domain boundary. Imagine you were in this workshop and a head of product said, "Applied for Membership is one of the most important events because the product relies heavily on network effects, and there is strong correlation between applications made per month and revenue." Many people in the group might not have realized the importance of this step and had been focusing their efforts on improving elsewhere. Now, they are aligned with the head of product on what's important.

Some of the other heuristics for identifying boundaries are also noticeable in this example and have been highlighted in figure 9.14. Firstly, notice how the word used to describe the customer is different on either side of the event: before the event, they are considered Non-members, but after the event, they are referred to as Applicants. In addition, the event is a trigger for two new processes where activity is transferred to two new actors. You'll also notice the different types of domain roles. Before the event, the purpose is to build a specification, the application request. After the event, it's about executing processes that the specification feeds into.

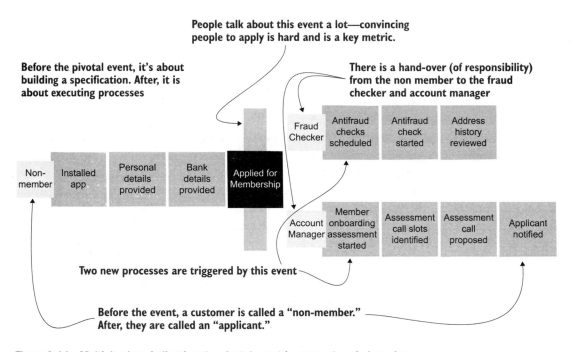

Figure 9.14   Multiple signs indicating the pivotal event is near a domain boundary

Sometimes, a group may struggle to limit the number of pivotal events. It may seem like almost every event is a pivotal event. This usually occurs in high-level workshops where large parts of the business are covered in fewer events. As a result, there may only be one or two events on the timeline for some subdomains, meaning most events could be considered pivotal events.

To use pivotal events effectively in these types of higher-level workshops, I would offer two pieces of advice. The first piece of advice is to encourage pivotal events that are relative to your level of detail. If you are running a high-level workshop in an area that covers many scope 2 domains, look for pivotal events that are important at that level. A good enabling constraint is to add a hard limit like "Please identify the 5 to 8 key transition points in this EventStorm." If you get the boundaries right at this level, you can then follow up with more detailed workshops to identify the subdomains within each scope 2 domain.

The other piece of advice I would offer is to zoom in on two pivotal events that are very close together and try to understand why. Usually, it's because a lot of information is missing, which might be because the people who understand that part of the domain aren't in the workshop. It might be important to get their insights before proceeding too far ahead. Remember, the sticky notes on the wall do not fully represent the domain. They only represent what the people in the workshop decided to put there.

9.4.2   Chunking the timeline

Pivotal events will get the group nicely warmed up by talking about various transitions and handovers in the domain. Building on this momentum, you can then start to identify domains and subdomains by slicing up the EventStorm into chunks. The pivotal events may have already done some of this for you. Essentially, this is the *align with process and journey steps* heuristic from section 9.3. It's about choosing sequences of events that belong together. For this step, I keep the instructions very simple, with something along the lines of "Group the sequences of events that seem to belong together," "Split the timeline up into steps," and "Which events feel like they belong together?" This terminology is intentionally vague because sometimes there is a desire to define what a domain is precisely, which can be distracting at this stage. It's sometimes good to visualize boundaries at multiple scopes, as figure 9.15 shows.

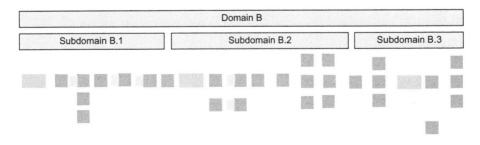

Figure 9.15   Visualizing a domain composed of multiple subdomains on an EventStorm

In a virtual setting, it's possible to copy and paste the EventStorm so that people can work in smaller breakout groups. This is an excellent technique for allowing the group to identify multiple options and compare the pros and cons. Smaller breakouts enable everyone to participate more.

9.4.3   *Looking for scattered subdomains*

Not all subdomains will appear as a series of events that sit neatly together on an EventStorm. Some subdomains will be represented by events that are scattered across multiple parts of the timeline. In the context of an EventStorming session, I refer to these as *scattered subdomains*. After chunking the timeline, or even at the same time, it's a good idea to start looking for scattered subdomains. Look for a particular domain concept, or just a word, that appears in multiple places, and consider it a potential subdomain. This is the practical application of the heuristic *centralize concepts that appear in multiple processes or steps* from earlier in the chapter.

At the same time, you'll need to balance this heuristic with the heuristics *align with existing semantic boundaries* and *define purposeful semantics*, as shown in figure 9.16. Even if a concept does appear in multiple places, it may be wiser to treat them as different subdomains, with the concept having different semantics in each of them relative to the purpose of the subdomain. As always, you'll need to analyze both of these options and others before making a final decision.

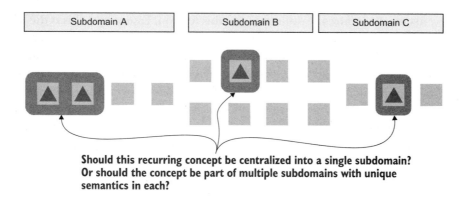

Should this recurring concept be centralized into a single subdomain? Or should the concept be part of multiple subdomains with unique semantics in each?

Figure 9.16   Not all subdomains have events next to each other on the timeline.

9.4.4   *Subdomains versus user journeys/processes*

A common mistake that beginners make when using EventStorming to identify domain boundaries is assuming that processes and steps in a process always align with domain boundaries. As discussed in section 9.3, *align subdomains with journey and process steps* is just one of the possible heuristics that can be applied to identify subdomains; yet, it's not always the optimal choice.

To help clarify the relationship between processes/steps/journeys and subdomains, I often find it useful to describe three different ways that the concepts can be related:

- *Fully aligned*—A subdomain is fully aligned with and shares the name of a process, journey, or process step.
- *Aligned with delegation*—Similar to the previous concept, except the subdomain delegates some of the rules or logic to other subdomains.
- *Unaligned*—No subdomain is aligned with the process, journey, or process step, which instead is a composition of multiple subdomains aligned to other purposes.

Let's use the example of a generic onboarding process to demonstrate the three possible scenarios. Figure 9.17 shows the *fully aligned* scenario. There is an Onboarding subdomain that handles all the steps of an onboarding user journey.

The fully aligned pattern is not suitable when the complexity is too high for a single subdomain, or multiple concepts and capabilities are unrelated and should not be coupled. In this scenario, the Onboarding subdomain still manages the process of Onboarding but delegates some aspects to other subdomains, like an Identity Verification subdomain or a Wallet subdomain, as shown in figure 9.18.

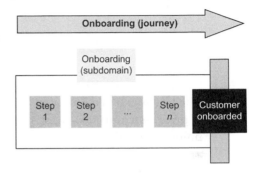

Figure 9.17 Subdomain and user journey are fully aligned.

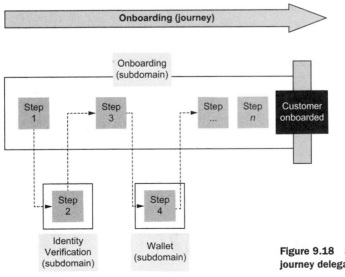

Figure 9.18 Subdomain aligned to user journey delegates some parts of the process.

When each of the steps within a process, journey, or process step involves drastically different domain concepts that are also used in other places outside the Onboarding journey, then the unaligned pattern (figure 9.19), where there is no Onboarding subdomain at all, is necessary.

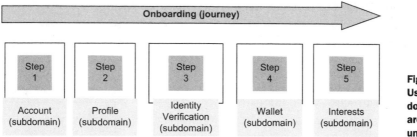

Figure 9.19
User journey and domain boundaries are completely unaligned.

The timeline-based format of EventStorming tends to bias us toward thinking in terms of processes, journeys, and steps. Sometimes these will be domain boundaries and sometimes not, so it's important to keep each of these three patterns in mind and decide on a case-by-case basis which is the best fit. The analysis tips covered next can help.

9.4.5 Analyzing subdomains

After you have identified a candidate domain boundary, it's useful to spend some time analyzing the cohesiveness and exploring alternative options. One way to do this is to write a short description of the subdomain. What is its purpose, and how does it achieve that purpose? Then, you can pose the following questions: "Does each event in the subdomain seem consistent with the name and description of the subdomain?" and "Do all of the events seem related to each other?"

Figure 9.20 uses the example of a Pickup and Dropoff subdomain from an online car dealership. The purpose of the subdomain is to deliver cars to customers and take their old cars away. At first glance, the first three events seem clearly related to the name and purpose: Picked Up New Car From Warehouse, Arrived at Customer's

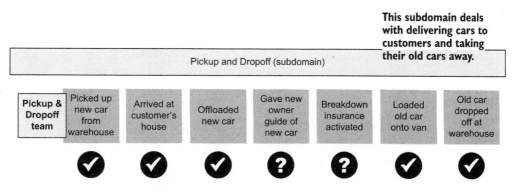

Figure 9.20   Analyzing the cohesiveness of a candidate subdomain

House, and Offloaded New Car. But then the fourth and fifth events feel different—Gave New Owner Guide of New Car and Breakdown Insurance Activated—so they have a question mark underneath them.

At this point, it's ok to put a question mark if something feels out of place, even if you can't articulate precisely why. In this example, the two question marks suggest an *aligned with delegation* subdomain. Pickup and Dropoff is concerned with the logistics of moving cars around. While giving the new owner a guide of the car and activating breakdown insurance happen at the same time, the domain concepts and logic have little relationship with the other steps in the subdomain, so those two events could be part of other subdomains.

There are a few basic, sense-check questions I recommend using to assess and refine options in the situations:

- Would it make sense for a single team to be responsible for all of the events?
- Have there been and will there be business rules and features that require these concepts to change together?
- Are there people (internal or external) who only care about some of these concepts and not others?

When going through this analysis process, I also find it valuable to visualize the key details of each subdomain using the subdomain overview canvas shown in figure 9.21. You can find the canvas on this book's Miro board (http://mng.bz/M9OD).

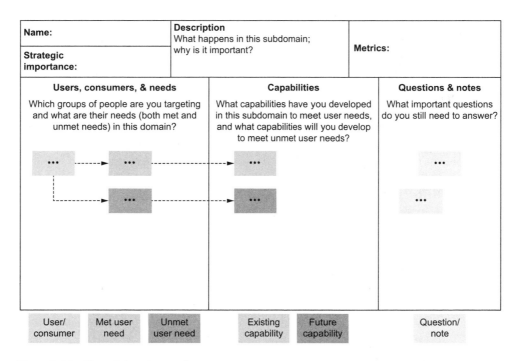

Figure 9.21 The subdomain overview canvas

9.4.6 *Planning a series of workshops*

Identifying domains and subdomains will take more than just a few hours or a few days. You can use big picture EventStorming to map out high-level boundaries and then use process modeling and software design EventStorming, along with techniques introduced in the following chapters, to get further into the details, allowing you to validate and refine the boundaries and have the confidence to commit to them. This means that expectations will need to be set accordingly with all stakeholders about the speed of progress. Unfortunately, I'm not comfortable giving even a ballpark figure for how long to estimate, because it varies so drastically from organization to organization. Some domains are far more complex, with decades of legacy software to factor in and people who are uncomfortable with collaborative techniques like EventStorming. The rate of progress is much slower in these environments.

If you want to get a sense of how long it takes and how much effort is involved in identifying domains and subdomains, I recommend starting with a big picture Event-Storming session for an important end-to-end process or a scope 2 domain—basically an area that covers around five to eight teams and contains reasonable domain complexity. If it's too simple and easy, it won't be representative enough of what to expect in complex areas. You should set aside two to three full days for the big picture session. After the workshop, you can then organize deep-dive workshops for two or three of the candidate subdomains identified. These workshops will be narrower in scope and more detailed, using process modeling EventStorming to map the current and possible future states along with some of the techniques introduced in the following chapters. I recommend allowing two full days per subdomain. At this point, you'll have a general idea of how long and how much effort it will take. Try to pick a complex subdomain to ensure that your findings are representative.

You've now reached the end of this chapter. There is much to think about when it comes to identifying effective domains and subdomains, but it's comforting that there are many tried and tested principles and techniques. Independent value streams require far more than just good domain boundaries, however. The next chapter looks at validating the strategic fit of a candidate subdomain. You can find interactive examples of this chapter's content on the book's Miro board (http://mng.bz/amd9).

Summary

- A business is broken down into conceptual business domains to identify different parts of the business that are related in some way.
- Larger domains are composed of multiple, more granular domains called subdomains.
- Business domains and subdomains are used as the basis for defining organizational and software architecture.
- Well-defined subdomains encapsulate cohesive domain concepts that are related and change together, enabling teams to have a clear purpose and reducing coupling in software.

- There are many ways to shape domain boundaries in a given organization. All have trade-offs, and there is usually no perfect solution, so it's important to explore multiple models.

- You may be inspired by external factors like competitors and subject-matter literature, but ultimately, you choose the domain boundaries that are most effective for achieving your desired business and organizational outcomes.

- There are many ways to shape domain boundaries because domain concepts are often related via multiple criteria—for instance, colored shapes can be grouped according to their color or shape.

- Some dependencies are more costly to remove or support than others, so understanding the cost to remove and support each possible dependency is key.

- Vlad Khononov's formula is a great way to reduce the guesswork in assessing the cost of a dependency. His formula for assessing coupling is *Pain = Strength * Volatility * Distance.*

- Domain boundaries are important decisions, so it's important to get into the details of the domain before committing. Some ideas make sense at a high level but prove to be suboptimal when further complexity is revealed and assumptions are broken.

- Defining domain boundaries is not a one-shot activity; you should start with constant evolution in mind.

- Heuristics are useful for identifying the different ways a business can be modeled as domains and subdomains. Each heuristic provides a different perspective, leading to different options.

- This book proposes five guiding heuristics for finding domain boundaries covering business, domain, organizational, technical, and user experience–related perspectives.

- More granular heuristics are used to define the boundaries of individual subdomains. These heuristics provide ideas like aligning subdomains with steps in a process or centralizing recurring domain concepts into a single subdomain.

- Semantic boundaries allow the same concept to have different meanings in different subdomains; for example, a tomato is a fruit in the botanical domain and a vegetable in the culinary domain.

- Grouping subdomains into scope 2 domains is important because it helps to reduce the cost of change across related subdomains by indicating how software and teams should be organized.

- Various heuristics are used to determine how to group subdomains, such as grouping subdomains to form products and grouping subdomains relative to a specific type of user.

- EventStorming is a recommended technique for identifying domain boundaries.

- Pivotal events are important events. Identifying them can lead to important conversations and insights about where to place domain boundaries.

- An EventStorm can be chunked into domains and subdomains by grouping events that seem related.
- Not all subdomains will have events that sit neatly together on the timeline, so it's important to look for these as well.
- It's useful to analyze candidate subdomains by writing down the purpose of the subdomain and checking to see if each event feels relevant enough.
- The subdomain overview canvas is a useful technique for visualizing the key information about an individual candidate subdomain to help decide if it looks like a good option.
- It usually takes a whole series of workshops to define domain boundaries, starting with big picture EventStorming and moving deeper into the details with process modeling EventStorming and other techniques.

Strategic IT portfolio

A key challenge for modernization leaders is ensuring that modernization efforts deliver the greatest business impact, which means avoiding underinvesting in high-priority areas and overinvesting in areas with limited return on investment. A bad decision could result in thousands of people-hours wasted modernizing low-value capabilities and missed opportunity costs of moving the business forward in key strategic areas. For technologists, it's crucial to discern that a brilliant technical architecture using the latest technologies and patterns in an area where a simple CRUD interface would suffice is a bad decision, regardless of the technical brilliance. One of the goals of architecture modernization is to enable fine-grained business investments, which requires a value-driven, portfolio-based approach.

Business subdomains are the perfect model for applying portfolio thinking to architecture modernization. Each business subdomain is an investment opportunity within the portfolio. The level of architecture modernization in each subdomain can vary according to the potential returns. In subdomains that play a crucial role in achieving desired business outcomes, investment can be higher, whereas in subdomains that have little effect on the business strategy, investment can obviously be lower. Strategic subdomains can be built in-house where maximum speed and control are needed, while off-the-shelf tools and outsourcing are options that can be used in less important subdomains.

Investment in the portfolio applies broadly, far beyond just finances. Investment touches on organizational aspects like the type of people who are part of a team and how they work together. In subdomains of strategic importance where innovation potential is high, it is much easier to justify investing in product discovery and collaborative techniques like EventStorming. Investment also touches on technical aspects of architecture. In low-importance domains where the focus is delivering good enough solutions for the lowest cost, simple technical solutions like simple forms over data or low-code solutions will often be cost-effective solutions, whereas more advanced architectural patterns may be more suitable in more complex and strategically valuable domains.

This chapter's purpose is to provide principles and tools for enabling a portfolio-based approach so that you can make globally optimal decisions. They will also help you to validate that candidate value streams are a good fit from a strategic perspective (see figure 10.1). For instance, a domain boundary may encompass both highly strategic and highly generic concepts, which may better serve the business as separate subdomains with different strategies.

This chapter introduces *Core Domain Charts,* a technique for mapping out domains as a portfolio and determining the optimal investment strategy in each area. The technique also helps to define target domain boundaries by choosing the candidate domain boundaries that align best with the desired strategic business investments. In addition, the chapter looks at some example patterns and provides guidance on how to invest appropriately in each type of domain. Before that, this chapter starts by looking at Martin Fowler's utility versus strategic IT dichotomy to better understand some of the fundamental principles in this space.

While reading through this chapter, keep in mind that it is necessary to maintain an overview of the portfolio and not just focus on isolated investments within each domain to avoid local optima. This is because there will always be dependencies between domains. The optimal investment strategy for two domains individually might not be the best investment overall. Some compromise and joined-up thinking are needed. This is especially the case where legacy systems are involved, and there is tight coupling and a lack of well-defined boundaries between the code for each subdomain.

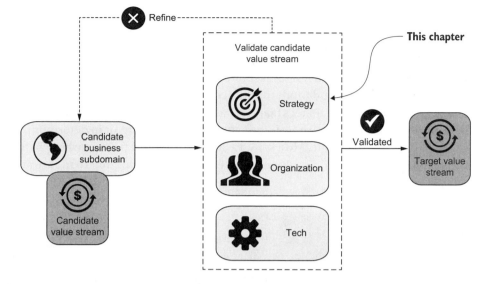

Figure 10.1 **This chapter shows how to take a portfolio perspective and verify each candidate value stream fits into the bigger picture.**

10.1 Utility vs. strategic IT dichotomy

Determining the optimal modernization strategy for each part of the portfolio will be driven by the potential level of business value that technology can bring. Software may be the principal factor in creating business value in some areas, while in others, it may provide little value, even if the area is a key part of the business strategy. To help determine the potential of architecture in each area, modernization leaders should ask, "Does IT play a strategic role in this area or is it just a utility?" This is what Martin Fowler refers to as the *utility versus strategic IT dichotomy* (http://mng.bz/lVod).

Martin's criteria for determining if IT is strategic is "It's all about whether the underlying business function is a differentiator or not. If how you do this function is a crucial part of what makes you better than the competition, then the software that supports this function needs to be as good as you can make it." In brief, where software contributes to capabilities that help your business differentiate, IT is strategic and needs to be as good as possible. Otherwise, IT is considered utility IT and must only be good enough. It needs to work reliably, but after a certain point, developing new features returns little or no benefit, and the effort would be better spent on strategic IT. One important caveat is that utility IT is not an excuse to create poor-quality software, as this may cause negative effects like reduced employee productivity or unhappy customers.

When I worked with a large transport company, their capabilities of optimizing the loading of freight onto trucks and itineraries and dynamically calculating live ETAs were highly strategic. Their software enabled them to do this better than their competitors, helping them to win more business, improve customer retention, and improve efficiencies, leading to reduced operating costs. In contrast, the company had a number of applications that contributed little to differentiation, like their invoicing system, which was treated as utility IT (because building a better invoicing system wouldn't give any advantage in the market).

Rather than a simple binary classification, I recommend looking at the utility versus strategic IT dichotomy as a range, as shown in figure 10.2, because this allows for more nuanced prioritization and modernization decisions. At the extreme left of the range, IT does not affect the company's market share; it offers little differentiation. Therefore, it's a clear utility. On the extreme right, software is the only factor in determining market share and is totally strategic. Most software applications will be somewhere between the two extremes and will even evolve over time, as Wardley Mapping demonstrated.

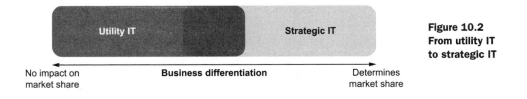

Figure 10.2
From utility IT
to strategic IT

10.1.1 *Tailored operating model*

Remember that the utility versus strategy IT dichotomy is not an academic exercise with little real-world applicability. It's the exact opposite. Classifying IT within a particular domain as utility or strategic should fundamentally affect the level and type of investment, covering financial, organizational, and technology aspects. As a general guideline, the more IT contributes to business differentiation, the more justification there is for a higher level of investment in each operating model aspect. The following is an example list of operating model aspects that should be tailored per team based on the strategic contribution of IT.

- *Team size*—The number of people working in a team should generally be higher for strategic IT, where greater investment leads to a greater return.
- *Team composition*—The skills and attitudes within a team should be tailored to the circumstances. Strategic IT generally benefits from having more senior and skilled people.
- *Collaboration*—Higher levels of collaboration between domain experts and software engineers with techniques like EventStorming is more valuable for strategic IT because it fosters a more innovative environment.
- *Discovery*—When there is greater opportunity for business differentiation, more discovery work increases the chances of discovering new ways to differentiate.
- *Prioritization*—The greater the strategic value of IT, the higher the precedence it should take when making prioritization decisions.
- *Dependencies*—Dependencies that reduce the rate of change for strategic IT are far more costly than those that affect utility IT. This means it is more justifiable to invest in removing and minimizing dependencies affecting strategic IT.

- *Architecture*—Investing in more advanced architectural patterns that allow a faster rate of change, advanced product capabilities, or better scalability is more justifiable in strategic IT.
- *Domain modeling*—Developing rich domain models takes time but results in greater collaboration and helps to sustain the rate of change over the long term. This is a good trade-off in strategic IT.
- *Code health*—Code quality is always important, but in strategic IT, code health enables the business to continue adding differentiating features at a high rate of change over a long period of time for lower cost and with fewer risks and is therefore vital.
- *Build versus buy versus partner*—Using off-the-shelf solutions makes sense when there is little opportunity to differentiate. Martin Fowler argues that conforming to off-the-shelf products makes sense rather than customizing them. For strategic IT, building in-house gives the most opportunity to differentiate so is nearly always the right approach.
- *Risk tolerance*—For strategic IT, the risk is being out-developed by competitors, whereas for utility IT, the risk is unreliability or excessive costs.

10.1.2 Identifying strategic IT

A successful architecture modernization is all about optimizing the business impact of strategic IT. So, it is essential to accurately determine which IT is strategic and which IT is utility. But this is easier said than done and shouldn't be left to gut instinct, which is susceptible to cognitive biases and politics. Firstly, it's important to have a clear understanding of how each domain contributes to business differentiation, and then it's necessary to determine IT's potential contribution to creating the differentiation. If a domain is highly differentiating and IT plays an important role, then strategic IT is needed in the domain.

To address the first part of the task, Wardley Mapping will reveal the areas where business differentiation is likely to be highest. Capabilities in the custom-built phase have been validated, and the focus is on developing them to exploit the potential, while capabilities in the first half of the product phase are at their most profitable and still have some scope for development. Commodity is unlikely to be strategic because capabilities in this phase are highly convergent, and there is little potential for differentiation. Capabilities in the early genesis phase might be considered strategic, but their potential is highly unknown, so it may be best to gain more confidence in the idea through research and experimentation before considering it strategic and making a big investment. Figure 10.3 highlights this area of the Wardley Map where candidates for strategic IT are likely to be found.

Not every component in the shaded area in figure 10.3 will be of equal strategic value; some may even be low enough in strategic value that they are still considered a utility. Not all software that is built in-house is strategic. Martin Fowler argues that only between 5 to 20% of a company's IT will be strategic. In any case, the Wardley Map should be considered as a starting point for identifying strategic IT candidates and not as a 1:1 mapping between evolution stages and strategic IT. It's important to

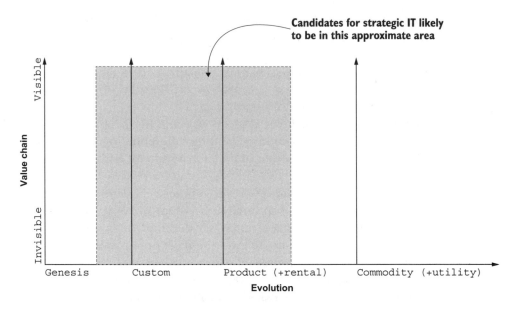

Figure 10.3   Identifying strategic IT candidates on a Wardley Map

follow up by getting into the details of each component and understanding exactly how it contributes to the strategy by creating business impact. This will then also help to understand the role of IT.

USING THE PRODUCT STRATEGY TO HELP IDENTIFY STRATEGIC IT

A good product strategy is one of the best sources of information for identifying strategic IT. It helps to move from high-level discussions into concrete details of how IT can contribute to business outcomes. The following list shows EdTech company Chegg's "hard to copy advantages" from their 2010 product strategy, according to Gibson Biddle, who was their chief product officer at the time (http://mng.bz/BAYw). The company's vision was to be a market leader in textbook rentals and expand into other student services like jobs and internships.

- "Create a 'student graph.' (We built a dataset of all courses on each campus. It included all the textbooks and content that were part of the course.)"
- "Develop unique personalization technology. (We built this capability using the student graph data above.)"
- "Achieve economies of scale through high-volume, used textbook purchases."
- "Build a viral brand, spread campus-wide through large, highly visible orange boxes."
- "Create a network effect through a 'homework help platform' where tutors around the world provide answers on Chegg's platform."

The *hard to copy advantages* section of Chegg's product strategy specifically called out which capabilities would help the business to differentiate and be hard to copy, like the student graph, personalization technology, and homework help platform. These all seem to be candidates for strategic IT because software plays an important role in enabling them. However, not all business differentiators require strategic IT. In this case, building a viral brand was also a key differentiator for Chegg, but placing large orange boxes on campus isn't something that is likely to necessitate a strategic IT approach.

Chegg's product strategy also contained specific criteria about how their capabilities would contribute to differentiation (similar to the north stars technique shown in chapter 3). For example, their *student graph* strategy had a clear success metric— *% of campuses with complete class, course, and textbook data*—and tactics for achieving the metric, like *scrape and parse data from 100 campuses*. In addition, the strategy contained high-level roadmap items per quarter.

TECHNOLOGY SHOULD INFLUENCE THE PRODUCT STRATEGY

Before moving on to the next section, which provides a practical technique for mapping out a portfolio and identifying strategic IT, there is an important nuance I'd like to clarify. It's not simply the case that technology leaders should reverse-engineer the product strategy to determine which parts of the architecture are strategic. Technology leaders should play an important role in helping to define the product strategy. Their contribution is needed to understand the true potential of technology and the effort needed to achieve it. In brief, it is the act of collaboratively building a product strategy that results in the identification of clear strategic IT initiatives. In my experience, the best results come when product people and technologists work closely together as a cohesive unit when defining the product strategy.

10.2 *Core Domain Charts*

Core Domain Charts (https://github.com/ddd-crew/core-domain-charts) is a technique from the domain-driven design (DDD) community that is designed to help with the challenge of utility versus strategic IT. It is used to map out an architecture as a portfolio of subdomains according to their business differentiation and model complexity, as shown in figure 10.4. Model complexity is a measure that represents the effort needed to discover, design, build, and maintain a software model of a business subdomain. The tool serves as both a way to collaborate and discuss the value of IT within each subdomain and as a visualization to capture the output. It is most effective when domain, business, product, and technical experts all work together to collectively define and align on the strategic importance and complexity of each subdomain.

In DDD terminology, a *core domain* is a subdomain that is both highly differentiating and complex. It fits Martin Fowler's definition of strategic IT and lives in the upper-right section of a Core Domain Chart, as shown in figure 10.4. A *generic subdomain* is a subdomain that has extremely low business differentiation potential and corresponds to Fowler's definition of utility IT. In between the two is a *supporting subdomain* that doesn't neatly correspond to either of Fowler's classifications. Supporting subdomains are strategic in the sense that they help to create differentiation in

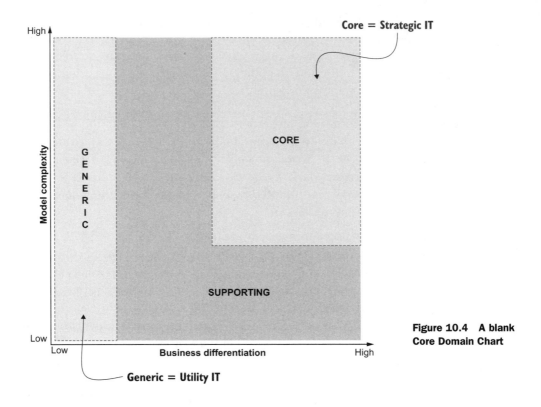

Figure 10.4   A blank
Core Domain Chart

core domains, yet they are utility in the sense that alone they don't offer much opportunity for differentiation.

> **NOTE**   Even though a core domain is considered to be a subdomain like the other two, it is nearly always referred to as a core domain and not as a core subdomain, although core subdomain is also correct. It's a useful shorthand because core domains are talked about the most, and core domain is quicker to pronounce and sounds better. This inconsistency in DDD is just something to be aware of. It's inconsequential.

Core Domain Charts are most commonly used at the level of subdomains, where each item represents an area small enough to be owned by a single team and to have its own dedicated domain and codebase. This is because fine-grained investment decisions are made at this level regarding the team, domain model, and software. It's common to see varied operating model characteristics, even between teams that own subdomains within the same domain (scope 2).

10.2.1 *Example Core Domain Chart*

To demonstrate how to use Core Domain Charts, I've put together a hypothetical example of a shared electric scooter company. This company's business model is based on the idea of placing physical scooters on the streets, which members of the public can easily use by downloading the app and scanning the QR code of a scooter. The company's key strategic objectives for the year are to grow revenues by increasing the number of journeys taken by customers and to make journeys more fun for customers, which is core to how they position the company's cool and trendy brand. Three strategic areas have been identified for achieving these objectives:

- *Improving placement of scooters*—Product managers and data scientists conducted in-depth analysis and came to the conclusion that between 25 to 50% more rides would be taken by customers if scooters were placcd in better locations.

- *A loyalty program*—The chief product officer believes that loyalty could be a differentiator by increasing the lifetime value of customers if executed well. The company has never done anything like this before, so there are a lot of questions about how to do it effectively. But this type of initiative has been done in many other industries, so there are established patterns that can be used as inspiration.

- *Robot tour guides*—The new CTO wants to make his mark on the company and believes robot tour guides that can plan bespoke, dynamic journeys and talk to customers will make the company look cool and lead to a huge rise in the number of journeys taken, particularly among tourists. There is little evidence yet to support this idea, but it would be a revolutionary innovation if successful.

Figure 10.5 provides a visualization of how the group perceives the strategic significance of each subdomain with regard to achieving the strategic objectives.

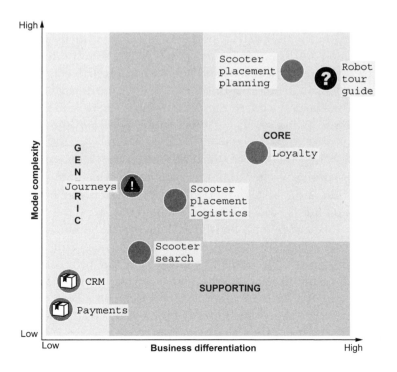

Figure 10.5   Core Domain Chart for the hypothetical shared scooter company

The *scooter placement planning* subdomain is considered to be a potential source of high differentiation, a big opportunity to grow market share. From an engineering perspective, it was concluded that improving placement would be possible but very complex, requiring the ingestion of many new data sources and building a richer calculation engine that operates at a high level of scale. This is seen as a long-term opportunity where investment over multiple years will be necessary to continue driving differentiation and would be hard to copy.

To unlock differentiation in the *scooter placement planning* core domain, the company must make an additional investment in the *scooter placement logistics* supporting subdomain. This subdomain involves moving scooters from one place to another. It's a combination of in-house software and human technicians who physically move the scooters. Currently, it will not support a more dynamic, real-time process.

Another core domain on the chart is *loyalty*. Differentiation is high, but complexity is lower. This reflects the fact that it is an easier subdomain to extract value from, but that also means it will be easier for competitors to copy and won't remain as a high-value core domain for around more than a year. It could have a big effect in the short term but will gradually drift toward becoming table stakes as the industry converges. Conversely, the robot tour guide subdomain has the potential to be a vital core domain and long-term source of differentiation, but extracting value will be much harder because the concept is highly novel, and it's unclear if customers will even be interested. The mix of high potential and high uncertainty is represented with a question mark on the Core Domain Chart.

Journeys is considered to be a fairly high complexity supporting subdomain. It manages the process from when a rider starts a journey on a scooter until they have arrived at their final destination and completed their journey. The software for this subdomain operates at a high level of scalability and needs to be as reliable as possible. Any downtime in this subdomain means that riders cannot take journeys, and no revenue can be generated. The warning icon on the Core Domain Chart is an indicator that failures in this subdomain could have a big effect on the customer, the business, and the brand reputation.

You might be wondering why the subdomain *journeys* is not a core domain. After all, isn't taking a journey on a scooter the core capability for which the customers use the company? And without the ability to take a journey, there is no business. Surely, this is the core of the business? From a differentiation point of view, it is not core. The organization does not see any potential to differentiate in this subdomain; it is table stakes. The company just needs it to remain solid and reliable with a continuous stream of minor improvements. So, while this subdomain may be a core part of the company's value proposition, it is not a core domain in the strategic sense because there is little opportunity for differentiation. It may have been a core domain when the company was a startup, but now the industry has moved on, and this component has evolved toward the late product and early commodity phase.

CRM and *payments* are not considered to be sources of differentiation in any way for the business. These are just considered a cost of doing business, so the company would rather buy off–the-shelf solutions that cover their basic needs for the lowest reasonable price. These subdomains are, therefore, considered to be generic. The package icon is used to indicate that SaaS products are used in these subdomains. *Scooter search* is also not considered to be a differentiator for the business. It's a basic table-stakes feature, but it does require custom code and logic that are not available off the shelf so is considered to be a supporting subdomain that requires a higher level of investment to maintain.

10.2.2 Assessing model complexity

In a nutshell, model complexity is the total complexity involved in discovering new ideas, designing a model, implementing the model in software, evolving the model and software, and supporting the software. There isn't a precise formula for determining the model complexity of subdomains because there are a number of factors that contribute to complexity, and ultimately, an element of subjectivity will always exist. But the main purpose of a Core Domain Chart is not to create precise definitions; it is to create alignment between all stakeholders on the level of value and effort needed within each subdomain, which then serves as the basis for making investment decisions. Approximations are usually good enough, provided they are arrived at through logical reasoning with input from multiple perspectives rather than the pure gut feeling of a single person.

This subsection lists the different types of complexity that contribute to overall model complexity. Making your group aware of these different types of complexities can help to mitigate the effects of cognitive biases and ensure the whole group has the same definition of model complexity, leading to more accurate assessments and more effective conversations.

USER NEEDS DISCOVERY COMPLEXITY

User needs discovery complexity refers to the amount of effort and level of unpredictability involved in identifying unmet user needs. For subdomains in the genesis phase of Wardley Mapping, user needs discovery complexity is high due to the fact that the concept is novel and unproven, and lots of research and experimentation is needed. User needs discovery complexity is also high as the concept matures toward commodity, where the industry converges on functionality, and it becomes increasingly difficult to find new ways to differentiate. Determining this type of complexity requires input from product and UX specialists.

PRODUCT DESIGN COMPLEXITY

After unmet user needs have been discovered, new product features and enhancements need to be designed that will address the unmet user needs in an effective and user-friendly way. The level of effort needed will vary on a case-by-case basis. Designing solutions to address some unmet user needs may require months of wireframes and user testing, as I mentioned in the business property tax example from the previous chapter. Determining this type of complexity also requires input from product and UX specialists.

DOMAIN MODEL DESIGN COMPLEXITY

Domain model design complexity refers to the difficulty of designing and evolving a conceptual domain model in a given subdomain. Some subdomains will have far more complicated calculations, algorithms, business rules, and business processes than others. As a result, it will take far more time and effort to design a model that can meet all of the product requirements and cover all of the necessary happy paths and edge cases.

An example of this is Gran Turismo, a racing game for the PlayStation that has an online mode. Every user gets frustrated by the penalty system—the model that decides if you have broken the rules like cutting a corner or crashing into another car. Sometimes, another car will hit you, yet it will be you who gets the time penalty. The makers of Gran Turismo (Polyphony Digital) are aware of this, and they have been constantly trying to improve the model for years to make the experience more enjoyable and less frustrating. Even though the user need is clear regarding how they want the product to function, designing an effective model that accommodates all scenarios and enables a great user experience is proving to be immensely complex.

CRUFT (AVOIDABLE SOFTWARE COMPLEXITY)

Martin Fowler defines *cruft* (https://martinfowler.com/articles/is-quality-worth-cost .html) as "the difference between the current code and how it would ideally be." Effectively, it's avoidable complexity that exists within software that could theoretically be removed without affecting how the software functions. Cruft is an important concept because the more complex software is, the harder it is to understand and the more risky and expensive it is to change. Cruft can take many forms in a software system, like poorly defined boundaries and interactions between different parts of the code, tight coupling, and bad naming. The more a business can use a subdomain to differentiate itself, the more expensive the costs of cruft will be as it reduces the rate of change where time to market is most crucial.

SCALE COMPLEXITY

Some subdomains are more complex due to the level of scale they are operating at. The business rules and domain logic may be simpler than other subdomains, but the overall complexity could be higher due to the sheer scale where more things can go wrong, things are more likely to go wrong, and the consequences of things going wrong are more severe. More robustness is needed, which adds to the complexity and maintenance costs. This is like the difference between a booking system that processes tens of thousands of orders per day where very minimal downtime can be tolerated versus a booking system that processes tens of orders per day, and the effects of downtime are minimal.

INTEGRATION COMPLEXITY

Integration complexity is high when a subdomain has to integrate with many other subdomains and systems, especially when each of those other systems has unique or weird data formats and is unreliable. While the internal domain model may not necessarily contain complex domain logic, all of the code to interact with other systems, transform data, and handle error conditions can add significant complexity.

Every software developer has experiences of high integration complexity. I once worked on a holiday booking application that had fairly simple business rules. However, it had to integrate with more than 10 other systems to fetch and integrate holiday deals and metadata. Each integration was totally bespoke because each system had completely different APIs, data formats, error codes, glitches, etc. The documentation was mostly poor, and getting responses from the API developers was slow.

OPERATIONAL COMPLEXITY

Operational complexity is complexity that exists outside of the software and in the organization, such as manual processes that involve calculations and decisions being made by employees using a variety of tools, usually including spreadsheets. Operational complexity is often caused by poorly designed products and software. By default, operational complexity is not considered to be part of model complexity because it is complexity that is managed outside of the software. However, very often, it's important to articulate complexity that exists outside of the software and its associated costs. Typically, this will be necessary when putting together a proposal for building software to replace the operational complexity. When this is the case, I find it useful to add an annotation to the Core Domain Chart to indicate that operational complexity is included, as shown in figure 10.6.

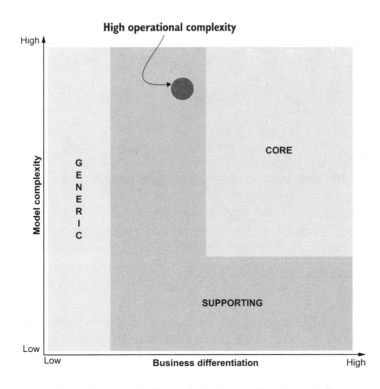

Figure 10.6   Using annotations to indicate operational complexity

Because model complexity is a composite measure that includes multiple types of complexity, sometimes annotations are useful to articulate the major type of complexity within a subdomain, even if it is not operational complexity.

10.2.3 *Core domain evolution*

Classifying subdomains as core, supporting, and generic is relative to a point in time. What is core today may be supporting or even generic at some point in the future as the landscape evolves and the business growth areas change accordingly. This evolution can be visualized on Core Domain Charts using arrows. As shown in figure 10.7, generally, an upward arrow indicates embracing more complexity by developing new features and capabilities that improve differentiation, while a downward arrow implies reducing complexity to reduce costs.

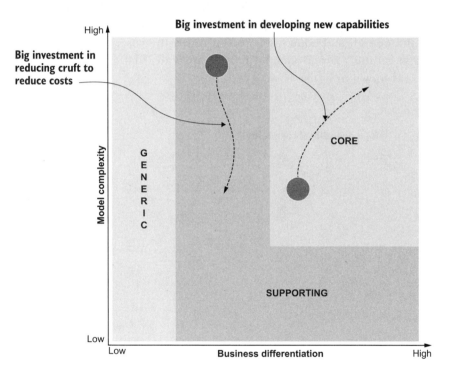

Figure 10.7   Using arrows to show subdomain evolution

Even if no investment is made in a subdomain, it will naturally evolve over time. It will become less differentiating and drift left as competitors develop new innovations, and it will move upward and grow more complex as the technology stack and infrastructure become dated. The implication is that some level of investment is required, even to keep a subdomain in the current position.

10.2.4 Industry example: Events industry scale-up

Two colleagues and I had the opportunity to work with an organization in the events industry. At the time of contact, the company was at a major transition point. They had built a successful startup around innovations in one small aspect of the events (typically music concerts) value chain. They had recently taken on a major round of funding based on their ambition to own the full value chain, including organizing their own events, having relationships with music stars, and managing travel and accommodation for customers. The organization was going to grow significantly, and the CTO was looking for help to understand how their architecture and organization would need to adapt to support the growth.

It quickly became clear that their current mode of operation was similar to many startups. There was a focus on moving quickly at the cost of long-term sustainability, and there was a lack of well-defined ownership, meaning every software developer touched every part of the codebase. They were already feeling some pains due to this when they were at around 30 engineers, and this wouldn't scale if the number of engineers doubled or tripled. So, one area of improvement was establishing clear areas of ownership for independent teams.

The organization needed architecture and design skills to be spread throughout the company to help them identify business domains and shape software and teams around them. While the organizational challenges were clear, choosing where to start was less obvious. The engineering leads had documented around 100 problems and challenges with the architecture and ways of working. They couldn't make a decision about where to begin establishing areas of ownership and introducing new ways of working due to analysis paralysis and fear of making the wrong choice.

This is where we used a Core Domain Chart to visualize effectively the opportunities and build a proposal for delivering their first slice of modernization. As a group, we talked through each of their subdomains and placed them on the Core Domain Chart based on their current differentiation and complexity. We then talked through each subdomain, discussing the challenges and opportunities that lived within it, and we added an arrow to each subdomain representing the potential investment. Figure 10.8 shows the three subdomains that were shortlisted. There are two core domains (*subdomain A* and *subdomain B*) with arrows moving up and to the right, which represent investing in key new differentiation features. There is also a supporting subdomain (*subdomain C*) with an arrow pointing down, representing the investment needed to reduce the cruft and improve the design so that the code was easier to evolve and the high operational costs were reduced.

Much of the benefit supplied by the Core Domain Chart was the structure it provided to our conversations and the visual representation of how the group perceived the relative importance and complexity of their subdomains. After a couple of hours of conversations, this helped us to converge on a clear step forward, and we began putting a business case together. Initially, *subdomain A* and *subdomain B* were the leading candidates. These were the core domains that could move the business forward, so

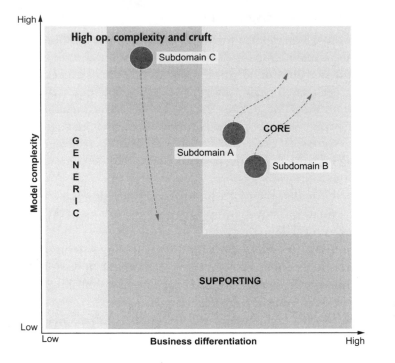

Figure 10.8   Three subdomains shortlisted for the first modernization step

the group naturally wanted to invest in those areas. However, the group took a U-turn and unanimously settled on *subdomain C*, the supporting subdomain.

Subdomain C was chosen as the first step for business and organizational reasons. On the business side, it would remove a complex manual process that took up a lot of important people's time, resulting in high lead times for the process. This perspective was crucial for getting buy-in from leadership. On the organizational side, this was a good move because the current code was scattered among multiple codebases; the organization didn't realize the scattered code made sense as a subdomain. This was perfect for giving the team an opportunity to practice modeling domains with techniques like EventStorming and designing loosely coupled architecture. They could take those learnings and insights and apply them to their whole business. Another benefit was the fact that *subdomains A* and *B* depended on *subdomain C*. By reducing the cruft in *subdomain C*, it wouldn't be a bottleneck when the team switched focus to innovating in *subdomains A* and *B*.

The Core Domain Chart was also used as part of the proposal that was put to leadership to get buy-in for the initiative. The Core Domain Chart was evidence that the team carefully considered the whole portfolio and picked the most appropriate option for business and organizational reasons. It proved they weren't just techies who wanted to play around with new technologies and architecture patterns.

10.2.5 *Comparisons with Wardley Mapping*

Some people comment that there are similarities between a Core Domain Chart and a Wardley Map. Bearing in mind that Wardley Mapping has been mentioned multiple times during this chapter, there is clearly a lot of truth to the observation. In my experience, while there are similarities and overlaps between the techniques, they serve different purposes.

Whereas Wardley Mapping is concerned with mapping out a whole landscape from an industry-wide perspective, a Core Domain Chart is designed to capture your choices about which parts of your architecture are strategic IT. Core Domain Charts focus on just two aspects: complexity and differentiation, which are the keys to assessing strategic IT. You can use Wardley Mapping for this, too, but you need to rely on additional annotations to emphasize complexity and differentiation that cannot be inferred from the evolution phase alone.

Wardley Mapping provides much more context about why something is differentiating. The stages of evolution indicate how mature the concept is, and value chains show components are linked and affecting each other. Wardley Mapping can also include all types of components and be applied at all scopes, meaning it can be used at any time. Core Domain Charts, meanwhile, are usually used only at a subdomain level and show only subdomains without value chains. It is usually used after candidate subdomains have been identified. Overall, I find both techniques to be very useful. Wardley Mapping is more advanced and useful, but Core Domain Charts are great for reaching and communicating strategic IT decisions.

10.3 *Core Domain Chart patterns*

This final part of the chapter looks at different patterns that appear on a Core Domain Chart and what that implies in terms of investment and tailoring the operating model. This list isn't exhaustive, and it's not recommended to try and force every subdomain into one of these patterns. The goal of this section is to cover a broad range of possibilities to show the appropriate approach in each type of subdomain can vary significantly and is more nuanced than just a simple utility versus strategic choice.

> **NOTE** You can find interactive versions of the following patterns combined into a cheat sheet on the book's Miro board (http://mng.bz/ddxg).

10.3.1 *Decisive core*

A *decisive core* is close to the top-right-hand corner, as shown in figure 10.9, meaning it is both highly differentiating and highly complex. Whichever organization gains an advantage in this area will have a decisive advantage in the market, like being the market leader or catching up with an established market leader. The high level of complexity reflects that developing an effective solution is extremely hard, meaning it is also hard to copy, which is why it has the potential to be so differentiating.

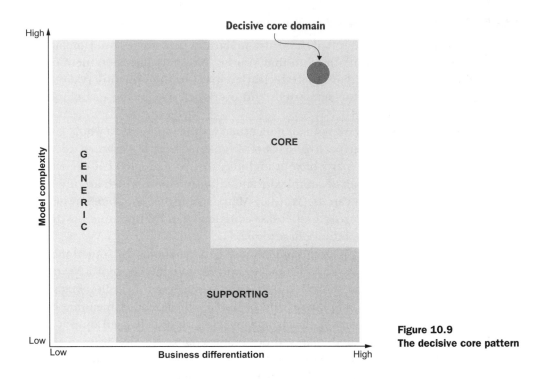

Figure 10.9
The decisive core pattern

The mindset for a decisive core is geared toward maximum exploitation of the business opportunity with a fast flow of changes because innovating more in this subdomain is likely to have a greater ROI than in other subdomains. However, sustainability is equally important because a decisive core is likely to be a medium- to long-term investment. Due to the highest strategic importance and complexity of a decisive core, it is an obvious decision to build in-house where you have full control.

A well-staffed team who are fully dedicated to this subdomain is crucial. And it makes sense for the team to be formed with a majority of senior and highly skilled people. Collaboration across roles is also likely to pay dividends. Closer collaboration between engineers, product, UX, and subject matter experts in both discovery and development will increase the chances of identifying new innovations and implementing them more rapidly. As a result, collaborative techniques like EventStorming are a great investment. Anything that reduces the flow of changes within a decisive core will likely have a higher negative cost than in other subdomains. As a result, dependencies need to be managed carefully, with priority given to the decisive core.

From a technical perspective, architecture, domain modeling, and code health are likely to be of high importance. A well-designed architecture aligned to well-designed domain boundaries will reduce coupling. In addition, applying more advanced architectural patterns and technologies can be justified here. A well-designed domain model is important in a decisive core because the essential complexity of the domain is high, and any unnecessary complexity could push the team's cognitive load over the edge. Keeping the code healthy is important so that the subdomain can continue to evolve over the long term. Any shortcuts that affect code health will become expensive in the long run as they reduce the rate of change.

A few questions to think about with this type of subdomain are

- Can the subdomain boundaries be further refined to remove any concepts that aren't as high value as the rest?
- Have multiple decisive core domains been identified? If so, can the organization afford to invest in all of them without excessive compromises?
- What would be the results if the decisive core doesn't turn out to be as differentiating as expected?

10.3.2 *Indefensible core*

An *indefensible core* is toward the right but much lower in complexity than a decisive core. Due to the lower complexity, the likelihood that competitors will be able to develop their own version is much higher, and therefore, the differentiation provided by this subdomain exists only for a shorter period of time—for example, 6 to 12 months, as shown in figure 10.10. I always remember an astute comment a chief product officer made during a workshop regarding their indefensible core domains: "Even though it's hard to protect our advantages for a long period of time, we want to be seen as the company that is always first to market with new innovations. It has a big impact on our brand."

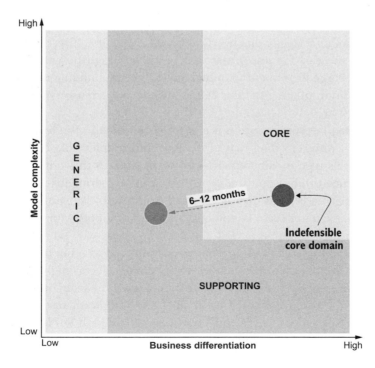

Figure 10.10   The indefensible core pattern

While an indefensible core may be a crucial component of the product strategy for one year, its role in the following year's strategy is likely to be much reduced as focus switches to other areas where a chance to differentiate exists. Therefore, the mindset should be geared toward exploiting the short-term opportunity and knowing when to reduce investment. In the initial stages, it makes sense to staff the team with a majority of senior and skilled engineers. During this period, collaboration between engineers and domain experts and techniques like EventStorming, along with product discovery techniques, are likely to be highly effective in getting to market first with the new capability. As a result, this also benefits from an in-house approach.

Investing in architecture, domain modeling, and code health requires a balanced approach. On one side, there is the need to get to market first and exploit the limited timeframe when the subdomain can provide differentiation, so spending too much time on design could have a negative effect. Yet, on the flip side, complexity can build up very quickly, which can reduce velocity even over the course of 6 to 12 months. The software is still likely to exist for many years with a steady stream of improvements and bug fixes, so it's not advisable to cut too many corners.

A few questions to think about with this type of subdomain are

- Could it grow into a decisive core? Have you invested enough time in searching for ways to make the subdomain more differentiating and defensible?
- Do you have a plan for what will be the core domain(s) when this subdomain is no longer a major differentiator, or are you too focused on the short term?

10.3.3 *Big bet future core*

A big bet future core is a subdomain that has the potential to be a decisive core, but there is a high level of uncertainty that needs to be validated first. Effectively, this type of subdomain is in the early genesis phase and has a very high potential for future worth but requires a large investment to unlock it. As a result, building in-house is the obvious choice. To differentiate on a Core Domain Chart, we can use a question mark, as shown in figure 10.11.

Even though a big bet future core is a type of core domain, the team's mindset needs to be radically different than that of decisive and indefensible core domains. People working in this type of subdomain need to be able to thrive in uncertainty. Software engineers need to be comfortable with running experiments and changing direction on a regular basis. And they need to be comfortable creating low-quality, throwaway code. This type of team is not suitable for developers who like structure and predictability in their work.

Once the potential for differentiation has been validated as a big bet, the future core becomes a decisive core, and the characteristics change accordingly. At this transition point, it may be necessary to change some members of the team or hand over to a different team who are more focused on quality and long-term sustainability. It's often necessary to rewrite the code at this point due to the high levels of cruft that have accumulated during the experimentation phase.

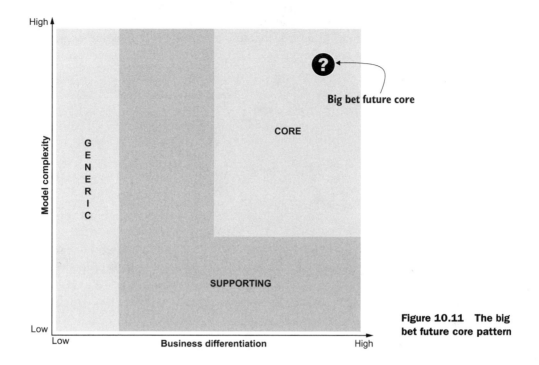

Figure 10.11 The big bet future core pattern

I find that prioritization is a crucial topic for upcoming big bet future cores. Because this type of subdomain does not yet deliver value, other subdomains that are delivering value are seen as more important. I've seen on multiple occasions how team members will be pulled away from big bet future cores to help in other subdomains. It's problematic because it may help to meet deadlines in the short term, but it can seriously compromise long-term success.

A few questions to think about with this type of subdomain are

- How will the importance of this subdomain be communicated so that it is treated equally or more importantly than subdomains that are already providing value?
- Will the organization try to measure the success of this team in the same way that teams in more established subdomains are measured?
- What signs are needed to validate the potential of this idea and increase investment or shut it down?

10.3.4 *High-leverage supporting*

A *high-leverage supporting* subdomain is a medium-to-high complexity supporting subdomain that is depended on by multiple other high-priority subdomains, as shown in figure 10.12. The presence of dependencies is crucial because the costs of good and bad decisions within this subdomain will be amplified and potentially affect all of the dependent subdomains. For instance, if the team does not invest wisely in architecture, domain modeling, and code health, it could easily become a bottleneck that slows down the other teams that are working on the highest business priorities.

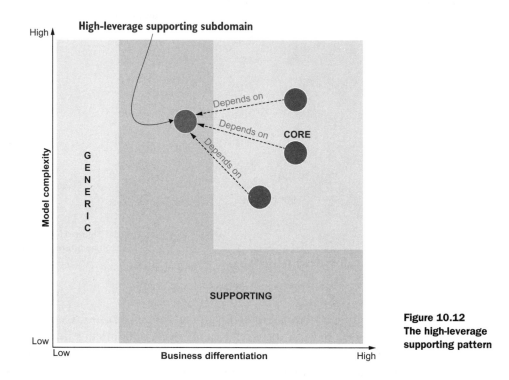

Figure 10.12
The high-leverage
supporting pattern

Even though a high-leverage supporting subdomain is not a core domain, it does play a highly important supporting role and is highly complex, which demands a team with experienced and skilled members. In addition, the weighty nature of the dependencies requires people who are skilled in building relationships with other teams and also able to understand the concepts in their subdomains in order to build what they need.

In these types of subdomains, collaborative techniques like EventStorming can be valuable, often in relation to the bigger picture of how this subdomain supports other subdomains. This is also one of the key domain modeling challenges: creating a model that supports the needs of multiple consumers while remaining supple and easy to evolve. Architectural patterns that keep change coupling low and reliability high are especially good investments here.

A few questions to think about with this type of subdomain are

- If the supporting subdomain is so complex and plays an important role in helping many other subdomains, could it play a bigger role in contribution to differentiation than you think—that is, should it be treated as a core domain?

- Do the dependencies need to exist? Could it be a sign that the domain boundaries are wrong? For example, the high-leverage supporting subdomain in figure 10.12 could be sliced into three parts, which are moved into the three core domains.

10.3.5   *Table stakes supporting*

A *table stakes supporting* subdomain is a basic supporting subdomain that is fairly low in both complexity and differentiation, as shown in figure 10.13. Identifying good enough and not overinvesting are key, while at the same time ensuring that any changes required to support improvement in core domains are implemented quickly and effectively. On balance, it usually makes sense to build in-house to avoid compromising initiatives in core domains.

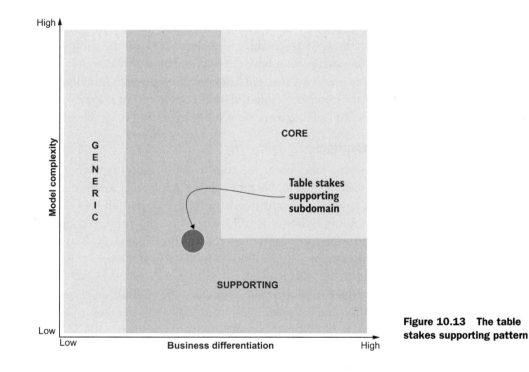

Figure 10.13   The table stakes supporting pattern

All investments will typically be reduced in a table stakes supporting subdomain compared to more complex and differentiation subdomains. The team will typically be smaller, and the level of experience and expertise within the team can justifiably be lower. For example, this type of subdomain may be a good opportunity for more junior employees to work and build their experience. Likewise, investing in advanced architectural patterns, practices like EventStorming, and coding patterns is less justifiable in this type of subdomain.

One media company I worked with identified *search* as a table stakes supporting domain. It didn't offer much opportunity for positive differentiation, but without some investment in search, customers just wouldn't use the product, meaning all of the innovations developed in core domains would have been to no avail. The company put together a team of four engineers, two of them senior and two of them more junior, who spent an initial six months building the search API. After six months, the search capability had reached a point where further improvements would have had little noticeable effect, and it was decided that the team would switch their focus to the *recommendations* subdomain, which was seen as a bigger opportunity for differentiation. The team continued to own and make small improvements in the *search* subdomain, but most of their time was spent developing capabilities in the *recommendations* subdomain.

A few questions to think about with this type of subdomain are

- Is continued investment even justified, or could the software be shut down?
- How much of the work in core domains will involve changes in this subdomain?
- If this is such a table stakes feature, are there now off-the-shelf products that provide this functionality that have recently become available?
- How will you ensure that sufficient knowledge of this subdomain and the code remain within the company while the level of investment is low?
- Will a team be motivated to work on a subdomain that is low in importance?

10.3.6 *Mission-critical supporting*

A *mission-critical supporting* subdomain contains a risk of high negative differentiation but limited positive differentiation. Negative differentiation is something that causes damage to the brand reputation and needs to be avoided at all costs. Even though complexity is low, building in-house is still likely to be the preferred option to have full control over preventing incidents that cause brand damage. A warning sign is used to highlight critical supporting subdomains on a Core Domain Chart, as shown in figure 10.14.

While mission-critical supporting subdomains are still supporting domains in terms of positive differentiation, the inherent risk requires some differences in approach. Seniority and expertise are required within the team, while more advanced architectural patterns and code health, especially those that limit the potential for risks, will be justified. Stakeholders who interact with the team need to be mature and not put pressure on the team to take any shortcuts or cut any corners. Even if no new features are being added, an ongoing investment to keep the system up-to-date is needed.

In December 2022, Southwest Airlines had to cancel 15,000 flights due to a meltdown caused by its scheduling system (http://mng.bz/rjPx). News sites and social media were full of negative publicity for the airline, and the company brand had taken a huge beating. The airline's CEO, Bob Jordan, was in full damage limitation, appearing in the media apologizing and asking for forgiveness (http://mng.bz/VRPN).

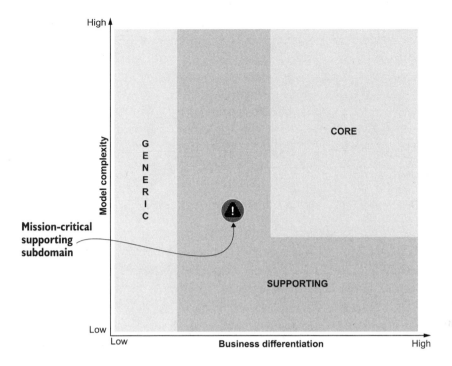

Figure 10.14   The critical supporting pattern

Reports suggest that the airline's mission-critical scheduling systems were still running on decades-old software (http://mng.bz/xjl7).

A few questions to think about with this type of subdomain are

- Does everybody in the company realize the risk that exists within this subdomain, especially senior leadership?
- How out of date is the technology being used in this subdomain?
- If there is a major incident, will you be able to provide evidence that you did everything possible to avoid the problem?

10.3.7 *Suspect supporting*

A *suspect supporting* subdomain sits toward the top left of a Core Domain Chart, as shown in figure 10.15. Often, a high-complexity supporting subdomain is a warning sign. How can something that's not highly differentiating be so complex? Sometimes, it's a prioritization mistake. Too much investment is being poured into subdomains where the payback is not justified. Most often, it is due to avoidable software complexity. The existing solution has become needlessly complex to maintain due to the accumulation of cruft. This is an important pattern to recognize because the high level of complexity results in a higher maintenance cost, which could be taking up investment that is better invested in more differentiating subdomains.

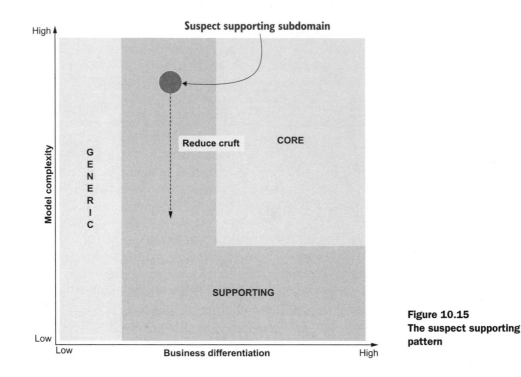

Figure 10.15
The suspect supporting pattern

There are multiple possible courses of action to take with suspect supporting subdomains. If there is a need to continue evolving the subdomain with new features and enhancements over the course of multiple years, reducing the complexity is a primary objective in order to reduce the cost of change and enable new features to be built. This will require a highly skilled team who are able to work with and modernize legacy software. However, if there is no desire or need to make changes to the subdomain, then it would be a waste to put together a large team of highly skilled engineers. It's likely to be more effective to have a smaller team composed of people who will be content to keep the system running and fix small issues that arise.

Often, when software has a high level of cruft, the boundaries are poorly defined and the code may resemble a big ball of mud, where the code for many subdomains is monolithic and tightly coupled. If this is the case, then it may be important to look at all of the affected subdomains as a collective whole, with the teams working very closely together toward a common modernization strategy. It's not possible to have a fine-grained strategy when the software is tightly coupled because teams will need to coordinate their work and deployments.

One of the risks with a suspect supporting domain is that the level of complexity can give a false impression that it's a high-priority core domain. This was exactly the case with a large European-Asian client I worked with. As one of my colleagues and I mapped out a Core Domain Chart, the group placed their *order management* subdomain close to the top right. We were confused because it didn't sound very differentiating, but the engineers argued that it must be core because it was the most complex engineering challenge in the company and was often being talked about by leadership. However, the group was unable to articulate how it enabled them to differentiate from competitors. After further conversations, we established that the subdomain was mission critical but offered little potential for differentiation.

The reason it was so complex was because a new and an old version of the system were running in parallel, and migrating was proving to be a long, drawn-out challenge. The new system didn't have all of the features of the old system, so internal users had to use both. We reached a consensus that it was important to continue the work in the supporting domain to reduce the complexity and create a better experience for internal users. More importantly, in that moment, the group realized what their real core domains were.

A few questions to think about with this type of subdomain are

- If the complexity was reduced, how could engineering effort be invested more effectively elsewhere?
- How long will it take to reduce the complexity?
- Is everybody in agreement that new feature development will need to be reduced or stopped while the code is being modernized?

10.3.8 *Hidden core*

A hidden core domain is a subdomain that is perceived to have high differentiation but low complexity, usually because there is complexity outside the software that would be more of a differentiator if brought into the software, as figure 10.16 shows. Any

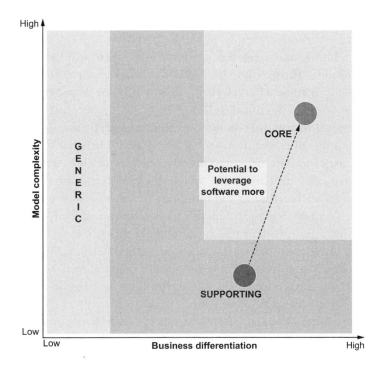

Figure 10.16
The hidden core pattern

subdomain in the bottom right should always raise suspicion: if a subdomain is low in complexity, it's an easy capability to develop, which means it is easy for other competitors to develop as well. I am always curious when leaders talk about certain high-priority initiatives, yet the requirements are basically simple CRUD systems. It's not always the case that a subdomain in the bottom right is a hidden core. There are genuine reasons why differentiating complexity is outside the software and cannot be brought into the software, like domains that rely heavily on human knowledge and skill.

To work out the most effective approach in this type of subdomain, we must first quantify the benefits that moving complexity into software can bring. Cross-skill collaboration with techniques like EventStorming and product discovery are likely to be key elements in gaining this clarity. Engineers will need to understand how the domain currently works and advise on the potential for replacing the current manual approaches with more advanced digital capabilities. This will require experienced engineers who are effective at collaborating and are experienced in product and domain discovery. If the subdomain is confirmed to be a hidden core, then the investment characteristics of a core domain should be applied, whereas if there is no benefit to bringing more complexity into software, it should continue to be treated as a supporting subdomain.

A few questions to think about with this type of subdomain are

- Who is using the capabilities provided by this subdomain, and what are they trying to achieve? Could software be more helpful?
- What evidence is being used to make the decision that this is so highly differentiating?

10.3.9 *Black swan core*

A *black swan event* is a highly unexpected occurrence with a profound effect and may seem obvious in hindsight (http://mng.bz/A8Ne). A black swan core domain is a domain that demonstrates these characteristics by starting out as a generic domain and becoming a core domain, as shown in figure 10.17. In theory, this should never happen because generic domains are commodity offerings with little to no differentiation potential, so when this does occur, it is a big surprise with weighty consequences.

Slack, the enterprise chat system, started life as a black swan core. It was originally an internal chat system used by Tiny Speck, which was building a video game called Glitch. IRC was a popular chat tool at the time, but the team chose to build an in-house chat solution. The Glitch project failed, which was the trigger for turning the internal chat system into the product that became Slack (http://mng.bz/ZReN). In December 2020, Salesforce announced it was acquiring Slack in a $27.7 billion deal (http://mng.bz/RmPR). The story of AWS is also similar in some respects—managing infrastructure wasn't Amazon's core business, but they became so good at it that they were able to spin it off into a separate business.

Traditional advice suggests SaaS, open source, or off-the-shelf solutions for generic domains, and this is still generally good advice. However, if you feel that there is even

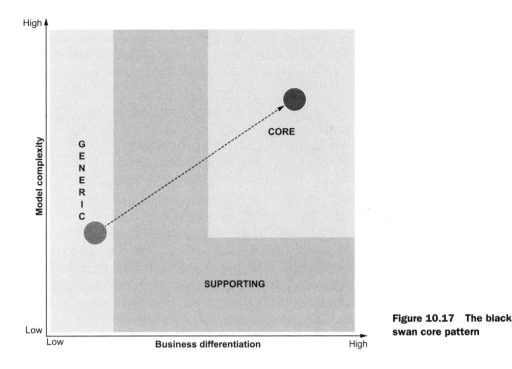

Figure 10.17   The black swan core pattern

a possibility that you may actually have a rare black swan core, building in-house may be worth considering to keep your options open—though this isn't an excuse to build everything in-house.

10.3.10 *Portfolio patterns*

All of the patterns in this section have focused on a single subdomain or a small cluster of closely related subdomains. This is useful because investment and approach should be tailored on a per-subdomain/per-team basis. However, it is also important to look at the portfolio as a whole and notice broad trends. One way I encourage people to do this is to ask, "Imagine there was no text on this Core Domain Chart, what would the visual patterns tell you?" The following are some examples to give you ideas and watch for on your Core Domain Charts:

- *A single core domain that is moving left into supporting*—This raises the question of what is coming next? Does the company have a longer-term plan? Should it be investing some effort into those initiatives now? Where are the big bet future cores?
- *Five or six core domains*—This is a concern that there may be too many high priorities, and investment is spread too thinly.
- *All/most generic subdomains built in-house*—Why are so many generic capabilities being built in-house? Is there a fundamental problem with the company's approach to build versus buy versus partner decisions?

When looking at the overall portfolio for trends, it's useful to indicate the investment in each team. Finances are usually too complicated, so I use team size as a proxy. As figure 10.18 shows, this can reveal important trends that need investigation, like a higher level of investment in supporting subdomains than core domains.

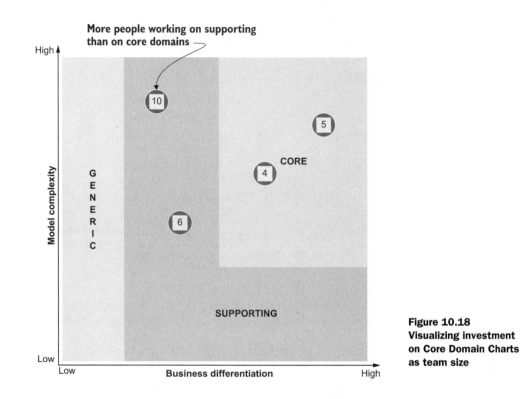

Figure 10.18
Visualizing investment on Core Domain Charts as team size

10.4 *Industry example: Strategy-aligned architecture at Vinted*

Established in 2008, Vinted is the first Lithuanian tech unicorn that is a global C2C online marketplace where its members can trade their pre-loved fashion and lifestyle items across many different categories, such as clothing, pet care, books, and video games to name a few. Originally, Vinted focused on a single vertical, women's clothing, and gradually expanded into others.

> **NOTE** This industry example was coauthored with Ornela Vasiliauskaite, an agile coach at Vinted. I highly recommend checking out her excellent DDD and socio-technical architecture-related talks (https://www.youtube.com/watch?v=joSgTOUy7eQ).

As the company grew from 30 engineering team members colocated in Lithuania in 2018 to 460 people spread across multiple locations in Europe at the beginning of 2023, growing pains started to become apparent. The time it took to implement new features continued to increase as more and more developers were all working in the same monolithic codebase. One reason adding new features was more complex than it could have been was the assumptions baked into the architecture. Many of the core abstractions were still heavily based on the assumption of a single vertical (women's clothing). Supporting multiple verticals had been forced into the current model rather than redesigned from a blank canvas.

In 2021, the growing pains had become untenable, and everybody agreed that it was time to modernize the architecture to speed up innovation. Developers found it hard to understand the code, and it took too long to compile, test, and deploy it. Hiring more developers didn't lead to the expected productivity increases, and onboarding them took longer. The system was also growing in fragility as changes in one area started breaking unrelated functionality.

Engineering leadership, including staff engineers, collectively agreed that a loosely coupled, modular architecture and teams that owned parts of the system were needed to bring back their ability to innovate at speed. That was seen as a prerequisite to grow from a successful startup to an even more successful scale-up.

One example of their growing pains was in the domain of categories. As Ornela explains: "Categorization at Vinted is done hierarchically and uses a tree metaphor. The broadest category is known as the 'root'; Vinted uses departments, such as 'Women' or 'Men' for these broader groupings. From there, we have parent-child relationships: the root will have one or more child categories, each narrower in scope than the parent category using an 'is a' relationship. For example, the Women root category can have children such as 'Footwear' or 'Clothing,' as those subcategories are narrower than the broader concept of women's fashion. The parent-child structure can continue indefinitely depending on how granular the structure needs to be" (see figure 10.19).

Over the years, the variety of items being traded on Vinted's platform grew, and now there are six distinct departments (Women, Men, Kids, Home, Entertainment,

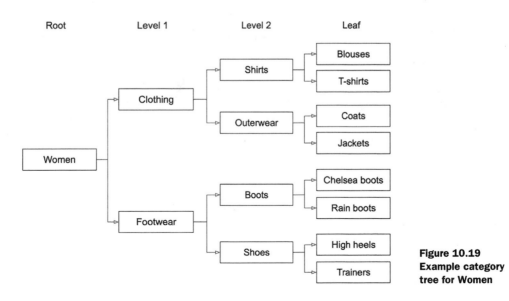

Figure 10.19
Example category tree for Women

and Pet Care) that Vinted members could choose to sell and buy items from. Deepening and widening the categories tree was crucial, so a new team was formed to focus on this area. However, the software architecture was a blocker.

Immediately from its inception, the newly formed categories team struggled to deliver value. Categories were not a well-defined part of the code that one team could easily work on without dependencies on other teams. Quite the opposite, category functionality was scattered throughout many parts of the architecture. As a result, the effort required to both understand the current code and implement new features was extremely high.

To tackle this challenge, the team decided to try domain-driven design as an approach to modeling categories as an independent, loosely coupled subdomain that would enable the categories team to have a clear purpose and achieve fast flow. If things went well, the organization wanted to apply concepts like DDD and Team Topologies more widely.

However, things didn't get off to a great start, as Ornela explains: "The first sessions we ran were really difficult. There was a lot of misalignment. Some people felt that the chosen approach (DDD) was to blame, while in reality the domain was just very complex. It was especially frustrating for the domain experts. Their conviction in the existing model made it difficult for them to listen to others and see why other options were also possible. I was also convinced I was right in my understanding of the domain model."

Introducing new approaches like DDD always takes time and patience. So, despite the shaky start, Ornela and her colleagues persevered. They looked for an external expert who could help kickstart their endeavor and decided to hire Marco Heimeshoff, a leading DDD consultant. It seemed like the perfect solution to hire an unbiased external facilitator who is skilled in domain modeling, and it proved to be the case. Marco helped them go deeper into the domain and define two potential models, as shown in figure 10.20.

But the group was still split. Half of the group preferred one model, and the rest preferred the other. After a few sessions of EventStorming and context mapping, the

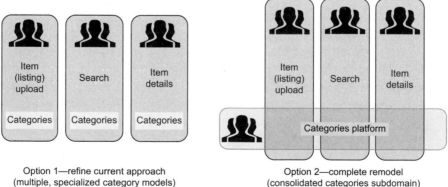

Option 1—refine current approach   Option 2—complete remodel
(multiple, specialized category models)   (consolidated categories subdomain)

Figure 10.20 Multiple competing models for categories

group realized that their split was more fundamental than their choice of model. The two groups had fundamentally different beliefs about the product strategy, and they had chosen the model that best aligned with their understanding of the product goals. "It was difficult to define boundaries and team structures without a clear product strategy to organize around," said Doug Wieand, product manager.

It had become clear to Ornela and the team that architectural decisions must be driven by business and product outcomes: "We needed to align on the product strategy before we could choose the right model. However, that was another hurdle. We were not aligned on what we wanted to optimize for. I think we were not accustomed to thinking about the architecture decisions in conjunction with product goals; thus, seeing two different approaches requiring two entirely different team and code structures forced us to think about what each of those models will help us to accomplish and which of these scenarios we actually prefer for our long term ambition."

With a clear understanding of the key challenge they faced, the team switched gears and began exploring strategic modeling approaches. They began with Core Domain Charts, explains Ornela: "We started with Core Domain Charts because it wasn't possible to pinpoint what we wanted to optimize for by focusing on categories alone. We needed to see it in a wider context so that we could understand the different types of complexity each option would introduce into the overall system and how the differentiation provided by categories compared to other investments we were considering."

After multiple strategic modeling sessions with Wardley Maps and Core Domain Charts, the group began to converge on a preferred option. Figure 10.21 shows a

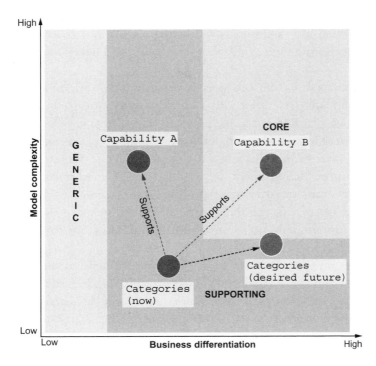

Figure 10.21   Mapping the strategic portfolio with a Core Domain Chart

fragment of the strategic model the team came up with in their latest iteration of their Core Domain Chart. It shows how the group converged on the idea that categories would be a vital enabler of their core domain (capability B) as well as supporting other important areas like capability A. The more investment in improving the power of categories and the ability to iterate quickly, the better they could achieve their ultimate business outcomes.

Adding strategic modeling of their portfolio into the mix helped the team to close the full feedback loop and consider the modernization efforts from the angles of code structure, team structure, and product and business strategy. Finally, everybody was 100% aligned on what the socio-technical architecture should be optimized for, says Ornela, and the group unanimously chose the model of categories that best suited the product vision: "Before all of the DDD efforts, we were solely focusing on adding new categories into the system as it is and we were getting slower and slower. After adopting various modeling approaches, we started to see how we could add these new categories at accelerating pace. Taking longer time horizons into consideration, and seeing and discussing different models in front of us allowed us to build confidence, justify certain technical investments, and align on a long-term vision. We chose the approach to invest into the categories platform that supports all the other areas where the category context is needed."

There was still a huge effort ahead of the group to decouple the architecture, but everybody knew exactly what they needed to do and why it was important. As the team's taxonomist, Charlie Lapin, puts it: "A holistic rework of the categories meant that we were both more proactive, such as with trends—capturing what's trending and allowing for categorization within that framing—as well as being more reactive by removing categories that are confusing, overlapping, or are not relevant to users." The whole team was motivated and able to focus their full energy to achieve their desired outcome.

One of the key takeaways from this story is perseverance. Despite the turbulent first few sessions, the team persevered with a domain-driven approach to improving their architecture, and it turned out to be a success. The outcome of their work and the approach taken were impressive enough to be noticed by business leaders and colleagues from other areas of the business. This quote from the Vinted Marketplace CEO, Adam Jay, captures the sentiment well: "At the scale Vinted operates, we need our teams to be fully empowered to make product and architecture decisions. I'm glad to see examples of such dedication and perseverance to make the needed yet difficult changes in our organizational structure and architecture to fuel Vinted's success."

Another key takeaway is the importance of sharing learnings and successes across the organization. People were excited by what the group had achieved and how they achieved it. Ornela and her team were asked to share their learnings in other domains and spread the ideas to other parts of the organization facing similar scaling challenges. "With their success, Ornela and her team helped unlock our next stage of engineering productivity and created an example to be followed by other teams. While we're on the journey, I'm already confident that the impact of their work will have positive reverberations throughout Vinted's technology team," remarked Mindaugas Mozūras, VP of engineering.

This story shows that proficiency in using DDD methods alone is not the key to gaining valuable insights. Focusing on the problem they were trying to solve and experimenting with multiple methods to figure out the solution they were most confident in worked for Ornela and the team at Vinted. A kind of freestyle problem-solving approach, drawing inspiration from many sources and adapting them to their own context as needed. To build that confidence, the team used visual models, and by comparing and assessing them, collecting feedback from various stakeholders, and iterating on the models quickly and collaboratively, they managed to come up with solutions relatively quickly and achieve buy-in across the board.

This chapter is now complete. You've seen how to identify strategic IT, which is crucial in making key modernization decisions, like how to shape domain boundaries and how to organize teams effectively. These two themes continue in the next chapter, which looks much more closely at the socio-technical aspects of architecture: how to codesign teams and architecture to achieve the optimal overall system, using the principles and patterns of Team Topologies.

Summary

- Architecture should be treated as a portfolio, with a level of investment and operating model tailored to the specifics of each area.
- A well-designed technology architecture may just be gold plating that wastes effort that could have been better invested in more strategic areas.
- Martin Fowler's utility versus strategic IT dichotomy classifies IT applications as utility or strategic according to their contribution to business differentiation. Software that helps organizations to differentiate is considered strategic, while software that is considered just to be a cost of doing business with little or no differentiation is considered to be utility.
- Classifying IT as utility or strategic is not to serve an academic or theoretical purpose; it should have specific impacts on many aspects of the operating model, including team size, team composition, product discovery, prioritization, domain modeling, architecture, code health, and build versus buy versus partner.
- Candidates for strategic IT are likely to be found on a Wardley Map between late genesis and mid-product. This is not a hard and fast rule, and not all components within these areas are guaranteed to be strategic IT.
- The act of collaboratively defining a product strategy based on research and data will make clear which parts of IT are strategic.

- Business domains are a great model for enabling architecture to be treated as a portfolio with investments aligned to business outcomes. Each business domain and subdomain can have tailored investment and operating model characteristics.
- Core Domain Charts is a technique from the domain-driven design community that helps to identify and make decisions about strategic IT and the approach to be taken in each subdomain.
- A collaborative approach involving business, product, technology, and other stakeholders is ideal when defining Core Domain Charts.
- In DDD, each subdomain is considered to be core, supporting, or generic based on a combination of business differentiation and model complexity.
  - Core domains (which are subdomains) are high in differentiation and complexity, so they should nearly always be built in-house. They align with Fowler's definition of strategic IT.
  - Supporting subdomains are less complex and differentiating but require industry- and company-specific domain logic, so they are typically built in-house.
  - Generic subdomains have little or no differentiation potential, and where possible, off-the-shelf solutions usually make sense. They align with Fowler's definition of utility IT.
- The classification of a subdomain can change over time. What is core at one point in time will most likely drift left into supporting at some point in the future. Arrows can be used on a Core Domain Chart to show this evolution.
- Model complexity is a composite measure of complexity that represents the effort required to discover user needs, build and evolve a domain model, implement it in software, and support it in production.
- Operational complexity is usually not considered to be part of model complexity but often plays an important role in strategic discussions, so it can be highlighted on Core Domain Charts using annotations.
- There is some overlap between Core Domain Charts and Wardley Mapping; however, Wardley Mapping is a much more advanced technique that takes an industry-wide perspective and can be applied to all scopes. Core Domain Charts are used more specifically to visualize strategic IT choices according to differentiation and complexity.
- There are a variety of patterns that can be observed on a Core Domain Chart, like decisive core, indefensible core, suspect supporting, and table stakes supporting. Each pattern has implications on how the subdomain should be treated.
- A decisive core typically necessitates a big investment in talented people, collaborative practices like EventStorming, and more advanced architectural patterns.

- A table stakes support requires a much smaller investment to achieve a good enough solution, providing that there is no negative effect in core domains.
- While fine-grained investments can be made on a per-subdomain/per-team basis, it's important to look at the investments in the portfolio as a whole because there are dependencies between subdomains, and decisions taken in one may affect others.

Team Topologies 11

This chapter covers

- Designing Team Topologies
- Validating candidate value streams
- Sensing and evolving Team Topologies
- Grouping teams that work on related challenges

Modern architecture requires a socio-technical approach. Jointly optimizing the organization and software architecture is necessary to achieve optimal organizational performance. More than a well-designed software architecture is needed to achieve fast flow because teams may be organized in a way that introduces friction and bottlenecks into their workflow. Teams must work on the same code and, as a result, must synchronize their changes and deployments or risk tripping over each other.

Ideally, teams should form part of *independent value streams*. As explained in chapter 6, a value stream is all of the steps a team goes through, from discovering unmet user needs in a subdomain for which they are responsible to designing solutions, implementing them in software, and deploying and supporting them in production. Fast flow is enabled by independent value streams, where teams have

240

responsibility for everything in the value stream, from the conceptual subdomain to the software needed to implement the subdomain's capabilities.

Independent doesn't mean isolated. In practice, some dependencies will always exist, and most value streams will not be 100% independent. But we should still aim for value streams that are as independent as possible by challenging every dependency and obstacle to a team's flow, like decisions that affect them by people outside of the team.

In 2019, the book *Team Topologies* by authors Matthew Skelton and Manuel Pais was released. It contains a toolkit for shaping socio-technical architecture and creating the conditions for teams to achieve fast flow. This chapter introduces the principles and patterns of Team Topologies and shows how they can be used to refine domain boundaries by validating the organizational aspects of candidate value streams, as highlighted in figure 11.1

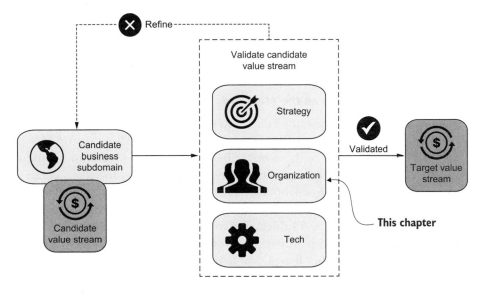

Figure 11.1   Refining and validating domain boundaries with Team Topologies

11.1   Team Topologies principles

At the heart of Team Topologies is a core set of principles for organizing teams for fast flow. These principles were included in Team Topologies because they have proven effective in organizations that develop their products with a high velocity. While the patterns are helpful and often easier to remember, the principles are the most critical aspect of Team Topologies and should always be front of mind. My personal experience over more than a decade corroborates these principles. Likewise, you may already apply some of these principles in your company. Team Topologies isn't a proprietary framework that tries to reinvent organization design. Many of the ideas have proven to be effective in the industry.

11.1.1 *Sustainable fast flow*

The subtitle of the *Team Topologies* book is *Organizing Business and Technology Teams for Fast Flow*. Some people misinterpret this as churning out code as fast as possible while neglecting quality. So, the first thing to remember is that fast flow means *sustainable fast flow*—the ability to maintain a high velocity over multiple years. The other vital thing to remember is that speed versus quality is a fallacy. Keeping a codebase healthy by reducing cruft means that code is easier to understand, easier to change, and less likely to have bugs or downtime (http://mng.bz/27Xo). These are key enablers for reducing the cost of change and improving flow.

In their 2018 book *Accelerate* (http://mng.bz/1JzQ), Forsgren et al. presented research findings that showed high-performing teams deployed to production multiple times per day yet still had less production downtime and were able to recover faster when they did. For many, achieving sustainable fast flow requires deep changes—not just to the organization structure, but every aspect of building products, from technical practices to leadership mindset.

11.1.2 *Small, long-lived teams as the standard*

Team Topologies recommends that teams should generally be "a stable group of five to nine people who work towards a shared goal as a unit." There is scope for deviation, but this is considered to be the sensible default. The sizing recommendation is based on trust. Team Topologies argues that once a team gets beyond five to nine people, it becomes difficult for team members to retain the same high -level of trust. In my anecdotal experience, going beyond that size makes it difficult to keep up with everything happening in the team, and subteams start to form anyway. On the other end, going below five can result in too little capacity or the risk of losing a large chunk of knowledge when a team member leaves. Stable teams don't have to be static, however. The section on dynamic reteaming later in this chapter covers team fluidity patterns.

The long-lived aspect of a team is important for both social and technical connotations. From a social perspective, long-lived creates an opportunity for teams to better know each other and continuously improve how they work together. They are responsible for a part of the product and motivated to keep improving it. From a technical perspective, long-lived incentivizes teams to keep code healthy and evolvable in the long term because people know that they have to support the code that they write. One of the worst culprits of poor flow is legacy code, and it is one of the most expensive problems to fix. Therefore, the importance of organizing teams to incentivize long-term code health cannot be overstated.

11.1.3 *Team-first thinking*

Some traditional approaches refer to software engineers as "resources." They are seen as interchangeable units whose work is micromanaged. They can be partially allocated to multiple projects simultaneously and moved around on a whim. Nowadays, the flaws in this approach are widespread. Context switching has a high cost on productivity, and engineers can contribute much more than just code when they are immersed in the domain and aligned with business goals. Team Topologies embraces this mindset by considering teams as the individual unit. It's the team themselves who collectively decide what each member will work on. All work is routed to the team and not the individual.

Team-first thinking also applies to goal setting and recognition. When individual team members have their own targets, they are incentivized to act as individuals, whereas when the team has shared goals and is recognized for their collective efforts, cooperation is incentivized. I worked for one organization that had cascading objectives that cascaded all the way down from the CEO to every individual employee. One example, in particular, stands out in my memory, where one team member had worked with his line manager to set his goals. His primary objective was to write a certain number of stored procedures. This was baffling because the team had little work that seemed like it needed stored procedures, and this team member was looking for work to achieve his objectives that weren't consistent with the team's product goals.

In organizations that lack team-first thinking, one antipattern to look out for is standardized processes and ways of working. There is a belief that if all teams follow the same agile process and use the same Jira workflows, every team will be highly productive, and it will be easy to rotate people to different teams. I've never seen this to be effective in practice. The best teams I have worked with owned their process and were able to continuously improve it. Standardized workflows stifle improvement and result in lower productivity. The benefit of a consistent process is also a fallacy. As a software engineer, when I moved from one team to another, the process was the easiest thing to learn. Learning the code and the domain and building relationships with team members took far longer. Standardized workflows and processes often ignore this human element.

11.1.4 *You build it, you run it*

One of the prominent trends of the 2010s that emerged from the DevOps space was *you build it, you run it* (http://mng.bz/PRA8). This approach puts teams thoroughly in control of the software they build. Teams design, write, and deploy their code to production and then support their code in production. The idea behind this approach is that teams will be incentivized to create more reliable software if they are responsible for it. *You build it, you run it* results in more independent value streams and faster flow because there are fewer handovers. For these reasons, it is central to the ideas in Team Topologies.

I had my first *you build it, you run it* experience at 7digital in 2012. Every morning during daily standup, each team would observe the dashboards displayed on monitors hanging off the walls around their team area. We would look at API traffic, performance, error codes, and custom metrics relevant to each subdomain. Whenever we built new features, we always thought about instrumentation we could add to verify that the feature was working or that would quickly alert us to the source when there were problems in production. This way of developing features, with operability (https://www.stevesmith.tech/blog/category/operability/) in mind, is something I have yet to observe in teams that do not run the code they create.

To someone unfamiliar with *you build it, you run it,* this may be perceived as extra work that reduces the productivity of software engineers. But this is not the case in my experience. By owning every aspect of our software, each team deployed to production multiple times per day. As a result, no time was lost coordinating with other teams to deploy the code. When there were problems in production, the team could resolve them quickly, not forgetting there were already fewer production concerns and bugs due to adopting this approach.

It's not necessary to apply *you build it, you run it* everywhere. In some circumstances, relying on the traditional model of a separate ops team running code in production is more effective. Steve Smith makes the case that *you build it, you run it* becomes more critical as product demands and reliability needs increase (http://mng.bz/Jdyz).

11.1.5 *Good boundaries minimize cognitive load*

Excessive cognitive load is a significant inhibitor to sustainable fast flow. When teams have a high cognitive load, there are many risks: the quality of the team's work may diminish, the team will work in unsustainable ways, and team members may burn out as they try to keep up with everything expected of them. A team's motivation may drop as they context switch between different initiatives and lacks a clear sense of purpose. A team's cognitive load capacity varies based on factors like the size of a team and its expertise.

There are several aspects to keeping a team's cognitive load manageable. Well-defined boundaries is one of them. No subdomain should be too large or complex that it results in cognitive load that is too high for a single team. Once a subdomain reaches that point, it should be split into multiple smaller subdomains. Likewise, if a team owns multiple subdomains, then the collective complexity cannot exceed the cognitive load of a single team. This includes the costs of context switching that will be necessary as the team switches from working in one subdomain to the others.

Subdomains include various types of complexity, as discussed in the previous chapter, including the current state of the software, which could be complex due to high levels of cruft. Visualizing team boundaries on a Core Domain Chart is a helpful way to quickly identify where high team cognitive load may appear, as shown in figure 11.2.

Team Topologies makes a distinction between three types of team cognitive loads, which are each handled in different ways:

- *Intrinsic cognitive load*—This type of cognitive load refers to the inherent difficulty of a task. Designing a function to calculate the total price of a simple order has much less intrinsic cognitive load than learning a new programming language. It is difficult to reduce this type of cognitive load without changing the requirements of the task.

- *Extraneous cognitive load*—This type of cognitive load is caused by environmental factors that aren't intrinsic to the task and could potentially be avoided. For example, legacy code that couples unrelated concepts makes it harder to pick out the specific concepts necessary for a given task.
- *Germane cognitive load*—This type of cognitive load is related to the mental effort required to structure and organize the material being learned into long-term memory, like learning new business domain concepts.

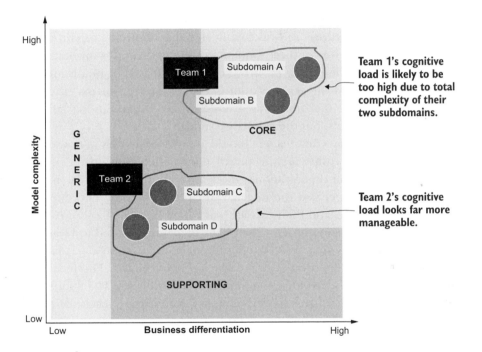

Figure 11.2   Identifying potential high cognitive load on a Core Domain Chart

No precise formula exists for measuring cognitive load, but it is possible to get a good, reasonable understanding by asking teams to describe how well they can achieve their tasks and how overworked they feel. This should be a recurring conversation as a team's cognitive load can increase as their responsibilities grow.

11.1.6   Embrace Conway's law

The idea that organization structure and communication patterns are strong forces on software architecture goes back to 1968 when Melvyn Conway coined what later became known as Conway's law: "Any organization that designs a system (defined broadly) will produce a design whose structure is a copy of the organization's communication structure." As mentioned in chapter 2, Conway's law is essential for modern architecture because the relationship between organization and software architecture is so strong.

Conway's law is a crucial component of Team Topologies due to its implications on flow. The organization and the software need to be purposefully architected and jointly optimized to enable independent value streams. For example, suppose the organization is aligned to one set of domain boundaries, and the software is aligned to a different set of domain boundaries. In that case, teams will be working in the same codebases, needing to coordinate their work and tripping over each other.

Despite being a common topic, Conway's law is still under-acknowledged. Martin Fowler gets to the crux of the problems seen in many organizations: "A lot of what we see out in the industries is people ignoring [the forces of Conway's law] and trying to come up with architectures or just not really thinking about the organizational design and trying to pretend it isn't there, and as a result, you get this mismatch where people are trying to do something in software design and their organizational design is pushing against it, and the result is a lot of friction and problems" (http://mng.bz/wjBB). Sometimes it's the other way around, where organizational changes ignore architectural constraints, but the results are similar.

To embrace Conway's law, leaders should always look closely at how organizational dynamics affect the software architecture. Unfortunately, this wasn't the case when I worked with one travel organization. One team owned customer-facing capabilities, and another group operated the internal API platforms. The customer-facing team reported to marketing, and their mission was to sell holidays by showcasing the company's products and taking orders. The platform teams reported to IT and owned the systems and databases that were the source of truth for the data, like itineraries, prices, and special offers used in the marketing applications. The teams had a rock-bottom relationship and avoided communication at all costs. Their software architecture reflected this and was excessively complex, leading to substantial problems that inconvenienced customers and internal stakeholders.

The marketing IT team had grown frustrated with the unreliable platform APIs, which were slow and error-prone. The problem was that customers and managers in the company saw it as a website problem, and the marketing IT team was held responsible. When the marketing IT team was delayed adding new features because they were waiting for backend API changes, they also got the blame and felt unfairly treated.

The problems here are predominantly on the social side: the two groups needed to work together to find a solution for the problematic APIs, and the organization needs to incentivize them to collaborate by not blaming the marketing IT team when there is little they can do to help. However, the solution taken was a technical one. The marketing IT team built a data importer that sucked all of the data out of the platform APIs and stored it in their own local database. As a result, they improved website performance and reliability and could add new features faster, all without needing to talk to their enemies in the platform teams.

Unfortunately, the new architecture created a whole new set of problems. In addition to the considerable investment in building the synchronization system, there were other consequences, like data consistency errors where new holidays would be missing from the website or out-of-date prices being shown. This also resulted in a blame game between marketing IT and the platform IT teams about whose fault it was. People in other teams, like the content management team, would have to mediate between the two teams to find out what caused the problem.

Overall, a large portion of the team's cognitive load was taken up with the maintenance of the synchronization system. The software architecture truly was a mirror of the organization's communication dysfunctions. The company was paying a dear price for not adhering to the implications of Conway's law. If both groups had tried to build better relationships and been open to collaborating with each other, the system would have been much simpler and the problems far fewer. In reality, personality clashes can't always be resolved, which means leadership needs to be aware of the consequences of this type of problem and step in before things get out of hand.

11.2 Team Topologies patterns

Team Topologies introduces patterns for modeling organizations: four team types and three interaction modes. These patterns build on top of the principles and are a useful tool for designing and evolving organizations in contexts where the principles have been fully embraced. However, applying the patterns without also adopting the principles is unlikely to lead to much of an improvement. That's structure-and-process-fallacy thinking.

11.2.1 The four team types

Team Topologies introduces four team types for modeling organizations. Determining the type of each team is important because it helps the team understand their role and their expected behaviors, which can also surface problems. For example, when a team feels like they consist of multiple team types, it could be a sign that they have too many or too diverse responsibilities. The four team types, shown in figure 11.3, are an aspirational model, meaning that the existing teams in your organization may not fit. Rather than forcing every team into one of these types, you can indicate

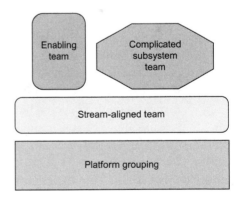

Figure 11.3   The four team types of Team Topologies

that they will remain outside the Team Topologies model until those areas have been modernized. Otherwise, you risk just using a new label to describe what you have always done.

NOTE The Team Topologies notation uses specific colors and shapes. You can find full-color, interactive versions of all the notation shown in this chapter on the book's Miro board (http://mng.bz/qjMN).

STREAM-ALIGNED TEAMS

Most teams within an organization will be *stream-aligned teams*. Stream-aligned teams are fully responsible for independent value streams that usually contribute to product capabilities, from discovering unmet user needs within a subdomain to a *you build it, you run it* operating model. The team should contain all of the skills necessary for their value stream, such as a product manager, tester, and UX specialist. A stream-aligned team is not just an IT team that is separated from "the business." A stream-aligned team has both business and IT responsibilities.

Common examples of stream-aligned teams include

- A team that is responsible for domain APIs
- A team that builds embedded software for hardware devices
- A purely UI team like the mobile app team or web team
- A full-stack team that owns the backend API and UI pages for an end-to-end product feature like a search component

PLATFORM GROUPINGS

Platform groupings exist to provide shared capabilities that reduce the cognitive load of stream-aligned teams, which frees those teams up to focus on their core mission and improves their flow. In Team Topologies, the term platform is used in a general sense. A platform can refer to an internal developer platform (IDP), which provides capabilities to help teams build software like infrastructure and tooling. A platform can also refer to a horizontal, which contains domain logic like Uber's fulfillment platform discussed in chapter 6.

A key priority for platforms is ensuring that the platform doesn't become a bottleneck and add cognitive load to stream-aligned teams. For these reasons, developer experience (DX) is a principal focus of teams working as part of a platform. In a nutshell, this means that a platform's teams should invest in the usability of their platforms through concepts like self-service capabilities, which are documented well. If stream-aligned teams regularly create tickets for the platform's teams, it is a warning sign that needs further exploration. Platforms and DX are covered more extensively in chapter 13.

In Team Topologies, a platform may represent a single team or a group of teams that each own part of a cohesive platform or act as enablers, as shown in figure 11.4. Platform groupings can even contain nested platform groupings. There was an example of this in chapter 6, NAVs internal technology platform, which consisted of the infrastructure platform, data platform, and design system.

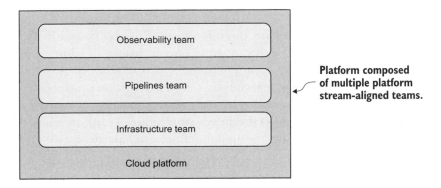

Figure 11.4   Platform groupings are typically composed of multiple teams (they can be any of the four team types, including nested platform groupings).

COMPLICATED SUBSYSTEM TEAMS

Complicated subsystem teams exist to deal with capabilities that require a high level of specialist knowledge to work on. The benefit of this is that the specialist skills do not need to be embedded in multiple stream-aligned teams. They can be concentrated into a single dedicated team, effectively encapsulating the complexity and making it easy for others to consume. There are many potential candidates for a complicated subsystem team like software that needs ultralow latency or requires degree-level education in a particular domain like physics. This poses the risk that hiring people to work in the team will take longer, and the costs of a team member leaving will be higher.

ENABLING TEAMS

Enabling teams exist to help other teams become more effective at their work and more autonomous. They differ from the other three team types because they don't own parts of the product or infrastructure. An enabling team's responsibility is to support other teams through education and empowerment, not by doing their work for them.

A common pattern is establishing enabling teams for skills the organization lacks, like continuous delivery, EventStorming, workshop facilitation, or chaos engineering. The enabling team will spend time with other teams in various forms, like teaching new concepts, facilitating workshops, and even spending time with the teams to introduce ideas while doing real work. Enabling teams can also be project-based, such as an enabling team that is put together to ensure a particular project is delivered on time. I recommend creating an architecture modernization enabling team (AMET) to ensure modernization stays on track and maintains momentum. AMETs are covered in chapter 15.

One integral aspect to be aware of regarding enabling teams is that the team should have expiry conditions. This means that when the enabling team has achieved its purpose, the team no longer has a need to exist, and the members can move to other challenges. This contradicts some of the principles in the first part of the chapter, but as mentioned, enabling teams are a bit different.

11.2.2 *The three interaction modes*

Supporting the four team types are three interaction modes shown in figure 11.5. They describe the relationships that can exist between teams, in addition to no relationship at all. Team Topologies argues that more collaboration does not necessarily mean more effective teams. One reason is that some interaction modes carry a higher cognitive load cost than others, so they are expensive to maintain. Consequently, it's important to choose the most effective interaction mode. Team interactions should evolve as the context changes, like the amount of work in a particular domain.

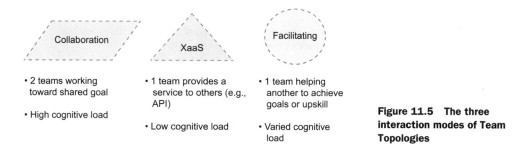

Collaboration

XaaS

Facilitating

- 2 teams working toward shared goal
- High cognitive load

- 1 team provides a service to others (e.g., API)
- Low cognitive load

- 1 team helping another to achieve goals or upskill
- Varied cognitive load

Figure 11.5   The three interaction modes of Team Topologies

COLLABORATION

In *collaboration* mode, two teams work together toward a shared outcome. Each team is making changes in their area, and success is collective. Due to the close nature of collaboration, teams need to synchronize their work through shared rituals, joint decision-making, and various forms of communication. This means that collaboration can have a high-cognitive load cost and reduce the team's output. Collaboration is the obvious choice when staying aligned, and moving together in the same direction is more important than each team producing maximum output. But when the benefits of close alignment don't justify the loss in production, the relationship should be switched to X-as-a-service or removed.

X-AS-A-SERVICE

X-as-a-service (XaaS) is an interaction mode associated with lower cognitive load. One team may use the capabilities of another team, like calling their API, but there is no need for repeated synchronization of work, shared rituals, or high levels of asynchronous collaboration. There may be onboarding costs, feature requests, and support from time to time, but they are generally minimal overall compared to a collaboration relationship.

FACILITATING

One team supporting another to achieve a single team's goal is an interaction model called *facilitating*. This is similar to the role of an enabling team; however, any team can temporarily adopt the facilitating interaction mode in support of another team. An example is when one team has an urgent deadline, so another team switches focus to help them.

Facilitation could also involve upskilling, with people from one team dedicating some of their time to teaching the other team a new skill. One of my clients introduced mob programming in this fashion. After one team tried it and saw a clear benefit, they helped other teams to learn and apply the technique.

11.2.3 Industry example: Global cosmetics brand

Visualizing Team Topologies with team types and interaction modes can uncover organizational problems or help to explain certain known problems. This was the case when my colleague Maxime Sanglan-Charlier (https://mastodon.social/@__maxs__) and I worked remotely to help a global cosmetics brand begin its architecture modernization initiative. The name of one team came up in all of our listening tour sessions, usually in a negative context. The team was responsible for an integration platform. Their goal was to ensure that teams based in all geographical locations could access all of the data they needed to build product experiences for their customers and for internal analytics purposes.

We decided to set up a call with the integration platform team to get their perspective on the matter and try to make sense of all the comments raised about them. During the call, we started to map out their team topology, shown in figure 11.6, so we could better understand the situation. The crux of the matter became clear: the team was interacting with at least four other teams using the collaboration mode. This interaction mode carries a high-cognitive load cost due to the level of coordination required. That's why the team was perceived as a bottleneck by other teams. But what had caused the team to end up in this topology?

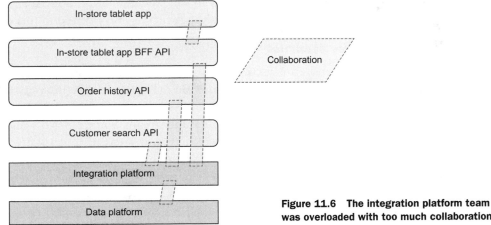

Figure 11.6 The integration platform team was overloaded with too much collaboration.

At first, we thought the team was just using the word collaboration in a general sense to describe their relationships with other teams. But as we discussed each dependency with the integration platform team, they explained that they were building and maintaining custom endpoints for each team because the stream-aligned teams lacked the skills or the budget to do it themselves.

A high level of coordination was involved, and the integration platform team even had to maintain the integrations they built for other teams. Ultimately, the integration platform team was caught in a difficult situation, and they tried to do their best to make everyone happy. Unfortunately, this amount of coordination exceeded what they were capable of.

With the principles and patterns of Team Topologies, we were quickly able to visualize and gain shared agreement on the problem. Everybody agreed that the team needed to discontinue accepting work that belonged outside of the platform, and it was clear which existing responsibilities needed to be handed over. While the vision was clear, it would take a sustained effort to undo some of the previous choices and embed new ways of thinking throughout the company. To avoid these types of problems, both managers and team members should always pay close attention to the team's cognitive load by making it a regular topic during retrospectives.

11.3   *Validating candidate value streams*

The Team Topologies principles and patterns covered so far in the chapter are generally good concepts that modernization leaders should always keep in mind. They are also effective when validating a candidate value stream: verifying a proposed domain boundary to see if it makes sense as a team and software boundary and ensuring other conditions are in place for the team to be effective. To validate a candidate value stream using Team Topologies concepts, a technique called *independent service heuristics* (ISH) (http://mng.bz/7vXV), provided by Team Topologies, can be used. It's a set of heuristics that can be used to assess a value stream's independence and flag any concerns. Other techniques can also be used to validate the organizational aspects of a value stream, like John Cutler's mandate levels, which is also covered in this section.

11.3.1   *Independent service heuristics*

ISH is a checklist of ten heuristics. Each heuristic includes questions and guidance to help apply it. The checklist is there to ensure the right people have the right conversations, covering all important aspects of a value stream before investing in changes. After applying each heuristic to a candidate value stream, you will have a higher level of confidence that it is suitable, or you will highlight areas of uncertainty and concerns to address with follow-up sessions. This technique is best used collaboratively with a mix of people representing different perspectives: business leadership, product, engineering, etc.

For each heuristic, you will need to establish satisfaction criteria. I recommend a simple approach, using *thumbs-up, thumbs down,* or *more investigation needed.* This subsection covers a selection of the heuristics to give a flavor of what ISH is about and how it can be used. Remember that when you are applying ISH to assess your candidate value streams, it's important to go through all of the heuristics, and you are free to use other tools and techniques to complement each heuristic.

ISH: IMPACT/VALUE

The *impact/value* ISH is about determining purpose: would the team responsible for the value stream be motivated by interesting and engaging domain and product challenges that create value for the business and customer?

Some questions to ask when discussing this ISH are

- Is the scope big enough to provide impact?
- Would the scope be engaging for talented people?
- Is there sufficient value to the customers and the organization that the value would clearly be recognized?

Answering yes to these questions indicates a value stream with high impact and value and a strong sense of team purpose that all stakeholders recognize. A clear thumbs-up. Answering no to any of the questions is not necessarily a thumbs down. For example, realistically, not all areas will be as interesting to work on, like some supporting and generic subdomains. If you believe some people would be motivated to work in this value stream, it can still be considered a thumbs-up if that constraint is clear. Alternatively, refining the domain boundaries or other aspects of the value stream may be better to provide a higher sense of purpose.

Any uncertainty around the value provided by a value stream shouldn't be glossed over. If you can't articulate the value it will or could bring, how can you be sure that you are making a good decision? It is good to follow-up with sessions on techniques like Wardley Mapping and EventStorming to get a clear picture of the value provided.

ISH: PRODUCT DECISIONS

A growing sentiment in modern product management is that the people building the product are among the best sources for product ideas. They know how the product works, follow up on how customers use it, and know what is possible with the technology.

The *product decisions* ISH is there to determine whether a value stream is independent enough for teams to discover unmet user needs, determine their own roadmap to create better products, and ensure the team isn't just ordered to build what other people and teams dictate to them. That negatively affects innovation, team motivation, and flow due to the value stream being subject to external factors.

When teams own their roadmap, they can make more decisions within the team, which improves flow and puts decision-making with people closest to the customer.

Some questions to ask when discussing this ISH are

- Does this thing provide discrete value in a well-defined sphere of execution?
- Can the team define its roadmap based on what they discover is best for the product and its users, or is the team always driven by the requirements and priorities of other teams?

It's a warning sign if a team has little or no product-decision autonomy, although the level of product-decision autonomy can vary for legitimate reasons. For supporting subdomain value streams, it can be reasonable to expect that work in core domain value streams will heavily influence their roadmap and backlog. My main concern is when the team has little say in the process and is simply told what to build. The supporting sub-domain team should be involved in the discovery and design process and have the final decision on any work in their value stream. They should understand why work is important and want to do it because it is the right thing for the product, not just because they are being ordered to build something by others outside the team.

ISH: TEAMS (COGNITIVE LOAD)

Cognitive load is a fundamental concept in Team Topologies and is explicitly called out in the *teams* ISH. When assessing a candidate value stream, you should consider everything the team is responsible for to measure their total cognitive load, not just the particular value stream being assessed.

Some questions to ask when discussing this ISH are

- Would the cognitive load (breadth of topics/context switching) be bounded to help the team focus and succeed? Does the team have a defined list of responsibilities, and are they realistically manageable considering the costs of context switching?
- Would significant infrastructure or other platform abstractions be needed? In other words, would a lot of the team's capacity be taken up with infrastructure work or extraneous work that isn't connected to their core mission?

These questions touch on the different types of cognitive load a team may face to ensure their full cognitive load is considered. If either of these questions raises alarm bells, a number of actions are available, like adjusting domain boundaries, reducing roadmap expectations, and pushing complexity out of the team into platforms. Team Topologies also provides a cognitive load assessment questionnaire on its GitHub page (http://mng.bz/mjBy).

ISH: COST TRACKING

The *cost tracking* ISH helps identify how easily the costs and ROI of a value stream can be isolated. The more distinguishable the costs to run a value stream and the value produced, the more independently the value stream can be treated. When costs and ROI are hard to distinguish in isolation, there will be investment risks, such as not understanding if the value stream is delivering an acceptable ROI. It may put the team under pressure if their contributions are not distinguishable—a common problem for teams that work on platforms.

Some questions to ask when discussing this ISH are

- Are the full costs of running this thing transparent or possible to discover? Consider infrastructure costs, data storage costs, data transfer costs, license costs, etc.
- Does the organization track this separately?

In large organizations with internal platforms consumed only by other internal teams, it's not always possible to ascertain the precise ROI of a value stream. This isn't a reason not to proceed with the value stream, but it does need to be fully understood by all involved to ensure the team's work is appreciated and they aren't negatively affected further down the line. There are ways to measure the value of internal platforms through metrics and internal customer surveys. The point of this ISH is to ensure that these things have been thought of in advance so that measures can be put in place.

ISH: DEPENDENCIES

Too many dependencies on other value streams prevent a value stream from becoming independent and achieving fast flow. It's always imperative to look beyond the surface for any dependencies that are not obvious but could be problematic. The *dependencies* ISH is a first line of defense by bringing together people familiar with different aspects of the value stream. Unexpected dependencies are more likely to be discovered.

Some questions to ask when discussing this ISH are

- Is the subdomain logically independent from other subdomains?
- Could the team "self-serve" dependencies in a nonblocking manner from a platform?

As discussed in previous chapters, some dependencies will always exist. This ISH is a chance to properly discuss which dependencies are acceptable or unavoidable and which are too expensive and should be removed by reshaping domain boundaries, allowing duplication to exist, or pushing responsibilities into platforms.

Talking about dependencies with a diverse group is a great start but often isn't enough in isolation. You'll see in the next chapter how techniques like domain message flow modeling can be used to design end-to-end business flows as a software architecture that uncovers dependencies between subdomains. It's also a good idea to look at the product roadmaps and map out which subdomains will need to change for each initiative.

INDUSTRY EXAMPLE: ISH FOR REGULATED E-COMMERCE

While working with Matthew Skelton and other colleagues to help a North American e-commerce market leader operating in a regulated industry kick off its modernization journey, we used ISH to assess the suitability of a candidate value stream as the first slice of modernization. After being the market leader in one market for over 10 years, the organization was establishing two new verticals as it became a multiproduct company. They had been market leaders in the existing vertical for the past decade and saw only marginal future growth opportunities. The two new verticals presented significant growth opportunities, one in particular that was earmarked to grow company revenue by three to five times if executed successfully.

The organization wanted to explore benefitting from commonality across multiple verticals to reduce operating costs and improve time-to-market, so the candidate value stream was a horizontal that would potentially support all three verticals. If successful, this first slice of modernization would not only deliver direct business value but also help the company build a playbook for developing other horizontals. They had never done this before, and there were many question marks around whether it would work and how it would work within the organization's unique operating context.

Figure 11.7 visualizes this challenge as a Wardley Map. Some key questions that needed to be answered were as follows: Could three verticals at different stages of evolution really be satisfied by a single horizontal? Would there be any clashes or mismatches due to the varying characteristics of each vertical? Could the horizontal team become a bottleneck? And where exactly should the boundaries be drawn between the verticals and the horizontal, considering there were high levels of product, domain, software, and operational complexity?

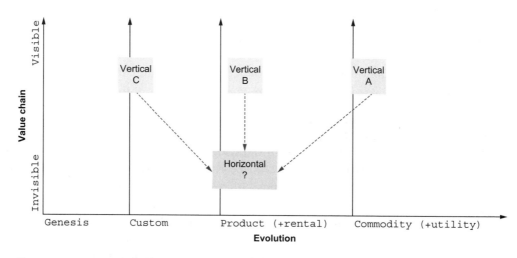

Figure 11.7   Could a single horizontal support three diverse verticals?

Initially, we ran discovery and modeling workshops with techniques like EventStorming to sketch out domain and technical boundaries. We then applied ISH to understand the organizational implications. From a value proposition perspective, everything looked good: it was easy to imagine the platform as a completely separate product. There were discussions that one day maybe it could be externalized.

From an organizational perspective, however, there were some thumbs down. Most notably, the team would have no dedicated budget. They would be funded exclusively by verticals, and their roadmap would be highly constrained to build only what verticals were willing to pay for. The team was not empowered to make product decisions that they believed were best aligned with the company's long-term interests. Further, the existing capability was formed of multiple legacy systems and only had a team of three engineers working on it, meaning the cognitive load would be far too high.

You might be surprised to hear that the organization decided to proceed with the initiative, which reinforces a key point: a red flag doesn't mean you can't proceed. It means you need to be aware of the problem and understand how you will deal with it. Some problems, especially cultural ones, can take a long time to address, so it's better to get started and chip away at the problem as you go rather than not starting at all. Being pragmatic is a necessity for architecture modernization, although it shouldn't be used as an excuse to avoid addressing the hard problems.

The most important thing for modernization leaders is that concerns like these are identified early when there is still time to act on them, and the cost of doing so is cheapest. Bringing together diverse stakeholders who each understand different aspects of the proposed value stream and using ISH as a checklist to structure conversations and activities is a good approach for covering the organizational aspects of the value stream.

> **NOTE** You can learn more about this case study and ISH in general by checking out a joint talk (https://bit.ly/ms-nt-ish) delivered by Matthew Skelton and me at the Domain-Driven Design Europe 2022 conference.

11.3.2 Mandate levels

When discussing independent value streams, it's easy to use words like autonomy and empowerment ambiguously. John Cutler's mandate levels (http://mng.bz/5oaZ) is an excellent technique for assessing the independence of a value stream with a precise and structured definition of autonomy. It enables you to have clear and productive conversations covering the nuances of the topic so that you can more deeply assess your candidate value stream and avoid missing important details.

There are nine mandate levels, from level A to level I, which can vary from team to team, as shown in figure 11.8. Each mandate level represents a level of work, starting

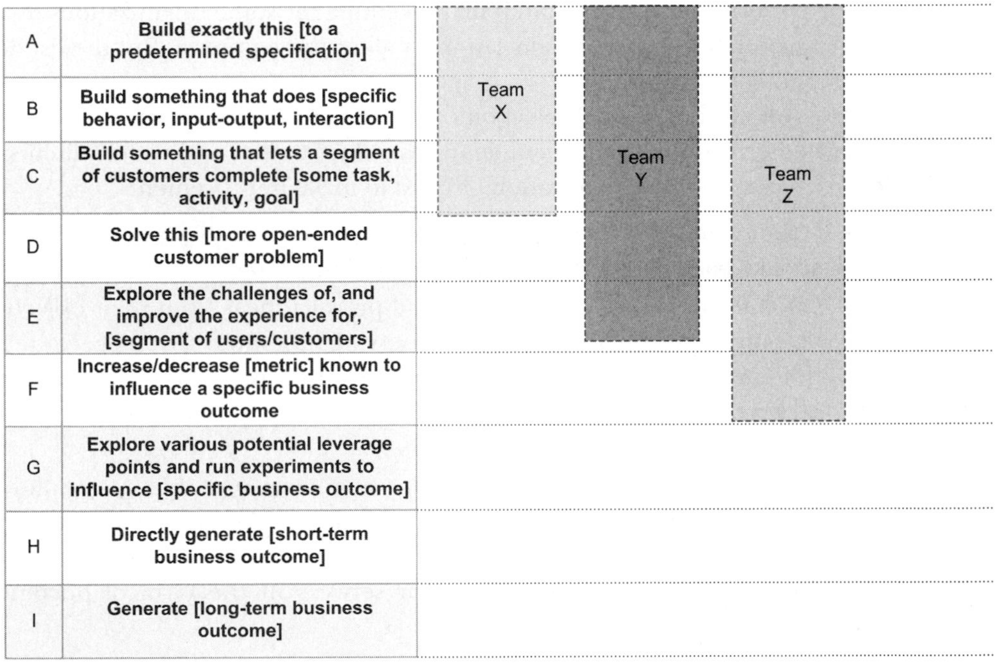

A	**Build exactly this [to a predetermined specification]**	Team X		
B	**Build something that does [specific behavior, input-output, interaction]**	Team X		
C	**Build something that lets a segment of customers complete [some task, activity, goal]**		Team Y	Team Z
D	**Solve this [more open-ended customer problem]**		Team Y	Team Z
E	**Explore the challenges of, and improve the experience for, [segment of users/customers]**		Team Y	Team Z
F	**Increase/decrease [metric] known to influence a specific business outcome**			Team Z
G	**Explore various potential leverage points and run experiments to influence [specific business outcome]**			
H	**Directly generate [short-term business outcome]**			
I	**Generate [long-term business outcome]**			

Figure 11.8 Different teams may have different mandate levels.

from highly specific to highly general. Level A is the most specific: "Build exactly this [to a predetermined specification]." A team with only a mandate at level A has extremely low autonomy because they are told exactly what to build. Many of the decisions affecting their work are made outside of the value stream; therefore, it is not independent at all. Level I is the most general: "Generate [long-term business outcome]." A team with this mandate up to level I is, therefore, empowered to make almost every decision affecting the work they choose to do, so the value stream will be highly independent.

There isn't a specific mandate level that is optimal for all value streams. It's okay for different teams to have different levels. However, in most cases, value streams not going beyond level C (like Team X in figure 11.8) would make me concerned that the team lacks autonomy, which is likely to affect the product quality and the flow.

Even when a team has a greater mandate level, there is no guarantee their value stream will be independent. They are empowered to make decisions, but that doesn't prevent dependencies across multiple value streams from arising when a new product feature requires changes to multiple subdomains. Mandate levels address a key chunk of autonomy, but it doesn't tell the whole story of how independent a value stream is.

11.3.3   *Good product team/bad product team*

Another checklist-like tool for assessing the organizational aspects of a value stream is Marty Cagan's list of characteristics that differentiate good and bad product teams (http://mng.bz/6nQZ). There are 19 criteria in the list. Not every criterion will apply to all types of teams equally, and it may take time for some organizations to achieve a level of maturity where any team can meet all of these criteria. But the list does serve as a general benchmark.

The following is a small selection of Marty's criteria. For each of the criteria, discuss whether it would be achievable in the value stream, and if not, discuss whether you are happy with the justification or need to make improvements.

- Good teams have a compelling product vision that they pursue with a missionary-like passion. Bad teams are mercenaries.
- Good teams get their inspiration and product ideas from their objectives (e.g., objectives and key results), from observing customers' struggle, from analyzing the data customers generate from using their products, and from constantly seeking to apply new technology to solve real problems. Bad teams gather requirements from sales and customers.
- Good teams have product, design, and engineering sit side-by-side and embrace the give and take between the functionality, the user experience, and the enabling technology. Bad teams sit in their respective functional areas and ask that others make requests for their services in the form of documents and scheduling meetings.
- Good teams ensure that their engineers have time to try out the discovery prototypes every day so that they can contribute their thoughts on how to make the

product better. Bad teams show the prototypes to the engineers during sprint planning so they can estimate.

- Good teams know that many of their favorite ideas won't end up working for customers, and even the ones that could will need several iterations to get to the point where they provide the desired outcome. Bad teams just build what's on the roadmap and are satisfied with meeting dates and ensuring quality.

11.4 Sensing and evolving team topologies

A core theme of Team Topologies is the need to sense and evolve socio-technical architecture continually. It's not a linear process that starts with designing an ideal future state and is then followed by a big reorg. It's an ongoing process with no end state. Organizations are always evolving due to internal and external pressures, so stakeholders at all levels of the org chart need to fully embrace continuous evolution.

11.4.1 Organizational sensing

Organizational sensing is about continuously scanning for clues that the existing team topology is no longer optimal and will benefit from evolution. The following are symptoms that the team topology may need to evolve. Keep in mind, though, that these symptoms could also point to other problems that don't require changing the team topology, like team practices or leadership behaviors.

- *Too much collaboration*—If multiple teams collaborate excessively, it may be due to excessive coupling in their domain concepts resulting from suboptimal domain boundaries or simply the wrong interaction mode.
- *Excessive context switching*—When a team is trying to juggle too many responsibilities, their cognitive load will be overstretched. This could result from poorly defined boundaries and interaction modes or a sign that their domain(s) has grown too large for them to manage. It could also result from the business trying to do too much work in parallel.
- *Delivery cadence is slowing down*—Deploying less frequently is another sign that the team's cognitive load has grown too high. This could be due to either their domain or infrastructure responsibilities growing or the level of cruft in their code becoming too much.
- *High delivery coordination*—If business outcomes frequently require coordinating the work of many teams, team autonomy and flow across the organization are likely to suffer. This could also indicate boundaries that no longer align well with changes occurring in the domain.

As you might be aware, the people in the teams doing the work are the people who are often closest to these types of symptoms and will notice them first. Accordingly, everybody needs to be aware of the signs of suboptimal topologies and be encouraged to speak up when they feel these pains. It's not only the job of managers and architects to sense and evolve topologies. Many people, however, aren't aware when they are feeling pain due to suboptimal topologies, as was the case with the fragrance company example. This means it's important to invest in learning opportunities to create a sensing organization that can constantly evolve rather than requiring large reorgs every few years.

11.4.2   *Industry example: Awkward interactions when becoming multiproduct*

I had the chance to work with a smaller logistics company that had successfully established a market presence with their first product and was developing a second product. Clearly, it was a positive step for the company, but also a source of additional organizational complexity because the new product depended on the first product. As shown in figure 11.9, the team responsible for the new product was in genesis mode, rapidly trying to validate the product idea. However, the existing product team was in full product mode—they had scaled to a large customer base and needed to balance stability with adding new features.

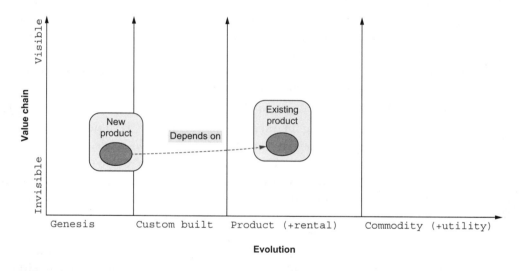

Figure 11.9   New product depends on the existing product.

The new product team asked for small tweaks and improvements daily, but the existing product team didn't have the confidence or the cognitive load to move at their pace. Both teams saw each other as a problem, and there was no quick fix to make the problem disappear. They both had ambitious targets, but the dependency meant one had to compromise. The team interaction was undoubtedly awkward, which was a sign that some aspects of the topology may require evolution.

One option for the logistics company was to evolve its boundaries, like the e-commerce example, where a platform was extracted from the first vertical and shared with multiple verticals. But reshaping boundaries and reorganizing teams isn't the solution to every awkward problem. These changes can be expensive and even exacerbate the situation if the fundamental problems remain. It makes sense to analyze the situation more closely and look for more fundamental problems.

The first fundamental concern the logistics company needed to address was the competitive dynamic between the two teams. Both teams had their own ambitious goals, but that was pulling them in separate directions when a dependency between them required closer collaboration. Leadership needed to ensure that the overall priorities were clear and where compromises were acceptable: more risk in the established product or more speed in the new product. Both teams could then be jointly responsible and jointly rewarded for collaboratively delivering the optimal overall solution.

The key takeaway is that overall company priorities should be made clear, and teams should be rewarded for their contribution, even if that means supporting another team rather than maximizing their objectives. A common problem I see is that leadership loads up teams with competing priorities and keeps pressuring all teams to deliver as much and as quickly as possible, even when there is a strong dependency between them and some compromise is needed.

There would be no awkwardness in the interaction between the two logistics teams if the old product could move at the pace required by the new product without risking the reliability of their product. As discussed earlier in the chapter, when teams are empowered and incentivized to maintain the health of their code, and they have a *you build it, you run it* operating model, moving reliability at speed is definitely achievable, which could enable both teams to get closer to their ideal outcomes. It pays to invest in the fundamental capability of continuous delivery.

> **NOTE** As Figure 11.10 shows, Wardley Mapping is a useful tool for anticipating awkward interactions that may arise. This is a good reminder of why regularly running Wardley Mapping sessions can help you identify these warning signs early and implement measures to deal with them before they become too problematic.

11.4.3 *Evolutionary patterns*

After sensing opportunities, it's important to evolve topologies most effectively. Knowing about various principles and patterns is highly beneficial. Evolution may involve reshaping boundaries, changing interaction types, or removing interactions. Just because two teams collaborate at one point in time, it doesn't mean that they should collaborate indefinitely. Team Topologies covers some evolutionary patterns, but technology leaders should be familiar with other great work in this space, especially Heidi Helfand's work on dynamic reteaming.

DISCOVER TO ESTABLISH

A common and intentional pattern of topology evolution is *discover to establish, as* shown in figure 11.10. This pattern is characterized by teams working closely together in a novel domain with the collaboration interaction mode, but as certainty increases, there is less need for collaboration, so the interaction mode becomes XaaS, or sometimes no interaction at all.

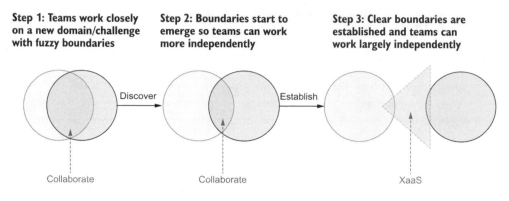

Step 1: Teams work closely on a new domain/challenge with fuzzy boundaries

Step 2: Boundaries start to emerge so teams can work more independently

Step 3: Clear boundaries are established and teams can work largely independently

Discover

Establish

Collaborate

Collaborate

XaaS

Figure 11.10   The discover to establish pattern

Discover to establish is a widespread pattern applied in all types of organizations in all contexts. It's a pervasive pattern when organizations embark on a journey to build a platform.

When I worked with a financial services organization that kicked off its modernization journey by developing its first cloud-based application, the plan was for the first stream-aligned teams to build their applications, including all of their platform needs, which would gradually be extracted out of the team's code and into a dedicated platform. During the initial phase, the platform engineers worked very closely, attending the teams' daily standups, for example. They focused on giving the teams all the support they needed to develop their serverless applications on AWS while simultaneously preparing for a future where they would own a platform that was used by many teams across the organization.

In the initial stages, they were focused heavily on helping the teams achieve their objectives and not spending too much time trying to create the platform. It was a difficult balance between short- and medium-term needs, but they got it spot on. Trying to extract a platform too early risks slowing down the teams delivering the initial slice of modernization and is likely to result in a platform design based on speculation rather than actual needs and usage patterns.

DYNAMIC RETEAMING PATTERNS

One of the misconceptions associated with Team Topologies is the idea that long-lived teams are equal to static teams, where the same people must always be working together on the same team. This is an oversimplification of a nuanced concept. Long-lived implies that a team should be stable but not necessarily static. Some flexibility of team members is more than permitted; it is encouraged to keep things fresh and adaptable as priorities and constraints shift around. It is even argued that keeping a team together for too long results in them becoming stale. Heidi Helfand is one of the leading voices in this area, and her book *Dynamic Reteaming* (2nd ed.) (http://mng.bz/orP2) is one of the leading resources. One of Heidi's catchphrases is, "Team change is inevitable. So get good at it," indicating that organizations are constantly evolving as new people are always joining and leaving.

Dynamic Reteaming includes several patterns for evolving Team Topologies and the individual members within a team. The patterns are based on the five reasons that teams need to change:

- *Growth/attrition*—Growth is a natural factor in most organizations, like when startups take on more funding and need to scale to achieve the ambitious vision of investors. Growth always has a big effect on an organization's culture. Equally, scaling down is sometimes necessary, which can also have a big effect.
- *New work or priority*—A change in strategy or investment in new growth opportunities, like entering new markets, can cause reteaming.
- *Knowledge sharing*—When there is expertise in one team that can benefit other teams, it can be a good idea to rotate people around on a temporary or permanent basis to spread the knowledge.
- *Stagnation and learning*—People's motivation can drop when their work doesn't offer new and interesting challenges, so moving them to other teams to work on different capabilities and learn new things is a good reason for change.
- *Surprise reasons*—Unexpected events that require organizational changes, like a pandemic.

The following is a sample of Heidi's reteaming patterns and how they relate to these five reasons for change:

- *Grow and split*—When teams grow too large, it's necessary to split the team into multiple smaller teams. Some signs that a team has grown too large are meetings that last too long, lots of communication within the team that is hard to keep up with, and subteams forming around distinct objectives.
- *Merging*—The opposite of grow and split is merging, where multiple teams come together to form a single team. This is one approach to dealing with dependencies, like when a dependency between two teams is so strong that it is more effective to work as a single team.
- *Isolation*—Sometimes, work needs to happen away from the organization's current culture, like when introducing new approaches. This is the isolation pattern, establishing teams that are shielded from some aspects of the organization.
- *Switching*—The switching pattern involves moving a team member from one team to another to spread knowledge and make work more interesting and varied. This is a great technique for improving retention.
- *One by one*—As new people join a team, it takes time for them to become familiar with their new teammates and vice versa. The one-by-one pattern proposes to grow teams by one person at a time so that the team and the individual can gradually adapt to the change.

I'm a believer in dynamic reteaming. Some of the best experiences in my days as a junior software engineer were when I switched to different teams for a short period. I learned a lot by pair programming with so many different people, and it made my work fresh and exciting. But there is a lot to consider, such as how often to switch and the complexity of each subdomain. Each person is unique, with their own preferences, so it is best to experiment carefully and gradually and ensure the people involved are included in the decision-making process and given a chance to share their feedback.

When switching is involved, I'm often asked about estimates. Some organizations use story points to measure team productivity, like the predictability of delivering a fixed amount of story points per sprint, but this isn't possible when people move around and cause their team's output to be inconsistent. I've never worked in teams that use story points or similar estimation techniques, so I'm unable to answer that question from experience. My advice is that there are many benefits from applying dynamic reteaming, and they are too valuable to miss out on, so I recommend experimenting with ways to make the estimating technique flexible enough to support these approaches in your unique context.

INDUSTRY EXAMPLE: MONTHLY SWITCHING AT GROCERY CHAIN

In 2018, I saw an effective use of dynamic reteaming at a large grocery chain in one of their domains (scope 2), which was composed of four teams, each owning a subdomain within the domain. Every month, one person would rotate from each team into another team (within the domain), as shown in figure 11.11. This way, everybody would know the whole domain and would be able to contribute to any codebase in the domain. The arrangement resulted in four teams who thought about work collectively and built good social relationships as if they were a single team.

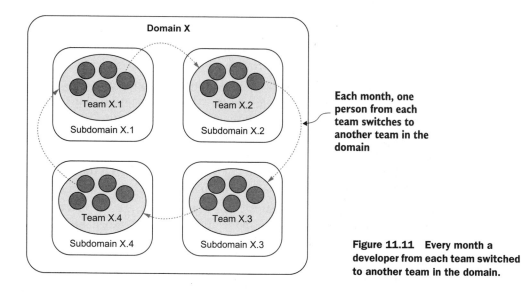

Figure 11.11 Every month a developer from each team switched to another team in the domain.

Another benefit to this approach was that when anybody left the team, no knowledge was lost. Due to the monthly rotation and practices like pair programming, knowledge sharing was extremely high. This was important because the team was approximately 50:50 full-time employees and contractors, resulting in relatively high staff turnover. Their commitment to knowledge sharing helped to minimize the costs of onboarding and rolling off team members.

Overall, my observations were very positive, and I was genuinely impressed. Each team worked well, and overall, the teams worked well together. People from all four teams would often go for lunch together, and the teams had regular shared rituals like planning which had a very positive ambiance. I have since encouraged other organizations to experiment with this pattern, and I wholeheartedly encourage you to as well.

11.5 Team grouping patterns

Teams that work on related challenges like the same domain, area of a product, or platform will generally need to have some communication bandwidth in order to coordinate their work and design the optimal end-to-end solution for customers. Chapter 9 looked at various heuristics for grouping subdomains into domains as a way to determine which teams should be grouped together, like *group subdomains into product-focused domains, group subdomains into horizontal domains*, and *group subdomains into process-focused domains*.

When considering how to group teams, it's also important to think about the skills within a team. For example, will teams be responsible for both the user interface and the backend domain logic and data, or will there be separate backend and frontend teams? There is no globally correct solution here. Some teams enjoy being frontend and backend specialists and want to continue working that way, and sometimes a backend is consumed by multiple frontend applications, so it's not feasible for them to own all of the UI.

When there is a high level of co-change between domain logic and the parts of the UI that expose those domain concepts, it may be beneficial to have teams that own both the UI and backend components. A domain will then be composed of multiple teams that each own the UI and backend for a specific subdomain(s), as shown in figure 11.12.

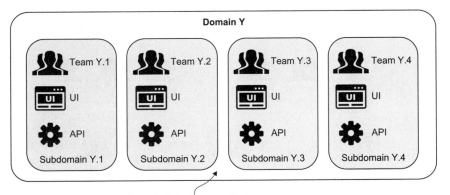

Domain Y is composed of
4 teams who each own all
of the UI and API code for
a single subdomain.

Figure 11.12 Domain composed of multiple front-back teams

Alternatively, if the different parts of the UI change together often, it may make sense to have one frontend team that owns the entire frontend for the domain alongside multiple backends, as shown in figure 11.13. With this grouping, it may be possible to have slightly larger subdomains because the backend teams will not be using up some of their cognitive load dealing with parts of the UI.

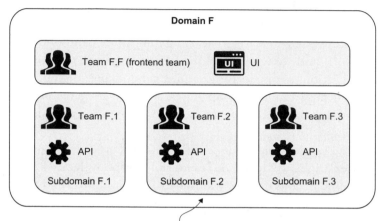

Domain F is composed of 4 teams who each own either frontend or backend code.

Figure 11.13   Domain composed of dedicated frontend and backend teams

A very common pattern is when the frontend and backend are totally separated. Multiple teams who each own a part of a frontend will be grouped together—such as the web team and the mobile team. Domain groups are then composed of teams who own backend logic only for their subdomains, as shown in figure 11.14.

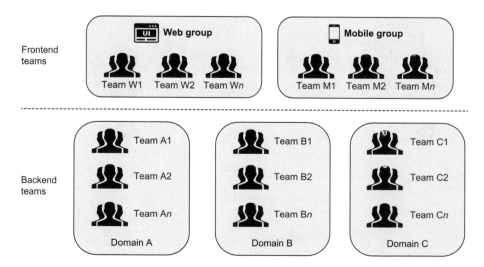

Figure 11.14   Dedicated frontend and backend groups

With this pattern, all of the people working on the frontend sit together so they can optimize the end-to-user experience and make it more consistent. However, the distance between frontend and backend teams is greater, which often blocks flow because collaboration between the teams is less fluid.

In my experience, all of these patterns are common, and there are many nuanced variations of them, too. There is definitely no perfect solution. While some domains and products are more suited to some patterns, it's also a very personal choice based on people's career aspirations and how they prefer to work. Remember, the purpose is to find the optimal balance of BVSSH (Better Value Sooner Safer Happier). But I will say that I have seen situations where people were reluctant to let go of a frontend/backend split (they wanted to remain silos) even though it resulted in too many dependencies and poor communication. Personal choice doesn't overrule other factors; reducing dependencies and improving flow is equally important.

While each of the patterns will likely involve some form of dependencies between teams, each team should still have the autonomy to deploy their technical artifacts in isolation—for example, a frontend team should be able to deploy the frontend independently of backend APIs and vice versa. This is achieved by designing loosely coupled architectural subsystems with contract coupling (covered in the next chapter). These can still be considered independent value streams if they represent the optimal socio-technical architecture with the least coupling pain.

NOTE The topic of dedicated frontend and backend teams versus full-stack teams has been hotly debated for a long time. There are many pros and cons on either side. If this is something that feels relevant to you, it's definitely worth digging deeper into the topic and getting more opinions. A conversation on LinkedIn started by Yan Cui provides a variety of perspectives (http://mng.bz/n1Pe).

Summary

- Jointly optimizing organization and software architecture is necessary to achieve fast flow.
- Poorly aligned team and software boundaries can result in shared resources, like teams working in the same parts of the code, which causes more expensive and riskier changes.
- Team Topologies is a socio-technical toolkit for organizing teams around independent value streams with fast flow.
- Fast flow should be sustainable, meaning it can be continued over many years. This requires an investment in technical practices and a good engineering culture.
- Teams should generally contain five to nine people to enable a high level of trust and avoid information overload.
- Teams should be long-lived so that they can become experts within their subdomain, contribute new product ideas, and are incentivized to work sustainably and keep code healthy.

- Software developers should not be seen as resources that are partially allocated to multiple streams of work. This has high context switching and doesn't create conditions for people to do their best work.
- Standardized processes and ways of working stifle teams and prevent continuous improvement.
- Team Topologies encourages a team-first approach, where the team decides who will work on each task and how they will work.
- *You build it, you run it* is an approach where teams are responsible for supporting their code in production. It can improve flow by reducing handovers and incentivizing teams to build more reliable software.
- Team cognitive load needs to be carefully managed. When cognitive load is too high, a team's velocity and quality can drop, and there is a risk of burnout.
- Good domain boundaries minimize cognitive load by reducing the scope of a team's responsibilities to a manageable level.
- Overlaying team boundaries onto a Core Domain Chart can indicate where cognitive load may be too high, like a team responsible for multiple highly complex subdomains.
- There are three types of cognitive load in the model used by Team Topologies:
  - *Intrinsic*—The inherent difficulty of a task
  - *Extraneous*—Additional complexity added by the environment
  - *Germane*—The effort to learn a concept
- Conway's law implies that the communication structures in an organization will influence the design of a software architecture.
- Implications of Conway's law are ubiquitous, and the concept should always be kept in mind when architecting systems.
- There are four team types in Team Topologies:
  - *Stream-aligned teams*—Own a stream of work that contributes to the product
  - *Platform groupings*—A group of teams owing shared capabilities that empower stream-aligned teams and reduce their cognitive load
  - *Complicated subsystem teams*—Own a complex part of the system that requires specialist knowledge
  - *Enabling teams*—Support the growth of other teams
- Three interaction modes exist in Team Topologies:
  - *Collaborating*—Two teams working toward a shared goal
  - *X-as-a-service*—One team consumes the capabilities of another
  - *Facilitating*—One team helps another
- Collaboration has a high-cognitive load, so it should be applied carefully. More collaboration is not always a good thing.
- The Team Topologies patterns alone will have little benefit if they are not applied in combination with the principles.

- Independent service heuristics is a checklist of heuristics that can be used to assess the level of independence of a candidate or existing value stream.
- There are 10 ISH heuristics covering value, product decisions, dependencies, and more.
- ISH should serve to structure conversation for a diverse group of stakeholders, not as a tick-box exercise for a lone architect-type person.
- John Cutler's mandate levels consist of a structured model of a team's autonomy over their work and can be used to assess the independence of a value stream.
- Team Topologies are in a constant state of flux because organizations are always evolving.
- Teams should continually be sensing awkward interactions and signs that the topology should evolve, like excessive collaboration or a reduction in delivery cadence.
- Discover to establish is a pattern that starts with two teams working closely using collaboration mode and then gradually drifting apart to XaaS as boundaries and responsibilities become clearer.
- Dynamic reteaming is a series of principles and patterns documented by Heidi Helfand that concern the fluidity of teams and Team Topologies.
- Dynamic reteaming defines five reasons for reteaming: growth/attrition, new work or priorities, knowledge sharing, stagnation and learning, and surprise reasons.
- There are five patterns for reteaming: grow and split, merging, isolation, switching, and one by one.
- The principles and patterns of Team Topologies and dynamic reteaming also exist at the group level.
- Teams can be grouped into different topologies, such as dedicated frontend and backend teams or groups of teams that are responsible for both the frontend and backend parts of a subdomain.
- Choosing the appropriate grouping of teams involves analyzing the product, domain, organization, and preferences of the people involved.

Loosely coupled
software architecture

12

This chapter covers

- Minimizing coupling in software architecture
- Designing software architecture aligned to the domain
- Validating the design of individual subsystems
- Determining the optimal level of modernization for each subsystem
- Migrating subsystems from the current to the target state

Achieving independent value streams in software development requires a loosely coupled software architecture. Loose coupling in the software means lower change coupling across value streams, resulting in few organizational dependencies that affect flow. For some leaders, grasping the importance of loosely coupled architecture takes time. But there are no quick fixes to address the technical requirements of fast flow; doing the hard work of confronting the legacy systems cannot be avoided.

The first step to a loosely coupled software architecture is grasping a deeper understanding of loose coupling. Even engineers can struggle with this somewhat nebulous idea, as there are no established standards for describing coupling in

270

software. However, there have been attempts to develop models for describing coupling. This chapter introduces Vlad Khononov's modern approach.

Designing a loosely coupled software architecture involves aligning software subsystems with the target subdomains. Feedback from the design and implementation of the software may also flow in the opposite direction, prompting refinement of the domain boundaries and team structure. This chapter presents various techniques for designing software architecture driven by the domain.

> ### Subsystems
>
> This chapter uses the term *subsystem* to refer to a part of software architecture. A subsystem could be a microservice, a module in a monolith, or possibly something else.
>
> Most concepts in the chapter apply similarly to both forms unless stated otherwise. The ideal scenario is for subsystems to be aligned to optimal subdomains, but this will not always be the case when referring to subsystems in a legacy system.

Modernization involves more than just designing a target state for each subsystem. It also requires determining the extent to which each subsystem should be modernized and devising a strategy for migrating from the current to the target state—a task that is often considered to be the most challenging. A thorough understanding of the complexity of the current state is critical to determining the optimal modernization return on investment (ROI) and migration approach for each subsystem. This chapter provides guidance and recommended resources for navigating this intricate aspect of modernization (see figure 12.1).

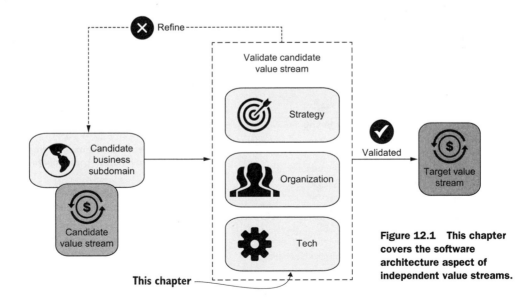

Figure 12.1   This chapter covers the software architecture aspect of independent value streams.

The next chapter delves into another technical aspect of modernization, *internal developer platforms*, which are also vital to flow by enabling teams to make changes to the architecture frequently and rapidly.

12.1   *Coupling types and strength*

Designing a loosely coupled software architecture requires careful consideration of trade-offs. A thorough understanding of the different types of coupling and their intricacies is crucial in making informed architectural decisions. Although various approaches have been proposed over the years for describing the different types of coupling in software systems, none have gained widespread acceptance.

Fortunately, Vlad Khononov, an experienced architect, has conducted extensive research on the classical approaches and developed a modern classification that builds upon previous works while adapting them to contemporary settings. Vlad identifies four types of coupling, arranged according to *integration strength*, which indicates the degree to which one component knows about another.

> ### Knowing about other components
>
> Vlad uses the terminology *knows about* to describe the level of coupling between two components. This is more of a metaphor rather than implying a component is able to think and reason. It represents how much information about one component can be found inside the other component.
>
> For instance, if you look inside the codebase for component A, what can you learn about component B—its public interface, database persistence format, private methods, etc.? Because component A *knows* those things, it might break if they are changed in component B.

Figure 12.2 illustrates the types of coupling in order of increasing *integration strength*, with stronger coupling leading to a higher likelihood of cascading changes and, therefore, changes are riskier.

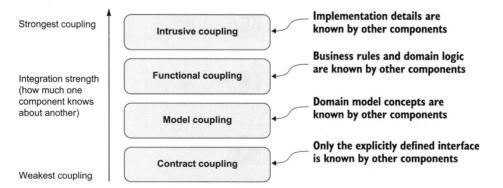

Figure 12.2   Vlad Khononov's coupling types

In Vlad's model, the strongest form of coupling is *intrusive coupling*. As shown in figure 12.3, this type of coupling is where one component knows potentially everything about the other, making every change risky.

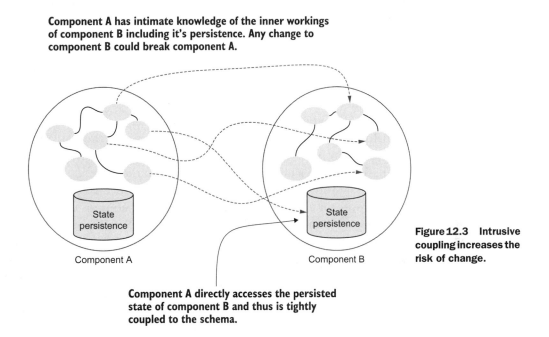

Component A has intimate knowledge of the inner workings of component B including it's persistence. Any change to component B could break component A.

State persistence

State persistence

Component A

Component B

Figure 12.3 Intrusive coupling increases the risk of change.

Component A directly accesses the persisted state of component B and thus is tightly coupled to the schema.

In concrete terms, intrusive coupling takes various forms, like accessing private methods via reflection and directly accessing persisted state or shared code. An extreme example of shared code is the *god class*, a large class in the software that combines and tightly couples disparate logic from multiple subdomains.

Unencapsulated persistence is a common form of intrusive coupling at an architectural level. A subsystem can easily break other subsystems unknowingly just by changing the format in which its state is persisted.

What is a component?

In Vlad's model, the word *component* is used in the general sense to mean a part of a software system. It could refer to a function, a class, a microservice, or even an entire system. It depends on your level of analysis (e.g., analyzing a system of microservices versus analysis classes in the same code module).

In other contexts, the word *component* has more specific definitions. In this chapter, components are architectural subsystems like microservices or modules in a monolith.

Functional coupling is weaker and less fragile than intrusive coupling, although it can still be highly problematic. It's where components need to change together even though there isn't a visible connection like an API call or shared code. A common manifestation is the same business rules duplicated in different components needing to be updated at the same time. I worked on one system where different user interfaces were showing different prices. It turned out that the logic for calculating prices and discounts had been duplicated in three or four components (one of those places was JavaScript embedded in HTML). When the developers made changes to introduce special discount pricing, they weren't aware that it had to be changed in all of those places.

Model coupling is a weaker form of coupling, but the consequences can still be significant under certain conditions. This form of coupling arises when one component is aware of the domain model of another, like the names of concepts, their structure, and the relationships between them. At Salesforce, for example, the domain model of an advertising subsystem was copied from Facebook's marketing API. Initially, this decision was beneficial, as it facilitated optimal time-to-market.

Looking at the Salesforce code and understanding how it is related to Facebook was easy. However, over time, Facebook introduced new versions of its marketing API with completely revised domain models. As a result, the Salesforce domain model failed to keep pace with these changes, resulting in difficulties in understanding how the Salesforce code correlated with the Facebook domain model. This situation made learning the codebase and making changes more challenging and time-consuming.

Contract coupling is the weakest form of coupling (other than no coupling). This form of coupling relies on two components integrating via explicitly defined interfaces with no knowledge of anything that sits behind the interface. Contract coupling is the sensible default when designing loosely coupled subsystems, whether microservices or modules in a monolith. With this form of coupling, anything internal to the subsystem behind its interface can be changed more confidently and rapidly. As long as the contract is not broken, the change is safe, as shown in figure 12.4.

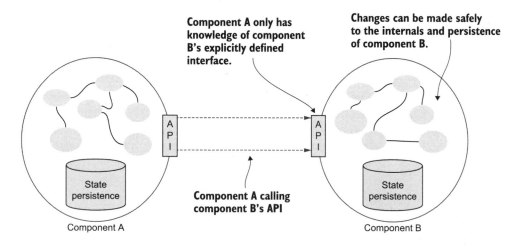

Figure 12.4   Contract coupling is the weakest form of coupling, resulting in safer changes.

While internal changes are generally low risk and faster to implement, changes to the contract of a subsystem need to be performed much more carefully. Versioning may even be necessary. As a result, it's critical to design interfaces studiously. Anything exposed via the contract has a higher cost of change than internal details, so good design only exposes what is required to avoid unnecessary coupling. The techniques in the remainder of the chapter cover this in more detail.

The forms of coupling aren't exclusive. Two components might, for example, be coupled via an explicit interface yet still have functional coupling as well. If making an assessment, such as determining how much investment is needed to modernize (covered later in the chapter), the safe option is to specify the strongest form of coupling to avoid underestimating the effort and risk involved.

As introduced in chapter 9, Vlad's model for assessing the coupling between two parts is *Pain = Strength * Volatility * Distance*. When two concepts are coupled but have low volatility due to rarely changing together, the overall pain of the coupling is likely to be low, even if the two parts have intrusive coupling. Remember that volatility is not just how often things changed in the past, it is how often they could change in the future, so understanding the product direction is essential for determining volatility.

Distance represents the level of socio-technical coordination required to implement a change. Chapter 9 touched on the social aspect with the example of a greater distance between teams who report to different managers and are located in different offices. Technically, distance starts with lines of code. Two variables in a 10-line function have a very low distance. Two classes in the same codebase is a greater distance, whereas two classes in separate microservices would be an even greater distance, potentially being in separate codebases and integrating over the network at runtime. A change at this distance could require coordinated changes and deployments in two codebases involving two teams, much greater coordination than a single team changing a few lines of code in a single function.

NOTE This chapter touches on some of the key concepts in Vlad's work on coupling and complexity. However, Vlad's work goes much deeper. You can learn more in his book *Balancing Coupling in Software Design: Successful Software Architecture in General and Distributed Systems* (Addison-Wesley Signature Series [Vernon]).

12.1.1 Local versus global complexity

When architecting a system, it's important to be aware of the effect of size on coupling. In the early microservice days, it wasn't uncommon to hear cliches like "Every microservice should be 100 lines of code or fewer. Then they are straightforward to understand and change and can even be thrown away and rewritten easily." While there is some truth to the idea that smaller means simpler, it's only half the story. For this reason, Vlad also articulates the importance of balancing *local complexity* and global complexity (http://mng.bz/Xq0E).

Limiting the size of a microservice to 100 lines of code will make the microservice simpler and easier to understand compared to a 10k lines of code microservice.

However, the logic and complexity of those other 9.9k lines don't just magically disappear. They're just somewhere else—possibly spread across hundreds of microservices. This means that the system as a whole is more complex. In other words, the global complexity is higher due to more interactions between each microservice, as shown in figure 12.5. Furthermore, because each microservice communicates over the network, the complexity could be far more expensive than a single monolithic application (the network increases the distance, which increases pain through the lens of Vlad's model).

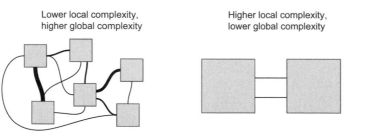

Figure 12.5   Balancing local and global complexity

Finding the perfect balance between local and global complexity is hard to achieve in constantly evolving systems. The best mindset is to ensure all engineers and architects working on the system understand the different types of coupling and complexity and their trade-offs. This will ensure they make good design decisions and can spot when a design has drifted too far from the optimal. The techniques in the following sections are useful for exploring different aspects of architectural design and finding the optimal balance.

12.2   Modeling architectural flows

One of the best ways to identify coupling in an architecture design is to map out flows. These are sequences of interactions between multiple subsystems collaborating as part of an end-to-end use case or process. The interactions between subsystems are coupling. Once the coupling has been visualized, you can assess it and explore alternative designs that may have lower or less harmful coupling.

12.2.1   Model exploration whirlpool

My recommendation for effectively navigating the design process is Eric Evans's model, exploration whirlpool (https://www.domainlanguage.com/ddd/whirlpool/) —a valuable tool for uncovering coupling in a design by continuously challenging it with concrete scenarios. This iterative design process—which can be applied at different scopes, from designing the domain model of an individual subdomain to architecting the model of multiple subdomains interacting to fulfill an end-to-end flow—emphasizes the importance of working through concrete scenarios, as shown in figure 12.6.

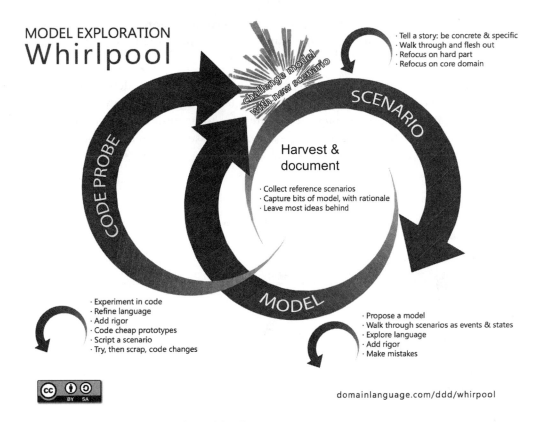

MODEL EXPLORATION
Whirlpool

challenge model with new scenario

SCENARIO

· Tell a story: be concrete & specific
· Walk through and flesh out
· Refocus on hard part
· Refocus on core domain

CODE PROBE

Harvest & document

· Collect reference scenarios
· Capture bits of model, with rationale
· Leave most ideas behind

MODEL

· Experiment in code
· Refine language
· Add rigor
· Code cheap prototypes
· Script a scenario
· Try, then scrap, code changes

· Propose a model
· Walk through scenarios as events & states
· Explore language
· Add rigor
· Make mistakes

domainlanguage.com/ddd/whirlpool

Figure 12.6 The model exploration whirlpool

By repeatedly working through concrete scenarios, key details are less likely to be missed, which is a common risk when staying high-level and abstract. In fact, the whirlpool encourages going even deeper into the details where necessary by creating code spikes to verify that the conceptual model will be effective when implemented.

To implement the various steps of the whirlpool, you can use whichever techniques you feel are most relevant in your context. In the next section, we'll explore how big picture EventStorming can be used as a source for the reference scenarios, while Domain Message Flow Modeling can be utilized to model the architectural flows aligned to the domain. Additionally, later in the chapter, we'll see how software design EventStorming can be used to go a level deeper, fulfilling a similar purpose to a code probe.

12.2.2 *Domain Message Flow Modeling*

Domain Message Flow Modeling (http://mng.bz/yZre) is one technique for designing and visualizing high-level domain flows involving multiple subdomains. As a result, it can be used to design or uncover the coupling between the architectural subsystems that represent each subdomain. This technique makes it easy to explore and iterate on architectural models.

NOTE You can find interactive and full-color versions of all the diagrams in this chapter on the book's Miro board (http://mng.bz/amwX) along with links to all of the techniques mentioned.

The recommended notation for Domain Message Flow Modeling, illustrated in figure 12.7, is centered around the domain while also aligning closely with the implementation. As a result, it enables the architecture to be designed based on domain-specific vocabulary while also providing a reasonable assurance that a well-designed system on paper will translate into an effective architecture in reality.

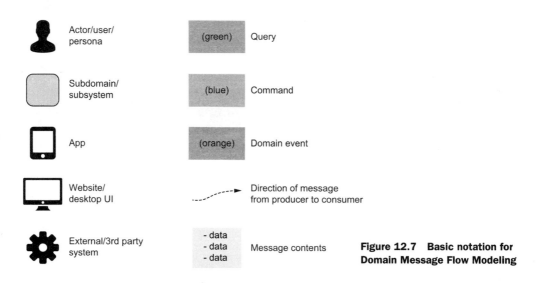

Figure 12.7   **Basic notation for Domain Message Flow Modeling**

Observing the whirlpool, we must first collect reference scenarios. Figure 12.8 shows a scenario extracted from a big picture EventStorming session. This is a simplified, theoretical example of an online car dealership. The scenario is Winning a Car at an Auction. Figure 12.8 shows the first seven domain events of the scenario, which begin with the acquisition crew inspecting a car and end with the system recommending that the car be purchased.

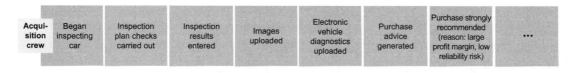

Figure 12.8   **Extracting scenarios from big picture EventStorming**

I prefer to model message flows step by step. I walk through each domain event in order and design the part of the architecture needed to enable the event to happen. However, before getting started, there is a crucial modeling principle to understand: strive to create a design that best fits the business needs rather than trying to model the real world too closely. In simple terms, the architecture doesn't need to be a 1:1 mapping of your EventStorm (e.g., figure 12.8) or other domain artifact.

So, let's get started and see what this looks like in practice. The first event in the scenario is Began Inspecting Car. Let's imagine we ask the domain experts to walk us through this step again, and they respond, "A member of the acquisition crew will look at the inspection details on the iPad screen, like checking the paint for scratches, and start inspecting the car." If we try to boil this down to the simplest possible solution, all the software must do is show the inspection details on the iPad screen. Figure 12.9 shows that one way this can be modeled is with a query, Get Inspection Details, from the iPad app to an *inspections* subsystem.

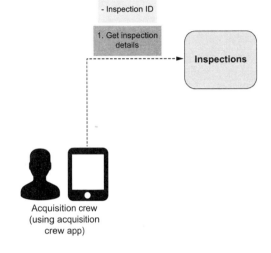

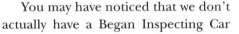

Figure 12.9   Step 1: showing inspection details

You may have noticed that we don't actually have a Began Inspecting Car event in the model. That's because it seems like no requirement depends on this being tracked in the software. But it's good to verify with domain experts by testing various requirements that may not have been considered:

Us: What if two people look at the inspection details at the same time, and they both try to inspect the same car?

DEs: Realistically, that will never happen because people know what jobs they have been assigned to well before the inspection, and we never have more than one team attending the same auction anyway.

Us: How about the time the inspection took place? Wouldn't you like to keep track of this information?

DEs: We only need to know what day it occurs, and we already have access to this. The exact hour and minute isn't something that could help us in any way.

Based on this conversation, it seems that the system does not need to track when an inspection begins. While it is a domain event that happens in the physical world, it's not needed in the software model (yet). So, we can proceed with the current model that uses only a query.

Good modelers challenge

We're already starting to see a key dynamic in healthy modeling: challenging the requirements. Good modelers don't just accept requirements at face value. In this example, we checked for new requirements that might improve the product or be needed in the future. It can also work the other way, trying to simplify, remove, or refine requirements to simplify the architecture.

The insights that emerge could significantly affect how you architect the system. Uncovering them earlier (e.g., in these design sessions) means you won't be in the position later on where you need to evolve an architecture that has been built around the wrong assumptions (e.g., realizing you do need to track when an inspection begins even though you built an architecture that assumes this will never be necessary).

Returning to the scenario in figure 12.8, we encounter the next event, Inspection Plan Checks Carried Out. Imagine that the dialogue plays out as follows between us and the domain experts:

Us: Can you talk us through this step again?

DEs: This is where the acquisition crew has looked at the inspections on the iPad screen and carried them all out, like checking the bodywork for scratches.

Us: How can the app help in this scenario? How should it process the results of the inspections?

DEs: Well, our only objective at that moment is to generate the purchase advice. But the inspection results alone aren't sufficient. We need the images and vehicle diagnostics as well. So, the inspection results alone provide no value.

Us: So what would you call that moment when those three bits of information have all been gathered, and you can generate the purchase advice with them?

DEs: We don't really have a word to describe that. But effectively, that's when the inspection is finished. Let's refer to it as Inspection Completed.

Refining the domain during design

Notice here how we've defined a new domain concept, Inspection Completed, that wasn't uncovered during EventStorming. This is an important takeaway: when designing a model, you can still change or refine the domain.

Like with requirements, it's not a one-way street. Trying to architect a system throws up new insights and perspectives that make you think more deeply and differently about the domain, leading to new ideas for improving the domain or how you reason about it.

So, with this information, how would you evolve the design in figure 12.9? You can see my solution in figure 12.10. I've again tried implementing the known requirements with the simplest possible solution. A single command, Complete Inspection, takes all the information needed to generate the purchase advice. I could have had one command representing each step (inspection results, images, vehicle diagnostics), but

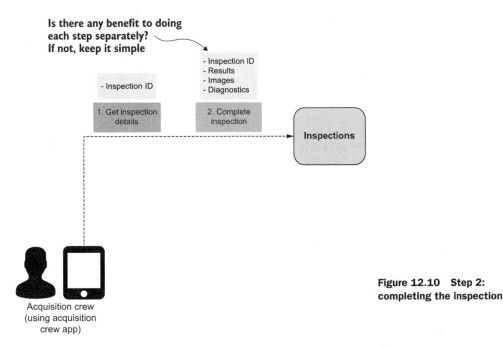

Figure 12.10   Step 2: completing the inspection

there was no requirement to do so. The requirements from the domain experts implied it was all or nothing, so there was no need for the *inspections* subsystem to keep track of incomplete information. There may be technical reasons why this solution won't work, so we could stop and create a code probe to verify, but for now we'll continue modeling this scenario.

After the inspection is completed, the system has all of the information needed to generate the purchase advice, which is the next event in the scenario. How would you evolve the model to implement this functionality?

Generating purchase advice doesn't sound like a responsibility that belongs to *inspections*. We could broaden the scope of *inspections* and rename it accordingly, or we could introduce another subsystem that deals with generating the purchase advice. The two responsibilities feel substantially different, so let's go with the latter and introduce a second subsystem called *purchasing advice*, which is a term the domain experts use to describe the general capability.

Uncovering and refining domain boundaries during design

A new subdomain, purchasing advice, has just entered the picture. This is a good example of the iterative and evolutionary nature of defining domain boundaries.

Not all subdomains will necessarily emerge in discovery sessions like EventStorming. As you begin to architect the system, you may uncover new edge cases and requirements. In turn, these may trigger you to define new subdomains or evolve existing ones. Even as you start to implement the software, new insights may cause you to rethink domain boundaries. They're never really fixed.

Following this design direction with the new *purchasing advice* subsystem, we now have to determine how the new subsystem will know when to generate the purchase advice and how it will get the information from *inspections*. The inspections subsystem could publish an event, or it could invoke a command. Figure 12.11 shows an updated model with the two possible choices for step 3.

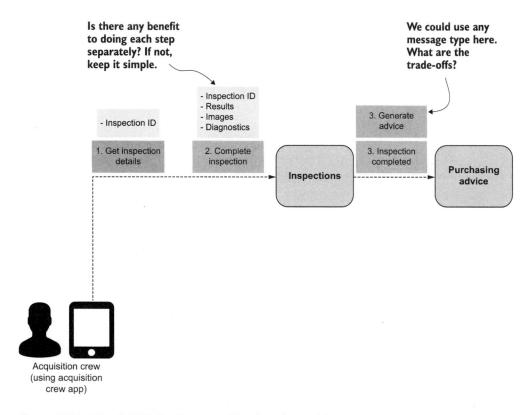

Figure 12.11   Step 3: initiating the generation of purchase advice

This discussion highlights a fundamental design concept, *decision coupling*. With a command, the sender decides what happens next. In this case, *inspections* would initiate the next step of the process by telling *purchasing advice* to Generate Advice. With an event, it's the recipient who decides. In this case, *inspections* would simply announce Inspection Completed, and then *purchasing advice*, after consuming the event, would decide that it is going to generate the purchase advice. So which is best, and how do we decide?

It's always good to play around with both options and see how each option affects the overall complexity. One benefit of events is that whenever a new subsystem needs to know about the event, the publisher of the event doesn't have to change. Let's assume that in this example, other subsystems need to know when an inspection is completed and there will be more in the future, so we'll model this step with the Inspection Completed event rather than a command.

The next step is for *purchasing advice* to generate the purchase advice. The reference scenario (figure 12.8) shows three parts to the advice—a profit margin element, a risk element, and the overall recommendation. Should purchasing advice be responsible for all three of those responsibilities, or would it be better to have multiple subsystems? Figure 12.12 shows the option where *profit margin calculation* and *risk calculation* subsystems are introduced.

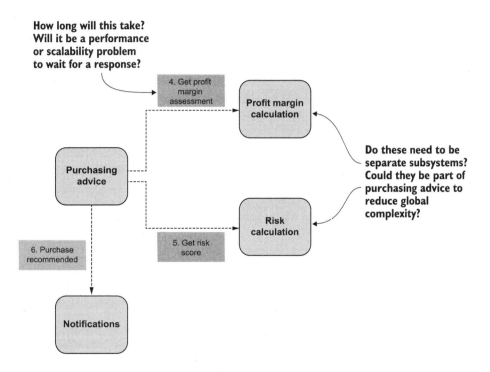

Figure 12.12   Steps 4–6: Generating the purchase advice

As always, there are multiple ways to model the communication between subsystems. Figure 12.12 explores the possibility of two queries (steps 4 and 5). After receiving both responses, *purchasing advice* will combine all the information and make an overall assessment (step 6).

But are queries a good choice here? Typically, queries are synchronous, meaning the caller waits for a response before continuing. If it takes more than a few seconds for *profit margin calculation* to produce a response, an asynchronous workflow involving events may be better for scalability and performance reasons. Synchronous communication is usually more fragile, too. If the *profit margin calculation* or *risk calculation* subsystems are experiencing downtime, *purchasing advice* cannot perform its role. Its uptime would be coupled with their uptime. This highlights a design subtlety: the design should be driven by the domain, but technical factors must be considered as well.

The decision to introduce two new subdomains in the previous step (figure 12.12) was somewhat arbitrary. My default is to start by going too granular to provoke deeper conversations about boundaries. But what if this is too granular and would result in a distributed big ball of mud? How do we get the granularity just right? By following the whirlpool: explore more scenarios to uncover more coupling and complexity at this level or get deeper into the details with a code probe (or another technique, such as software design EventStorming [covered later in the chapter], which is a step closer to code but still visual and collaborative and enables rapid experimentation).

This example finishes here, but why not continue your learning by taking a moment to try the technique yourself. You could model some flows from your domain or continue my car dealership example. There is more information on the book's Miro board. If you prefer to learn the technique collaboratively, why not instead schedule a 2-hour session with your colleagues for some time in the next few weeks?

12.2.3 *Industry example: Modernizing an accounting system*

Maxime is a consultant who specializes in DDD. He works with clients in various industries to map out domains, define boundaries, and implement domain models in code. One of his clients maintains a portfolio of products aimed at farmers, cultivators, and wine growers. They wanted to modernize their product offerings by moving from desktop-based rich clients to a SaaS model. Such a change required an extensive modernization of their fragile old systems. There wasn't an easy lift-and-shift approach, and even if there was, they needed the ability to innovate quickly, which required a faster flow of changes than the current architecture could allow.

> **NOTE** This industry example was coauthored with Maxime Sanglan-Charlier. Max has extensive experience with domain-driven design, architecture, and modern engineering practices. He is one of the most skilled facilitators I have worked with.

The company chose their accounting domain as the starting point for their modernization journey, and they hired Max to help them. Within the accounting domain, the fixed asset subdomain had been identified as the optimal starting point. So they began with big picture EventStorming sessions facilitated by Max. It helped all the stakeholders align on the same level of understanding and decide the best area to focus on for an MVP, and crucially, what could be descoped from the MVP to reduce the time-to-market. The group also started paying extra attention to their domain terminology and building their shared language.

An output from the EventStorming sessions was candidate subdomains. However, as an experienced domain modeler, Max knew that further modeling was needed: "The outcome of Big Picture Event Storming sessions was a perfect starting point to identify boundaries in the domain. Using a set of design heuristics, we quickly drew boundaries and started shaping the future architecture. But you should never consider those boundaries as the final ones! You need to refine them to gain more confidence." So Maxime organized some domain message flow modeling workshops: "That's where Domain Message Flow Modelling came in handy! This tool helped us to refine the boundaries by testing them against real use cases from our domain."

Figure 12.13 shows the message flow of the depreciation–fixed assets sales scenario. This was the first scenario involving the fixed asset subdomain that the group modeled. It involved three other subdomains and 10 messages.

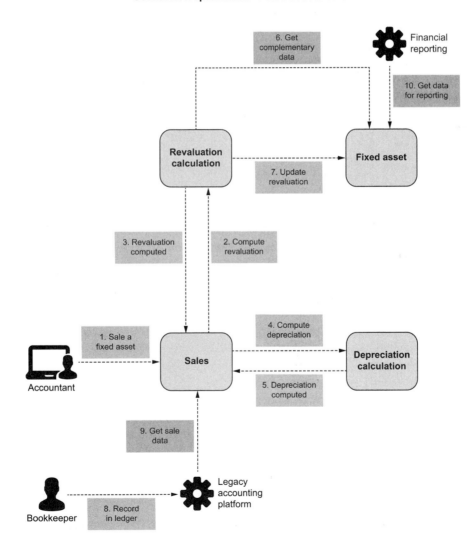

Figure 12.13   First iteration with fine-grained boundaries

Modeling the first scenario proved an important moment for the group: "Visual Collaboration Tools are powerful: just looking at this diagram, people realized that too many messages were sent to fulfill a quite common and simple scenario. This triggered a lot of interesting discussions, and one of the outcomes was that in the real world, the *revaluation* and the *sale* would always go together. So we decided to give it a try, and we joined them both into a single subdomain." This is shown in figure 12.14.

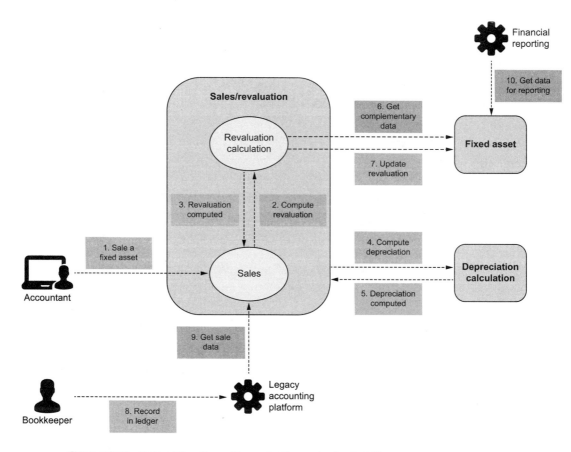

Figure 12.14   Second iteration with revaluation and sales together

Diagram messiness

Note that the diagrams in this example have been tidied and polished for physical book format. In reality, they were much messier and more organic. When using Domain Message Flow Modeling, or any technique to design, explore and refine models, don't get distracted by creating pretty diagrams and instead allow yourself to focus on modeling.

Messy diagrams are completely fine, akin to sketching out ideas on a whiteboard. You can see the original, unpolished versions of Max's diagrams on the book's Miro board (http://mng.bz/amwX).

As with most modeling endeavors, one improvement unlocked new insights to refine the model further: "People agreed that it was better like that, but then someone said that the *Sale* was actually a behavior of the *fixed asset* subdomain and that *revaluation* and *depreciation* were both computing behaviors. So a third iteration popped up where we decided to put the *sale* as a responsibility of *fixed asset,* and we created a dedicated boundary for computing tasks." Figure 12.15 shows the group's third iteration.

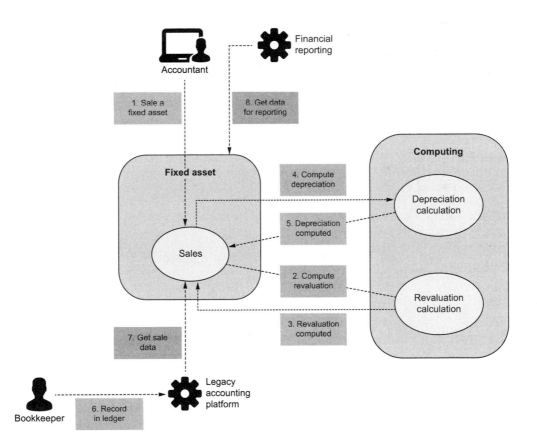

Figure 12.15   Third iteration with fixed asset and computing

As discussed earlier in the chapter, just making parts of a system smaller doesn't lead to simpler systems. Balancing local and global complexity is vital. This was something Max and the group discovered. Fewer, but larger, subsystems reduced the global complexity and the overall complexity: "The diagram looked much more simple than the first two. We increased cohesion within the boundaries. People had the feeling that everything was in the right place. We first started with four different boundaries, but in the end, we had only two left. We tend to think that the refinement cycles always lead to smaller boundaries, but sometimes it's the other way around! In this case, we started with too fine-grained boundaries that would have brought a lot of complexity if people would have started building their new architecture based on that."

Max and the group also demonstrated first-hand why concrete scenarios are a crucial aspect of Eric Evans's model exploration whirlpool: "Validation through real use cases was extremely helpful. It was pretty easy to visualize how systems communicate and identify dependencies. In general, you can easily spot design smells and try new options. It helps to better define boundaries that all the team agrees on. And on this project, it definitely resulted in lower coupling and higher cohesion."

12.3   *Individual subsystem design*

Before committing to an architecture, it is wise to conduct a review of the overall design of each subsystem. The process of examining multiple scenarios enhances the quality of the design. However, it is beneficial to consolidate the information gathered from various scenarios into a cohesive and unified view to ensure overall optimization.

In accordance with the model exploration whirlpool, it is also crucial to delve deeper into the details to gain confidence in the design's suitability. Building proof of concepts in code is one method, while software design EventStorming is another that moves close to code-level detail yet retains visualization and collaboration, enabling quicker experimentation.

12.3.1   *Using a canvas*

Canvases are a great way to visualize the overall design of a subsystem and enable greater collaboration. The bounded context canvas (https://github.com/ddd-crew/bounded-context-canvas) is one option. It's another tool from the DDD community that can be used to verify that the overall design of an individual subsystem is loosely coupled and tightly bound to the domain. The canvas comprises eight sections, each representing an important design aspect.

Figure 12.16 provides an example canvas to demonstrate each section. It shows the canvas for a *discounts* subsystem, which is a software subsystem that implements an organization's *discounts* subdomain capabilities.

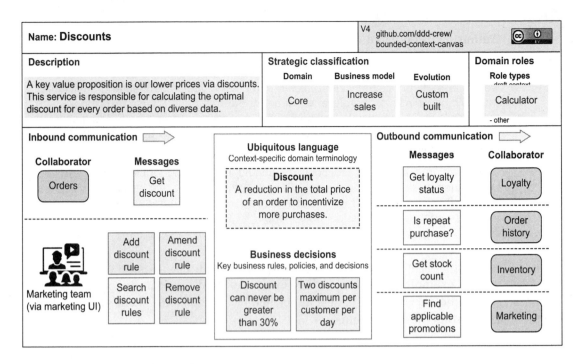

Figure 12.16 The bounded context canvas

The first section of the canvas is the *name* section. It might seem trivial, but the name of a subsystem can have a big effect on its design and evolution. Generic names attract behavior, meaning the more generic a name, the more likely it is that unrelated functionality will be lumped together. A good name is precise enough that it helps to spot when responsibilities that shouldn't belong together are being combined.

The second section of the canvas is the *description* section. This section is used to summarize the purpose and responsibilities of the canvas. Writing down a clear purpose is a great way to highlight misalignment in a group. People might agree on a name but then when each person shares their definition, inconsistencies arise. The example in figure 12.16 clearly explains in business terms the value of the *discounts* subsystem.

The third section of the canvas is *strategic classification*. How does the subsystem fit into the business strategy? There are three suggested placeholders. The first is the core, supporting, generic classification introduced in chapter 10. The second placeholder is for the subsystem's role in the business model. The *discounts* subsystem's business model role is to increase sales. Other options could be to improve productivity, increase engagement, reduce costs, or improve compliance. The third placeholder is evolution in the Wardley Mapping sense.

> ## Definition of bounded context
>
> The term *bounded context* was coined by Eric Evans in his 2003 book *Domain-Driven Design*. He defines it as "A description of a boundary (typically a subsystem, or the work of a particular team) within which a particular model is defined and applicable" (http://mng.bz/p1zw). Therefore, you'll see the terms bounded context, model, and subsystem used somewhat interchangeably in practice—for example, the discounts subsystem is the boundary (the bounded context) within which the discounts domain model is applicable.
>
> Eric advocates that bounded contexts should be loosely coupled: "Explicitly set boundaries in terms of team organization, usage within specific parts of the application, and physical manifestations such as code bases and database schemas." This is akin to contract coupling in Vlad's model.

The fourth section of the canvas is *domain roles*, which was introduced in chapter 9. Common examples are specification, execution, and analysis. But in the *discounts* example, the *calculator* role has been specified because this subsystem's main duty is to calculate something (discounts).

The fifth and sixth sections, *inbound* and *outbound communication*, visualize the interactions with other collaborators, like other subsystems and external services. This part of the canvas helps to surface important design information like the level of coupling, the number of responsibilities the subsystem has, and the design quality of the subsystem's interface. In the *discounts* example, we can immediately observe a number of queries on the outbound side. This subsystem depends on four other subsystems to be able to fulfill requests from the *orders* subsystem when it asks for a discount. We need to look closer and understand if this will result in a high level of change coupling (http://mng.bz/OPva) or runtime reliability risks.

In general, it's good to challenge every dependency. What is the pain of each dependency according to Vlad's formula, and what would be the cost to remove it? In the *discounts* example, perhaps *discounts* and *marketing* could be combined to remove one of the dependencies. It would reduce the global complexity, but would the resulting subsystem be too large and complex and result in excessive cognitive load for a single team?

The final two sections sandwiched between the inbound and outbound communication are for capturing key domain terminology and important business rules. A good exercise is to ask the group to list the top five most important domain terms and the five most important business rules. It doesn't take long, yet it can surface misalignment in the group and help to share important knowledge.

While each part of the canvas is useful in isolation, the true benefit comes when collectively looking at the whole canvas. Do all parts, like the name, description, and communication, seem cohesive? For example, do the names and messages in the communication sections align with the name and descriptions sections?

NOTE This chapter introduces a variety of techniques that enable a visual and collaborative approach to the design of architecture and software. For a deeper dive into the topic, I highly recommend the book *Collaborative Software Design* (http://mng.bz/YRxa) by Evelyn van Kelle, Gien Verschatse, and Kenny Baas-Schwegler. In addition to software and architecture design advice, it covers a range of topics, including facilitation, decision-making, and the effects of cognitive biases in the design process.

12.3.2 Software design EventStorming

Software design EventStorming (aka design-level EventStorming) is the third flavor of the technique. It introduces additional software-relevant notation and is used to model narrower scopes in finer detail. It allows a group to visualize a model that is close to the implementation in software, so it's a good way to verify a design by going a level deeper into the details. It's a great technique to use for validating proposed architectural boundaries because of the collaborative nature and the ability to explore and refine models quickly.

Figure 12.17 shows the complete notation for software design EventStorming. Compared to process modeling EventStorming, there is only a single change: the addition of the large yellow *aggregate* sticky. This concept represents a collection of objects in code that are considered to be a single atomic unit.

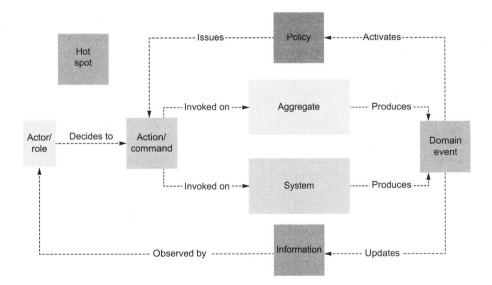

Figure 12.17   Software Design EventStorming notation

Figure 12.18 shows a small extract from the *disputes* subdomain of a utility bill provider. The bill dispute process has been modeled using software design EventStorming. It begins with a customer reviewing their latest bill and raising a dispute. When the customer performs the action, a *dispute* aggregate is the piece of code responsible for deciding what should happen.

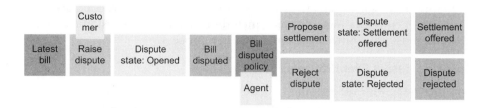

Figure 12.18   Designing the software for a utility provider's bill dispute subdomain with software design EventStorming

Usually, aggregates have multiple states, which change after operations on them. They are like state machines, so I prefer to make the states explicit. In Figure 12.18, you can see three of the *dispute* aggregate's states shown: Opened, Settlement Offered, and Rejected.

Software design EventStorming derives its name from the visual model being very close to the software implementation. Listing 12.1 shows how the visual model in figure 12.18 could be implemented as code using a traditional object-oriented approach.

Listing 12.1   Disputing aggregate pseudocode

```
class Dispute {
    DisputeStatus status
    List<DomainEvent> events

    raise(customerId, billId, message) {
        //...
        status = Opened
        events.add(new BillDisputed(...))
    }

    proposeSettlement(amount, message) {
        //...
        status = SettlementOffered
        events.add(new SettlementOffered(...))
    }

    //...
}
```

The *dispute* aggregate stickies are represented in code by a class called *Dispute*. Each blue action applied to the aggregate corresponds to a method on the aggregate—for example, *proposeSettlement()*. The state on each aggregate sticky represents the *status* field on the class, and the orange domain event stickies are implemented as separate classes—for example, *BillDisputed()*—which the *dispute* aggregate publishes (via adding instances of them to its *events* list).

> **NOTE**   For engineers seeking guidance on implementing domain models in code, check out the recommended resources on the book's Miro board (http://mng.bz/amwX).

It's important to remember that software design EventStorming isn't an exact 1:1 mapping with code. While it does help to validate that a design will work as code and can surface problems early, it doesn't compile. You may still find surprises when you start coding, and sometimes, it is better to skip software design EventStorming and go straight to code, depending on factors like the group of people, the time available, and the complexity of the subdomain. Once you have applied the technique a few times on real domains, you will be able to judge when it's appropriate to use it.

12.4   Subsystem modernization strategies

So far, this chapter has focused chiefly on the desired future architecture. If that's not hard enough, there is still the challenge of figuring out how to migrate from the current state to the target state, which is arguably even harder, having to deal with challenges like whether to run the new and old versions in parallel for a while. But that's when business value is finally delivered, so it cannot be avoided.

Before that, the optimal modernization investment strategy needs to be determined for each subsystem. You could rewrite each subsystem with new technologies, a new domain model, and new capabilities. But would the ROI be worth it? And what costs of delay would be introduced by fully modernizing every subsystem? Finding the sweet spot is crucial.

This final section of the chapter looks at principles and patterns for modernizing individual subsystems. However, looking at the bigger picture and making decisions based on a higher-level strategy and roadmap is also necessary. This is the topic of chapter 16.

12.4.1   The modernization strategy selector

During the journey of modernizing a system, choosing a modernization strategy for each subdomain is generally advisable based on its unique requirements. For instance, while a lift-and-shift approach from on-premises to the cloud may be the optimal choice for one subdomain, a complete rewrite in entirely different technologies might be ideal for core domains with a significant opportunity for differentiation. It's crucial to identify the point of diminishing returns.

Often, making fine-grained decisions may not always be feasible due to the coupling in legacy systems that are not aligned with the target subdomains. In those scenarios, a common approach is to lift and shift an entire monolith to the cloud and then apply other modernization strategies for each subdomain. This highlights that modernizing each subdomain can be a gradual progression and doesn't need to be a big bang. When determining how much to modernize each subdomain, the *Modernization Strategy*

Selector shown in figure 12.19 can help (gathering information to help choose a strategy involves concepts from previous chapters, notably chapters 5, 8, and 10).

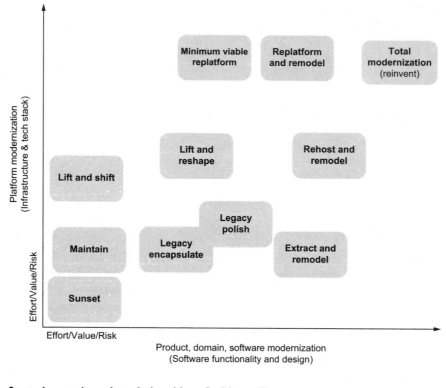

Strategies are shown in typical positions. Positions will differ on a case-by-case basis, e.g., the cost of a rewrite is sometimes less than evolving the current codebase.

Figure 12.19   The Modernization Strategy Selector (to be used per subdomain)

The x-axis represents the level of modernization applied to changing the behavior and design of the code so that it provides more value or is easier to work with, which basically consists of a range:

- *Expose*—Making existing functionality from the legacy subsystem available to other subsystems (e.g., by creating an API or publishing an event) with the least amount of effort and invasive changes possible
- *Polish*—Cleaning up some of the low-hanging technical debt without addressing more fundamental concerns
- *Replicate*—Rewriting the subsystem, maintaining the existing functionality but cleaning up all the technical debt
- *Remodel*—Rewriting the subsystem, maintaining existing functionality but investing in a complete redesign of the domain model so that it is easier to evolve

- *Rethink*—Recreating the functionality and domain model from a blank canvas, typically involving large amounts of user research and domain discovery and modeling

The y-axis represents the level of modernization applied to the technologies used to build the subsystem. It's about answering questions like: How different will the programming language, frameworks, databases, and infrastructure be in the modernized world compared to the current state?

It includes

- *Infrastructure*—e.g. from on-prem to the cloud or from VMs to Serverless
- *Programming language and runtime*—e.g. from C# .NET to Kotlin on the JVM
- *Data storage and integration*—e.g. from Oracle SQL to a MongoDB and RabbitMQ
- *Libraries and frameworks*—e.g. adopting new web frameworks, persistence frameworks, and testing frameworks

A simple option for producing an overall score is to choose high (3 points), medium (2 points), or low (1 point) for each criterion.

The following are some example strategies. This isn't an exhaustive list, so don't feel a need to try and fit what you are doing exactly into one of these:

- *Sunset*—The subsystem will be discontinued and shut down (there is no modernization, but this could still involve a large amount of effort and risk).
- *Maintain*—Try to keep the current subsystem running for the least cost. There might still be some effort involved in keeping the technologies up to date with the latest security patches, etc.
- *Legacy encapsulate*—As in the previous example, but expose the legacy capabilities to other subsystems.
- *Legacy polish*—Similar to the previous example but also addressing small amounts of technical debt.
- *Extract and remodel*—Pulling a subsystem out of the legacy system and rebuilding with a brand-new domain model (existing functionality and tech stack remain largely the same).
- *Lift and shift*—Move the current code onto new infrastructure with minimal or no changes to the application code.
- *Lift and reshape*—As in the previous example, but cleaning up some parts of the code so that new features can be added more easily, or it runs more reliably in production.
- *Rehost and remodel*—Rebuild the system with a fresh domain model and deploy to more modern infrastructure, using largely the same programming languages and frameworks.
- *Total modernization*—Every aspect of the technology, functionality, and domain model is completely modernized to the highest degree possible. It is likely to be a very expensive option but justifiable for subsystems that are a major source of

competitive advantage or innovation. In some cases, this might actually be easier than trying to work with very messy legacy.

12.4.2 *Migration patterns*

Modernization is exciting. It starts with discovery and design and ends with systems that provide greater value and are easier to evolve. Sandwiched in between, however, is the tough part—the journey of migrating from the legacy to the modernized. Fortunately, modernization is a ubiquitous challenge, and several useful patterns have emerged to help with the arduous task of migration.

Some patterns have the concept of gradual and iterative migration baked into their definition. But even where not, it's advisable to chunk a migration into smaller steps to deliver some value sooner and reduce the severity of any incidents.

STRANGLER FIG

The *strangler fig* pattern (http://mng.bz/46BQ), defined by Martin Fowler, is used to migrate an existing architecture to a new architecture gradually. While this pattern applies at an entire application or systems level, it will naturally apply to all nested subsystems. It's based on the behavior of the strangler fig plant, which grows around a host tree, eventually killing it and taking its place. It involves creating a new system that delegates to the existing system. Over time, more responsibility is added to the strangler, and less delegation is needed until no delegation is needed at all. SoundCloud used the strangler fig pattern over an eight-year migration journey (http://mng.bz/QRx4).

Figure 12.20 shows how the strangler fig can be applied as a migration from a legacy monolith to modernized subsystems. A routing component processes all requests arriving into the system. The router routes each call to the legacy monolith or a modernized subsystem. In the beginning, most calls will be routed to the legacy system. Over time, as more modernized subsystems are developed, fewer calls will go to the

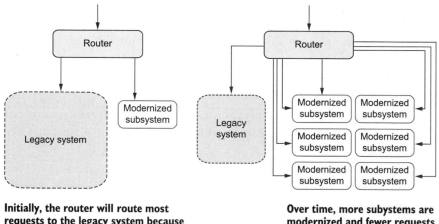

Initially, the router will route most requests to the legacy system because not much has been modernized.

Over time, more subsystems are modernized and fewer requests are routed to the legacy system.

Figure 12.20   Gradual system migration with the strangler fig pattern

legacy system. The legacy may disappear altogether at some point, although some parts could remain.

Strangler fig is a very common technique. It's one of the most common choices when adopting a gradual migration rather than a complete rewrite. The gradual nature reduces the risk of a big bang switchover, which can go wrong for many reasons. However, the pattern can introduce additional complexity and risks, such as the following:

- *Data synchronization*—For example, the modernized subsystems have separate data storage that needs to remain consistent with the legacy system.
- *Legacy integration*—For example, changes need to be made to the legacy code to process incoming requests or integrate with extracted subsystems.
- *Legacy decoupling*—For example, the legacy is tightly coupled, and all of the logic for a single subdomain cannot easily be broken, so decoupling in the monolith is required first.
- *Harder to debug*—For example, due to the extra moving parts, it may be harder to debug, particularly where synchronization is involved.
- *UX*—For example, users may now have another application they need to use to achieve their tasks.

Resources for practitioners

For engineers and architects that will be designing and implementing migration, it's essential to have an in-depth understanding of the topic. You can find a list of recommended resources on the book's Miro board.

In addition, other approaches to learning and upskilling for practitioners, like book clubs, communities of practice, and mentoring, are all extremely valuable. These are covered in chapter 17.

BUBBLE

The *bubble* (aka bubble context) pattern defined by Eric Evans is a similar pattern to the strangler fig, but it applies more granularly at the level of an individual subsystem. The basic idea of this pattern is that a new subsystem, the bubble, is placed in front of an existing subsystem(s). This allows a fresh domain model to be designed and implemented that is unconstrained by the legacy model, as shown in figure 12.21.

Like a strangler, it may handle some logic internally and delegate to the legacy subsystems where necessary via an *anticorruption layer* (ACL), a translator from one model to another. Over time, more logic is added to the bubble until the legacy has been replaced. At that point, the bubble is effectively gone.

One crucial challenge with the bubble is the complexity of the ACL, which should not be overlooked. ACLs can take on a life of their own and be more complex than the domain model. When this is the case, the cost of the bubble pattern may not be justified, and another approach, like addressing the legacy head on, may be necessary or even conforming to the legacy model.

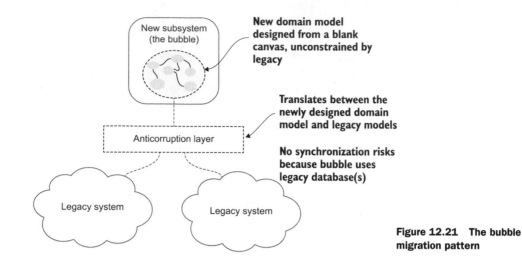

Figure 12.21   The bubble migration pattern

AUTONOMOUS BUBBLE

The *autonomous bubble* pattern, also from Eric Evans, is a variation of the bubble. In this version of the pattern, the bubble has its own data store. Integration with the legacy subsystem(s) is via asynchronous data synchronization, as shown in figure 12.22.

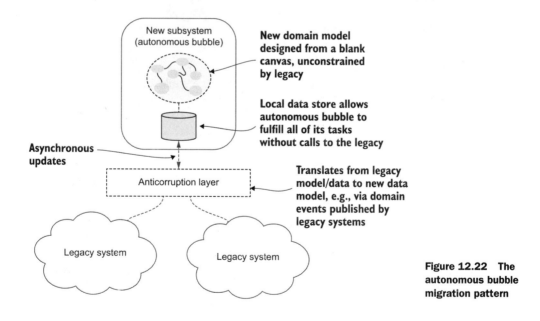

Figure 12.22   The autonomous bubble migration pattern

Both bubble patterns involve the creation of a bubble, enabling the development of a fresh domain model, unconstrained by the legacy, that can be easily evolved. However, the interplay with legacy varies greatly, creating unique trade-offs that require careful consideration.

A clear benefit of the non-autonomous bubble is the lack of data synchronization risks. As a compromise, however, the bubble doesn't have anywhere to store data, so any new fields need to be added to the legacy. If these types of changes are to be expected, then the level of change required to the legacy systems could make this pattern undesirable. That's where the autonomous bubble is likely to be a better fit. New fields can easily be added to the bubble without changing the legacy, but there's a cost—data synchronization. For instance, if data synchronization happens once per day, but users need to see real-time updates, the autonomous bubble may not be suitable.

WRAPPING LEGACY AND EXPOSING VIA DOMAIN EVENTS

When the cost of modernizing legacy is not justifiable, but capabilities of the legacy are still needed by modernized subsystems, legacy capabilities can be encapsulated and exposed via contracts. Contracts can be in various formats, like HTTP APIs or domain events, as shown in figure 12.23.

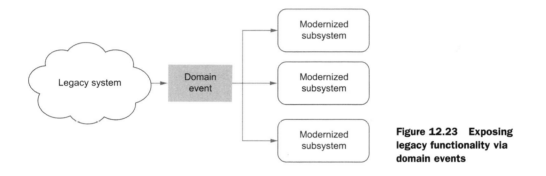

Figure 12.23   Exposing legacy functionality via domain events

While this pattern doesn't require extensive modernization of the legacy code, it usually does require modifying the legacy to publish these events. So, there is some work and some risk involved, and in fragile legacy systems, it could still be considerable, especially if there is no existing infrastructure for publishing events.

Another challenge with this pattern is the design of the events. You may not want all of your modernized subsystems coupled to the legacy domain or data model, so it may be better to put an ACL in between, similar to the bubble pattern, to isolate them from the legacy.

One of the worst migration disasters I've seen was when a large legacy database was converted into Kafka streams via change data capture. This isn't an inherently bad idea, but it was problematic because it put a huge amount of complexity into the many applications consuming the messages. They all had to understand the legacy database schema and be able to translate it into what was actually happening in the domain.

Imagine an *order* message that contains everything about the order and is published whenever anything about the order changes. A service that only cares about price updates has to consume thousands of messages per day and check each one to see if the price has changed. Now, imagine that complexity spreads across every subsystem. Encapsulating the legacy behind well-designed domain events, like Price Increased, would have resulted in much lower complexity and coupling on a local and global level.

PARALLEL RUN

The *parallel run* pattern involves running the legacy and modernized subsystems simultaneously for a period of time. During this period, both subsystems process the same input, although only the output from one subsystem is used. When the modernized subsystem's responses have been verified, its outputs are used. This allows the modernized system to be tested and refined in real-world scenarios while also providing a fallback option. Once the new system has been fully tested and is working as expected, the old system can be decommissioned, and the parallel run can be ended. Zalando used this pattern to break their returns capability out of a monolith into a new microservice (http://mng.bz/n1zd). They used a gradual approach where endpoints were switched over one by one.

REFACTOR FIRST

While it's nice to be able to rewrite subsystems or use patterns like bubble to allow clean code to be written from the get-go, on many occasions, the legacy will be too coupled or poorly designed that some cleanup will be necessary first. I first realized this when I was a junior developer, and I tried to use the bubble. I liked using the bubble because I got to work with a clean domain model and not have to be fully immersed in the legacy. But on one occasion, I made the mistake of creating a bubble on a codebase that already had multiple layers of incomplete refactoring attempts.

Working with a more skilled senior engineer, we flattened the layers of failed refactorings and the legacy underneath by basically inlining all of the methods using automatic IDE refactorings. We then sculpted and modeled the flattened logic. It was a little risky because we could have broken the legacy, but it was definitely the right choice, and it taught me an important lesson—you can't always build another layer on top of the existing legacy. Sometimes, you have to refactor the legacy first.

ANTIPATTERN: THE SEXY NEW CODEBASE

One migration antipattern I have witnessed on numerous occasions is the *sexy new codebase* antipattern. This is when all development in a legacy monolith is stopped, and all new feature work is built in a new codebase, which is much easier to work in and is much more exciting than being stuck in the legacy code. Unfortunately, the new codebase quickly loses its charm because it becomes tightly coupled and difficult to work with due to still needing to integrate and synchronize with the legacy.

This antipattern arises when teams want to stop developing in a legacy system and build a better architecture that enables a faster flow of changes. However, the problems occur because domain boundaries have been ignored, and the system is still coupled. It may be possible that some types of work can be developed faster because they don't depend on the legacy, but this anti-pattern applies when a significant amount of the new code depends on the legacy.

The best way to avoid this anti-pattern is to always ensure that architectural boundaries are based on carefully defined domain boundaries.

DEFINING A MIGRATION PATTERNS LIBRARY

A common theme I have observed in organizations investing in significant modernization is to establish a playbook of migration patterns (this is similar to the concept of golden paths covered in chapter 13). The patterns are tailored to the organization's context. Typically, they provide step-by-step guidance showing how to migrate a subsystem from the legacy system to approved technologies and architectural patterns. They can also include additional support like advice on which pattern to choose and related activities. AWS recommends (http://mng.bz/vP9a) that each migration pattern provides guidance on the following topics: current state, target state, preconditions, migration strategy, benefits, costs, skills, and migration factory (AWS terminology for a team that supports migration).

According to AWS, "20–50 percent of an enterprise application portfolio consists of repeated patterns that can be optimized by a factory approach." In my experience, this seems about right. As a result, I do agree that establishing a migration patterns' library is a sensible idea in medium to large organizations.

12.4.3 *Assessing current-state complexity*

Choosing the optimal modernization strategy and migration patterns requires an understanding of the current state of the system. This is an essential step in determining the level of investment required to achieve the desired level of return. While there is no simple metric, flowchart, or tool that can provide the perfect picture, many tools and techniques can help a great deal.

ASSESSMENT CRITERIA

Determining the health of a legacy system is notoriously difficult. There are no objective measurements or simple flow charts. Some aspects are quantifiable, but they don't tell the whole story and can be dangerous if misused, whereas some aspects are highly subjective. Being aware of the different criteria that contribute to system health is the first step. At least you know what to look for, even if you cannot perfectly measure it.

- *Technology age*—Assessing how old and how far behind modern technologies the current implementation is. This covers the programming language, libraries, frameworks, runtime versions, and so on.
- *Subsystem modularity*—Assessing how decoupled subsystems are. Vlad's model introduced earlier in the chapter can be used for this.
- *Subdomain alignment*—Assessing how well the current subsystems align with the target subdomains. In legacy systems, a lack of modularity and domain alignment combine to create extremely coupled software with *god classes*

(https://wiki.c2.com/?GodClass) that contain intertwined logic for a large number of subdomains, one of the hardest and riskiest legacy refactoring challenges.

- *Layering integrity*—Assessing how well the layers of application have been maintained. For instance, how much business logic is in the UI and database stored procedures?
- *DORA Metrics*—Helping to assess how quickly changes can be made to the software, deployed to production, and run reliably in a product.
- *Test coverage & quality*—Assessing how well-tested the current code is. The better the tests, the more confidence and less risky changes will be. Just remember that test coverage alone does not tell the full story so it's important to get into the code and look at how well the tests are written.
- *Quality attributes*—Performance, scalability, and security provide clues into how well the system has been designed.
- *Code understanding*—Assessing how many, and how well, people in the organization still understand how it works.
- *Cost to run*—Assessing how much needs to be invested in keeping the current software running. Does the cost seem excessive for the value it provides?

ARCHITECTURE ANALYSIS TOOLS

Software systems have been growing ever more complex as more of the world runs on software. Understanding and maintaining systems has unsurprisingly grown more challenging as a result. However, over the last few years, architecture analysis tooling has started to catch up, allowing us to understand our systems better and deal with their complexity. The most popular tool in my circles is CodeScene, and it is also my preferred tool, especially when trying to determine where, how, and how much to modernize.

When I was working with one CTO who had joined a company with the remit of modernization, he used CodeScene to quickly ascertain which parts of the system had no owners and which parts were worked on exclusively by contractors. He used the visualizations provided by CodeScene to explain these insights to the leadership group to justify some of the changes he wanted to make. This is a recurring theme in my experience—CodeScene is not just a tool for engineers and architects. It provides insights and visualizations that can explain systems to a nontechnical audience. This example was compelling because anyone could ascertain the high proportion of black (no owner, worked on by former employees) and red (worked on largely by contractors) dots. I can't share that particular example, but figure 12.24 gives a glimpse into how the feature works.

CodeScene analyzes multiple sources of information to identify complexity and challenges in a system and suggest actions to take. Firstly, it can assess a codebase and visualize the health of each part of the system. You can see an example in figure 12.25. The darker the color, the lower the health of that part of the system.

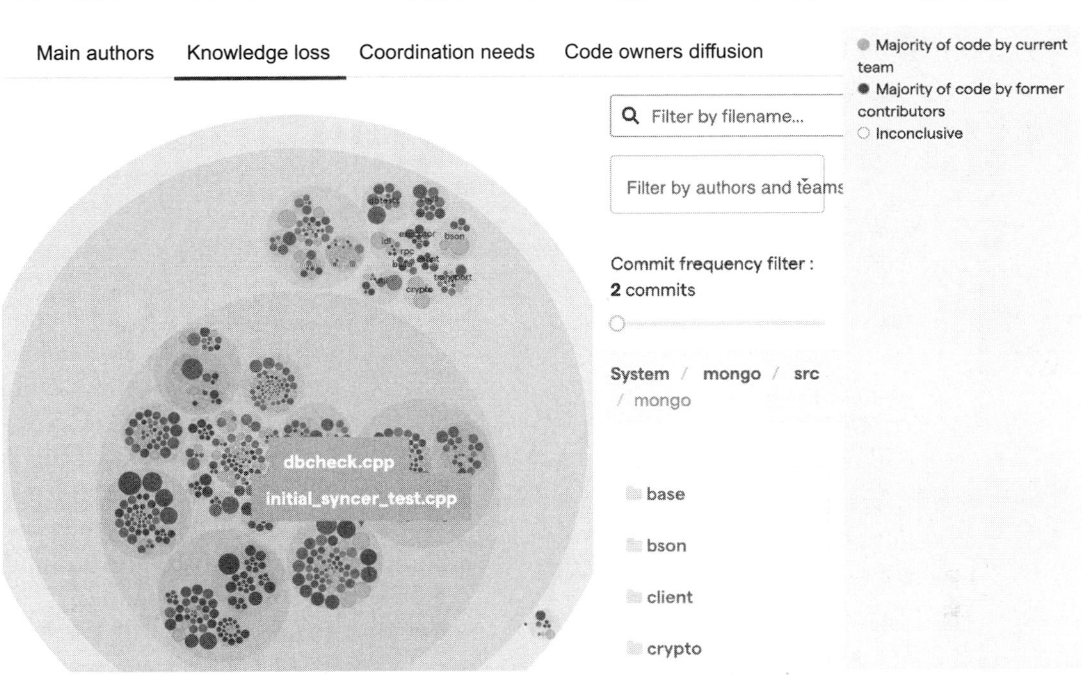

Figure 12.24 Identifying knowledge loss in a codebase with CodeScene

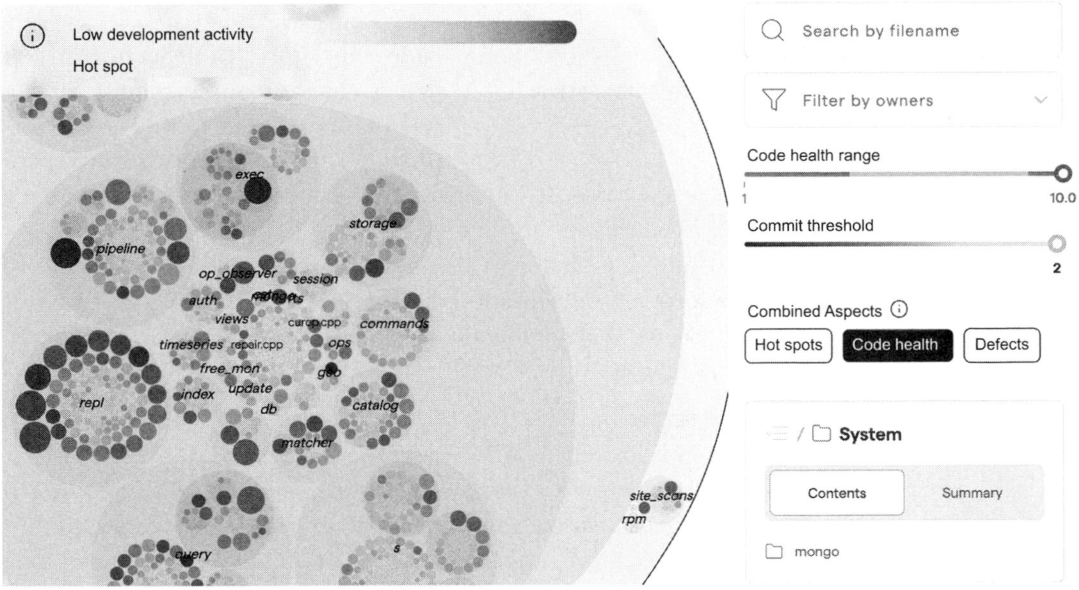

Figure 12.25 Visualizing code health with CodeScene

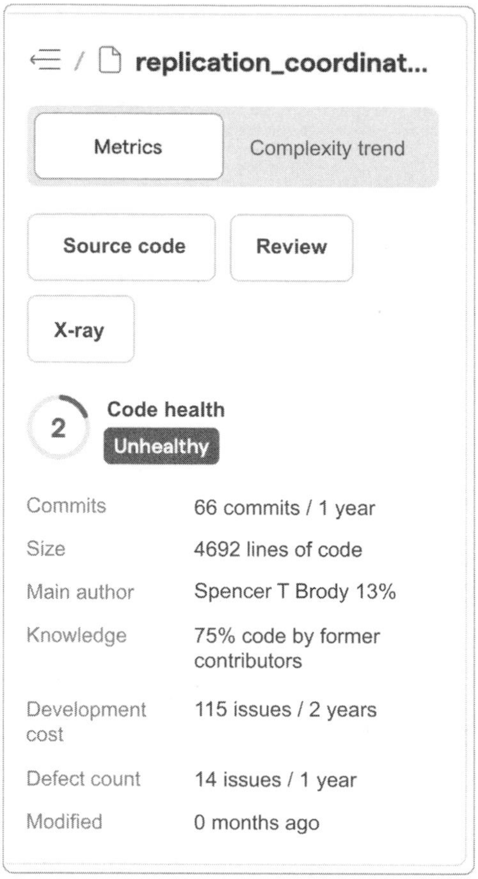

```
≡ / ⧉ replication_coordinat...

  [ Metrics ]    Complexity trend

  [ Source code ]    [ Review ]

  [ X-ray ]

  ⟳  Code health
  2   [ Unhealthy ]

Commits           66 commits / 1 year

Size              4692 lines of code

Main author       Spencer T Brody 13%

Knowledge         75% code by former
                  contributors

Development       115 issues / 2 years
cost

Defect count      14 issues / 1 year

Modified          0 months ago
```

Figure 12.26   Digging into parts of the system

If you click on a particular area, you get additional details like dependencies, defects, and complexity trends, as shown in figure 12.26. You can also perform actions like viewing the source code or digging into even more granular views, which assess individual functions in the code.

Even more impressive is that CodeScene combines information about the system with version control history. This means CodeScene can see how often each part of the system changes, allowing it to suggest hotspots—areas that are highly complex and change frequently. These are clear candidates for high-priority modernization initiatives, although I wouldn't make such significant decisions based solely on the suggestion of a tool.

Using version control history, CodeScene can also show you the change coupling in your system. Even if two subsystems are not part of the same code repository, CodeScene can still detect change coupling between subsystems and show trends over time, provided it has access to the version control history of both repositories. It's impressive how it covers both the technical and social aspects of architecture.

If you haven't used CodeScene before, I recommend you check it out. It can provide invaluable information for modernization discovery, design, and delivery. There's a live demo on the CodeScene website, which you can click around and explore to get an understanding of how it works.

ENGINEER EXPLORATION AND FEEDBACK

I've never seen tools used exclusively to analyze a system's health and used as the only source of input into modernization decisions, so I cannot recommend this approach. Tools can play a big part, but the knowledge and feedback from engineers who work in the system are equally, if not more, important. As a result, engineers will need to be given plenty of time to assess the current software using techniques like code review sessions, workshops (e.g., C4 current-state mapping workshops), and knowledge-sharing sessions. But it's not a competition. Tools enhance engineering capabilities by providing insights about where engineers should look and spend their time, like the parts of the system that are changed most often or the parts of the code that are touched by the most people.

EXPERIMENTAL DECOUPLING

Sometimes, the best way to understand how complex a part of the code will be to migrate is to jump right in, code for it, and see what happens. When I joined Salesforce, I did this as an experimental approach in the legacy monolith on my local machine. I wasn't expecting it to work (it definitely didn't), but it helped me understand how difficult it would be to decouple certain areas.

I picked a specific concept called *creatives*. We had discussed this being a separate microservice, so I tried to extract it as a microservice. I tried various approaches, like deleting the concept from the codebase, trying to fix all of the compiler errors, and creating an interface whose implementation I could replace with API calls to the microservice. I wasn't taking small, safe steps, and I wasn't adding unit tests. It was chaotic and messy, but that wasn't problematic because I just wanted to learn.

Before I began the experimental decoupling, I envisioned extracting creatives as a microservice in just a few days and completely wowing all my colleagues. "How hard can it be?" I thought. It seemed simple and isolated and should be easy to extract. After a week of experimental decoupling, my illusions were shattered, and I realized just how incredibly complex it would be to decouple the code and the database. But at least I was now thinking realistically and recognized the challenges.

This story demonstrates a heuristic I've mentioned previously. When you stay high-level, it's easy to fool yourself. An approach may look obvious or simple, but until you get into the details and verify, you should remain cautious before making any commitments.

12.5   Industry example: Domain-driven modernization of a gigs platform to support new markets

> **NOTE**   This industry example was written by Kenny Baas-Schwegler, Shannon Fuit, Chris van der Meer, and their colleagues and is based on their experiences as they began to modernize a match-making system that enabled employers and unemployed people to find each other for short-term jobs (gigs) without the need for recruiters. The system was three years old and had gradually turned into a big ball of mud. During that period, the time required to add new features increased significantly, and the system was becoming harder to scale as the business grew. The system had evolved into a substantial business liability. When leadership aimed to expand into markets beyond the Netherlands, such as Germany, it became crucial to modernize the system to facilitate a more agile and accelerated implementation of changes.

One of the major reasons for the system's decline into poor health was early architectural choices. Time-to-market and product-market-fit were key business drivers, so the team chose Ruby on Rails since this was the standard in the organization. Its convention-over-configuration approach allowed the team to progress rapidly in the early stages, but they were now paying the costs of those early wins. Rails had encouraged the team to couple their domain model and database model by using the active record pattern. As the system grew, the coupling of domain and persistence logic resulted in code that was harder to understand, change, and scale.

Expanding into new markets would introduce two new challenges. The first challenge was that the domain model would need to evolve to support regional differences. Germany has a completely different way of doing temping work compared to the Netherlands regarding contracts, procedures, and legal rules. In addition to having a different model, the platform had to be integrated with another set of third-party providers specific to Germany. The desire was to implement support for Germany in the software without affecting the stable product running in the Netherlands.

The second challenge was scaling up the development team to build and own the new business capabilities. Extra developers were added to the team to work on the rollout of the platform in Germany, which doubled the team's size. It turned out to be difficult for the new developers to create a mental model of the domain based on the code. First, because it was difficult to keep track of all the dependencies, and second, because a lot of important business rules were hidden implicitly within the implementation. Additionally, with so many developers working on the same codebase, they frequently obstructed each other, causing constant test failures and merge conflicts.

The team was split into two, with each team owning a different area of the domain. But the software coupling remained, meaning that when either team made changes, it would still affect the other team. It was at this point that Kenny was hired as a consultant. His purpose was to teach and help the teams apply domain-driven design to design and migrate to a loosely coupled, domain-aligned architecture that allowed teams to work independently with a sustainable, faster flow of changes.

The team began their DDD journey with EventStorming sessions. Initially, they chose to design the onboarding flow of a company because that problem wasn't too complex. This allowed them to decouple the company and contact rules between Germany and the Netherlands within a new bounded context while learning DDD at the same time. Feeling more confident, the team began to develop a model for each country tailored to its specific requirements.

The team used EventStorming once again to draw out their model. This time, they used software design EventStorming (figure 12.27) because they wanted to get close to how the model would look in software and begin implementing it.

As the team set their sights on implementing the model, they began researching how to do this in Ruby on Rails, without ending up in the same situation as before.

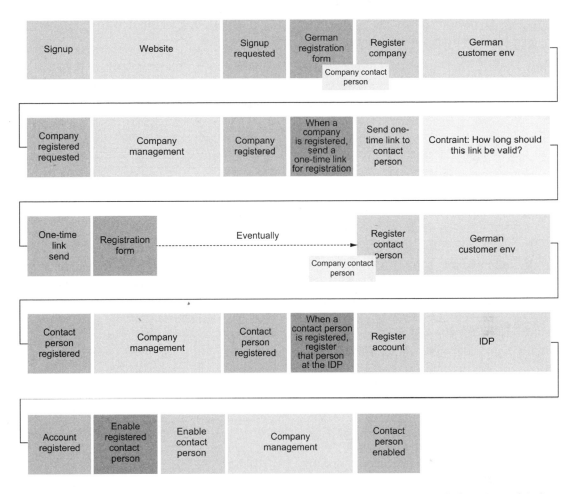

Figure 12.27 The software design EventStorming, showing the flow of a contact person in Germany registering on the platform and how that flow should be integrated with the current IDP (identity providers)

They followed the guidelines in the book *Domain-Driven Rails* by Arkency, which shows how to migrate from typical monolithic Rails applications to a domain-driven style.

Implementing the new bounded context (model) for the German market could be implemented seamlessly as a new codebase, completely decoupled from the existing code and functionality. After successfully doing a proof of concept for the onboarding of German companies, the domain-driven design approach proved itself. Then, the real challenge began, which was doing a ship of Theseus. We needed to introduce new features while also refactoring existing features into new bounded contexts.

For the initial steps of modernization, all the new and existing models continued to use a single shared database schema by using a bubble context, as in figure 12.28. The team consciously made this choice because refactoring the code first led to bigger improvements for less effort. Database decoupling is usually one of the hardest and most risky migration activities.

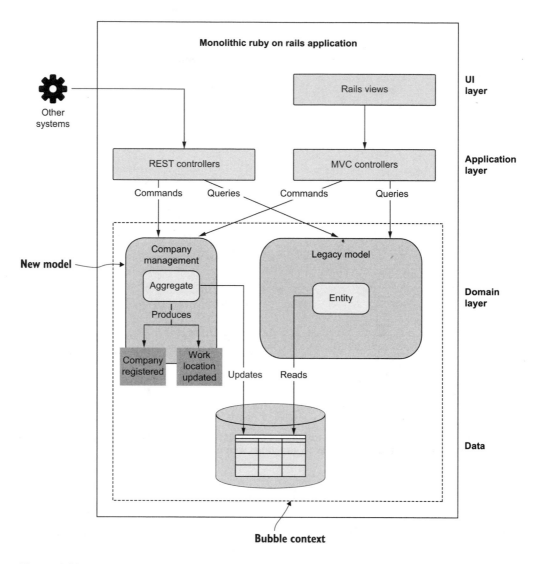

Figure 12.28   How the bubble context was implemented

But the database couldn't be ignored forever. It was still a major source of coupling between the models and teams. Each bounded context needed to have its own persistence schema and move to an autonomous bubble. With that, the team could change without worrying about breaking other bounded contexts, or the legacy model, as shown in figure 12.29.

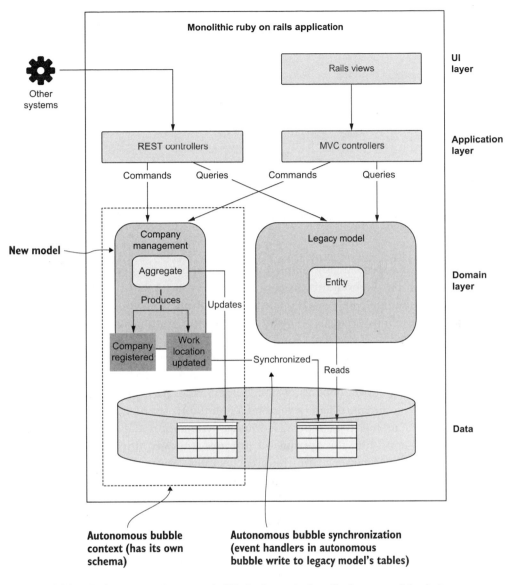

Figure 12.29 Moving to an autonomous bubble to decouple from the legacy model using an event handler to update the legacy model with changes from the bounded context

For that, we used an anticorruption layer (ACL). The ACL was used to hide the complexities of the old model in the monolith. The newly built bounded contexts would publish domain events that were intercepted by the ACL. The ACL would convert the new events to the old model. For example, as shown in figure 12.30, when implementing the new job drafting and job fulfillment bounded contexts, a Job Published event was raised, which the ACL intercepted and translated into the old model to a job.

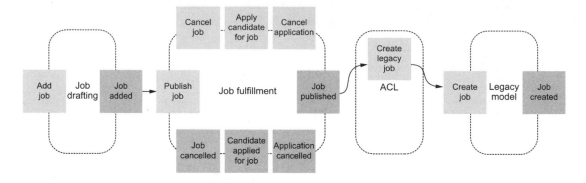

Figure 12.30   How the old legacy model is synced and updated through domain events from the new bounded context. The ACL is subscribed to the new domain events and then creates legacy jobs in the old legacy model.

This ACL approach also enabled a gradual approach where the team could A/B test changes. Throughout this process, the team ensured that the old model and its associated functionality remained operational, allowing for a controlled and efficient migration to the improved context while introducing new business functionality at a steady pace.

After roughly six months, the team was thrilled with their modernization efforts. They were able to implement new changes at a much faster pace even as the user base continued to grow, delighting stakeholders in all parts of the business. The team and their domain experts had developed a ubiquitous language.

The team felt that adopting a domain-driven approach was key to their success and saw first-hand how this approach can transform even the most complex and tangled applications. A larger team where each subteam owns a set of domain models could now work on the product. The team also wanted to emphasize a few other factors that were critical to their success:

- Cultivate a culture of continuous learning and improvement.
- Establish a ubiquitous language for direct stakeholder communication.
- Define a future vision for the organization.
- Celebrate successes and learn from failures.
- Incrementally migrate from monolith to bounded contexts.
- Implement domain-driven design in manageable steps.

Summary

- There are different types of coupling in software systems.
- Vlad Khononov proposes a model of coupling that includes four options for assessing the strength of coupling between two components. From strongest to weakest, they are intrusive coupling, model coupling, functional coupling, and contract coupling.

- We should always strive for contract coupling where possible because it is the weakest form and reduces the cost and risk of each change.
- Making subsystems smaller reduces their local complexity but may increase global complexity. It's important to consider the overall complexity rather than making lots of small pieces.
- Modeling flows and processes are key to uncovering coupling in a design and, therefore, reducing the coupling.
- Eric Evans's model exploration whirlpool is an effective guide for navigating the design process. It focuses on continuously challenging the model by working through concrete scenarios and getting deeper into the details where necessary.
- Domain Message Flow Modeling is a technique for designing architecture by modeling the interactions between subdomains and their subsystems. It uses a domain-oriented notation that maps closely onto the implementation.
- EventStorming can be used as a starting point for message flow modeling by extracting sequences of events as reference scenarios.
- It's important to challenge each aspect of a message flow model, like the types of messages, names, and boundaries.
- Choosing between commands and events can have a big effect on the design, especially the decision coupling, which is about deciding which subsystem determines what happens next in the flow.
- When designing architecture, the requirements and scenarios shouldn't be treated as fixed; you should always treat them as suspect and challenge them based on feedback from the design process.
- A good modeling process will involve exploring many possible models, not just one or two.
- Don't waste time creating pretty diagrams when modeling; messy is fine.
- Consolidating the information from various scenarios into a single unified design helps assess a subsystem's overall design. This can be achieved with visual canvases like the bounded context canvas.
- When the overall design for a subsystem is pieced together, bad design choices will stand out, like message names and responsibilities that aren't consistent with the name or purpose of the subsystem.
- Software design EventStorming (aka design-level EventStorming) can be a stepping stone from conceptual models to code. Each sticky note maps to a granular piece of code, and a new notation—aggregates—is introduced.
- Software design EventStorming can be used to move deeper into the details during the modeling process to get feedback on whether a design will work as code while still allowing visual collaboration.
- The modernization strategy for each subsystem should be decided on a case-by-case basis. Some subsystems will only benefit from lift and shift, while others

may benefit from a complete overhaul of the technology stack, infrastructure, functionality, and software design.

- Understanding the potential value and cost of investment needed is key to identifying each subsystem's optimal ROI and migration strategy.
- Migrating from the current state to the target state is probably the hardest part of modernization. There are many migration patterns, like the strangler fig, bubble, and parallel run patterns.
- Assessing the current state of a system can be achieved through various means like using tools, running workshops, and just diving into the code and trying to decouple it in an experimental fashion for discovery purposes.

13

Internal developer platforms

This chapter covers

- Creating a slick developer experience to enable fast flow
- Determining the capabilities of an internal developer platform
- Managing an internal developer platform with a modern product management approach
- Deciding when to build an internal developer platform

Independent value streams enable fast flow by empowering teams to make most of the decisions that affect their value stream, like giving them more responsibility to deploy and support their applications. However, the extra responsibilities will be counterproductive if the complexity of building, deploying, and supporting code is too high. Teams will spend too much time on extraneous tasks that don't contribute to product enhancements.

Making it as effortless as possible for teams to build, deploy, and support software through an outstanding *developer experience (DX or DevEx)* is essential to establishing truly independent value teams. Good DX enables teams to continuously deliver product enhancements rather than getting caught up in a web of intricate tasks just to get their code in front of users.

Internal developer platforms (IDPs) are one aspect of creating an exceptional DX that removes all the unnecessary friction in the workflow of development teams and allows them to focus on discovering and delivering value at a high velocity. However, building effective IDPs is a complex task. Moreover, it can be an expensive way to create serious problems that reduce flow. Therefore, it's essential to invest wisely and staff the team carefully with people with the right mix of skills and a mindset that is just as much customer-focused as tech-focused.

Platform engineering (IDPs are a subset of platform engineering) should be a central theme of any modernization journey. It's a vast topic that necessitates a high level of research. This chapter outlines some of the most crucial aspects of building an IDP, like examples of good DX and the capabilities of an IDP, and provides recommended resources for going deeper into the topic.

Figure 13.1 outlines the structure of this chapter. Firstly, look at the characteristics of a modern DX needed to achieve IVSs. Then, look at the capabilities of an IDP that are required to achieve the necessary DX. And finally, explore how to manage a platform, touching on organization design, strategy, roadmap, and product mindset.

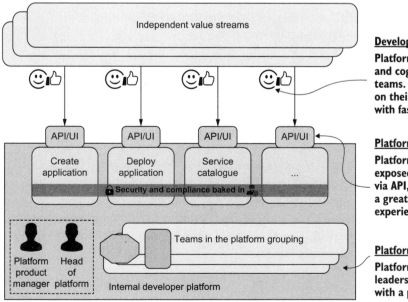

Figure 13.1   The role of IDPs in enabling independent value streams

> **IDPs are risky business**
>
> While reading through this chapter, please keep in mind that building IDPs carries significant risks. A well-thought-out IDP can amplify the productivity of a whole organization, while a badly executed IDP can be catastrophic to productivity and morale.
>
> I was in the audience at Craft Conf 2023 for Michael Nygard's talk *Lessons Learned Building Developer Platforms* (http://mng.bz/qjNx) and would advise anyone thinking of building an IDP to watch the video of this talk first. Also, keep in mind that an IDP doesn't have to be a huge endeavor, as Matthew Skelton explains: "A platform is a 'curated experience for engineers.' A good platform could thus be just a wiki page that specifies 5 or 14 AWS services that should be used together in a specific way."

13.1 Developer experience

When building an internal platform, the top priority should be DX. Almost every platform decision should be driven by how well it supports DX improvements. Whenever I've seen internal platforms go wrong, there has always been insufficient attention to DX and, usually, more focus on technologies like Kubernetes. Technologies alone will not enable fast flow and can worsen things if their complexity is not dealt with carefully. In one Austrian company I worked with, each team needed a dedicated team member to deal with platform responsibilities due to the high levels of complexity in the form of various Kubernetes configuration files and Git repositories. The DX was appalling.

Developer experience refers to the experience that developers have while building, testing, and deploying software (and even other parts of their job). It encompasses everything from the tools and technologies to the processes and workflows involved in the development lifecycle. DX is critical because it directly affects software developers' productivity, creativity, and motivation, affecting the overall speed and quality of product innovation.

DX enables fast flow by removing barriers to productivity and allowing developers to focus on discovering unmet user needs and delivering solutions to meet those needs. When developers have access to the right tools and technologies, they can work more efficiently and effectively, reducing the time it takes to develop and deploy software. When processes and workflows are optimized, developers spend less time on administrative tasks like setting up environments or managing dependencies and more time delivering value.

By continuously investing in DX, companies can also attract and retain top talent. Developers want to work for companies that value their skills and provide them with the resources they need to do their jobs well. When organizations invest in DX, they signal to developers that they are committed to creating a productive and enjoyable work environment, which can improve employee satisfaction and retention. Ultimately, prioritizing DX can lead to better software, faster development, and a more engaged and motivated team. My best experiences as a developer were in organizations with a great DX, like 7digital, where deploying code was trivial, and we got to spend most of our time doing interesting product work and not fighting infrastructure.

13.1.1 *Zero to production in less than a day*

For many software development teams, getting new software applications set up and deployed to production is a nightmare that can take weeks or months and consume much of their time. Clearly, this is not fast flow and is a blocker to fast flow. It also encourages teams to find workarounds that can create more significant architectural problems down the line, like one organization that built a CRM inside their trading platform codebase so they wouldn't have to go through months of hassling trying to get a new application into production. It worked in the short term, but in the long term, it compromised their speed of development in their differentiating trading platform and added significant barriers to transitioning to an off-the-shelf CRM.

Nowadays, the benchmark for spinning up a new application and deploying it to a production environment is hours or even minutes. This standard is easily achievable with modern cloud providers. And to be clear, all the way to production in a single day implies using a robust and secure deployment pipeline that bakes in quality and compliance requirements to the same standards as any other application running in production. Developers have a slick paved road that provides almost everything they need out of the box.

When spinning up a new application is not a blocker to flow, teams will not be forced to compromise between the optimal architecture and hitting a deadline. If a new application is required to implement a new capability, it can easily be achieved without adding much delay to delivery; therefore, engineers won't feel the need to wedge it into an existing codebase to save time. However, this does introduce a new risk. I've seen teams creating too many microservices because it was so cheap and easy, resulting in high coupling. Developing new applications should not be done on a whim. Carefully defining domain boundaries is compulsory.

13.1.2 *Roll out the red carpet for teams to do continuous delivery*

If you want to build a high-performing engineering organization with fast flow, a platform should make it as easy as possible for developers to deliver value to customers continuously. I encourage platform engineers to imagine they are rolling out the red carpet for developers. Not in the sense that developers are more important but that all their needs for getting code into production are well and truly taken care of. So much so that it is a pleasurable and frictionless experience, and they feel well looked after. They should have all the tools needed to develop, deploy, and support applications in production.

Continuous delivery capabilities should be exposed in a user-friendly manner. Doing the right thing should be the easiest thing. Life can be frustrating as a developer when you are constantly blocked, awaiting people outside the team to provide you with a service such as spinning up infrastructure, providing access to some tool, or installing software. A good DX removes the frustration of being blocked and prevents friction between development and platform teams through a self-service experience.

13.1.3 *Delightful onboarding experience*

Joining a new company is a time of optimism and positivity. But unfortunately, the positivity can be dampened for many developers during onboarding. Getting access to tools and getting the necessary permissions is usually frustrating, likewise for getting a development machine set up so you can be productive and write code. In some companies, this takes weeks and can be like a murder mystery game. You have to talk to many people and piece the clues together until your developer machine finally allows you to contribute.

In 2012, my CTO at 7digital, Rob Bowley, was passionate about "every developer pushing code to production on their first day." This implied doing it from their own machine and having access to all the required tools. I believe this should be every CTO's goal. On my first day, I paired up with a senior engineer. We picked up a piece of work for a nontrivial part of the system and used TDD (test driven development) to implement it. I pressed the button, which deployed it to production, and then we watched the monitoring for a few minutes to ensure everything appeared to be functioning correctly. A first day I'll never forget.

13.1.4 *Frictionless local development experience*

Naturally, developers spend a lot of time using their computers to code. When the DX is slick, a developer can focus on solving business problems and seamlessly performing the relevant tasks. When the DX is poor, a developer resents opening their laptop. As far back as 2013, I began using tools like Vagrant and Docker Compose to automate the creation of disposable development environments, and these days, the tools are even better.

A developer should be able to install the tools they need to do their job and have powerful machines and peripherals that provide an optimized, comfortable experience. They should have access to all necessary resources for building applications and gaining the necessary knowledge. Penny-pinching on developer equipment is a false economy and sends out the wrong message.

Using security as an excuse for completely locking down developer machines is rarely an acceptable excuse for adding friction. It doesn't need to be a choice between a great DX and security. Practices like ensuring developers cannot access production environments and giving them sandboxes should be applied to eliminate risks.

> **NOTE** Continuous learning and upskilling are necessities in modern software development, making them another critical DX component. It's the topic of chapter 17.

13.1.5 *Industry example: HMRC's Multi-channel Digital Tax Platform (UK government)*

In 2015, the benchmark for what I considered to be a good developer experience reached a new threshold. Working on UK government initiatives, I had the chance to witness and use an IDP that allowed around 60 UK government development teams, spread all over the country, to rapidly spin up new services and deliver improvements daily. The developer experience was top-notch for that time, especially considering the UK government had a poor track record with IT projects.

Even today, many technology leaders tell me that DX is just a buzzword and achieving these ideals is impossible, especially in large organizations building complex products. I show them what HMRC's IDP, the Multi-channel Digital Tax Platform (MDTP), was capable of back in 2015 to prove it is possible, and nothing is stopping them from achieving a great DX.

Spinning up a new application was basically adding a few lines of configuration and running a few jobs. HMRC's platform operations team (PlatOps) created libraries to make this as simple as possible.

The general process was

- Run a Jenkins (https://www.jenkins.io/) job via the UI, providing a few parameters like application name and type (e.g., microservice or frontend)
- Set up build and deploy pipelines (via a few lines of config)
- Set up metrics, monitoring, and logging (via a few lines of config)

The Jenkins job to create a new application was fully self-service. It would make a Git repository and populate it with the skeleton of an application based on the specified parameters. For example, setting microservice as the application type would populate the Git repository with a skeleton Scala Play Framework (https://www.playframe work.com/) application. The application would be prepopulated with various configuration settings and MDTP-specific conventions like libraries for dealing with authentication, metrics, and logging. Templates were powered by bootstrap libraries like microservice-bootstrap (https://github.com/hmrc/microservice-bootstrap).

Setting up the build and deploy pipelines was performed by adding some configuration using a Groovy DSL created by PlatOps. Listing 13.1 shows how it was possible to set up pipelines for frontend Scala applications that use the SBT build system. This is a real example from HMRC's open-source Jenkins-jobs repository (https://github.com /hmrc/jenkins-jobs). You can see more examples and job templates in the repository.

Listing 13.1   Setting up pipelines on MDTP

```
new SbtFrontendJobBuilder('paye-tax-calculator-frontend')
  .withSCoverage()
  .withScalaStyle()
  .build(this as DslFactory)
```

After adding configuration to the config file in a repository, a peer-to-peer system allowed anyone to approve the pull request. It wasn't only PlatOps that could authorize. Therefore, it was usually merged within minutes and didn't become a blocker to flow. Once merged, a team could immediately start deploying and testing the application in *dev* and QA environments. Getting to production was similarly automated. However, there was a platform policy that every application must be pen tested before being opened to a live environment.

The MDTP also provided a great DX for supporting applications in production and other environments. PlatOps created repositories for logging and monitoring. Teams needed only to add a few lines of config using a DSL, similar to Listing 13.1. They would get access to tools like Grafana and Splunk with out-of-the-box standard reports and dashboards showing things like the number of requests, the error rate, and response times. This ensured that every team had solid foundations for a *you build it, you run it* approach. Teams could also add customizations as necessary.

Thanks to PlatOps, there was a whole ecosystem of tools and support surrounding MDTP, like a preconfigured load-testing setup based on Gatling (https://gatling.io/). Furthermore, a high level of detail was paid to documenting the capabilities. If that hadn't been the case, 60 teams would have all been raising endless support tickets, which would not have been sustainable. In addition, there were many Slack channels for discussing different aspects of the platform, which were always alive with community members and people from PlatOps.

It helped that the MDTP had a dedicated product manager, but I also observed that all members of PlatOps had a strong desire to create a great DX for the many teams consuming the platform. Even though we developers gave them a lot of headaches, PlatOps continually strived to improve our lives, like when filling out a form to deploy to production was replaced with an entirely self-service capability. It was impressive that they had such a laser focus on DX and never got distracted by shiny technologies or creating some uberplatform that was technically brilliant but hard to use.

It's important to acknowledge that not everything about the MDTP was perfect. At that scale, there are always compromises. The biggest, at that time, was probably technology standardization. Teams had to use Scala and the Play Framework to develop backend microservices and frontend applications. This certainly wasn't to everyone's taste and resulted in hiring challenges. However, standardization allowed many capabilities to be provided out of the box and allowed teams to focus on solving problems and delivering value. In my opinion, it was the right choice, although it was certainly a contentious topic.

My former teammate Richard Dennehy describes other benefits that he experienced due to MDTP's standardization: "The team I was on for a couple of years ended up inheriting a lot of services from various teams, and it was nice having some common structure between them, as opposed to potentially having to learn everything from scratch." He also emphasizes another significant aspect of the platform's DX relating to the local development experience: "I highly appreciated how nice it was to be able to run basically everything locally, using the tools provided by PlatOps, like Service Manager" (https://github.com/hmrc/service-manager).

In summary, HMRC's MDTP provided an exceptional developer experience at scale all the way back in 2015. Through self-service capabilities, teams could spin up new services in minutes and deploy them to production daily with the tools needed to support their applications in production. Many essentials were provided out of the box by the platform operations team, while a rich community allowed everyone building on the MDTP to share knowledge and contribute improvements.

13.2   Platform capabilities

An IDP can be crucial in creating a great DX that enables fast flow. One of the first steps on the journey of developing an IDP is thinking about what capabilities the platform will provide and how to present them. Various approaches can be taken to achieve the optimal DX for a given capability, like UI, YAML, CLI, or GitOps-based experiences. This section touches on some of the most foundational and common platform capabilities.

13.2.1   Golden paths

A golden path (or paved road) is like a recipe for creating a new software application or other resources. Ideally, it is fully automated, but any manual steps should be well-documented. For example, a Java API golden path would be something that an engineer chooses when they need to develop a completely new backend API. The golden path would then follow the recipe of setting up a new Java API based on the organization's conventions, such as setting up code repositories, infrastructure, and common libraries, as the following industry example demonstrates.

INDUSTRY EXAMPLE: PAVING THE ROAD AT A NEOBANK

Chris O'Dell is a platform engineer who specializes in building and operating platforms that provide great developer experience that enables continuous delivery. She's worked on platforms for a number of high-scale organizations like Stack Overflow, Apple, and JustEat. Prior to her career transition, she was a software engineer who practiced continuous delivery. As a result, she understands both perspectives and sees the full picture.

This industry example shares Chris's experience of building and supporting a platform-paved road at a mobile-first neobank. The platform supported around 2000 Go microservices that lived in a monorepo and ran on Kubernetes, with around 150 software engineers working on them. It enabled teams to deploy to production many times per day so they could innovate much faster than traditional banks.

The platform was composed of multiple teams, each owning a different layer. The paved road was owned by the developer experience team, where Chris worked. Their goal was to provide a simple developer experience while balancing obfuscation: "Some people want to give devs a magic button—this leads to problems when things go wrong. We never hid Kubernetes, but we did offer lots of defaults," explains Chris.

Spinning up a new microservice and getting all the way to production usually took less than a few hours, thanks to the slick paved road shown in figure 13.2. A developer would run a command-line tool created by the platform teams. It would ask them a few questions like the type of application (e.g., website or database) and would then create a folder with the template of a Go application and Kubernetes configuration. That step took less than 5 minutes. The developer would then commit the code and create a pull request, which gave them a PR number.

Shipper:

• Manage deployments
• Auto run tests
• Hide Kubernetes complexity
• Bake in compliance

Shipper will not deploy code to production unless it has been reviewed by a 2nd person and been deployed to staging (compliance).

The 2nd person can be someone from the same team to prevent the platform being a bottleneck.

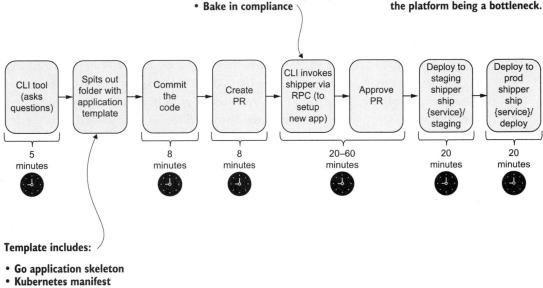

Template includes:

• Go application skeleton
• Kubernetes manifest
• Dockerfile (using shared base)
• Kustomize for manifest file inheritance (app name, CPUs, memory, etc.)
• RPC and messaging library/examples
• Monitoring and metrics

Figure 13.2   Paved road for creating a new microservice and pushing to production in just a few hours

After raising the PR, the CLI tool would send an RPC to another tool called the shipper service, which handled platform tasks like deployment. Developers could execute commands on their machine, like *Shipper ship staging* and *Shipper ship deploy* to deploy their code to the relevant environment once the PR has been approved. The PR could be approved by anyone, even someone inside the same team, so there were no bottlenecks in the process. The Go template produced by the CLI tool provided everything a team would need, including libraries and examples for RPC calls, messaging, monitoring and metrics, Dockerfile, Kubernetes manifest, and Kustomize for manifest file inheritance.

Behind the scenes, Shipper was doing a lot of important work, like hiding Kubernetes complexity and baking in compliance. For instance, it would only allow production deployments if the code had previously been deployed to staging. And it ensured that every piece of code had been looked at by at least two developers before going to production, which was a regulatory requirement. It enforced this policy by analyzing the Git history. "All developers need to know is *Shipper ship* thanks to all of the standards," says Chris.

The paved road made delivering new features equally smooth. Teams deployed to production as often as they wanted and were even encouraged to deliver small increments on a regular basis. New feature development would often start with the definition of a new feature flag to control the visibility of the new feature. The platform provided teams with the feature flag capability. Teams would then start to implement the feature around the feature flags. When teams were ready to deploy, they would create a PR in the monorepo, which could touch multiple microservices if necessary.

Teams would then run *Shipper ship staging* to deploy to staging where QA could test the feature on a phone. They would use the internal dashboard to control visibility of the feature using the previously mentioned feature flags. Once satisfied with the feature in QA, the PR could be merged, and *Shipper ship deploy* would be used to deploy the feature to production.

Once in production, teams supported their code using observability tooling and dashboards provided for free by the platform. The application template would configure all the plumbing for an application to start logging, including baked-in conventions like standard naming patterns for metrics. These capabilities were owned and operated by the platform infrastructure team whose remit was availability, monitoring, and metrics.

Building a paved road is not simply a project that starts by asking developers what they want and then designing the best possible developer experience. "Building and evolving a paved road is about constantly balancing what the developers want with what the platform needs," explains Chris. "On one occasion, the developers were complaining about builds taking too long. But the platform team identified that most of the time was spent waiting for PRs to be reviewed. So, the platform team built improved tooling to accelerate and improve the PR process." Similarly, the choice of standardizing on Go was a contentious decision: "New joiners usually had disbelief but then became a believer after experiencing all of the benefits the platform could provide by standardizing on technology choices."

GOLDEN PATH CATALOGS

Treat the engineers who use the platform as well as you would external customers and make golden paths as easy for them to consume as possible by providing clear guidance and removing things they shouldn't care about. Tools like Backstage (https://backstage.io/)—an open-source developer portal that makes creating a catalog of golden path templates easy—are an excellent example of this. Backstage improves the DX of discovering, defining, and executing golden paths. It's far more than static documentation. Figure 13.3 shows an example golden path catalog in a Backstage project populated with multiple golden paths. Choosing a template allows parameters to be supplied and jobs to be triggered within.

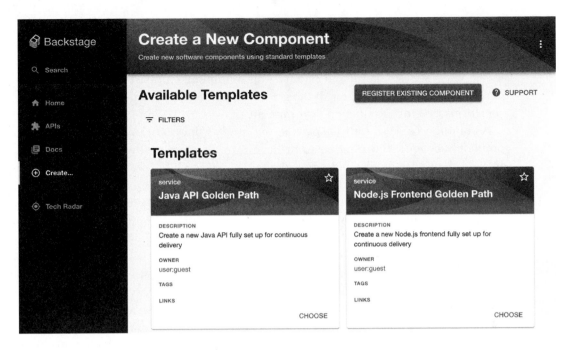

Figure 13.3   A golden path catalog in Backstage

13.2.2 *Pipelines and environments*

To move code from a developer's laptop to test and production environments, pipelines are needed to build and deploy the code. An opinionated platform can provide out-of-the-box build and deployment pipelines that set up every step from the moment a developer pushes code until the code is running in a production environment. Typically, build and deployment pipelines will form part of the golden path and can be fully automated (or almost fully automated in the case of the HMRC MDTP example).

A good metric for build and deployment pipelines is *lead time for changes,* which measures the time between a developer committing a piece of code and the code being deployed to a production environment. Many organizations are now at a level where lead time for changes is under one hour, and teams are deploying to production multiple times per day. Organizations operating below this threshold are likely to be disadvantaged.

Setting up environments has traditionally been one of the most time-consuming and frustrating activities for operations teams and developers. With the big leaps in technology in the 2010s, like infrastructure as code (IAC), creating environments should be fully automated and take just minutes. Spinning up test and production environments should be free with the golden path.

13.2.3 *Observability*

A trend since the mid-2010s has been for engineering teams to take on more responsibility for owning the operation of their applications in production. *You Build It, You build it, you run it* is the term that captures this sentiment, emphasizing that the people who write the code are those with the greatest incentives and opportunities to ensure it performs well in a production environment.

A common concern with *you build it, you run it* is that software developers will get completely bogged down having to manage infrastructure and will have no time to focus on their real job of building products. This concern is only valid when the cost of supporting an application in production is too high, which is a sign of bigger problems. A well-designed IDP provides the tooling, support, and education so that the cost of supporting systems in production is low enough not to distract engineers, as demonstrated in the HMRC MDTP example.

Monitoring, logging, and alerting are three IDP components that reduce the cognitive load of supporting applications in production. Getting them right is vital and requires a lot of effort, but the ROI is worth it. Good observability goes beyond monitoring and can greatly increase reliability and reduce maintenance costs. As Liz Fong-Jones explains, "[Monitoring] simply shows developers when something is wrong but doesn't give any insights into the reasons why it's wrong. As a result, organizations need a new way of thinking about things. This is where observability comes in. Observability allows developers to understand the internal state of an application by analyzing its external outputs" (http://mng.bz/7vGQ). OpenTelemetry (https://opentelemetry.io/) is an open-source tool for implementing observability in a variety of languages and is a great starting point for learning more about observability.

As part of the golden path, application templates can include logging and monitoring code libraries that hook into tooling like Grafana and Splunk. All engineers have to do is publish logs using the provided library, which will appear in centralized logging platforms thanks to automatically configured plumbing. In addition, common dashboards based on the *four golden signals* (http://mng.bz/mjN8) should also be provided out of the box.

13.2.4 *Software applications catalog*

Traditionally, the discoverability of IT systems has been poor. Identifying all the applications within an organization has often relied on tribal knowledge or out-of-date documentation. It's not uncommon to hear of engineers duplicating existing APIs because they weren't aware a similar API already existed in the company. A software catalog solves this problem by cataloging all APIs, frontends, and other applications in a centralized location. It captures key information like the team that owns the software and links to other useful information like dashboards, code repositories, and team communication channels. Figure 13.4 shows how Backstage can be used to catalog software applications.

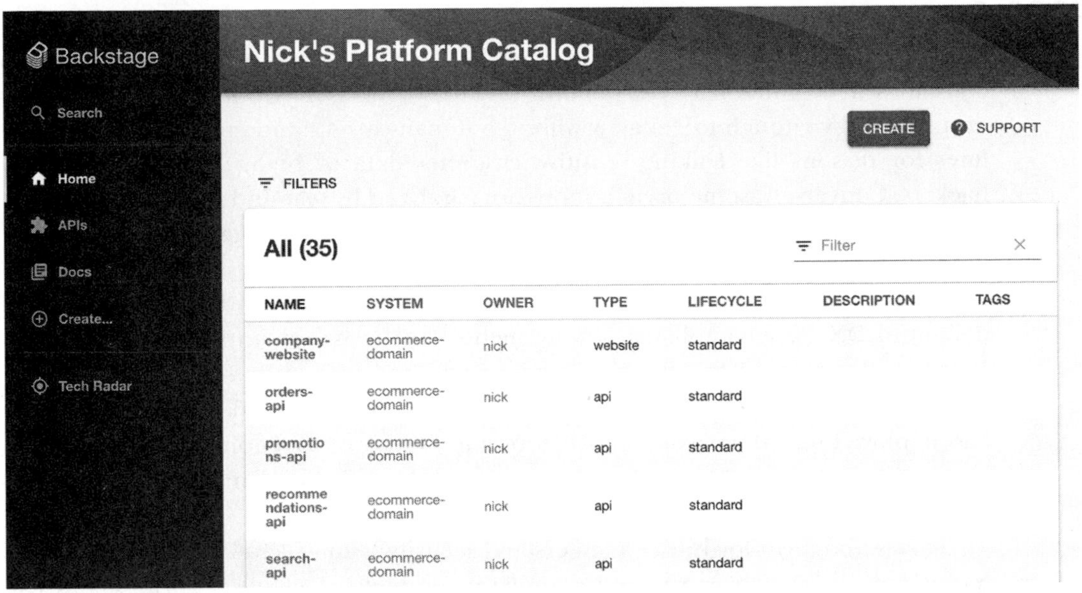

Figure 13.4   Using Backstage as a software applications catalog

In a modern context, live metadata should power software catalogs, not static documentation. For example, when a team is spinning up a new API by following a golden path, metadata should be automatically created and accessible to the software catalog. No manual effort should be required, meaning all IT applications are guaranteed to be discoverable and the documentation up to date. Backstage, for example, can include the current production status of the application in addition to team and code information.

13.2.5 *Great platform documentation*

A good IDP has great documentation. Engineers and other platform consumers should be able to find the information they need and complete the majority of their platform tasks just by following the documentation. If engineers constantly contact the platform's teams for help and advice, the DX starts to suffer, and platform engineers lose time to support activities that prevent them from improving the platform. This becomes especially important as the platform scales and is used by more and more teams. Poor documentation will result in accelerating support costs and unhappy platform consumers. Teams working in platforms should actively monitor their support activities and look for opportunities to improve documentation to reduce the support workload, just like a company building a product for external customers. Some companies hire dedicated content specialists to ensure platform documentation is high quality.

13.2.6 *Security and compliance*

One of the most neglected topics in many tech companies is security. In the rush to constantly deliver new features, building secure systems is overlooked. Some organizations are lucky enough to get away with it, but many aren't and end up as news headlines for reasons like leaking sensitive customer data or being held to ransom by hackers. Conversely, some organizations are paralyzed by fear and lock down their systems so heavily that software developers face a constant struggle to develop and deploy new features.

An IDP can play a crucial role in building secure systems while still allowing a delightful DX. Key compliance requirements can be baked into the platform. For example, deployment pipelines can be implemented with automated code scanning and other checks, like validating that the code has been reviewed by a second person and deployed to test environments before it goes into production. The platform can keep a full audit history of each change as proof that all compliance checks were successfully carried out.

This is a win-win for both engineers and security teams. Developers don't have to remember to follow security and compliance guidelines, while security teams can sleep easy knowing that their controls are automated as part of the platform.

For some organizations, improving security is a principal reason for building an IDP, as platform engineering expert Ivan Angelov explains in this short story: "One of our biggest competitors got taken down for more than a week by an attack. They lost tens of millions in missed revenue alone and spent weeks dealing with the breach. This prompted us to look at whether the same could happen to us, and it quickly became clear that not only could it happen, but it would take a huge amount of time to address the tens of thousands of known vulnerabilities we have. Without a platform and appropriately staffed security teams, we're finding ourselves in a situation where we need to rapidly increase investment in our platform to address them quickly and efficiently, so that's become a huge driver for building our IDP."

13.2.7 *API management*

Over time, software architectures have become significantly more distributed, particularly after the explosion of microservices. As a result, the ubiquity of APIs has grown. HTTP APIs are commonly used for frontend-to-backend integration, service-to-service integration, and integration with external systems. Consequently, the complexity of managing APIs has also risen. Nowadays, enterprises with more than just a handful of APIs typically adopt an API management solution.

An API management solution typically consists of capabilities like API lifecycle management, a portal for browsing and interacting with APIs, access control (developers apps, API keys, etc.), and monetizing externally published APIs. An expensive API management solution can seem overkill when you only have a few APIs and integrations. The intricacy of this problem is that the number of APIs can quickly grow over time. When you realize that an API management solution is needed, the cost of migrating all your APIs to an API management solution may take months or even years. A little upfront planning and regular reviews are key to making a move at the ideal time.

Commercial API management solutions sometimes market questionable design practices. In particular, the ability to write custom JavaScript that executes within the gateway should be used cautiously. I've encountered numerous situations where business and application logic ended up within the gateway, solving a short-term problem but causing long-term maintenance issues. Searching through code in both the gateway and the actual API when production issues occur adds complication and frustration. This problem is exacerbated when different teams own the code in the API platform and the code for the API.

13.2.8 FinOps

FinOps (financial operations) is becoming an increasingly prevalent concept. FinOps aims to track, manage, and optimize costs, usage, and optimization of cloud resources to help businesses save money and improve efficiency. There are many horror stories involving companies that accidentally ended up with huge cloud bills, so it's clear why FinOps is important. By implementing FinOps practices, platform engineers can gain greater visibility into their platform's costs and usage, make data-driven decisions, and optimize resource utilization to ensure that the platform remains financially sustainable over time.

Implementing FinOps requires additional effort, like tagging resources. When left to developers, it can easily be forgotten by accident because they have other things to focus on. Baking it into the platform removes the potential for errors and adds no extra work for developers. There's a lot to consider when introducing FinOps, so I recommend checking out the FinOps Foundation (https://www.finops.org/introduction/what-is-finops/).

13.3 Industry example: Platform-powered business model revolution at La Redoute

> **NOTE** This industry example was co-authored with Antoine Craske, former director of technology transformation at La Redoute. Now CIO & CTO of Grupo Lusiaves, he is also the founder of the QE Unit and the quality engineering framework, available at qeunit.com.

La Redoute is a leading French fashion retailer with more than 10 million customers worldwide and annual revenues reaching 1 billion euros. The company is almost 200 years old, having been established in 1837 with 99% notoriety in France. But this reputation alone wasn't enough to protect the historic company's status as a market leader. In 2014, the company CEO painted a stark picture: "We generate 50 million of negative EBITDA for 600 million annual sales. Our projects take months. Our position has declined. We have four years to transform or it's game over for La Redoute."

La Redoute was initially a pioneer of the mail-order business during the 1950s, but with internet business models starting to dominate, the company needed to modernize its entire business to have any chance of survival. It was a difficult period for the company. Not only did they need to find long-term innovations, but they had to massively reduce costs in the short-term, resulting in the loss of 50% of their 3500 employees. Yet, the most challenging of times are often the times where modernization has the greatest chance of success. La Redoute had to transform its business model and completely modernize its approach to developing products. Leadership knew this. They had nothing to lose and gave product and technology teams the license to go for all-out innovation. "We have to make 10x more with less. Find limitations, remove constraints, and enable the business to iterate at speed" was the mandate laid out by business leaders.

During my conversations with Antoine Craske, a technology director who has been at La Redoute since 2010, I learned many fascinating insights about the company's modernization journey, like how they revolutionized their warehouse operations and logistics through an integrated approach to software, hardware, and processes. Their warehouses are now among the most automated in Europe. Antoine articulated clearly why this was crucial to business prosperity: "An order placed on our digital channel has to be no more than 2 hours later in the truck for departure. We had no choice but to streamline the entire value-chain."

Building an internal developer platform with exceptional developer experience was a crucial enabler of La Redoute's turnaround. It used to take days for a commit to go from a developer's laptop to production; now, it takes less than 10 minutes. Creating new services used to take weeks; now it takes minutes. Overall, the company deploys around 100 times per day, which has directly supported the growth of the business—now active in 26 countries with 7 million unique visitors per month.

While exploiting the potential of modern technologies was important, Antoine and his colleagues put developer experience at the forefront of their platform, thinking "We knew that a successful developer experience was the cornerstone of better supporting the business, as most of our initiatives depend on technology. I personally pushed the developer experience to satisfy three criteria, where time-to-market was not the first one but a consequence of the others:

- *Quality*—The first imperative to deliver high standards of functionality, security, and infrastructure, among other requirements. Our key driver is to deliver a *built-in quality* in the first place, by the people producing the artifacts rather than chasing other teams (to ensure they complied).
- *Efficiency*—The second imperative for our DX, promoting a minimalist and incremental approach. For instance, we did not start with a fully featured internal developer portal, but rather a portal of standard pipelines that later evolved to GitOps and an IDP portal. This approach lets us build only what was really needed for our team.
- *Speed*—The last imperative largely derives from the first two. A streamlined platform enabling teams to deliver the essential quality requirements supports faster cycles of iteration. The speed imperatives translated into more autonomy and self-service, enabled by progressive automation.

We provide a paved path/golden path for our developers to follow, which includes self-service provisioning for pipeline, secrets, configuration, and exposition."

A good IDP supports more than just development; it provides teams with the capabilities to support their services in production as efficiently and hassle-free as possible. La Redoute was fully cognizant of this: "The operational stage is secured by the pipeline offering progressive deployments capabilities, and by design, all components must ensure observability foundations for logs and metrics. By default, components expose non-functional logs and metrics, allowing to industrialize the alerting for API errors for instance. Business metrics on another side, must be added by the developer, and are monitored across all services. An application missing the business monitoring is then tracked up with automated ticketing and review with the engineering managers. We also built a dashboard to measure our DevOps performance and make data-driven decisions with indicators like build frequency, success ratio, waiting time per stages, number of deployments in production, and SLIs among others."

Like a product, an IDP is a long-term, ongoing investment. And like many products, IDPs have various stakeholders with diverse needs, which means road mapping plays a vital role. At La Redoute, like many organizations setting out to build IDPs, the mindset shift for infrastructure-oriented people to start thinking about DX didn't happen instantly. "The shift to DX was a key step in prioritizing our roadmap better. The infrastructure-driven platform team gradually understood that their customers were the developers, which sometimes meant limiting technology optimizations to increase developer satisfaction instead. This broader, more cohesive vision was further strengthened by joining the CTO, solution architecture, and platform CoP practices to ensure that we were working towards common goals and keeping all considerations in mind."

As with a commercial product, it's also important to be somewhat data-driven to verify that the IDP is meeting the needs of stakeholders and investments are delivering a satisfactory return. La Redoute continuously monitors several metrics that help them keep track of platform adoption, usage, and effectiveness: "It's essential that we have metrics and KPIs in place to ensure that we avoid getting siloed in our optimization efforts. Metrics such as daily usage of the platform and the number of commits per developer can help us understand the usage and adoption of the platform. KPIs such as the number of deploys per day, lead time from development to production, and waiting time per stage can help us measure the efficiency of our development process. It's important to understand the difference between metrics and KPIs, that I like to restate as linkin the output and outcomes, and how both can be used to drive continuous improvement."

Antoine was also keen to emphasize the crucial role that organization design has played in establishing and sustaining their IDP (see figure 13.5): "Organizational design is also a crucial part of our platform development process. We have a dedicated platform team consisting of a lead and four engineers focused on developer experience. In addition to this, we have a CoP engineering tech lead responsible for adoption, continuous improvement, and knowledge sharing. We also have a CoE focused on cloud and infrastructure to help align our main priorities. Governance is also critical, and we have identified our sponsors and stakeholders who are responsible for ensuring the success of our platform development efforts. We also secure time to regularly share with teams in the form of talks and other sharing opportunities."

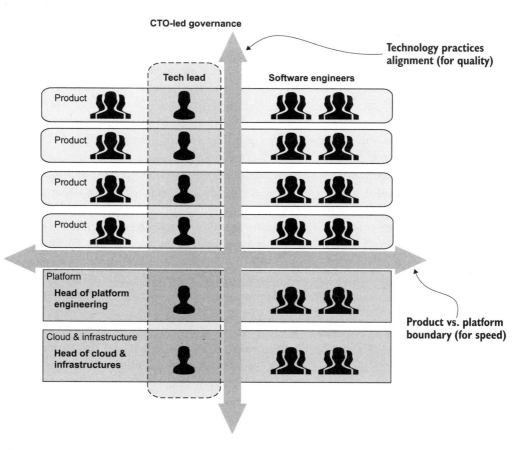

Figure 13.5   Organizational design to sustain the IDP

"The success of a platform is heavily dependent on the people working on it. At present, the engineering perimeter of the platform at hand is using about 60 to 80 individuals depending on the current workload. While the data perimeter is utilizing around 15 individuals and the middleware is not fully integrated, with only about 8 individuals currently involved. To ensure that the platform runs effectively and efficiently, there is a dedicated platform team consisting of 4 people who are focused on building and running the platform. Their objectives are to ensure that the developer experience is optimized for maximum satisfaction. Additionally, the Cloud Center & CoE play a crucial role in providing some common foundations and specific services to the platform team and the wider engineering team."

One fundamental, and oftentimes controversial, topic that cannot be avoided when building an IDP is technology stack and build-versus-buy choices. Rather than being seduced by fashionable industry trends or industry peer pressure, it's important to focus on your own unique context. As Antoine explains: "It is important to understand the trade-offs of technology choices in context. Our approach was to take the minimalist choice and iterate, rather than pre-optimize and over-engineer, as this would lead to maintenance costs and delay."

By focusing on what was important to them, Antoine and his colleagues decided that Kubernetes was the sweet spot for their needs: "We wanted managed services for efficiency and focus, but we also wanted to maintain some flexibility with an acceptable level of lock-in. We chose Kubernetes instead of a container or app as a service, as it provided us with desired level of flexibility because the other options were tied to cloud providers at the time. We also preferred to use the Spring framework rather than a PaaS solution on top of it, as it gave us the option of moving to a higher layer of abstraction in the future if needed."

Platform technology choices extend beyond just infrastructure and programming frameworks. There's a whole ecosystem of tools to consider, with many open source and vendor offerings to choose from. La Redoute took a principled and pragmatic approach and even built tools of their own that were open-sourced: "We believe in picking mature and community-supported solutions that will remain for some time, even if not always open-source. Examples of such solutions include Hashicorp Vault, ELK, Grafana, Jaeger, and Kubernetes. And sometimes, it is necessary to bootstrap yourself where you don't find what you need. We did that in 2010, building Cerberus Testing, now an open-source test automation platform, and in that journey with akhq.io as an Apache Kafka management console. We built it in a distributed OSPO (Open-Source Program Office) model, collaborating with three companies, and sharing the roadmap and resources. The product supported our use cases and grew with our needs and of the community, counting companies like BMW, Adeo, BestBuy, Decathlon, or Klarna. We were happy to see it appear in the ThoughtWorks technology radar at the end of 2022."

Another complex, unavoidable challenge of building IDPs is the trade-off between standards and flexibility. The more the platform is standardized, the more tooling and processes can be built around the common conventions. But the risk is that too much standardization can stifle teams, forcing them to use technologies and processes that limit their ability to innovate. Antoine explains that La Redoute made a best effort to identify what would be optimal in their unique context: "It's important to step back and consider the big picture. This includes taking into account the company's size and where the limiting factors may be. At La Redoute, some of the limiting factors were release/deployment dependencies and testing. As a result, we leveraged our IDP standards to evolve the software architecture to a finer grain of modularity aligned with business domains and functions (i.e., miniservices). In addition, we structured standard event-driven patterns, increasing functional and technical decoupling by design. We tackled the testing part with scalable test environments to support the systematic automated tests required as part of every deployment pipeline."

> **NOTE** Platform engineering is a vast topic. On the book's Miro board (http://mng.bz/qjMN), you can find recommended resources for digging deeper into the topic and keeping up with the latest developments.

13.4   *Managing internal developer platforms*

A platform's positive and negative characteristics will be amplified by the number of teams using the platform. Therefore, it's crucial that every aspect of building and maintaining the platform is well managed. From treating the platform as a product to choosing an appropriate funding model to optimize the experience of people working on platforms, there is a lot to think about and get right.

13.4.1   *Platform as a product*

The concept of *platform as a product* (http://mng.bz/5op7) has become increasingly popular because it is an effective approach to building and evolving modern platforms, which counteracts the mistakes from previous generations. It's the idea of applying modern product management practices to building IDPs, like having a value-driven strategy and product management expertise within the platform's teams.

PRODUCT NOT PROJECT

One of the biggest things to worry about when building an IDP is investing large sums of money and hundreds of people hours only to find that nobody wants to use the platform when it has been built. This does happen in reality and is usually the result of treating the platform as a project. Do not set out with the mindset of designing the whole platform up front, spending multiple years building and then expecting everybody to come and use it.

Building an internal platform should apply the principles and practices of modern product development. It should be developed iteratively based on feedback, driven by a clear strategy connected to a compelling business case, with sufficient expertise and genuine product management expertise on the team. Start small with proof of concepts and MVPs and scale the investment as value is validated.

SOLID BUSINESS CASE AND PRODUCT STRATEGY

Building an IDP should be driven by a clear understanding of the value it will provide. It's not a good idea to do it just because it seems fashionable and other organizations are doing it. It's essential to clearly understand the value the platform will provide and how it compares to the existing approach and off-the-shelf solutions.

Efficiency and cost reduction are benefits of an IDP. However, when focusing on these advantages alone, it's easy to develop a below-par platform that provides a poor experience to consumers through lacking features and poor usability. While cost is always an important consideration, the focal point of the business case and strategy should be lower cognitive load and improved productivity. Improved innovation, collaboration, and scalability are other benefits to articulate.

Many concepts used throughout this book can be applied equally to building business cases and designing IDPs, like listening and mapping tours, Wardley Mapping, and even EventStorming as a technique for mapping out internal processes and development workflows.

DATA- AND FEEDBACK-DRIVEN

A developer platform should reduce the cognitive load of the engineering teams that consume it and empower them to focus on their core business objectives. It's a major warning sign when the platform increases teams' cognitive load. Tracking key metrics enables a platform's teams to assess the platform's effect on DX, team satisfaction, and cognitive and system reliability. Further, these insights should be used as feedback to drive the platform roadmap.

Developer experience metrics measure how well the platform supports its users in accomplishing their tasks. These metrics can include

- Time to create a new service (from zero to running in production)
- Deployment frequency
- Lead time for changes
- Number of support tickets raised (indicator that self-service needs improvement)

In addition to DX metrics, surveys are an important tool for gathering feedback about the experience of platform consumers. On average, platforms send out a survey about once per quarter, containing questions along the lines of

- How satisfied are you overall with your experience of the platform? (1–10)
- How easy do you find creating a new microservice on the platform? (1–10)
- How happy are you with the process of deploying new changes to production? (1–10)
- In general, how easy is it to navigate the platform documentation? (1–10)
- What is your biggest pain point with the platform?
- If you could change one thing about the platform, what would it be?

Assessing usage is also a key measurement to determine the effect on the platform. Most importantly, how many teams are actually using the platform out of your total addressable market? Are all the relevant teams within the organization using the platform?

Engineers are using the platform not only to set up new services but to support them in production. Therefore, measuring production reliability is essential. Reliability metrics include uptime, latency, number of incidents, mean time to recovery, and change failure rate.

PLATFORM PRODUCT MANAGERS

It's so easy to invest a lot of time and effort in building a suboptimal platform or even a platform that provides a worse experience. I've seen countless occasions where it was considered acceptable to have low usability standards because a platform was internal only or intended to be used by developers. Maintaining a focus on the needs of platform consumers and delivering what they need in a usable form is critical. For this reason, an IDP cannot be staffed only by people with strong technical skills. It's equally important to have product management skills on the team. Like the MDTP example, the optimal scenario is that the whole team has a strong product mindset and is totally focused on providing a great DX.

Good platform product managers will spend a lot of time with developers who use the platform to understand how they currently work and their pain points. They will do this constantly and continuously seek feedback while developing and evolving a product strategy for the platform.

A good platform product manager will also ensure that the platform's roadmap is focused on the highest-value items for the organization as a whole. It's worryingly easy for teams on a platform to fall into the habit of developing ad-hoc features based on whichever team is shouting loudest. While feedback and adaptability are important, all work should be validated and prioritized accordingly rather than the team being reactive and building to spec.

REAL SELF-SERVICE

Self-service may sound like an exact and unambiguous requirement. Yet, there are some interesting interpretations out there that involve raising support tickets and manual tasks being conducted by platform team members. This is not what is intended when talking about self-service platforms. Self-service platforms enable platform consumers to perform their tasks, like creating a new application or deploying to production, without raising any tickets or relying on platform team members to carry out manual steps like creating servers or deploying code.

One way to test your platform's definition of self-service is to compare yourself with AWS. Anybody can create an account with AWS and spin up services like AWS Lambda or EC2 virtual machines. No support tickets are created, nobody at AWS is manually doing the work behind the scenes, and there is no need to talk to anyone at AWS. The AWS platform allows engineers to carry out their tasks immediately and without the support of any humans.

Obviously, things occasionally go wrong; therefore, there are genuine reasons for raising support tickets to the platform. But, there should be periodic analysis of support tickets to ensure support tickets are not being raised for routine tasks that should be automated or documented better.

FUNDING MODEL

New platform components and enhancements should not be funded on a per-feature basis by the teams requesting the features. A better funding model is for the platform to have a dedicated budget. Firstly, platform features and enhancements should benefit many teams, so one customer paying doesn't make sense. Secondly, platform components require ongoing maintenance beyond an initial payment. And thirdly, arguing about who is funding features creates politics and distractions that benefit no one and ultimately delays improvements to the platform.

13.4.2 *Adequately staffed*

Building an IDP is not a side project for people already fully occupied with other work. This can work when there are just a few teams, and people dedicated to the platform can't be justified, but it doesn't work as the number of teams grows beyond approximately six. Building a half-baked platform can be worse than building no platform at all. They can add more friction and complexity to the workflow of every team that uses the platform. So, if you feel there is a need to build an IDP, then take time to determine the necessary level of investment.

DIFFERENT SKILLS FOR DIFFERENT LAYERS

As the number of platform components increases and the number of teams consuming the platform grows, the number of people working on the platform will also need to increase. When the team gets too large, it should be split into multiple smaller teams, each owning an area of the platform. Adrian Cockroft's first principle for architecting platform groupings is that it isn't one platform: "It's layers of platforms that need different specialized knowledge, so it's usually many platform teams" (http:// mng.bz/6nAR). At HMRC, for example, PlatOps was mostly responsible for developer-centric tools and services, while other teams like WebOps (the web operations team) were responsible for lower layers like hosting and networking.

THE RISKS OF MULTIPLE TEAMS AND BACKLOGS

When a platform is composed of multiple teams responsible for different layers, one anti-pattern to avoid is what Evan Bottcher calls *the un-platform* (http://mng.bz/ orRD). In brief, each team has its own incentives and management structure and has no incentive for a joined-up end-to-end experience. As a consequence, the dysfunctions are exposed to consumers of the platform. Because there are handovers and bottlenecks inside the platform, work takes longer. And when teams have issues, they may get passed around between different teams when trying to resolve issues, for example.

To avoid building an un-platform, focus on the types of platform work and optimize end-to-end flows. And incentivize teams in a platform grouping to optimize for end-to-end performance rather than individual productivity.

13.4.3 *Build vs. curate*

There is no obligation to build and manage all platform layers. If you adopt Serverless, for example, there is no hardware or operating system to manage. Cloud providers take care of that for you. And it's not a binary choice. Some parts of your system may use Serverless, while others may need access to lower layers of the stack. When working with one organization that had chosen a Serverless-based platform, it surprised me how happy the security team was with the direction. I expected a lot of resistance and a long list of reasons why it would take months to obtain approval, but their response was the opposite. They liked that Serverless provided a much smaller attack surface.

Where off-the-shelf components exist, like API management solutions and software catalogs, you need a good reason to build them in-house. Remember Matthew Skelton's quote from the start of the chapter that emphasizes a digital platform should involve curating and adapting existing offerings: "A platform is a 'curated experience for engineers.' A good platform could thus be just a wiki page that specifies 5 or 14 AWS services that should be used together in a specific way."

When you build platform capabilities in-house, you effectively compete with cloud providers like Google and AWS. Even if you feel that developing in-house is cheaper, can you provide an equally good, or even better, developer experience? If not, your cost savings may be a poor trade-off when your development teams have higher cognitive load and are less productive.

13.4.4 *Technology standardization vs. flexibility*

Opinionated platforms improve the DX by enabling platform engineers to build more advanced and bespoke tooling. At HMRC in 2015, the only choice for building a new microservice API was using the programming language Scala and the Play Framework. It's fair to say that some engineers complained about the lack of freedom and flexibility. However, the results tell their own story. There were 50+ teams, all able to spin up new microservices and have them close to production-ready in just hours, with the ability to deploy to production daily. An IDP doesn't have to be this highly opinionated, but this example does make a clear case for diligently considering the level of standardization that is right in your context.

Rather than mandating the use of golden paths and paved roads, some organizations prefer to offer engineering teams more flexibility. Netflix is an example of a company that invests heavily in paved roads without strict mandates: "We don't mandate adoption of those paved roads but encourage adoption by ensuring that development and operations using those technologies is a far better experience than not using them" (http://mng.bz/wjp5).

The more technologies you use, the more golden paths and tools you must create. Some questions to ask yourself are

- Is it an effective use of your time and budget to support four programming languages and three cloud providers?
- Can you continue to provide an exceptional DX when you are spread thinly across a more diverse technology landscape?
- How will the cognitive load and flow of teams be impacted if they have to take on more infrastructure and tooling responsibilities (that could have been part of the platform)?

13.4.5 *Platform engineer experience*

While DX is extremely important, Paula Kennedy, the cofounder and COO at Syntasso, makes an equally valid point: "The challenge we're coming across is that cognitive load is shifting onto the platform teams. These teams have become responsible for providing the developer experience, but with many tools that need to be incorporated, as well as other concerns such as compliance and governance, they face huge cognitive load" (https://platformengineering.org/blog/cognitive-load).

Providing great experiences for developers shouldn't come at the expense of burning out platform engineers. We should also be thinking about platform engineer experiences, as Paula articulates. This means continually seeking feedback from platform engineers, analyzing their workflows and pain points, and optimizing their processes.

13.5 *When to build a platform*

Deciding to build an IDP and how much to invest can be tricky. There are numerous difficult decisions to make and a few key principles that everyone involved in the initiative needs to be aligned on. Firstly, an IDP should not be delivered as a big bang 12- to 24-month project. In Team Topologies, Matthew Skelton and Manual Pais advocate for a thinnest viable platform mentality: "A TVP is the smallest set of APIs, documentation, and tools needed to accelerate the teams developing modern software services and systems." The second important principle is that the IDP isn't a side project. It will be the foundation for many or all your engineering teams. It needs dedicated team members and long-term funding.

Smaller organizations with just a few engineering teams typically don't need an IDP. In 2021, a client of mine was a startup within a large European organization. The startup's raison d'être was to disrupt the entire industry, including its parent company. The startup's CEO did everything possible to create an innovative and product-centric culture. In particular, he pushed autonomy, empowerment, and flat hierarchy to the limit. Everybody reported to the CEO, and teams were fully empowered to make product and technology decisions. When I first met with the organization, they were just starting to encounter growing pains due to their success. They weren't sure if a platform team was needed.

On one hand, they didn't want a centralized team that could introduce bureaucracy into the organization. On the other hand, a few engineers were expected to maintain and build the common infrastructure and tooling as a side project in addition to their main job as engineers in product teams. The common infrastructure became neglected, increasing each team's cognitive load, and the side-project engineers were starting to burn out. Combined with the projection to double the number of teams, the signs strongly hinted that it was the right time to build a real platform with a dedicated team.

Size isn't the only factor that should influence the decision to build an IDP. Even in larger organizations, there are reasons not to create a platform. For example, when the chance of adoption is likely to be low. This happens for a number of reasons, such as teams not wanting to give up freedom they already have or not having the time to migrate from their existing technologies to the new platform. Or simply resistance to change from those who are happy operating more traditionally.

Summary
- To achieve independent value streams with fast flow, stream-aligned teams cannot be burdened with a high level of work just to build, deploy, and test their code.
- A slick developer experience (DX) is key to reducing extraneous cognitive load so teams can focus on continuously delivering product enhancements.

- The main purpose of an internal developer platform (IDP) is to provide a great DX and reduce the teams' cognitive load.
- DX covers many aspects of a developer's work like
  - Creating and setting up new applications
  - Developing code locally
  - Deploying code to test and production environments
  - Supporting code in production
- In a modern context, DX should allow teams to set up new applications in minutes or hours; deploy code to production in minutes' and have metrics, monitoring, logging, and advanced observability out of the box.
- IDPs can enable a slick DX with golden paths, which are highly automated or well-documented processes for performing common tasks like spinning up new applications.
- IDPs can expose capabilities in various forms like UIs, CLIs, and Git repositories.
- IDPs should provide an applications catalog that shows all of an organization's applications along with metadata like the team that owns the application.
- High-quality documentation is a key part of ensuring platforms are self-service and easy to use; without this, teams will struggle and may need to raise support tickets.
- IDPs should be treated as products with a value-driven, iterative approach and not treated as waterfall-style projects.
- IDPs should be staffed with skilled product managers who continuously seek out feedback from platform consumers and treat them like external customers.
- It's ideal when the whole platform is focused on DX and the needs of their internal customers.
- Not all of a platform needs to be built in-house; some or most of a platform could be a curated experience of off-the-shelf offerings.
- Not every organization needs a platform; it may be an unwise choice when there are only a few teams, adoption of the platform is likely to be low, or off-the-shelf solutions are sufficient.

14

Data mesh revolutionizing data engineering

If you thought modernizing your architecture would not affect your data, you would be seriously wrong. I won't try to convince you of the importance of data; anyone who has read this far into this chapter knows already. Many people nicknamed data the new oil, but modern data engineering goes beyond simple pipelines. Data feeds everything from dashboards and reports used by executives when making decisions to risk analysis and fraud detection, including AI. However, unleashing the true value of data comes at a severe operational cost if not done correctly. For sanity's sake, I will not name the organizations whose operating budget for maintaining pipelines and systems forbids them to do any forward-thinking; then, they hire many data scientists who spend 80% of their time on data discovery and engineering. Finally, most complain about the value data brings to the company. Sound familiar? In this chapter, I will walk you through how we came to this point, what the issues are with modern data management, why you can solve them with just four fundamental principles, what the various elements of the architecture are, and finally, how to get started.

14.1 Setting up the context for complex data

In this section, I will briefly cover the technology background and new needs around data. I will conclude with the issues most corporations face. Do not worry; I am not giving a history lesson, but I will attempt to explain how data morphed from this simple, structured element to a shapeless monster. But keep in mind, when I talk about a beast, I think more about Cookie Monster—a friendly creature, as long as you feed it.

14.1.1 The dawn of data engineering

For me, the real revolution surrounding data started around 1971, when MIT demonstrated Codd's idea (http://mng.bz/ZRrA) of a relational database. Along with the third normal form, engineers began to think more about data and how to use it.

Data warehouses were the next logical evolution: How can I aggregate data, let's say, from thousands of stores across the country so that I can understand what I am selling? At first, data warehouses seemed like a great idea until businesses demanded more agility from their data teams. The rigorous (and somewhat complex) modeling associated with data warehouses rendered the ingestion of new data sources very complicated.

The example in figure 14.1 is loosely based on an auto parts retail company with a B2C and B2B activity. The information is split into different buckets based on the source. Look at a store receipt: part of the information is stored in the loyalty customer dataset (process 3 in the diagram); it is recorded in the store transaction (process 6); and depending on whether it is a pro/B2B customer or a retail/B2C, customer it goes in two other buckets (processes 2 and 4). When the company added the loyalty program, a whole new process (3) had to be built to collect the loyalty information from the store receipt.

As shown in figure 14.1, even with a simple data warehouse, the ingestion process is not easy and can become increasingly complex as your input files grow. Because these processes are across the domains of the company, a centralized team, which has no domain expertise, is often building them.

Data lakes tackled the problems by hiding the ingestion complexity under the living room rug. Data lakes made it easy to ingest data but pushed the burden of accessing it onto consumers.

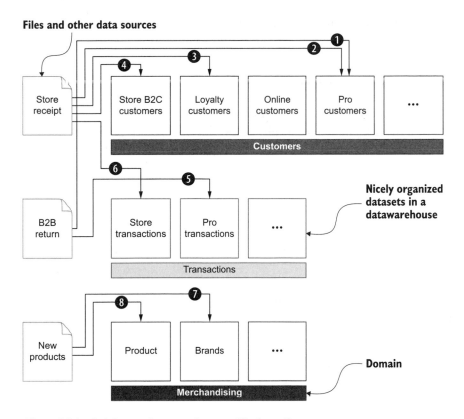

Figure 14.1 A data warehouse and some of its ingestion process

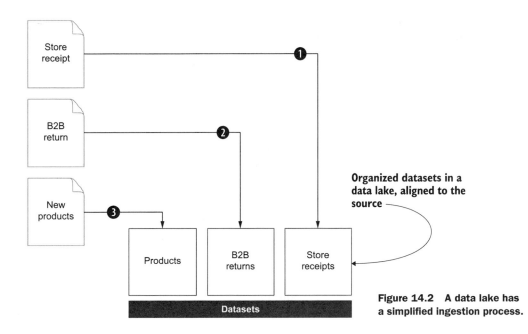

Figure 14.2 A data lake has a simplified ingestion process.

Figure 14.2 illustrates the simple ingestion processes. As you can see, it is much simpler: store receipts go into the store receipt bucket, B2B returns go to the B2B returns bucket, and so on. However, there are two issues:

- What happens when the store receipts change format or you open in a new country or add a special tax, loyalty program, or any other change? You may have new buckets or modifications of existing ones.
- As figure 14.3 indicates, it can become complicated really fast when you want to access the data.

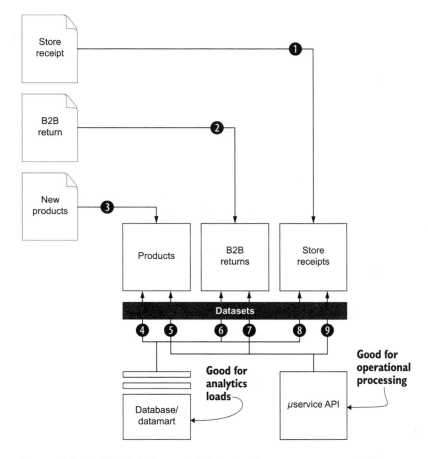

Figure 14.3   Getting data from a data lake is not as easy as you would like.

The numbers on pipelines/processes in figures 14.2 and 14.3 are not linked to figure 14.1; they simply illustrate that there is no obvious win in building pipelines.

Like the data warehouse, data lakes and their ingestion and consumption are handled by centralized teams with minimal domain knowledge in a project mode. This centralization thinking is very similar to the monolithic approach in software engineering.

The size of those projects, building and deploying a data lake or data warehouse, often calls for an enterprise engagement. Building a data lake for only your department is difficult as it will require enterprise-level oversight, governance, and resources. No enterprise wants a shadow IT data lake.

In both scenarios, the ETL (extract, transform, and load) and ELT (extract, load, and transform) pipelines are becoming expensive to maintain. Some enterprises' entire operational budget supports those pipelines and their maintenance, freezing any new developments. The lake house tries combining data warehouses and lakes without addressing the centralization issues around data.

14.1.2 New needs around data

The rigor around data is growing everywhere—a trend that will continue. Let's address the elephant in the room first: data breaches. They seem to happen all the time, and although the root cause of the breach is rarely (dare I say never?) the data itself, it is about how we manage the data. For the consumer, it can be devastating. However, for corporations, fines are only one consequence; reputational harm lasts longer. Corporations understand that they need to protect the data as data cannot protect itself.

Early in my career, I remember going to a customer at a single "mom and pop" shop (without even a mom). He was building and deploying a pharmacy management system out of his basement. I am sure that neither the details of the prescriptions nor the names of the patients were encrypted.

Another concern is how much information technology has become ubiquitous in our daily lives. States and governments have developed laws to manage how personal data is handled and used. Famous examples include Europe's GDPR (2016), California's CCPA (2018), and France's National Commission on Informatics and Liberty (1978). Corporations need to comply with privacy regulations.

A third issue is the abuse and inadequate practices that develop over time—inadequate reporting to Wall Street, complex (and voluntarily cryptic) financial products, abuse in collection calls and reach out, and so much more. Corporations have rightfully been the target of legislators for increased scrutiny and need to prove that they are willing to do the right thing. For example, in the United States, you should keep your financial data for 7 years, but in France, it is 10 years, and Australia is changing from 7 years to 10 years.

This assessment is in no way exhaustive or static. We live in a dynamic and global world. We need a governance system from an enterprise perspective that is flexible based on business and regulatory needs.

14.1.3 More problems than solutions

We are experiencing a constant run toward new technologies that do not

- Solve centralization of data and data engineering, far from the expertise of the factory floor
- Answer to more regulations and diverse compliance rules
- Provide lifecycles around data and its constant acceleration

- Grant access or allow users to manipulate data easily
- Ensure trust
- Support the growing scale of data

In the next section, we see how data mesh can directly solve some of these issues and help others.

14.2 *The four principles of data mesh*

In this section, I will detail the four principles driving data mesh; how they provide a solution to the problems discussed in the previous section; and, most importantly, why those four principles rely on one another. In May 2019, a brilliant engineer, Zhamak Dehghani, published a paper highlighting the basis of the data mesh called "How to Move Beyond a Monolithic Data Lake to a Distributed Data Mesh" (http://mng.bz/RmMv). In her paper, Dehghani sets the ground for four principles, which are refined over the last couple of years into the data mesh's four principles.

I like to compare those principles to how the agile manifesto by Kent Beck et al. (https://agilemanifesto.org/) disrupted the waterfall-based lifecycle in software engineering. Data mesh brings to data engineering many of the concepts you may have been familiar with in agile software engineering and domain-driven design, including product thinking, iterative development, ownership, and more. Let's discuss the four principles.

14.2.1 *Principle of domain ownership*

The term *domain* has been so overused in recent decades that its meaning is almost gibberish. Nevertheless, let's try to tame the domain and ownership in this context. Chapter 8 provides more detailed enlightenment about this notion.

A domain is a specific area of business on which you are focusing. If you are in the financial industry, it can be customer accounts or a specific area, such as individual accounts. Identifying the domain sets the boundaries and prevents you from falling into scope-creep situations (such as including all types of accounts in the project).

If you are familiar with domain-driven design, which was discussed previously in this book, the principle will come naturally to you. It is common sense: find the people who know a domain best and associate them with a data architect. The decentralized team has precious domain expertise; they know more about the data sources, data producers, rules, history, and evolution of systems than a centralized team that switches from domain to domain. Adding the data architect into the mix will bring security, rules, and global governance to stay compliant with enterprise policies. Problem solved: centralization of data and data engineering.

14.2.2 *Principle of data as a product*

In software engineering, Agile replaced the project with the product. It was only a question of time before data also became a product versus a project. Before seeing what a data product can bring, let's remind ourselves what a project is.

A project is a carefully planned initiative with a precise goal. A project is executed individually or as a team, although in software and data engineering, it is mostly teams. An essential attribute of a project is about time. A project is finite. It should end; its temporality is built-in.

Focusing on a data product will enable you to switch from a project-planning perspective to a customer-centric approach. Daunting? No, just remember DAUNTIVS; a data product must be

- Discoverable
- Addressable
- Understandable
- Natively accessible
- Trustworthy and truthful
- Interoperable and composable
- Valuable on its own
- Secure

In the next sections, I will describe the architecture and implementation to answer those requirements.

In software architecture, the smallest deployable element is called a quantum. When applied to data architecture, the data quantum is the smallest deployable element bringing value (figure 14.4). The data quantum is not related to quantum computing.

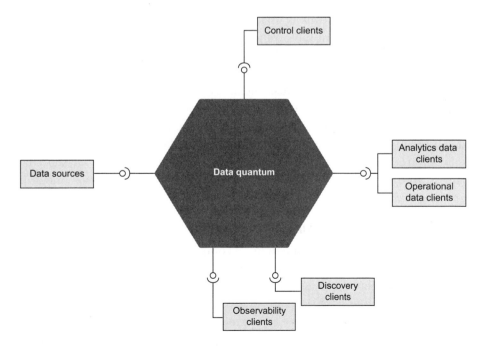

Figure 14.4 The data quantum takes the shape of a hexagon, highlighting its multiple endpoints, allowing access to data, metadata, observability, and control.

You're probably wondering, "Hey, how is that different from my data lake with a couple of data governance tools?" The answer is that size matters: instead of an entire enterprise-level lake, you focus on a single domain. It's more "byte size" and chewable. Thanks to its smaller size and scope, implementation is faster and the value from data is reinjected in the company a lot faster.

Let's consider a small example: Is it easier to build and deploy a smaller data product than a full data lake? By focusing on a smaller product at first, you can materialize value quicker. Our approach was to focus on six smaller datasets, each composed of one table and less than 200 columns, knowing that we could easily evolve it at a later stage based on customer needs. This allowed us to deliver quick results. Problem solved: provide lifecycle around data and its constant acceleration.

14.2.3 *Principle of the self-serve data platform*

When I was a kid, in France, I loved going to the local supermarket with my parents because it had a cafeteria where I could put all the food I wanted onto a tray. The self-service empowered me to make (bad) food choices. But what does that mean when it comes to a data platform?

Since its inception in 2001, Agile has proven to be a working methodology. Agile software engineering empowered software engineers. The way to empower data scientists is to give them access to data.

Data scientists and analysts spend (too much) time in their data discovery phase. In many situations, they find a piece of data in a random column in a table somewhere and assume that this is what they need. Sometimes it works, and sometimes your PB&J toast does not fall on the jelly side. (The peanut butter and jelly toast or sandwich is a rare American delicacy. As you can imagine, your toast falling on the jelly side is not the best experience.)

Empowering the data scientists means giving them access to not only a basic catalog of fields but also precise definitions, active and passive metadata, feedback loops, and much more. For a data engineer, self-service means the ability to create ad-hoc data pipelines and products. As you build a data mesh, they are your customers: you want to greet them in a five-star Yelp cafeteria, not this crappy one-star shack. Problems solved: grant access or allow users to manipulate data easily and support the growing scale of data.

14.2.4 *Principle of federated computational governance*

Every word of the principle of federated computational governance has a very important meaning, as I shall convey. Information technology has become ubiquitous in our day-to-day life. States and governments have developed laws to manage how personal data is handled and used. Of course, those constraints are not the only push toward governance in enterprises; most companies often have data governance rules and protections that may go beyond what the law requires. Those rules are established by a central (federal) governance team.

Your data governance team creates policies applicable to the entire organization, which the domain team will follow to achieve enterprise-level consistency and compliance. However, the domain team owns the local governance at the quantum level, maximizing the team's expertise.

But why push toward computational governance and not just data governance? Because data governance is simply too limiting. Even when you include metadata in your governance (and, of course, you do), you are still missing the entire ecosystem of computational resources linked to your systems. In a modern cloud-based world, you must account for many more assets. It simply makes sense to extend from data to computational governance (figure 14.5).

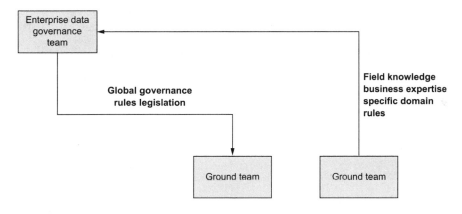

Figure 14.5 In a federated governance model, the enterprise data governance team works with each business unit.

For example, the company's data retention period could be three years, but some local teams may be required to keep the data for seven (or more) years. The central data governance team will say "three years," while the ground team can override this based on their needs and choose a "seven-year" value. Problem solved: answer to more regulations and diverse compliance rules.

14.2.5 *No principle lives in isolation*

Now that you know everything about the four principles driving a data mesh, let's focus on their interactions and understand the relationship between the principles. Each principle influences one another, and as you design and build your data mesh, you cannot look at one principle in isolation; you need progress on the four fronts at the same time. It is easier than it seems, but ignoring even one principle would be a big mistake, as figure 14.6 illustrates.

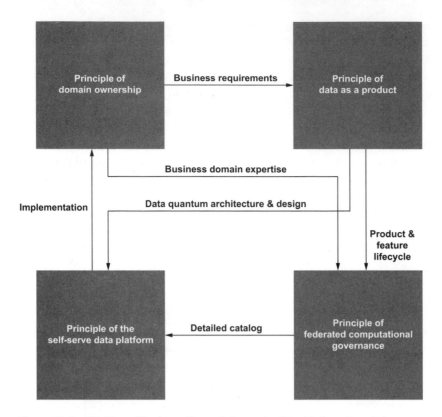

Figure 14.6   Thinking of implementing a data mesh without integrating all four principles would be a mistake.

Here is how to read figure 14.6. Following the principle of domain ownership, the domain drafts the business requirements. Those requirements will be used to design the product (principle of data as a product). The product enters a lifecycle in terms of availability and lifecycle that are managed by the principle of federated governance. Finally, the product's availability influences the self-service aspect of the data platform.

14.3   *Building your first data quantum*

After understanding the problem statements and the principles that will solve them, one of the hardest parts is how to architect (and then implement) a data mesh. Let's start small and expand from there. Let's build your first data quantum.

14.3.1   *The smallest element with value*

Whatever you do, the goal is to build value for your company. However, how can you create this value without boiling the ocean (which is cruel in many ways)?

If you are familiar with domain-driven design (DDD), you will quickly draw a parallel; if not, think of a limited scope for your project. What is the minimal set of (data) features you can deliver that will bring value to your consumers?

In this way, you are applying the first principle: domain ownership. Agile and product thinking introduced the notion of a minimal viable product (MVP). You are going to deliver a minimal viable data product. It may contain only some of the elements demanded by your customers, but like with Agile methodologies, you will deploy, let's say, 80% of the features within a (few) sprints.

Similar to Agile methodologies, after you deliver your first product, your customers will provide feedback, and you will add the features from your backlog. This delivery mechanism is hitting the second principle of data mesh: data as a product.

As you previously read, the smallest deployment element of an architecture is a quantum. The smallest deployment data product of an architecture is a data quantum. Let's build our first data quantum.

14.3.2 *Logical architecture*

You just learned that a data quantum is the smallest element you can deploy. Let's consider its main components.

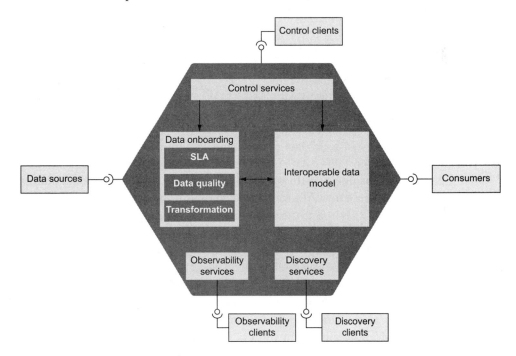

Figure 14.7   A data quantum (pl. data quanta) is the implementation of a data product and is represented as a hexagon.

You can divide the data quantum into five subcomponents (figure 14.7):

- The discovery & dictionary services
- The observability services
- The control services

- The data onboarding
- The interoperable data

The *dictionary services* provide the precious sesame to your passive metadata. I recommend that your data quantum users can connect, without authentication, to the dictionary. This facilitates the third principle of data mesh: the self-serve data platform. Their data discovery is then extremely simplified as they can browse the dictionary in a very interactive way without needing specific permissions, with additional description and access to data lineage. When they find what they need, they can easily check that they have access or request access to the data. The information exposed by the dictionary services is called passive metadata.

The *observability services* bring an interface between the built-in observability of the data quantum and REST clients. Observability can measure the availability of the sources and changes in the source schema; the services also include data quality. These services allow a data consumer to gauge the quality of the data within the data quantum and decide if the data quantum will match their service-level objectives (SLO) expectations. Collectively, you can call those metrics active metadata.

> **NOTE** Check out this post on Medium at http://mng.bz/27Wa for a quick introduction to the dimensions of data quality.

The *control services* offer access to a REST API where you can control the onboarding and data store(s). If you want to create a new version of your dataset in the data quantum, there is an API call for that. Do you need to control which data quality rules should be applied in your data onboarding? There is an API call for that. This interface is mainly oriented for data engineers managing the data quanta.

As you can imagine, the three sets of APIs are similar for each data quantum: there is no need to learn a new API for each data quantum. To simplify your usage, you can wrap your REST APIs in a Python API accessible via a notebook or a web application.

The *data onboarding component* is your old data pipeline on steroids. In many (if not all) predata mesh data engineering projects, the focus was on the data pipeline. The data mesh puts the pipeline back in its place. The pipeline is important but is an element of the data onboarding, such as observability or the application data quality rules. Adding all those functions in this component secures the classic, often failing, fragile ETL process. Yup, the days when the pipeline is the team's quarterback are behind us. (More details about the evil side of the data pipeline can be found here: http://mng.bz/1Jgq.)

Last but seriously not least, the *interoperable data model* is your critical data in a consumable way. I could have represented this component as the classic cylinder in older architecture diagrams. However, remember that the data a data quantum exposes is not always relational. The data quantum promises to separate the application from the data. This promise has an impact on the data modeling inside the data quantum. Before jumping into the physical architecture, let's discover what is gluing all that together: the data contract.

14.3.3 *Your new best friend: The data contract*

You have just learned about the components forming a data product, but how do you keep all those components in check? How can you define a base layer guaranteeing that all components speak the same language? This is the role of the data contract.

The data contract has multiple roles and benefits (figure 14. 8). The contract is a lingua franca used by many of the internal components of the data quantum. It creates a clear list of expectations between the data producer and the data consumer. The term *contract* is a powerful word that binds the different parties. It is precisely that. If I have data I want to sell (or give) to you, the data contract will describe all the information about the product I am selling you. I also like to think of the contract as the brochure I am giving you to advertise my data product.

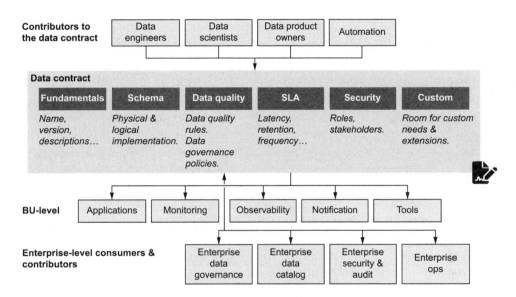

Figure 14.8 The data contract is a rich document defining the internal and external behavior of the data product.

In terms of responsibility, the data product owner owns the data contract. But data engineers, scientists, curators, stewards, and a lot of automation can contribute.

The data contract contains

- Fundamental elements like names, versions, and descriptions (including links to video tutorials, etc.)
- Schema from the exposed data, both logical and physical, including the connection between the two worlds
- Data quality rules and governance policies
- Service-level agreements (SLA)

- Security, more specifically, roles and stakeholders
- Room for expansion with custom attributes

The data contract is used by many (if not all) of the internal components of the data quantum. It is also used both at the business unit (BU) level and enterprise level. At the BU level, it is used for applications, monitoring, observability, notification, and other tools.

At the enterprise level, the data contract can be used by many teams as well that need to oversee data usage. Recently, PayPal has decided to release in open source, under an Apache 2 license, its internal template for a data contract, which is a YAML file. I would encourage you to read it, use it, and contribute to it. The data contract is essential for the internals of the data quantum, but it is even more critical to the outside world, as you will discover in the next section.

> **NOTE**   The Linux Foundation is now hosting the Open Data Contract Standard (ODCS) as an open standard. You can read more here: http://mng.bz/ PR1R. The standard can be found here: http://mng.bz/JdxZ.

14.3.4 *Physical architecture*

Before you implement your data product, you will need to clarify your physical architecture.

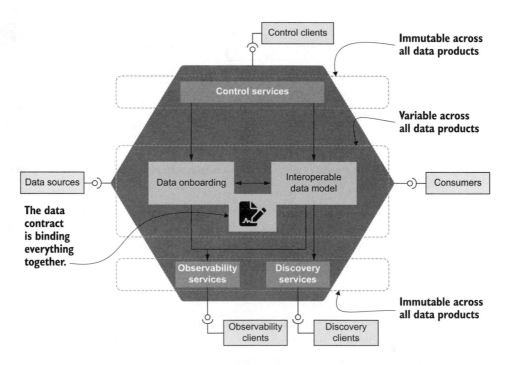

Figure 14.9   Only a few things change from data product to data product: onboarding, model, and contract.

Over the past year, I talked to many implementers, and although there are a few common points, I realized that the physical architecture is highly dependent on your existing infrastructure. Let's focus on those common points, and you can integrate them into your infrastructure (figure 14.9).

When you build a data product, the variable parts include

- The data onboarding
- The model itself
- The data contract

NOTE When you compare building a data product to a data pipeline, the data contract is the only additional element your data engineers handle. Later in your project, use the data contract to ease the data engineers' work.

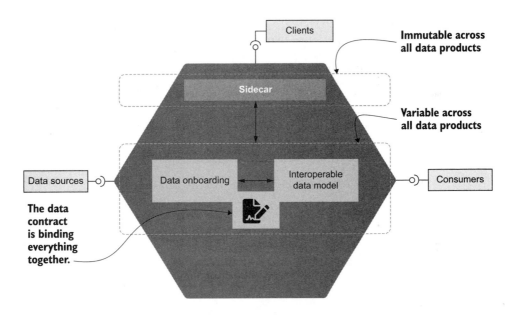

Figure 14.10 A good practice is to isolate the immutable parts in a single sidecar that can be deployed with each data product.

By isolating all your elements in a sidecar that uses the data contract as a configuration file, you create a viable component that you will be able to reuse in all your data products (figure 14.10).

NOTE Handling cross-cutting concerns is a good use case for the sidecar pattern. The name is an analogy with a motorcycle and its attached sidecar, with which it has strong ties. The difference between a sidecar and a library is that the sidecar is active (it has processes and services) and a library is passive code.

The sidecar will contain all your microservices, libraries, etc. The implementation will rely on your infrastructure: container and K8S, lambda functions on AWS, or a good old VM on your preferred cloud. The choice is yours (or, in many cases, imposed on you), but you still control the behaviors consistently.

14.4 *Navigating through the planes*

At this stage, you should understand everything you need to build multiple data products. However, numerous data products do not form a data mesh; they form a constellation of data products. You are transferring the issues with management elsewhere but still need to solve them. In this last section, I will drive you through the experience planes that will build the mesh.

They consist of

- The infrastructure experience plane
- The data product experience plane
- The mesh experience plane

14.4.1 *The infrastructure experience plane*

The infrastructure experience plane is undoubtedly the easiest to understand. This plane is regrouping all your infrastructure artifacts, including core producers. It includes network elements, SaaS applications, virtual machines, and more (figure 14.11). The infrastructure does not depend on the data mesh but strongly depends

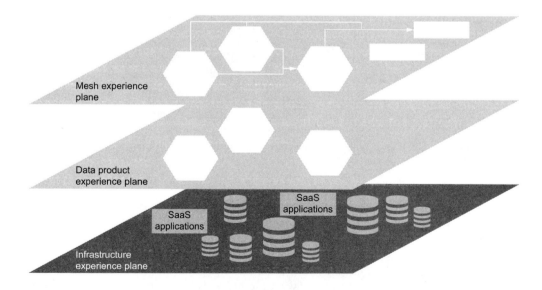

Figure 14.11   The infrastructure experience plane focuses on databases, security, networks, SaaS applications, and all the other low-level elements.

on this plane. A mix of data engineers and system engineers manages this plane. Your security should be the strongest on this plane. In most cases, when building a data mesh, you do not need to modify this plane, but you need a good understanding of it.

14.4.2 The data product experience plane

The data product experience plane is the home of your unlinked data products. This plane regroups all your data products but ignores the link between them. It heavily relies on its infrastructure to offer data products and access to data (figure 14.12). Usually, data engineers use this plane in their capacity to build data products.

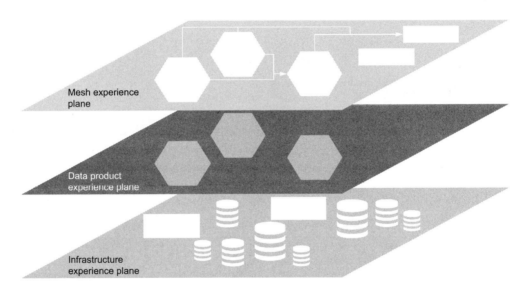

Figure 14.12 The data product experience plane feeds from the infrastructure plane to offer data products.

14.4.3 The mesh experience plane

Finally, the mesh experience plane is where the meshing happens. This plane creates the link between the data products, and naturally, this is where the meshing happens. The data quanta can talk to one another and share their information to centralization tools like a data discovery system (catalog), monitoring solution, and many more, as only the imagination is the limit (figure 14.13).

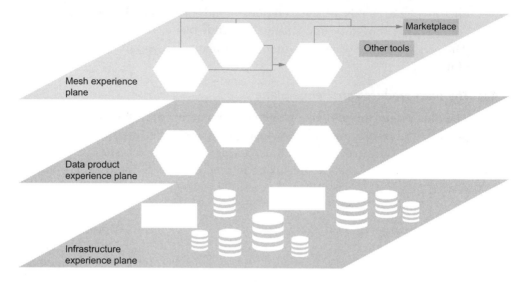

Figure 14.13   The mesh experience plane provides the full experience.

As you can imagine, the mesh experience plane heavily relies on the data product experience plane. The users of this plane are anyone producing or consuming data. They have many different roles in the organization. Figure 14.14 shows the three planes together.

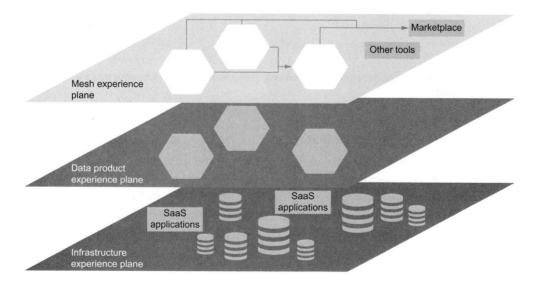

Figure 14.14   The three experience planes working in synergy.

Let's imagine a couple of scenarios. As a data scientist, I want to look for data so I can start by searching the marketplace. Once I have the right data product, I can access its internals directly, like detailed descriptions, sample data, ratings, and more. Finally, if I use its data, I will control it through the infrastructure experience plane.

As a data engineer, I am building a pipeline between a couple of sources and a target database, which will become a data product. I work within the data experience plane to build the data product from the work done in the infrastructure plane. When ready, I will register (or expose) the data product in the mesh experience plane.

14.5 First and next steps

You are now ready to build your data mesh. Here is some final advice for your journey:

- As with any disruptive technologies and methodologies, be prepared to guide your users through this transition. The *cognitive load and innovation will scare* and block some. Many data engineers live by the sacrosanct data pipeline, and reducing their idol to a mere component in a mesh can be traumatizing.
- Prepare your leadership for time to stand up a new platform; they should not expect results two weeks after you start (or even three).
- Limit your dependency on the infrastructure experience plane as you build your prototype.
- As with all product development, identify clearly who your users are and what tools they currently use. Share your personas. You may need to transition or extend their tooling, and this may create friction and resistance.
- And the truth is there is no "data mesh product" out there. There might be bricks, elements, or components that can be assembled to help you build your mesh (Spark remains a fantastic engine to perform your data transformation at scale; for more on this, I recommend the following book: https://jgp.ai/sia). However, there is nothing like an OTS (off-the-shelf) commercial or open source platform. In late 2022, Zhamak Dehghani founded Nextdata; her work is very promising but is not yet available.
- The lack of software vendors in the field fosters innovation but equally chaos.

Summary

- The data mesh paradigm comes from the natural evolution of data management.
- In many ways, data mesh is the application of Agile software engineering to data engineering.
- A data mesh is driven by four principles: domain ownership, data as a product, self-serve data platform, and federated computational governance.
- When building a data mesh, the four principles are intertwined. One cannot build a data mesh with only one (or even three) of the principles.
- The smallest deployable component is the data quantum.

- The data contract rules the internal and external behavior of the data product/data quantum.
- The plural of data quantum is data quanta, and by composing them, you build the data mesh.
- You can implement all your common services in a sidecar that is reusable across all your data products.
- The data mesh combines data products (or data quanta) in the mesh experience plane.
- Data products live in the data product experience plane.

15

Architecture modernization enabling teams

This chapter covers

- Identifying the need for an architecture modernization enabling team (AMET)
- Winding down an AMET when the mission has been achieved
- Staffing an AMET with suitable team members
- Establishing an enduring architecture operating model

If the most challenging part of modernization is getting started, then the second most challenging part is sustaining the momentum. Modernization is technology change, organizational change, and cultural change. You are swimming upstream against how things have always been done, and if you don't maintain high levels of commitment, your modernization will get washed away, and things will be back to the way they were before.

An *architecture modernization enabling team* (AMET) is one solution for countering the forces of inertia. An AMET's mission is to ensure modernization keeps progressing via various means, from organizing workshops to coaching leaders and teams to keeping modernization high on the agenda when other priorities, like BAU work and bug fixes, compete for people's limited time.

An AMET should not be confused with or become *the modernization team*. This is an antipattern where one team does all the modernization work. Equally, an AMET is not a centralized team of architects who do all the architecture and design and then hand it over to teams to implement. An AMET is more focused on supporting stream-aligned teams and other stakeholders during modernization (see figure 15.1) and upskilling the organization's architectural capabilities, creating long-lasting, durable change so that an AMET is no longer needed.

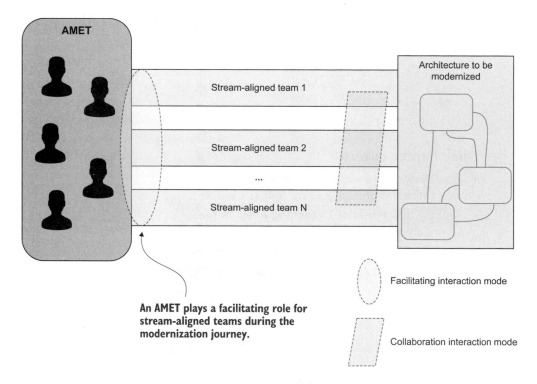

Figure 15.1   An AMET is an enabling team that facilitates stream-aligned teams (and other stakeholders) during the modernization journey.

The benefits are profound when an AMET focuses on upskilling just as much as delivering modernization. There is less need for significant modernization initiatives in the future. Because an organization's architectural capability is higher, the architecture will age more gracefully, and modernization will become an organic and ongoing activity.

Forming an AMET should be done carefully. Team members require a high level of maturity. They need to be comfortable engaging with all stakeholders involved in an initiative, from senior leadership to teams doing the work. And they need to know when to lead, when to facilitate, and when to step back and allow teams to take control. This chapter looks at the responsibilities of an AMET, how their purpose changes over time, and some suggestions for establishing effective AMETs.

15.1 AMET primary purposes

The concept of an AMET is not new. It's a pattern that has existed for many years. Eduardo da Silva (https://www.linkedin.com/in/emgsilva/) and I coined the term to describe an effective approach we have observed and applied on modernization journeys. We believe that there are six fundamental challenges most modernization initiatives will face, and we observe that effective AMETs focus on six primary responsibilities that each address one of the challenges, as shown in table 15.1.

Table 15.1 Fundamental architecture modernization challenges linked to AMET's primary responsibilities

Architecture modernization challenge	AMET primary purpose
Struggling to get things moving, stuck in analysis paralysis, lacking a compelling business case	Kickstart the modernization initiative
Progressing slowly due to conflicts with other work (e.g., business as usual) and deprioritization	Keep the momentum high throughout the journey
Lacking up-to-date knowledge and experience in designing modern architectures	Facilitate the design of better architecture
Failing to sustain new approaches and falling back to how things were	Facilitate long-lasting, durable change
People outside the initiative get confused by modernization or are unsure of the value	Keep people informed of the vision and progress being made
Learnings in one area do not benefit other areas	Promote success stories and learnings

15.1.1 Kickstarting modernization

Investing in modernization is a big decision. It's a gamble and a sacrifice. It's a choice to commit time and money that could be spent elsewhere, like continuing to add new product features and enhancements or developing new products. It's also daunting; with a legacy built up over many years and many opportunities for improvement, where to begin? For reasons like these, just getting started with modernization is hard. The path of least resistance is to keep operating as normal and ignore the problems (unless you have been doing that and are finally at the point where they can no longer be ignored).

Sometimes, being bold and sacrificing other investments in favor of modernization is the right course of action for an organization. And this is the first primary purpose of an AMET: to help all relevant stakeholders realize that architecture modernization will unlock major strategic business opportunities. The kickstarting analogy emphasizes that an initial boost of energy is needed to get things up and running to transition from a steady BAU state to an energetic enthusiasm for modernization.

As discussed in chapters 3 and 4, building a compelling vision and starting with a listening and mapping tour can help to kickstart a modernization initiative. This is a good initial focus for an AMET to conduct a listening and mapping tour to discover people's problems and the opportunities for modernization before switching into solution mode. One particular activity that I highly recommend is the Kickstarter workshop introduced in chapter 4. After meeting people individually or in small groups, this workshop is a chance to get together in person for a few days to get aligned on the vision, explore the domain, and start building a concrete plan of action for delivering a first slice of modernization within three to six months.

Delivering an initial slice of modernization within three to six months builds excitement, belief, and, perhaps most importantly, trust. Management has shown that they are willing to invest in and support modernization when there is a well-articulated vision, and teams have shown that they can deliver business value. So often, I see the lack of trust as a major inhibitor to getting modernization off the ground. Management is weary of committing to a large investment that may turn into techies playing around with fashionable, shiny technologies rather than delivering value. And engineers don't believe that management will invest to a level that is truly needed, so they are also wary and hesitant to commit to modernizing.

15.1.2 *Sustaining modernization momentum*

After kickstarting modernization, some momentum has been built. But it can quickly and easily be lost. An AMET works with all stakeholders as needed to keep modernization on the agenda and sustain or increase the momentum.

Numerous factors contribute to a loss of momentum, such as

- Lack of a clear vision, strategy, and priorities
- Other work being given a higher priority (e.g., BAU and bug fixes)
- Blocked by dependencies (e.g., teams not involved in modernization prioritizing nonmodernization work)
- Corporate red tape (e.g., taking months to get approval to deploy on the cloud)
- Not getting the investment needed (e.g., funds to hire additional people and skills relevant to the type and level of modernization needed)
- Going around in circles, unable to make significant or complex architectural decisions
- Concerns spanning multiple teams that fall through the cracks

To be able to deal with all these kinds of challenges, an AMET needs people who are comfortable dealing with all types of stakeholders and are able to use all of the techniques in this book, from mapping out strategy with Wardley Mapping to facilitating domain discovery with EventStorming, to designing and implementing domain models with domain-driven design. Not every team member will need to be an expert in each skill (although it's a worthwhile ambition), but the team needs the full range of skills collectively. It may need to bring in outside help, and AMET team members will very likely need to have opportunities for training and upskilling themselves.

It's crucial to remember that an AMET is not intended just to fight fires and fix whatever problems arise. An AMET's purpose is to establish solutions so that the organization can deal with these types of issues without the need for an AMET. For example, suppose teams working on related challenges cannot make collective decisions in a timely fashion. In that case, the AMET may introduce a decision-making approach like *The Architecture Advice Process* (http://mng.bz/j1Ve), which is covered later in the chapter.

15.1.3 *Facilitating better design*

Even if an architecture modernization gets off to a good start and momentum remains high, it's still possible for the initiative to deliver underwhelming results if the new architecture is not designed well. If teams have been working in a legacy system and haven't had opportunities to learn modern skills and practice designing good architecture, it's unrealistic to expect them to design the system well. The new system may have as many flaws as the old one.

This was the case for Segment (http://mng.bz/W1qW), who rebuilt their system twice. First, they went to microservices and then back to a monolith because their microservice design caused too many problems. Alexandra Noonan articulates one of their key learnings: "If microservices are implemented incorrectly or used as a band-aid without addressing some of the root flaws in your system, you'll be unable to do new product development because you're drowning in the complexity." This principle can apply to any modernization, not just microservices.

An AMET needs to look out for a lack of adequate design skills to prevent the type of expensive problems Segment experienced. A recurring theme is that people struggle with the concept of domains and identifying domain boundaries. One CTO told me, "We're moving from on-prem to the cloud, but I feel like we're repeating our old mistakes. I'm concerned that we don't understand what domains are. I thought if we did some EventStorming they would just fall out, but that wasn't the case at all." Another example was a technology leader who said, "We need to modernize our 20-year-old system, but we've got people who have been here for 15 years, and they've started by creating a big entity relationship diagram for the entire database. This seems completely the wrong way of designing systems after what I learned in the DDD workshop."

Both examples demonstrate somebody realizing ineffective architecture practices and a skills gap. This is precisely the kind of observation an AMET should be making and then supporting and upskilling teams so they are equipped to design modern architecture.

15.1.4 *Facilitating long-lasting, durable change*

At the start of a modernization initiative, there is excitement and openness to try new techniques and ways of working, using techniques like EventStorming. But over time, it's easy to fall back into old ways of working. This can happen for several reasons. Sometimes, there is too much reliance on external consultants, and when they leave, there is insufficient knowledge and expertise within the organization to sustain the new ideas and approaches. On other occasions, the organization drifts back into old habits, like when teams are piled up with work and don't have sufficient time or support to continue the new techniques and continuously improve their practices.

An AMET is strongly focused on enabling long-lasting, durable change so that the organization continues to benefit from modernization long after modernization is finished. An AMET will work with teams to help them develop the skills necessary to design and evolve architectures to a high standard and collaborate effectively with other teams and stakeholders. An AMET will also work with leadership to ensure they continue incentivizing better ways of working and help them adopt modern approaches to leadership.

INDUSTRY EXAMPLE: COMMUNITY OF PRACTICE SUPPORTING THE TRANSITION TO A PRODUCT-CENTRIC APPROACH

When I was part of an enabling team to help an organization move from a project-centric to a product-centric approach, we established a community of practice (CoP) for heads of product and platform. These people managed a group of teams responsible for either external-facing products or internal platforms consumed by the external-facing products. Before the shift to products and platforms, the product and platform leaders had worked in a strong project culture—their focus was delivering scope on time and budget, communicating progress, and managing risks.

The CoP allowed the product and platform leads to raise issues they were facing and get advice and support from other product and platform leads and external experts hired to help with the transition. It was an hourly session held every two weeks.

Just moving to a product-centric structure didn't magically lead to a faster time to market and better products. Initially, the leads were still trying to work in a project-centric fashion despite now being product and platform leads. For example, on one occasion, a platform lead had asked to speak at the next CoP about resource utilization. He opened the session by proposing a format. It was an Excel spreadsheet where each column was a day, and each row was a team member. He could show what each person in his teams would work on for any given day in the following three months. This approach gave the team no autonomy or flexibility in deciding how to do their work. It rebranded how the company worked before, just with a different spreadsheet and names, like avoiding the word *project* and using *product*.

When we asked the platform lead to explain the thinking behind this approach and why he needed something this detailed and rigid, he explained that he needed a way to show his stakeholders what each person in his team was working on. But that wasn't the case; it was just his perception of what he thought they needed based on how the company had previously operated for many years. Collectively, the CoP came to the agreement that fine-grained, rigid resource utilization was not necessary and that teams themselves should be able to decide who works on which tasks on a more flexible basis. It was also agreed that, generally, nobody outside the team needed to know which team members were working on which tasks (unless there was a clear need, e.g., for collaboration). It was still possible to communicate with the team via their chat channels and team leads to gain information or make requests.

As time went by, the CoP similarly addressed many topics, helping product-centric approaches to become the standard. The nature of the CoP itself also changed; enablers like myself became less involved, and the product and platform leaders themselves continued to drive their continuous improvement. The product-centric changes were long-lasting and durable, as was the approach to continuous improvement. There was no longer a need for an enabling team. The scaffolding could be removed safely. This is one way an AMET can support long-lasting, durable change.

15.1.5 *Communicating the vision and progress*

While modernization can be exciting for some, it can be confusing and worrying for others, like teams that aren't yet involved in the modernization journey. Sometimes, people are angry or jealous: "Why was that team chosen first instead of us?" "How come they get to do all the cool AWS and DDD stuff, and we're stuck fixing bugs in the legacy monolith?" Not everybody can be involved in modernization from the start, so concerns like these are likely to arise. Good communication helps to minimize these problems. If you bring people along on the journey, they are more likely to understand decisions, even if it's not what they would ideally like.

Communicating the vision and progress can also help people outside of modernization who feel stuck in a limbo state: "We've been asked to implement some complex new functionality. Should we keep working on the legacy tech stack or wait for modernization to establish a foundation and build our solution in the new world?"

Sometimes, people aren't aware of the modernization work that is happening in other parts of the business and how it could benefit them, so they continue building as usual when they could have waited for modernization to make their lives easier.

Some people may be skeptical or not even see the need for modernization. They may have been at the company for many years and are comfortable with the status quo. They may have even lived through similar initiatives that didn't deliver any value. Good communication can help to bring these people along, too, and allow them to see the value and spark their enthusiasm gradually.

An AMET shouldn't be the voice and face of modernization. It shouldn't be the team communicating the vision and progress. However, it may need to take on some of these responsibilities, especially at the start of a modernization journey, until it has established sustainable communication patterns. This may involve supporting technology leaders to set up rituals like monthly modernization progress sessions and working with teams to help them share their progress in various formats like text and video. There are many other possibilities, like internal conferences, communities of practice, and office hours sessions.

15.1.6 *Promoting success stories and learnings*

Building on the previous point, it's especially good to elevate modernization success stories and learnings. This enables successes and learnings in one area of the business to inspire and enable improvements in others. In organizations with a large amount of legacy technology and deeply ingrained legacy ways of working, getting from the current state to modern architecture and fast flow can feel impossible. But when one area of the organization has proved it is possible, it can invigorate teams in other areas. They realize that they don't have to be stuck deep in legacy, and they can see the steps other teams took as a guideline for planning their own modernization journey.

Allowing teams to share success stories at all-hands meetings and other events where large parts of the organization gather is a great idea. Equally, engineering off-sites are something I've seen work well. When I worked at Salesforce, hundreds of engineers were brought together from different offices across the US and Europe to discuss modernization of the legacy systems. But, the opportunity was also used for teams to share case studies of what was working and ideas from which other teams could benefit. I remember Ryan Tomlinson (https://www.linkedin.com/in/ryan-c -tomlinson/) talking about how his teams had achieved continuous delivery through engineering practices like TDD and fully automated infrastructure. Engineers from other teams dealing with a huge monolith that took hours to compile started to see that this wasn't just a nice theoretical idea, but it was 100% achievable, and there were people in other teams who could help them.

I've noticed that speaking publicly about success stories can have a positive effect internally. It's inspiring when people see their colleagues talking at meetups and conferences and having their blog posts praised on social media. They, too, want to do outstanding modernization work that is recognized and appreciated. So, I highly recommend that your organization establishes a tech blog and supports employees to speak at meetups and conferences. These are also great strategies for hiring—show the great work you are doing and the great engineering culture you have, and talented people will want to work for you.

If the infrastructure and rituals aren't in place for sharing your modernization success stories as widely as possible, this is definitely something an AMET should help with, even if it's just a case of finding people outside the team who can be responsible for them.

15.2 Industry example: Enabling modernization at a European telco

At the beginning of the 2020s, a major European telco had an ambitious, dual-focus growth strategy. On the one hand, the company was conducting an internal macrolevel restructuring, splitting itself into a NetCo, which manages physical assets like pipes and cables in the ground, and a ServCo, which offers products directly to customers. This change was driven by a desire to allow different parts of the organization to evolve at different rates. On the other hand, the telco was exploring product development and growth strategies by doing more for its existing customer base in nontraditional areas. The executives knew they had to be more responsive to opportunities in the market. They were concerned about their inability to move at speed in an increasingly competitive marketplace.

The telco knew its existing operating model was a significant sticking point. Regardless of their desired growth strategies, the organization needed to be more effective with a faster flow of product enhancements. They had tried transitioning from a Waterfall model to the Spotify model with generic Agile processes, but this shallow effort resulted in teams that were too large with many dependencies between them. Supported by João Rosa (https://www.joaorosa.io), the executives of the telco agreed to a more evolutionary approach tailored to their specific challenges and the nuances of their operating context. They were already aware of some of the biggest bottlenecks the transition to the Spotify model exposed.

What would your approach be to helping this telco modernize its systems and organization? For João, a key principle shaped the approach: durable change must come from within the organization. Many companies will outsource large parts of modernization to external consultants, but João has seen firsthand that this rarely works out. Instead, their first step was to establish an internal operating model exploration team, which aimed to explore the different evolution options for the operating model.

This team comprised João (the external consultant) and four diverse people from within the organization. They were either business-oriented department directors or technology-oriented IT architects. The team's stated purpose was to explore, facilitate, and advise on modernization efforts across the organization.

João acted as the coach within the team, bringing his previous experiences in similar initiatives to the table. He facilitated conversations within the group, helped them identify connections across the organization, and taught them how to use tools and concepts like Wardley Mapping, Value Stream Mapping, and Team Topologies. Effectively, João was empowering them to drive durable change rather than creating a dependency on himself.

The team's first challenge was to zoom into the current bottlenecks and understand what potential organizational changes were needed to facilitate a sustainable improvement in the flow of work. They began by meeting with some of the teams in *e-commerce* and *e-care* areas to try and answer a fundamental question: What are your current boundaries, and how did you choose them? This is a great opening question when communicated openly and genuinely because it creates a space for interesting insights and themes to emerge and doesn't bias particular solutions or answers.

Once problems begin to emerge, a follow-up question that João recommends is: What would it take to do X (where X is the insight that has emerged)? A common problem that teams face is that the limitations and constraints of the current environment make it hard to envision a different reality, and this question helps us to think beyond those current constraints. The other crucial benefit of this question is that it empowers the teams to identify improvements. Suppose you are used to offering solutions and making decisions but would like to become more of a facilitator and coach who can enable durable change. In that case, this is an ideal type of question to learn.

After interviews, João helped the operating model exploration team use multiple techniques, including EventStorming, Capability Mapping, and Value Stream Mapping, to map the organization and identify candidate domains and service boundaries. Each technique was applied to help facilitate valuable conversations as opposed to being seen as the ultimate artifact.

As a result of the diverse perspectives, discussions, and deep insights that surfaced about the business, they settled on five high-level domains for the organization. One of those domains was *product fulfilment*. It included the capability *customer self-fulfillment of an internet broadband package*. Figure 15.2 shows some key steps the team mapped out in the operational value stream for this capability: *place the broadband order, prepare the broadband equipment, ship the broadband equipment, deliver the broadband equipment,* and *self-install and activate the broadband.* These were the initial candidates for team and software boundaries.

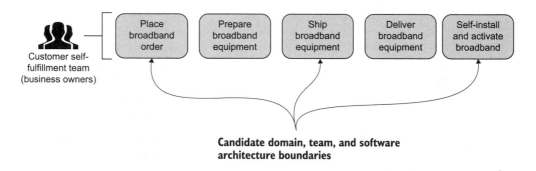

Figure 15.2   Partial view of the customer self-fulfillment of an internet broadband package operational value stream

From a business perspective, these boundaries made sense. The next step was to validate that they made sense from a team perspective. They used Team Topologies to map the team relationships and identify any problematic dependencies with the proposed structure. They followed a three-step approach:

- What is the to-be Team Topology that fits a telco context and allows fast flow?
- What are the as-is Team Topologies and challenges within the context?
- What are the options for team evolution and architecture modernization?

Figure 15.3 shows the as-is Team Topology that they mapped out. Both the number and nature of dependencies are problematic. All the steps in the *customer self-fulfillment of an internet broadband package* operational value stream require the involvement of multiple teams. And nearly all the interactions between teams are handover or collaboration, meaning higher levels of coordination and team cognitive load.

Figure 15.3 also highlights department boundaries, accentuating handovers between departments that represent more significant challenges to flow due to even higher levels of coordination, like the website platform shared between departments, testing and deployment done outside of the teams creating the software, and most of the steps of those processes being performed manually. The operating model exploration team also identified many escalation paths with the as-is approach, meaning teams were blocked, waiting for decisions or for work outside the team.

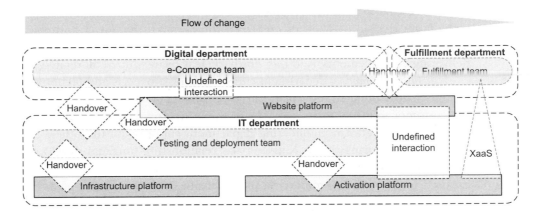

Figure 15.3   As-is team topology for the self-fulfillment of an internet broadband package value stream

Working closely with the teams involved, the operating model explanation team collaboratively designed a to-be team topology, shown in figure 15.4, which resulted in a big
improvement. They clubbed together related responsibilities and removed the need

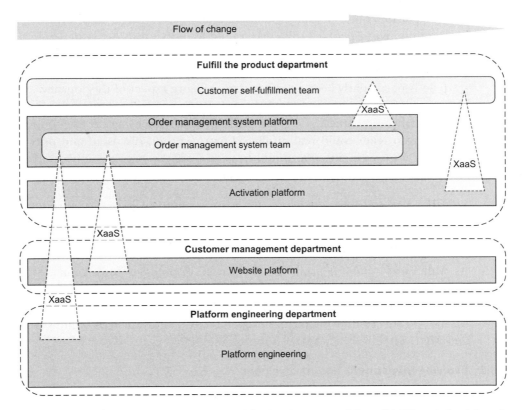

**Figure 15.4   To-be Team Topologies with few minimal paths to support the self-fulfillment of an internet
broadband package value stream**

for many escalation paths, so teams had fewer dependencies and were empowered to make faster decisions. They also replaced the high-cost handover and collaboration interactions with X-as-a-service relationships, so teams had more capacity to focus on delivering enhancements. And they ensured clear ownership of all related IT systems.

The *fulfill the product* department clubs together processes and technology related to their scope: the activation platform, the order management system platform, and the customer self-fulfillment team. All of them interact via an X-as-a-service relationship. And the platform engineering department supports all the other stream-align teams and platforms via an X-as-a-service relationship (internal development platforms are the topic of chapter 13). Lastly, all the self-fulfillment functionalities are exposed to the telco customers via their website, and the website platform exposes capabilities that the order management system team and the activation platform can consume via an X-as-a-service relationship.

Throughout the journey of identifying boundaries, João and the operating model exploration team not only supported the organization in identifying good candidate boundaries but also helped the organization establish a playbook and principles while removing no longer useful principles. This allowed the organization to scale out the approach to modernization, ensuring all improvements were aligned with the company's purpose.

The playbook also became a valuable tool for analyzing and prioritizing modernization initiatives—people at the telco could identify unnecessary dependencies, mismatches between boundaries, and excessive team cognitive load. The playbook gave them guidelines and techniques for addressing the challenges and improving flow.

João is particularly keen to emphasize one core aspect of this journey: "Our modernization efforts at the telco needed to take a sociotechnical approach: the joint optimization of the technical and the social systems. By focusing on the boundaries and what a given team could realistically achieve, we then discussed and prioritized the technical improvements that would best support the organization's purpose. If we ignored the social aspects, we would not have been able to achieve fast flow".

> **NOTE** You can find full-color, interactive versions of João's Team Topology diagrams on the book's Miro board (http://mng.bz/PRO8).

15.3   *Winding down an AMET*

As with every enabling team (in the Team Topologies sense), an AMET is not intended to exist forever. Once the team has achieved the purpose it set out to achieve, it can start to wind down. For an AMET, the mission is to empower the organization to successfully modernize its architecture and practices without the need for an AMET. Effectively, an AMET is scaffolding.

15.3.1   *Evolving investment and involvement*

Figure 15.5 nominally shows how the need for an AMET evolves as the organization's architectural capability increases. Initially, an AMET plays a leading role in making decisions and shaping the initiative's direction. Over time, however, the AMET starts to step back as modernization is delivered, and teams have the expertise and structures to continue the journey without the AMET. Team members may reduce the time they spend supporting AMET activities. Some members may roll off the team altogether.

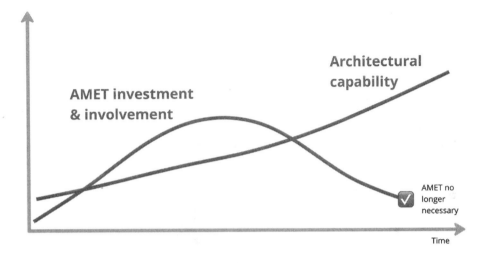

Figure 15.5   AMET involvement decreases as the organization upskills

As an AMET starts to wind down, its focus will be ensuring that long-lasting, durable change has truly been achieved. As the scaffolding is slowly removed, the team must confirm all structures remain in place. For example, AMET team members will attend and observe sessions without organizing or facilitating them and may run one-to-one coaching sessions to ensure leaders are equipped.

15.3.2   *Establishing an architecture operating model*

An AMET is a temporary team that may take on some architectural responsibilities during the early part of its lifecycle. However, you must consider what architecture means to your organization in the long term when the AMET no longer exists. What will be the architectural roles and responsibilities, how will decisions be made at each scope, what architectural standards will be established, and who defines them? An AMET's purpose of creating long-lasting, durable changes involves helping to establish the desired architecture operating model that will endure beyond the AMET's lifetime.

ARCHITECT ORGANIZATION MODEL

Defining architectural roles and responsibilities is the first consideration when designing your architecture operating model. Gregor Hohpe proposes four broad options (http://mng.bz/E92R) (based on Stefan Toth's work): *benevolent dictator(s), primus inter pares, architecture without architects,* and *the inmates running the asylum,* as shown in figure 15.6.

Benevolent dictator(s) is the traditional model of an architecture team that designs the architecture and hands over the designs for teams to implement. This is generally best avoided in product-led organizations where fast flow is required.

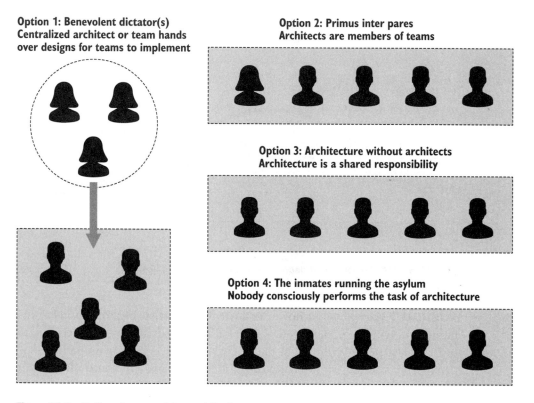

Figure 15.6   Options for organizing architects

Primus inter pares is where each team has a dedicated architect. Architecture is still the responsibility of a single person, but at least they are within the team, meaning fewer dependencies. *Architecture without architects,* meanwhile, relies on multiple members of a team sharing architectural responsibilities without a dedicated architect.

Finally, *the inmates running the asylum* means, effectively, that nobody is doing architecture, and it is neglected. Organizations don't choose this model by accident. For example, some just lack knowledge of architecture, and some believe there is no need for architecture in agile environments.

I consider the four models to be quite general. Each can be implemented in different ways. For instance, I think the personality and attitude of architects have as much of an effect on the quality of architecture (if not more) than the organizational model chosen. With *primus inter pares*, an architect embedded within a team could tend more toward an expert individual, much like a benevolent dictator, or they could be more of a facilitator who helps to upskill the team and move toward *architecture without architects*. Equally, a *benevolent dictator* team of architects with an enabling mindset could be more effective than architects embedded in teams in some circumstances. So, in addition to an architecture organization model, it's a good idea to define how you would like architects to operate in their role.

Architecture organization topologies (AOTs)

The options for organizing architects presented in figure 15.6 are largely focused on architecture at the team level. In medium and large organizations with multiple architectural scopes (covered in chapter 6), it's also important to architect responsibilities that span multiple teams, like a group of teams, each owning a subdomain within a larger domain.

Eduardo da Silva has documented a variety of patterns and their trade-offs. He refers to them as architecture organization topologies, and you can find them on his website (https://esilva.net/architecture-topologies).

ARCHITECTURE GUILDS

After determining architecture roles and responsibilities, it's necessary to think about architecture on a larger scale. How will architectural ideas and knowledge be shared across large parts, or even all, of your company? How will cross-cutting standards and principles be established that affect hundreds or thousands of engineers? Traditionally, centralized architecture teams and review boards have filled this void. But in organizations looking for more autonomy and decentralization of architecture to achieve fast flow, architecture guilds are likely to be a more effective solution due to the avoidance of a centralized bottleneck.

An architecture guild is a decentralized approach to making architectural decisions in medium and large organizations. A guild should be designed to meet the specific needs of your organization. As a starting point for establishing a guild in your organization, Jakub Nabrdalik's architecture guild example repository (http://mng.bz/NVYd; if for any reason this repository is deleted, you can find a snapshot on the book's Miro board, http://mng.bz/PRO8) provides an example structure containing the following elements:

- *Motivation*—Why your architecture guild exists, for example, to maintain high architectural standards while empowering teams to achieve fast flow.
- *Roles and responsibilities*—What the guild does, for example, identifying shared problems and identifying solutions that are globally optimal.
- *How the guild works*—When the guild meets, processes the guild follows, and the people that are involved.
- *How the guild cooperates with others*—How, when, and why other teams interact with the guild and vice versa; for example, all developers are welcome to join the guild.

- *Contact*—Details for contacting the guild, for example, chat channel or email address.

INDUSTRY EXAMPLE: COMCAST ARCHITECTURE GUILD

Comcast is America's largest multinational telecommunications conglomerate with an annual turnover of more than $120 billion (http://mng.bz/D9RV) and approaching 200,000 employees (http://mng.bz/lVlo). In 2019, they published a report describing their approach to architecture guilds (http://mng.bz/BAR2). They had already adopted decentralized approaches to architecture, which empowered teams to make decisions and move faster, and were seeking a way to maintain those advantages while still making effective decisions at scale that were optimal for the organization overall.

Comcast established a strategic architecture team at the top of their architecture guild structure to identify technical capabilities "where more commonality in implementation would be warranted." It would be exceptionally easy for a team with this remit to make decisions that looked good at a high level but didn't work out in practice and frustrated teams affected by the decision. However, Comcast had a very clear policy for mitigating this problem: "We stick to capabilities where our teams' needs are well understood and where there are multiple mature solutions available; it is much more likely we can find a 'one size fits most' solution in that setting and expect that to be a reasonable solution for several years."

When establishing an architecture guild, it's essential to understand what will work best for your unique organization and avoid unquestioningly adopting practices that worked elsewhere but may not be a good fit for you. For Comcast, distributed ways of working had been broadly adopted throughout the technology organization, so this was core to how their architecture guild operated: "We are a distributed technical organization, with both remote staff as well as geographically dispersed office locations, we decided to emphasize an asynchronous, written approach to work in the Guild to ensure everyone has an equal chance to participate. The core construct is a dedicated '#architecture' channel in our chat tool and an associated email distribution list."

Within the architecture guild, working groups are formed to address certain topics, like source control. Each working group has a charter that clearly outlines what is inside and outside the group's scope. Each working group has a dedicated Slack channel and two to three cochairs. Comcast's advice for identifying suitable cochairs needs little clarification: "Experience has shown that good facilitation skills are more critical than technical expertise for co-chairs!"

When making recommendations, working groups are expected to create architecture decision records (ADRs) composed of four sections: context, decision, rationale, and consequences. And to ensure groups don't jump too quickly to decisions, there is a four-step process that begins with allowing everyone to bring ideas and identifying the must-haves of the solution. Then, allowing anyone to propose a solution followed by evaluating each one. All these steps are documented in the ADR. To make the final decision, a vote is held where participants choose a score from 1 (best solution ever) to 5 (terrible mistake). Following the vote, any concerns are explored to try and improve the overall score to a 3 (acceptable).

Over time, Comcast noted that their architecture guild continued to gain traction and serve a greater purpose than originally intended. It led to the emergence of an architecture and design community, accelerated decision-making, and crowd-sourcing of working group chapters.

THE ARCHITECTURE ADVICE PROCESS

If you aim to adopt an architecture operating model that improves flow by avoiding dependencies on centralized architecture teams, one technique to be aware of is the architecture advice process (http://mng.bz/dd4w), which an AMET can help to establish. It's designed to maintain high levels of architectural quality while allowing teams to move at speed without being blocked when making architectural decisions. It can work well for decisions that affect multiple teams yet don't need the full weight of an RFC process of an architecture guild working group.

The architecture advice process allows anyone to make an architectural decision. But it's not a free-for-all where people can decide to design a system however they want to or introduce new technologies on a whim. The person making the decision must first discuss the idea with people affected by the decision and experts in relevant topics. One possible outcome is that the decision should be referred to an architecture guild working group.

Andrew Harmel-Law has been applying the architecture advice process and promoting it through conference talks and written articles. He offers the following advice for getting the most value out of the architecture advice process:

- Use ADRs to capture decisions that were made in addition to the conversations that took place with affected parties and experts.
- Establish principles and an internal technology radar (https://www.thought works.com/en-gb/radar) to guide people when making decisions.
- Remember that an architect's role is to help and facilitate, not to make all of the decisions.
- Hold a weekly hour-long architecture advisory forum (http://mng.bz/rjyy) where active decisions can be reviewed and discussed, and early warnings can be presented of upcoming decisions that may soon need to be made.

NOTE The Domain-Driven Design Europe 2022 opening keynote was an interactive session where the audience got to participate in various formats to explore the topic of the architecture advice process. I was there, and it was a great experience. You can find more information on GitHub, including all attendee responses (http://mng.bz/G9dJ).

15.4 Staffing an AMET

Team members are the most integral part of any AMET. Not only does the team need to have a broad range of expertise and be able to work effectively with all stakeholders, but team members also need a genuinely enabling mindset. Being part of an

AMET is not a fitting role for people who want to spend all their time doing modernization work or making decisions and dishing out tasks for teams to implement. Instead, being part of an AMET requires a strong desire to nurture and upskill others. Team members need to be comfortable leading and doing some of the work, knowing when to step back, being patient, and helping others grow.

15.4.1 *Patience and relationship building*

I've had the chance to work with a handful of technically brilliant people who are also highly skilled coaches and experts at switching between the two modes. One of them is Yogi Valani (https://www.linkedin.com/in/yogiv/). The following story is a short recollection of an experience working with Yogi. It deeply affected me, and I think it's a great example for potential AMET team members to decide if it's the type of role they would relish.

Technically, Yogi is as talented as any person I've worked with. He's got a PhD in math, worked in teams deploying to production multiple times per day, and played a pivotal role in building a data warehouse on GCP (Google Cloud Platform) at JustEat, which Google considered one of the largest in Europe at the time. It's effortless for people like Yogi to dominate or show how smart they are continually, but this wasn't the case at all.

On one project where we were moving a legacy system to the cloud and trying to improve flow, Yogi and I supported a team with no continuous delivery experience. We gathered in Amsterdam for an intensive week of planning the modernization and delivering some of the first pieces. We had a small office exclusively to ourselves; the environment was set up nicely.

After making a plan on the first morning and sketching out some designs on the whiteboard, Yogi suggested that we work as a whole group and use mob programming. As we tried this approach, the team's technical lead did not seem happy and got quite frustrated. The atmosphere was tense, and we weren't making great progress. We went for dinner as a whole team, and Yogi asked the tech lead what his thoughts were about the day's session and mobbing. He didn't want to engage, so Yogi didn't force the matter by trying to discuss it any further.

The following day followed a similar pattern. I clashed with the tech lead a few times. However, I could see that the tech lead wasn't clashing with Yogi, so I stepped back from the group and let them continue without me. During dinner in the evening, Yogi asked the question again. And this time, the tech lead responded. He was still frustrated, but he felt more comfortable sharing his honest opinion: "I don't see the point. I could do all of this work myself in half of the time. Why does it need so many people? Why are we wasting so much time?" Yogi responded calmly, "What we're trying to achieve by mobbing is to get the whole team to the level where they could do all this work by themselves in half the time. We want them to learn from you." At that moment, I could instantly feel everything change. The tech lead had been used to working in environments encouraging individual performance and expertise. At that moment, it clicked that we were trying to build a great team and that he, as the tech lead, was the key to making it work.

What Yogi achieved may appear simple, but it required a lot of skill and patience. Firstly, Yogi spent the first few days of the week building social connections with the tech lead. He never tried to argue or tell him he was wrong when the tech lead would get angry. When the tech lead didn't want to discuss the concerns on the first day, he stepped away, continued building trust, and gently tried to approach the topic again at other times. The tech lead began to trust Yogi because he knew that Yogi was genuine and cared about his opinion. Yogi could have used authority and forced the matter, but he genuinely wanted to make a social connection.

In this example, Yogi connected with a talented engineer and helped him see his work responsibilities from a different perspective. The tech lead was already technically brilliant. He could learn AWS concepts in minutes, but his approach was very individualistic due to the environments he had worked in throughout his career. The organization was trying to create a more collaborative approach, enabling faster flow. Yogi helped the tech lead to understand why this was important and how the tech lead could have a far more significant effect by coaching and upskilling those who worked with him, even if that meant individual productivity was sometimes lower.

Yogi explained to me that one of the turning points in his career was when he read the book *Non-violent Communication* by Marshall Rosenberg. "I realized that the words I used when interacting with people weren't conducive to creating effective relationships. After reading *Non-violent Communication*, I consciously tried to use words and phrases that couldn't be interpreted as aggressive and were more open and amicable. But I do also care about people and want to build good relationships."

One final point I would like to add about this example is that change doesn't always happen in a few days. Sometimes, it can take months of patience and respect and building trust with people to make those big breakthroughs. AMETs need to live and breathe this mentality, not just act nice when they want something.

15.4.2 Should an AMET be full time?

How important is modernization in your organization, and to what extent do you face the challenges outlined in table 15.1? No rule states that AMET team members have to be fully committed to the team. Still, if modernization is of utmost importance and the six recurring challenges pose a major risk, the sensible solution is for AMET team members to be 100% dedicated. Whenever I see people expected to do modernization-enabling work as a side project around their other responsibilities, they spend most of their time being sucked back into their other work, and modernization suffers.

The true picture is much more nuanced. By definition, an AMET supports other teams, so even when team members work full time for an AMET, they will still be helping other teams address challenges and deliver modernization. And not every team member needs to be 100% part of the AMET. Some people may be brought in and out of the AMET as needs change over time.

At a minimum, I would suggest a core group of at least two people who are 100% dedicated to the AMET. Everything they work in is connected to the AMET's purpose. In addition, there should be periodic points where all people involved with the AMET get together. For example, an AMET planning session every two weeks and a monthly AMET retrospective.

15.4.3 Bringing in external help

The topic of external consultants is always a tricky balancing act and sometimes controversial. I've been involved in projects where big chunks of modernization work are almost entirely outsourced to external consultancies. This approach results in numerous problems, but most importantly, it doesn't lead to long-lasting, durable change within the organization. I've also been involved in initiatives where the people within an organization don't have the skills and experience to carry out a fundamental rethink of architecture and practices, which also has numerous problems.

An AMET is one scenario where studiously bringing in outside help can pay dividends. The key aspect to focus on is long-lasting, durable change. Will your company be able to sustain your architectural capabilities when the external people have left? And will you be able to part ways with external consultants, or will you always depend on them? When a CTO wanted help kicking off a modernization initiative, I accepted the opportunity to lead a small tribe. But from day one, I worked closely with an existing tech lead who would be responsible when I walked away in 6 to 12 months. And it was evident in communications, so everybody understood the arrangement.

Finding external help willing to play this type of role can be tricky. Some consultancies have a firm sales culture. They are looking for ways to increase their business with you and get more people involved, not step away in six months because they've made themselves redundant. However, I have worked for consultancies where this isn't the case. When working for UK-based consultancy Equal Experts (EE) in 2017 for a client based in the United States, I faced numerous seeming conflicts of interest. But the advice I got from my contacts at EE was always "Do whatever is right for the client."

Choosing a reliable partner

I haven't worked with EE for many years, so I cannot recommend or discourage partnering with them. I've heard positive and negative experiences working with most consultancies (although some tend to be generally more positive than others). I shared this experience because I wanted to add balance to the argument and not appear to have an agenda against consultancies.

Working with consultancies who will act in your best interests is possible. Choosing partners is a very complex topic that requires a lot of care. I recommend starting by looking for consultancies with public content and case studies that align with what you are trying to achieve. I also advise asking them to explain in-depth how they will contribute to long-lasting, durable change.

15.5   Empowering an AMET

One of the natural concerns for an AMET, and enabling teams in general, is being toothless. An AMET is there to help others, but what if those teams don't want to cooperate with the AMET? It's not an uncommon scenario. How you address this will depend on the culture you are trying to foster, the personalities of the individuals involved, and other organizational dynamics like incentives and reporting hierarchies.

Ideally, people naturally respect the AMET team members and want to collaborate with them because they exist to facilitate solving a recognized challenge. It doesn't mean that the AMET should be experts whom others put on a pedestal and worship; it means the AMET should be regarded as knowledgeable in the topics they are advising on and perceived as being open to constructive feedback and being challenged. Everybody should feel that when they are working with the AMET, all conversations will be in good faith and aimed at identifying the overall optimal solution for the modernization effort. The first step to achieving this follows on from the previous section: staffing an AMET with people who are recognized by their peers as being knowledgeable and open to collaboration, aiming to build trust and relationships.

A second dimension to consider is the positioning of the team. This is about how people perceive the AMET based on how leaders explain the team's role and remit. It's up to you to decide what feels right in your context. As a default, my framing of an AMET is that it is an extension of the CTO (or other senior figure who is leading modernization) acting on the CTO's behalf. An AMET is helping other teams to adopt and implement the principles, patterns, and objectives that have been laid out in the modernization vision, strategy, and roadmap (covered in the next chapter) by the CTO (remember that enabling teams, in general, should always have a clear mission). The AMET members don't have carte blanche to do whatever they want based on a whim; they are guiding modernization based on agreements that have been made. But they do need public backing from senior modernization leaders.

Staffing an AMET with the right people and articulating the team's mission and remit play an important role in preventing the team from becoming toothless and allowing them to provide a greater effect. But what if you do those things and there are still conflicts or the team is struggling to have the desired effect? One key point to remember is that an AMET's responsibility is to maintain the momentum of modernization. They're not just advisors who offer optional advice to teams. If an AMET feels that the actions of a team(s) are negatively affecting modernization, the AMET is responsible for raising awareness and trying to resolve the situation. This means that the team needs to be prepared to deal with conflicts.

Organizational conflict is a deep topic, and it's best to consult expert resources on the subject to identify the approaches that will best work for you. There are multiple aspects to consider, like personal measures and escalation processes. On the Miro board, you can find a list of suggested learning resources curated by my colleagues Mike Rozinsky and Dan Young, who work in this field. It's also likely that the AMET team members themselves can benefit from coaching and enablement in this area.

Two things that have worked for me are openly discussing conflict and keeping stakeholders informed early. The first is about acknowledging there is a problem to the other person(s) and trying to amicably resolve the solution through direct conversation. It took me about 10 years or more in my career to have the maturity to do this (I believe it felt more natural after I began seeing a therapist). The second is about letting key stakeholders (like the CTO and HR) know early that there is some friction and difficulty. The reason I do this is that I don't want to raise awareness of the problem after it has already gotten out of hand.

15.6   Naming an AMET

Remember that architecture modernization enabling team is the pattern's name. You shouldn't name an AMET after the pattern. It's better to give an AMET a name that clearly describes its mission. Here are some examples: *Atlas Monolith Modernization Enabling Team, Logistics Monolith to Microservices Enabling Team, Payments Platform Rearchitecture Enabling Team,* and *Trading Domain System Evolution Enabling Team.*

When a team has a very vague or broad name, people aren't sure what the team does or when they should ask it for help. Equally, team members might take on extra responsibilities because they don't fully understand what is outside their scope. A precise, mission-aligned name helps everybody clearly understand the team's responsibilities and what they aren't.

In general, it's better to focus on the enabling aspect of the team rather than the architecture aspect because you don't want to give the impression that it is a team purely of architects. The team's purpose is to support the architecture's modernization, which requires a whole range of skills.

15.7   An AMET is not always necessary

One final point to add before the end of this chapter is that an AMET is not always necessary. This chapter outlines one possible approach for addressing the six challenges outlined at the start of the chapter, but it is not mandatory. For instance, if you already have a high level of architectural capability within the organization, and teams already have a great working relationship, the teams may already be equipped to self-organize and address the necessary modernization challenges. Adding an AMET could even backfire if teams don't feel it is necessary and that they aren't being respected and trusted.

If you're unsure about creating an AMET, refer to table 15.1. Do you see modernization challenges like trouble getting started or maintaining momentum? If so, establishing an AMET or something similar adapted to your unique context is wise.

Summary

- An architecture modernization enabling team (AMET) helps to kickstart modernization, sustain momentum, and enable long-lasting, durable change.
- As an enabling Team in the Team Topologies sense, an AMET should not do the work or make all the decisions but instead help other teams to achieve their goals and introduce sustainable practices—effectively, an AMET is scaffolding.

- AMETs should identify gaps in knowledge and expertise and upskill teams to be self-sufficient.
- An AMET should gradually wind down as the organization's baseline architectural modernization capabilities increase.
- There should be an established architecture operating model in place by the time the AMET winds down.
- An architecture operating model is your organization's approach to architecture covering things like structure, architecture guilds, roles and responsibilities, and decision-making processes.
- An architecture guild is an approach to establishing architectural principles and making decisions that affect large parts of an organization in a decentralized fashion that does not block team-level fast flow.
- The architecture advice process is an approach to making architecture decisions that allow anyone to make a decision, providing they consult affected people and subject experts.
- The most important part of an AMET is choosing people with the right skills and mindset.
- An AMET needs to be able to work with all stakeholders, from senior leadership to teams implementing changes.
- An AMET needs public backing from senior modernization leaders to ensure the team doesn't become toothless.
- AMET team members should be comfortable leading, facilitating, stepping back, and knowing when to adopt and switch between each mode.
- People don't need to be 100% committed to an AMET, but if you are serious about modernization, it is generally worth considering to ensure modernization doesn't lose focus.
- External experts can help AMETs to upskill, but the team and organization shouldn't become reliant on them.
- Establishing communities of practice is one way that AMETs can help to establish long-lasting, durable change.
- An AMET should be named according to its mission.
- You might not need an AMET; it's not an obligatory pattern. If you can achieve the purposes of an AMET without an AMET, then you don't need one.

Strategy and roadmaps

This chapter covers

- Building a compelling modernization narrative to generate excitement and buy-in
- Structuring a modernization strategy deck
- Starting with a small first slice and delivering value within three to six months
- Ramping up modernization across the organization
- Measuring and adapting continuously

Instead of continuing business as usual—developing new product features and working as you always have—modernization is an investment in a better future by spending time improving the architecture of a system and learning new ways of working. However, the idea of slowing down feature delivery is often perceived as bizarre by those without experience in software development and concepts like technical debt. So how do you persuade them that investing in modernization is in their, and everyone else's, best interests? Equally, how do you get buy-in from employees who might be happy with the current setup and be concerned by potential changes?

When crafted skillfully in a language that speaks to all stakeholders, a compelling modernization strategy is an inspiring vision that sets the scene for a united modernization journey. It helps everybody to see how modernization will benefit them, increasing the chances of securing their buy-in. A good strategy connects modernization initiatives to business outcomes, enabling modernization work to be prioritized and sequenced into a roadmap showing how the inspiring vision will gradually become a reality.

As figure 16.1 shows, modernization strategies and roadmaps need to be evolutionary. As teams work to implement modernization and deliver value, it's important to continuously learn by validating that architecture decisions worked out as expected and the modernization investment is providing sufficient return on investment and progressing at an acceptable pace. Modernization never goes exactly as planned, so be prepared from day one for continuous adaptation.

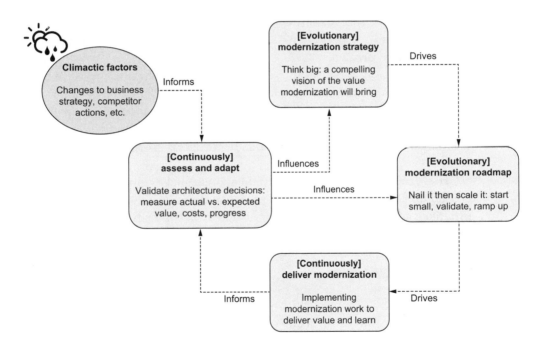

Figure 16.1 An evolutionary approach to modernization strategy and roadmaps

In this chapter, you'll see a *nail it then scale it* approach to modernization strategy and roadmaps. The principle behind this idea is to validate ideas on a small scale before rolling them out to larger parts of an organization. An additional benefit of adopting this approach is that you can start delivering value and learning within just three to six months. Delivering value early and often is a great way to sustain excitement and buy-in and secure ongoing investment. Modernization should not be a big multiyear project where a completely new system is delivered as one big bang at the end—a recipe for disaster.

16.1   *Think big: Building a compelling vision*

Many modernization journeys never make it past the first hurdle—getting started. Often, the cause is the lack of a compelling narrative. I see companies falling at this hurdle when modernization has a very technology-centric narrative. Engineering people are constantly using phrases like technical debt, refactoring, migrating to the cloud, and similar vocabulary, which usually doesn't inspire people outside of engineering to see the value of modernization.

A compelling narrative needs to inspire all stakeholders, including people in engineering. Some engineers and architects get used to working a certain way for years or decades. They built the current systems, know intricately how they work, and are very comfortable with the established development processes. Why should they step outside their comfort zone, take risks, and put their effort into something that replaces the systems they created?

Modernization initiatives that do get past the first hurdle can still falter and run out of steam before realizing even a fraction of their potential because it feels modernization is not delivering a sufficient return on investment. A compelling narrative can prevent this problem by bringing people along on the journey, helping them see the bigger picture, and accentuating the progress toward improved business outcomes.

There are a number of key ingredients that make up the recipe for an inspiring and compelling modernization vision. Some things are more quantifiable and objective, like business objectives, industry trends, and other types of data. But a compelling narrative isn't just numbers and facts; it also connects with people on an emotional level. It should include content like personal quotes, employee feedback, and the company's story.

16.1.1   *Crafting a modernization strategy deck*

There are many ways to structure a strategy deck and tell the story of your modernization journey. However, four key components are usually woven into the narrative, as shown in figure 16.2. What is the organization as a whole, and what are different parts of the organization ultimately trying to achieve? What challenges are holding it back? How will modernization help to achieve outcomes and deal with the challenges? And in what order and when will modernization work be carried out? I recommend telling the story and structuring a strategy deck in that logical order.

A diverse group of people should be involved in defining the strategy to create a compelling narrative that appeals to all stakeholders and genuinely addresses their needs and concerns. Feedback from a diverse group should be sought on a regular basis to ensure the strategy evolves with their needs.

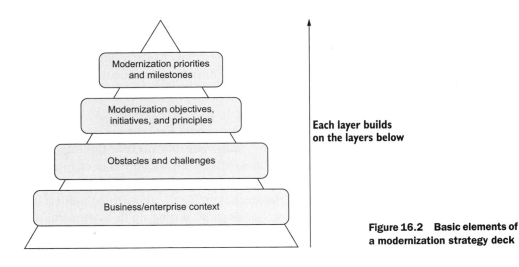

**Each layer builds
on the layers below**

**Figure 16.2   Basic elements of
a modernization strategy deck**

BUSINESS CONTEXT

Crafting a modernization vision begins by ascertaining the most important business objectives (covered in chapter 3), like north stars for products and portfolios. How does the business plan to sustain and grow its market share? To uncover these aspirations, you need to go out and start talking to people from across the organization (covered in chapter 4). Techniques like Wardley Mapping are a great tool for visualizing and exploring the strategy (covered in chapter 5). Wardley Mapping can help paint the picture of where the industry is heading and the opportunities that will arise. I recommend incorporating the visualizations into your deck.

As you gather this information, you can start to tell the business side of the modernization story. This would generally be the first section in a modernization strategy slide deck as part of a section called *business context, enterprise context,* or similar. This section aims to demonstrate that you have a deep understanding of the business strategy. This is crucial for gaining trust and buy-in from business leaders. You want them to feel like you truly grasp what the business is trying to achieve, and they couldn't have explained it better themselves. Having a strong business focus on the modernization strategy shows technologists the importance of speaking the language of the business when discussing modernization. Here is a list of items that should be included in the section on a strategy deck:

- Major business objectives, opportunities, and growth targets (e.g., revenue and other financial targets, launching into new markets, operational efficiency)
- Product and portfolio north stars and new capabilities that will enable them
- Wardley Maps and other strategy visuals to envision the future of the landscape, including what competitors are doing and other risks and opportunities that may arise
- The story of the company: In contrast to future evolution, how did the company get where it is today? How has the product and customer base changed over the past years/decades? What has worked well? How do customers perceive the brand?

- Personal quotes and survey feedback about goals and objectives (e.g., "I strongly believe that if we are first to market with our new product, we'll be well positioned as market leaders for the next 5 to 10 years" and "80% of the organization indicated that improving our offering in existing markets is a better idea than expanding into new markets")

OBSTACLES AND CHALLENGES

After telling the story of the business and the plan for creating new and better value, you can talk about the obstacles and challenges that prevent the organization from delivering *Better Value Sooner Safer Happier* (BVSSH was covered in chapter 1). A listening and mapping tour is also a great way to uncover obstacles and challenges.

In the following section of the deck, you'll talk about how modernization will address these challenges, so this section is about setting up that conversation. Accordingly, you'll want to focus on obstacles and challenges that modernization can address. For example, a common obstacle is being unable to innovate fast enough. It would be a good obstacle to mention if things like technical debt and organization structure were contributing factors because modernization can address those.

When talking about obstacles and challenges, I find a combination of both informational and emotional justifications to be effective in explaining the problem and what's causing it. For example, Value Stream Maps are a common visualization to show all the steps involved in delivering a new product/feature. This type of visualization makes it easy to accentuate the process's bottlenecks, such as prioritization, code review, or testing. While these visualizations are highly effective at conveying an accurate picture, they can feel a bit abstract. Supporting them with personal quotes can make the problem feel more real, for example, "I don't understand why everything takes so long here, even simple things. I asked for two text boxes to be put on a web page so we can improve SEO and six months later, it still hasn't been done. —Head of Marketing."

Further, you may want to consider showing how your organization stacks up against industry averages and high performers. For example, what is your deployment frequency, and how does it compare to the industry average (https://cloud.google.com/devops/state-of-devops)?

Another type of data to include is analysis from tools like CodeScene (covered in chapter 12). It can visualize things like coupling, complexity trends, and knowledge loss in a system in a format that nonengineers and nonarchitects can grasp. This is powerful because you can connect the dots and build an immensely compelling business case. For example, you can talk about a particular business objective and use the value stream map and employee quotes to show that the current operating model is a massive obstacle to achieving the outcome. You can then use CodeScene visuals to show information like how parts of the legacy code are tightly coupled, which is a major contributor to the bottlenecks in the value stream.

In this section of a strategy deck, it's important to choose words studiously. Many existing employees are likely to have been involved in building the current system and establishing current ways of working. You don't want to alienate them by making them feel like you are blaming them or being overly critical of their work. It's a difficult balancing act, so get feedback before publishing anything to a wider audience.

I've seen skilled leaders find a balance by being honest about the challenges but rationalizing them in a non-blaming fashion. One CTO I worked with explained that the challenges the company was facing were normal for an organization in its position that was transitioning from startup to scale up. Another found examples of old assumptions—that is, the system may have been built well to old requirements that have since changed. We've seen some industry examples of this, like Vinted in chapter 10, who designed core architecture abstractions around the assumption of being active in a single vertical, which no longer held as the company expanded into new verticals. Here is a summary of items to be included in this section:

- List of problems along with negative effects like metrics (e.g., average onboarding time is one week, but competitors do it in less than one day)
- Visualizations (e.g., value stream maps showing wait times, bottlenecks, etc.)
- IT industry trends (e.g., DORA metrics)
- Story of how the current operating model came to be (e.g., from startup to scale up or lots of M&A over the past few years) and design assumptions that changed (e.g., the system would only support a single market but then had to support multiple)
- Personal quotes pertaining to obstacles and challenges (e.g., "We have to use four different systems and two spreadsheets to process a simple case. This is a nightmare for my team.")
- Employee survey results (e.g., "73% of developers reported technical debt as the #1 reason they can't deliver features faster, while 92% reported that technical debt is increasing.")
- Architecture visualizations (e.g., CodeScene screenshots showing areas of the system with high complexity or knowledge loss) linked to obstacles

Avoiding the perception of copy-paste management

It's well known that when leaders join a new company, they often copy ideas that they have used in previous jobs. This isn't inherently bad, but leaders have a reputation for implementing approaches that have worked before without understanding if they are a good fit for the new organization.

Many people are wary of this. When they see a new leader join the company, and the leader immediately starts pushing new ideas, it can easily be negatively perceived as copy-paste management that will fail. The chances of getting buy-in will be much lower. But by well-articulating the business context and major obstacles, you can show that you have taken the time to understand the organization and are proposing solutions that are a good fit, even if you haven't been at the organization for a long time.

MODERNIZATION OBJECTIVES, INITIATIVES, AND PRINCIPLES

The next step is to build a compelling vision demonstrating how modernization will enable the business to achieve highly desirable outcomes that are impossible or unlikely without investing in modernization. If the previous sections are compelling, it will be easier to convey how modernization will directly contribute to improved business outcomes. However, just because you have made a compelling narrative of the business context and challenges, stakeholders are not guaranteed to buy into your proposed solutions. You still need to make well-reasoned pitches and avoid throwing around too many buzzwords like microservices and artificial intelligence that make it sound like you are using shiny technologies for the sake of it rather than for business reasons.

A good pattern to follow in this section is to start with modernization outcomes that are described in business-friendly language and work step-by-step, gradually getting more technical. For example, imagine the modernization outcome: "Improve time-to-market for new products and features: Currently, we ship every 4 to 10 weeks, an order of magnitude less frequently than our competitors and below industry averages. Our target is for every team to deploy new changes daily within two years, putting us ahead of our competitors and the industry average."

Next, you can describe themes, initiatives, and principles that are connected to the outcome. For example, a theme/principle that addresses the above outcome could be: "Project- to product-centric operating model: By organizing our teams and software around long-term, independent value streams, we will incentivize long-term thinking and sustainable fast flow. Teams will be empowered to make decisions and changes faster, putting us ahead of the competition."

Next, you can talk about specific initiatives connected to this outcome and theme. Where possible, I recommend describing the business architecture before moving into highly technical details. A product taxonomy (covered in chapter 6) is a good example of business architecture. It uses terms like product, portfolio, platform, domain, and value stream, which should be understandable by all stakeholders, allowing you to talk about architecture modernization in a language that everybody can follow to grasp the key ideas. In this example, you could talk about parts of the product taxonomy, like specific value streams that have been identified.

It is important to get into the technical details as well. However, it might not be necessary for all audiences, so you can have different versions of the deck tailored to different audiences. For example, you might want to talk about recommended architecture and migration patterns like the bubble (from chapter 12).

This section is also a good opportunity to show that modernization is more than just improving velocity and optimizing existing processes. You can make a compelling pitch showing how an investment in modernization will lead to direct improvements to the customer experience and create new types of value (covered in chapter 8) through modernized UIs, completely new capabilities, and such. Here is a summary of items that should be included in this section:

- Specific modernization outcomes (e.g., improving time to market, new and improved product capabilities)
- Modernization themes and principles (e.g., moving from project- to product-centric operating model)
- Details of target business architecture (e.g., product taxonomy)

- Specific initiatives (e.g., establishing the first independent value stream, migrating a specific legacy app to modernized tech stack)
- Software architecture diagrams and patterns (e.g., C4 architecture diagrams, recommended migration patterns like the bubble)

MODERNIZATION PRIORITIES AND ROADMAP

A strategy deck doesn't need to contain a super detailed target architecture and five-year roadmap, but I do think it's valuable to convey the top priorities and give some sense of when certain milestones are expected to be achieved. This helps to make the vision feel more tangible, and it helps people to see when they might be involved or when certain initiatives might affect them. I've been in a number of strategy presentations where leaders talk big about ambitious investments that then never transpire. As a result, a lot of people are skeptical of big talk until they see tangible commitments (and signs that progress is being made).

Showing the reasoning behind priorities helps to increase alignment. A portfolio overview can be a good starting point using techniques like Core Domain Charts (covered in chapter 11) that show how technology-centric modernization investments are based on business value. For example, you can emphasize how top modernization priorities enable innovation in business core domains, reduce maintenance costs and complexity in supporting domains, and move to off-the-shelf commodity services in generic domains.

The Modernization Strategy Selector (covered in chapter 12) can be used to articulate on a more granular level how the investment in each architecture subsystem has been carefully determined based on the potential business value and costs of modernization. Other tools that can be used are impact versus effort techniques like Modernization Core Domain Charts and scorecards that show more granular criteria that were used to make prioritization decisions (both techniques are covered later in the chapter). Here is a summary of items that should be included in this section:

- High-level roadmap of major milestones
- List of modernization priorities
- Portfolio view of priorities and investments (e.g., Core Domain Chart)
- Prioritization criteria (e.g., Scorecards, Modernization Strategy Selector, Modernization Core Domain Chart)

Ambitious deadlines are risky but can combat inertia in complex modernization challenges

There's always a risk in setting ambitious deadlines that they won't be reached, leading to concerns that modernization is failing, or people will rush to hit deadlines and make too many compromises. But when used effectively, setting ambitious but achievable date commitments can create a healthy sense of urgency and keep certain important outcomes high on the agenda that might otherwise be de-emphasized.

(continued)

For example, one client migrated to microservices, but they were all still coupled to the legacy monolithic database. Due to the level of effort needed, the database modernization kept getting pushed back, and investment couldn't be secured. If used well, deadlines can act as a countermeasure to inertia for these complex challenges. Put these items on the agenda early to emphasize their importance with a clear business case for modernizing that is compelling to all stakeholders while encouraging teams to continually chip away at these complex problems in the firm belief that eventually, a major goal will be achieved in the future.

16.1.2   *Industry example: Building and evolving a modernization strategy at IgluCruise.com*

Scott Millett has been the CIO at UK-based travel firm Iglu since 2015. I've known him since 2011, when we worked together and coauthored the book *Principles, Patterns, and Practices of Domain-Driven Design* (Wiley) in 2014. Scott has always been a very business-focused strategic thinker, and he's authored a book on this topic: *The Accidental CIO: A Lean and Agile Playbook for IT Leaders* (Wiley). So, I caught up with Scott in March 2023 and asked him to share his insights on his current approach to modernization and strategy at Iglu.

Nick: Could you summarize some of the key ways in which Iglu has modernized its technology and ways of working since you joined the company, and what was driving the need for those changes?

Scott: There were three big changes to our modernization effort. The most visible one is the new organization structure. Teams that were set up for transient projects are now formed around long-lived value streams or business capabilities, such as the booking fulfillment, or customer journey steps, such as the quote and book journey. Teams are also a fusion of technical and nontechnical people. This helps with embedding deep domain knowledge and expertise as well as creating a sense of ownership for the value stream outcome rather than just the technical aspects.

The second was how we solved problems. Historically, there had been a "build it all" approach. This led to a vast bespoke landscape and resulted in the limited development resources being spread thinly and having to focus on areas of the business that were not key to delivering the strategy. So, we began to take a more portfolio-based approach. We identified the generic and supporting capabilities and looked for off-the-shelf systems, managed services, or even outsourced them completely. This meant we could invest focus and effort in areas unique to our industry, aka our core domains. For example, in the CRM space, we had bespoke solutions for both lead management and customer services. 20 years ago, you could argue it made sense to build these; however, because of the evolution of technology and the cost-effectiveness of SaaS solutions, it didn't make commercial sense to keep these in-house. We replaced the bespoke solutions with Zendesk as that suited what we needed; however, the big impact was that I could consolidate the dev teams to focus on the cruise catalog which was unique to our industry and absolutely essential to achieve business success.

The last, and perhaps the biggest, change however was in decision rights. Previously the ops board made all decisions on what to focus on down to project level; however, this became a bottleneck, and there was no feeling of responsibility for the outcome at the team level. Now, we have clear decision rights at each flight level. The ops board is accountable for setting the strategic direction. Product managers at the tactical level are accountable for determining how we deliver against the strategic actions in the form of strategic initiatives. Then, at the operational level, product teams determine how best they can contribute to the strategic initiatives as well as juggling BAU needs. However, even though we have explicit accountability levels, everyone has a sense of responsibility for business success.

Nick: These types of changes aren't easy and can take a while to complete. Have the benefits been worth it?

Scott: That is a hard question to answer, as I don't know where we would be if we hadn't made those changes. However, these are my observations on the impact of our modernization program:

We have a quarterly eNPS survey, and our score is higher than it has ever been. We have quantifiable evidence that teams feel engaged, have clarity on what they are doing, and feel that they are making a difference.

Our attrition rate is very low, even during the height of the pandemic and the start of the "great resignation."

Our market shares are high, and we are hitting our business targets with digital channels, increasing in the revenue mix, which is a direct result of team contribution.

Feedback from my boss and my peers is positive. They understand IT's contribution and are encouraged by the proactive nature of the teams to identify solutions to opportunities and constraints.

Of course, there are also some things that didn't quite go according to plan. We had to make a couple of changes to teams as boundaries were not as well understood as first thought. During the first six months of the pandemic, we moved to a more command and control model of operating due to chaos and uncertainty of the impact of COVID. As we began to understand the new normal and pivot our top-level strategy, we could then give back decision rights to teams.

Nick: How did you start the journey of making such deep changes to the organization? Did you create some form of strategic vision?

Scott: I went back to first principles. In order to start a journey, you need to know where you are headed. I needed a strategy. In its simplest form, an IT strategy is the actions that you will take, in alignment with the rest of the organization, to achieve your business goals. Therefore, to work out the IT strategy, I really had to understand business strategy and the key factors impacting our organization in order to anchor my strategic actions.

I worked with my CEO and peers to explicitly map the choices our enterprise was making on where to play and how to win (Scott's approach to documenting business strategy is shown in figure 16.3). I spoke to my CEO to understand the aspirations of the board and my commercial director to understand the market opportunities. My marketing director helped me to understand our share of the market and market dynamics. I worked with the COO on the challenges and opportunities in sales and fulfillment. I then worked with my CEO on my assumptions to get feedback and clarify the strategic direction of the business. My experience has primarily been in SME businesses, and often there is a lack of explicit business strategy that you may find in larger organizations, so being able to tease the strategic direction is extremely important to anchor any technology actions.

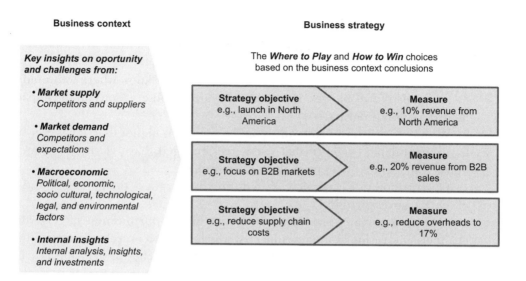

Figure 16.3   Scott Millett's approach to documenting business strategy

With clarity on our strategic objectives, I then looked for the barriers, obstacles, and challenges that stood in the way of the organization achieving them. These barriers were modeled as businesses' capabilities to understand what needed to be improved and what technology could contribute to that improvement. For example, one of the strategic objectives was to launch into new territories. I looked at all barriers and obstacles along the customer journey that would need to be improved, such as localized pricing management, content, rules and regulations, etc. I then consolidated them into groups of capabilities and, along with my peers in other departments, worked out what actions we needed to take (Scott's approach to determining IT strategic actions is shown in figure 16.4).

For example, a key capability improvement to support launching into new territories is localized content. This required the hiring of content creators that could speak the language of the target country, a process to obtain and keep up to date on changing content, and, of course technology to manage and deliver content. IT's strategic action in this instance was to provide a platform to manage and reduce the duplication of content as well as being able to deliver it based on a user's specific context.

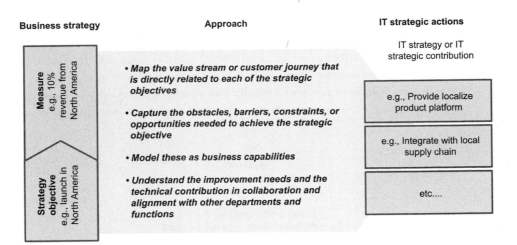

Figure 16.4   Scott Millett's approach to determining IT strategic actions

Nick: So you had a high-level vision of the key business objectives and the capabilities that needed to be developed to support them, how did you get from that vision to your new architecture and organizational design, which empowered teams to make decisions and innovate faster?

Scott: With strategic actions clarified, I worked with my enterprise architect on designing a target technical architecture. For this, we mapped the business capabilities to their evolution state: unique, supporting, or generic. We then looked at how we were currently approaching supporting these capabilities with tech and if that approach was appropriate. From this, we were able to create a target architecture—where we build versus where we buy, and some candidate solutions (Scott's approach to designing target architecture is shown in figure 16.5).

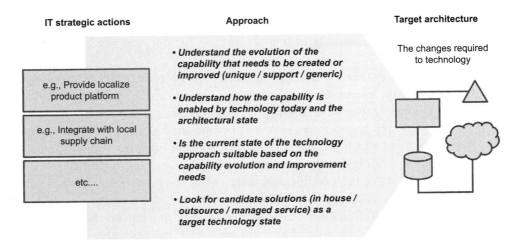

Figure 16.5   Scott Millett's approach to designing a target architecture

Lastly, we developed a target operating model aka how IT would be set up to do the work. So based on the target architecture, strategic objectives, IT strategic actions, and the wider business context, we designed a team structure, set out decision rights, ways of working, who we would partner with, how we would measure performance, the tools and tech we would leverage, and the talent we would need to achieve business success (Scott's approach to designing a target operating model is shown in figure 16.6).

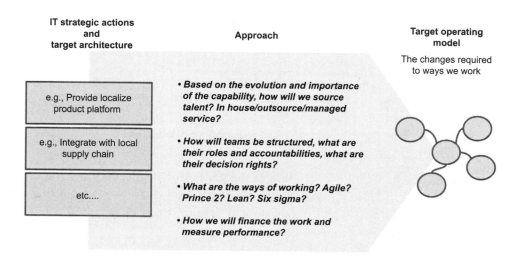

Figure 16.6   Scott Millett's approach to designing a target operating model

The most important thing in all of this was the red line that could be made from the decisions we made and the choices we took all the way to business success. This ensured I was aligned with what was going to help the business be successful. If my conclusions were wrong, it was because my assumptions were incorrect. Hence, any correction needed to be made on business assumptions.

Nick: How were you able to keep the strategy flexible and avoid it becoming a fixed five-year plan?

Scott: Strategy creation is not a once-and-done exercise. It needs to evolve based on changes to your assumptions and changes in the context, both business and technical, that your organization operates in. Your business context is made up of the key factors that can have a material impact on your organization that can cause a change in strategic direction, which in turn will have a knock-on effect to your technical strategy. The technical context represents the constantly changing technical landscape that expands the art of the possible and makes what was once unique into a commodity. Two big factors that impacted our business were:

COVID and its hangover obviously had massive impacts on the travel industry. At the outbreak it caused a need to focus on new capabilities to manage vast returns, reschedules, rebooks, and the complexities of COVID rules and regulations for itineraries that covered multi-countries, as well as highlighting capabilities that were exposed as being vastly immature and ill-prepared for a major incident. Post-COVID, there are still impacts to the strategic direction of the business, some as the result of external compliance and regulatory change.

In terms of the technical context, we started to embrace more forms of technology to increase our speed. Two big ones were low code platforms that enabled us to develop solutions rapidly and RPA solutions that enabled us to quickly solve the mass of manual back-office fulfillment tasks that were a constraint to business growth.

Nick: What kind of things do you do to be aware of changes that will impact your strategy?

Scott: The main thing is to continually scan your contexts to look for factors that may cause a trigger and change in strategic thinking. This is for both the business and technical context. Speak to your CEO and peers about what is happening in the macro- and microenvironments and what these mean to your business so that you can have a heads-up on potential impacts or opportunities for technology. Understand the impacts of what you are doing; are they working? Were your assumptions correct? Do we need to double down or pivot? In addition to the business context, keep abreast of technology advances. Go to expos and conferences, read white papers, consume as much as possible; you don't need to go deep, you need to go wide. You need to be aware of the art of the possible ready for when the wind changes.

16.2 Nail it: Delivering a first slice within three to six months

Getting modernization started as soon as possible by delivering a small first slice is a great way to prove the value of the concept, start building crucial momentum, and validate assumptions like technology choices and organizational readiness. I suggest aiming to identify a first slice that can be delivered within a quarter. But you can't just jump into delivery; you need to identify candidate first slices and time to decide and prepare. This can take anywhere from a couple of weeks to a quarter. You don't need to define a big strategy before starting with a first slice, in fact, delivering a first slice can be used as part of the narrative to make the business case for a larger modernization investment.

Starting with a single first slice is a sensible default. However, it's sometimes okay to have multiple initiatives as part of the first slice. I've seen examples where one initiative focused on something user-facing and involved front-end work running alongside another initiative to explore internal platforms. This made sense because both initiatives provided different types of learning opportunities that informed the long-term vision.

16.2.1 Planning a first slice

Figure 16.7 shows an example of how a detailed roadmap for a first slice could look in a hypothetical scenario where things go fairly smoothly. This isn't intended to be a step-by-step guide to copy and paste.

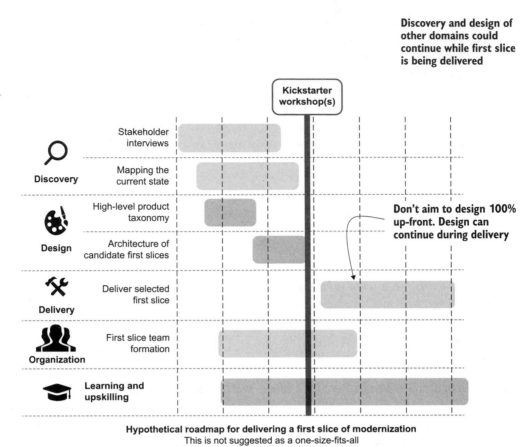

Figure 16.7 **Hypothetical roadmap for delivering a first slice within six months**

In this example, modernization begins with a short listening and mapping tour. This is about listening to diverse stakeholders to understand their goals and challenges and workshops to map out the current system and its problems. As this progresses, the higher levels of the future-state product taxonomy and some of the details can start to be mapped out.

After making progress with the tour and sketching a high-level taxonomy, it's possible to start thinking about a first slice. This is done by identifying candidate options and exploring each option's costs, benefits, and complexity (the next section provides techniques to help with this). And then, a kickstarter workshop can be used to choose the preferred option and start planning to deliver the first slice, which begins, ideally, soon after and is delivered within three months if all goes reasonably well.

At some point, before delivery begins, it's necessary to form the team(s) involved. Ideally, this will start as soon as possible to avoid any delays. One complication is that determining the people involved might not be possible until a candidate has been selected. In such a case, you can either prepare for multiple eventualities or delay the start of delivery.

A similar line of reasoning applies to learning and upskilling. If the first slice team(s) have a chance to learn new technologies and skills before delivery begins, they can hit the ground running. Alternatively, you can add two to four weeks of learning before delivery starts. In any case, some learning and upskilling will happen during delivery, so plenty of time for learning needs to be baked in. This topic is the focus of the next chapter.

16.2.2   Choosing where to start

When deciding where to start, or at any point on the journey when you need to decide on the next step, you'll need some way of assessing the options and picking the most suitable. I'm a big fan of visualizing the opportunity landscape and making the process collaborative using tools like the Modernization Core Domain Chart. When more detailed criteria are necessary, scorecard-style formats are commonly used.

MODERNIZATION CORE DOMAIN CHART

The Modernization Core Domain Chart is a variation of the Core Domain Charts' technique. As figure 16.8 shows, the horizontal axis represents the value of modernizing a particular subdomain, and the vertical axis represents the complexity of modernizing. Value is an overall measure that includes progress toward business outcomes like delivering new product capabilities and learning value, which is about gaining insights that support future modernization work like validating technology choices or patterns.

The bottom right quadrant, *low-hanging fruit*, represents subdomains with the most attractive ROI. The value of modernizing is

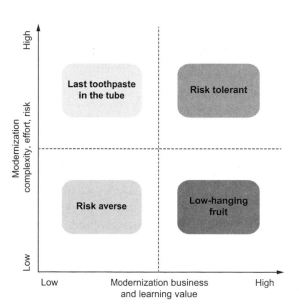

Figure 16.8   The modernization Core Domain Chart

high, while the complexity is low. An example would be a part of a legacy system that can be rewritten from scratch without touching the legacy systems, with new features being added that make a significant contribution to the product's north star.

The top left, *last toothpaste in the tube*, is the opposite scenario. The value of modernizing the subdomain is low, yet the effort is very high—like when you reach the end of a toothpaste tube, you have to roll up the tube and squeeze much harder to get the last small bit out. An example is one million lines of stored procedures full of business logic with no test coverage. Even when modernized, it's part of the system that is unlikely to see any noteworthy changes, so the effort to modernize will have minimal benefit in the long term.

Naturally, these subdomains should be left until later in the journey or not modernized. But there could still be convincing reasons, like being fragile and posing a brand reputation or security risk. (I would consider this a form of value that protects against loss, and accordingly, it wouldn't be in the top left.)

The bottom left and top right are the most common scenarios. The bottom left contains risk-averse choices. Complexity is lower, but equally so is business and learning value. In comparison, the top right is the inverse, representing opportunities where higher levels of risk must be tolerated for potentially greater business and learning value.

An example of risk aversion would be building a small API using the new platform and tech stack. The team gets an opportunity to learn the new stack, but they aren't addressing any complex legacy concerns or adding any noteworthy new functionality to the product. Conversely, a highly risk-tolerant approach might be extracting a core domain from the monolith, which is tightly coupled to everything and has no tests. It's hard to estimate what it will take, and it could break the system in many unexpected ways, but breaking it out will allow differentiating new capabilities to be added to the product.

Choosing between a risk-tolerant and risk-averse approach can be intricate, especially early on. On one side, engineers want to start with something small and low risk. But when the cost appears high, yet little business value appears to be delivered, sometimes it's hard for business leaders to see the point and give the initiative full backing. Sometimes, it is perceived as techies who want to play with shiny toys.

This type of scenario demonstrates the importance of a compelling strategy. It articulates the rationale behind technology-heavy decisions and why they are in the best interests of all stakeholders. The chances of buy-in are far greater.

The Modernization Core Domain Chart isn't only done once at the start of a project. It represents a highly dynamic landscape. Delivering one opportunity may provide insights or lay the foundations that reduce the complexity of others. It's also possible for items to move as they are gradually modernized. Showing dependencies is also useful to highlight where steps must be taken in a certain order.

Feel free to modify the axis labels if either axis is too generic and you want to be more explicit about individual measures like business value, learning outcomes, effort, or risk. Alternatively, use more suitable visualization formats like radar charts.

MODERNIZATION SCORECARDS

Visualizing the portfolio of opportunities can help see the big picture and how options compare. But when making important decisions, it's a good idea to get deeper into the details to better understand the pros and cons of certain options. Scorecards can be used for this purpose.

Creating scorecards involves identifying important criteria and scoring each modernization opportunity against each criterion. It's not just the output that's useful; assessing each opportunity against various criteria and having conversations are highly valuable alone.

Having a standard list of criteria and a scoring process would be ideal. Alas, it's a bit more involved. Your context is highly unique, meaning the most relevant characteristics and the importance of each will be specific to you. Even within the same organization, in different parts of the business, and at different times, the optimal characteristics for prioritizing opportunities will vary. One approach is to organize scorecards into three sections:

- *Business value*—What new value will be created that moves the business forward?
- *Delivery risks*—What are the potential causes and consequences for not delivering within certain timeframes?
- *Discovery/learning value versus complexity*—What insights will emerge that support future modernization, and how complex will it be to achieve each of them?

Figure 16.9 uses the hypothetical scenario of a *workflow automation* subdomain, showing the business value section of the modernization scorecard. The organization wants to understand if this is a good candidate as a first slice for modernization. High-profile customers have been promised new product features pertaining to this subdomain. They must either be built as part of this modernization initiative or in the legacy system. The scorecard will help to decide. A score of 0 represents no value, and a score of 5 represents very high value.

Architecture modernization scorecard		
Architecture area/initiative: **Extract *workflow automation* from monolith**		
Business value		
Delivers tangible business outcomes or moves forward important business and product metrics?	**5**	Defined as to top strategic priority by leadership. Expectation is a big uplift in revenue, lifetime value, new business
Is a source of long-term differentiation?	**4**	A sustainable fast flow of change in this area over the next 3+ years would be a major asset
Provides supporting functionality for other high-priority strategic initiatives?	**2**	May help sell some other services, but nothing major
Business value score (higher is better)	**11/15**	High business value

Figure 16.9 An example business value scorecard section

As Figure 16.9 shows, the business value is high. Leadership is aligned with this being a top organizational priority, and it connects clearly to key outcomes, notably revenue. But is there any benefit to building this in the new modernized world, or would the same value be delivered in the legacy monolith? The key indicator is that it's an essential long-term priority, and the ability to innovate faster would be a big advantage. That's not possible when building it in the legacy.

The initial sign is that this candidate would make a great first slice. However, the next section of the scorecard is the delivery risks section, which paints a different picture. The delivery risk is very high, making this an extremely risky first slice unless a loosening of the business deadline can be negotiated.

As figure 16.10 shows, the delivery risk is very high because it must be delivered within six months. Customers have been promised the new features will be available by then based on how long it would have taken to develop in the legacy. The number of dependencies on other teams is also high because the existing code is tightly coupled to many parts of the big ball of mud legacy monolith in which many other teams work.

Delivery risks		
Tied to key business deadlines?	5	Customers promised delivery within six months based on legacy implementation estimates
Requires a high level of coordination with others outside the team?	5	Highly entangled within the legacy monolith; high coordination needed with many teams
Will be problematic to resolve dependencies and other blockers that arise?	3	We have leadership buy-in, but there could be a lot of politics with other leaders who have their own priorities
Delivery risks rating (lower is better)	**13/15**	Very high delivery risk

Figure 16.10   An example delivery risks scorecard section

Figure 16.11 shows the final section of the scorecard. The organization has identified eleven priority modernization criteria. For example, *modernized APIs* represents the ability to learn about building modern APIs and establish principles and patterns for doing this effectively, which other teams can use for their modernization initiatives. *Integrating with existing data stores* represents learning about building modernized subsystems that integrate with legacy data and establishing patterns.

It might seem intuitive to create an overall score by combining the four individual scores and choosing the option with the best overall score. However, I don't recommend this approach because it puts too much faith in the numbers and doesn't account for certain criteria being of greater significance than others.

Discovery/learning value vs. complexity		
	Discovery/learning value	Potential complexity
Modernized APIs	3	2
Modernized frontend	2	4
Modernized data storage	2	5
Integrating with existing data stores	0	0
Modernized IDP	2	3
Integrating with existing infra	4	5
Modernized auth/identity	0	0
Modernized service-to-service integration	1	3
Untangling existing legacy systems	5	5
Other legacy integration	0	0
Local development experience	3	2
	22/55 (higher is better)	29/55 (lower is better)

Figure 16.11 An example discovery/learning value versus complexity scorecard section

In this example, the consequences of not delivering within six months would be severe. The company's biggest customers would not be happy, which could cause a storm and even derail the entire modernization initiative. Considering this is the first slice of modernization, many unknowns could pop up and cause delays of weeks or months. There is not much margin for error within six months. Therefore, this criterion alone is enough to rule this candidate out unless some of the constraints can be negotiated.

To avoid the inherent challenge of just relying on numbers, I always like to bring the group of decision-makers together and ask them to vote on the final decision. Creating the scorecards is still a crucial part of the process because it ensures people are voting based on diverse information and deep conversations. And the scorecards can be used as part of the activities that lead up to the vote.

Pro-con-fix list

Another useful technique I learned from Gien Verschatse is the pro-con-fix list (http://mng.bz/z0rA). Basically, this involves comparing the pros and cons of each option and identifying fixes to remove the cons.

> **(continued)**
>
> In the workflow automation scorecard example, a fix for the delivery risk might be to develop new workflow automation capabilities in the legacy monolith and the new modernized world. This approach, however, does introduce several challenges in addition to the costs of building the same thing twice.

16.2.3 *When to think about internal developer platforms*

Thinking about an IDP and developer experience needs to happen early in the modernization initiative. Delivering the first slice will depend on certain platform choices like infrastructure providers and preferred technologies. In addition, these choices will be necessary as part of the outcome of the first slice: patterns and insights that other teams can follow to begin their modernization journey, effectively the first steps in creating playbooks and golden paths.

But this doesn't mean that an entire platform needs to be built before modernization can begin—quite the opposite. The goal is to build just enough of the platform to allow the first slice to be delivered. This is a good example of *nail it then scale it*, but do remember to balance this with another key principle: think big, work small. Spend some time drafting a vision of what the platform could look like if all goes well to gain confidence that you are moving somewhat in the right direction.

In the simplest scenario, the first pieces that form the platform (i.e., the *Thinnest Viable Platform* (http://mng.bz/0lZv) can be extracted from the first slice after it has been delivered. I've seen this working extremely well when the platform and software engineers work closely together to deliver the first slice. They spend much of their time working together through daily standup sessions, planning sessions, and mob programming sessions. This is an example of the *discover to establish* pattern mentioned in chapter 11.

However, there is a risk with this style of approach. It assumes there won't be any major platform blockers or surprises that cannot be resolved quickly. In my experience, trying to establish a path to production is a scenario that throws up many risks that can take weeks or months to resolve, especially in large, bureaucratic organizations with a very traditional mindset regarding technology. Therefore, sometimes it is better to build a proof of concept that establishes a path to production before modernization begins.

In any case, one risk-management pattern I recommend for almost every project is the *walking skeleton*. The idea is to deploy a thin version of the application to production as soon as possible. This ensures a clear path to production, meaning there is a much-reduced risk of delays later in the project when trying to go live.

16.2.4 *What if things don't go to plan?*

Achieving an idyllic vision, like the one in figure 16.7, is possible but never guaranteed. In some instances, delivering the first slice can prove disastrous. The most extreme case

I have encountered was a first slice intended to take two months but ended up taking over a year due to roadblocks and crises at every stage. The signs were ominous even on the first day. The teams turned up ready to kick off modernization only to discover that no solution had been approved for hosting code in the cloud (due to misalignment between different streams of work), and due to firewall rules, the teams couldn't access the AWS console. Each setback took weeks to resolve. Even after being resolved, more problems arose, such as connecting cloud-hosted services to on-prem data and crippling fear of green-lighting any production deployments.

Despite the seemingly endless sequence of issues, I firmly believe that delivering the first slice of modernization as soon as possible was the right approach. It flagged the concerns at the earliest opportunity and prevented the problem from spreading to other teams. It's unlikely that more up-front planning would have surfaced these concerns sooner because many of these problems only manifest when trying to deploy working software into production. You could spend months thinking about every possible scenario, or try delivering a small slice and see what happens. We're always trying to find the sweet spot between too much upfront planning and recklessness.

Even though important discoveries were made, there were still extremely serious consequences. Commitments had been made to deliver within certain timeframes, and the delay in modernization by over six months affected the delivery of crucial work promised to senior stakeholders. This put a lot of pressure on everyone involved, and some people unfairly blamed the teams for the delay even though they were blocked.

Despite negative experiences like this, I continue to advocate for delivering the first slice of modernization as soon as possible. But I do encourage some caution. Be careful when tying the first slice of modernization to important business deadlines. Even if the timeframe seems generous, the first slice of modernization can still reveal major complications or many small ones that accumulate to delays that significantly overshoot deadlines.

16.3 Scale it: Ramping up modernization

Wouldn't it be nice to split modernization up into a list of tasks, prioritize them, and then work through them in priority order until all the modernization work is complete a few years later? Unfortunately, scaling up modernization is much more complex than that for many reasons, like dependencies between initiatives, other types of nonmodernization work, and complex environments where business and project strategy could change at any time.

16.3.1 Playbooks

A common way to scale modernization is with playbooks. A playbook lays out a standard pattern or process for a certain type of modernization. For example, a playbook could be created demonstrating how to modernize parts of a legacy on-prem as a Java API running in the cloud according to the organization's conventions. The playbook would be based on a real example that has verified the approach.

In addition to providing repeatable processes based on real examples, playbooks provide other benefits. They can allow modernization to scale up quickly, with many teams using the same playbook rather than needing the help of experts who have a limited capacity.

Playbooks can also reduce the need for centralized planning as teams can access and apply playbooks when they are ready to modernize rather than needing to commit upfront to specific dates. However, there is a downside; without an explicit commitment, modernization may keep getting pushed back in favor of feature delivery. In addition, understanding when certain teams plan to modernize may feed into the prioritization process for establishing playbooks, so playbooks are unlikely to completely eliminate the need for some central planning.

Adding some guard rails, especially at the start, is a sensible idea. For example, a team seeking to modernize via an established playbook needs some form of approval. It could be the AMET or another governance team, as long as they don't become a bottleneck. Over time the guardrails can gradually be removed—for example, as more teams have begun modernizing, peer-to-peer systems are possible where teams need the approval of another team that has applied the playbook. The following are examples of the type of information to include in a modernization playbook:

- General overview
- Criteria for choosing the playbook
- Prerequisites to applying the playbook
- The process or pattern to follow
- Examples of either initiatives that followed the playbook
- Teams responsible for the playbook and other contact details
- General advice and tips

Playbooks are usually accompanied by guidelines that help teams to decide which playbook to choose based on the modernization strategy that has been chosen for the subsystem. For example, different playbooks may be created for lifting and shifting a legacy Java API versus completely modernizing a legacy Java API.

16.3.2 *Seeding and spreading expertise*

One of the biggest constraints on scaling modernization is expertise and experience. Therefore, when delivering early modernization initiatives like the first slice, you may want to bring in people who are expecting to be involved in subsequent steps of modernization so that they can gain experience, allowing them to take the knowledge back to their team so they can hit the ground running when their initiative kicks off. It's always good to keep in mind the knowledge aspect of modernization. Typically, the more knowledge and experience of the modernization patterns spread around the organization, the more modernization can happen in parallel and, ultimately, the faster modernization will progress.

16.3.3 *Sequencing modernization work*

Playbooks can alleviate some of the need for explicitly sequencing modernization work by allowing teams to follow established patterns and processes when they decide modernization is right for them. However, some explicit sequencing of work is always likely to be necessary. The following is advice for dealing with the most common sequencing challenges you will likely face.

PRIORITIZING MODERNIZATION WORK

With a big landscape to modernize and many initiatives that will benefit from modernization, prioritization is a constant and dynamic challenge. It's made more complicated because many projects may already be in progress while some are scheduled to start soon. Should they continue as planned in the old stack or be replanned as part of the modernization effort, which could introduce new risks and affect existing commitments?

Effective prioritization starts with a clear and compelling modernization strategy that outlines the highest value modernization outcomes. You can ask yourself the following as a quick sense check: "Are we working on the modernization initiatives that will contribute most to the highest value modernization outcomes?" This isn't the only consideration, but I find it helps to better focus on what is most important in an ideal scenario.

The ideal scenario is not always possible, but at least you have a starting point to negotiate from. Maybe a quicker win on a lower value initiative would be a better next step, or maybe it's important to pick an initiative that supports a deliverable on the product roadmap. You've already seen two techniques that can help with these decisions: Modernization Core Domain Charts and scorecards. You can use them at any point during modernization.

There is usually value in a centralized resource that keeps track of all initiatives along with the approach and prioritization for that area. For example, some clients use a simple spreadsheet. Each row in the spreadsheet is a subdomain and columns in the details represent the modernization strategy being applied in that subdomain (e.g. lift and shift vs total modernization) along with some sense of prioritization like high, medium, and low or a numeric score. It goes without saying that priorities should be reviewed and reassessed on a regular basis.

IDENTIFYING DEPENDENCIES

If there is one thing to expect when modernizing legacy systems, it is a lot of dependencies. Dependencies can cause many problems from delays to extra work and increased costs. I've seen teams that have begun modernizing and committed to delivering important product features by certain dates only to be blocked for months because their new subsystems are dependent on changes to legacy systems and they had to wait. If not managed well, over the course of a modernization journey the total costs of dependencies could be catastrophic. As a result, sequencing work is never going to be easy, but there's a lot that you can do to minimize the risks and pains.

One of the biggest risks with dependencies is that lower-value initiatives negatively affect higher-value initiatives. A simple starting point for addressing this matter is ensuring that the highest value initiatives aren't losing people or resources to lower-value initiatives or being blocked by them.

Another problem caused by dependencies is work that cannot be started or completed because required foundational components aren't yet in place. Common examples are features related to identity platforms and IDPs, but there are many other possibilities. This is one of the reasons why longer-term planning is necessary. Understanding when certain initiatives need to be delivered by and the dependencies they have provides sufficient time for the required work to be done or the team to make alternative arrangements like tactical solutions.

Identifying dependencies doesn't happen by chance. It's important to be proactive by introducing rituals and habits that increase the chances of dependencies being identified as soon as possible or at least before they become problematic. There are a variety of measures to consider:

- *Collaborative design session*—Like EventStorming and collaborative design, where all teams involved in a piece of work map out the solution together, increasing the chance of identifying dependencies.
- *Architecture gatherings*—Sessions where teams come together and discuss the work their team is doing, including details of their architecture design, which can trigger other teams to raise awareness of hidden dependencies.
- *Boundary-spanning roles*—People who work across multiple teams or move between multiple teams and are able to identify a dependency that may not be obvious to members of each team.
- *Engineering off-sites*—In-person gatherings where large numbers, or all of engineering, come together to talk about their modernization work over the course of multiple days. Dependencies can be uncovered during presentations, conversations, or social interactions around the event.
- *Proof of concepts*—Building small proof of concepts can uncover previously hidden dependencies.
- *Make dependencies explicit on the roadmap*—This will accentuate potential bottlenecks and increase the chance of hidden dependencies being raised.
- *Continuous scanning*—Don't just look for dependencies when prioritizing; encourage everyone to continuously look for hidden dependencies.

LEGACY SYSTEM SCALING BOTTLENECKS

Some dependencies on legacy systems cannot be avoided. Even if you identify them early and are fully aware of them, you still need an effective strategy for managing them. Consider the scenario where three teams want to build new microservices in the cloud. Each of those microservices requires access to data from the legacy, on-prem, COBOL monolith's database. Currently, the data is not accessible, so APIs need to be created, and each team needs a unique API.

The legacy system is owned by a team of COBOL developers, who are the only people permitted to make changes to it. Due to the complexity and fragility of the legacy and the lack of people who understand it, it will take at least six weeks to build, test, and deploy each API. This is a problem because the three teams have all made commitments to deliver within three weeks, and other teams building new features depend on them. They had seen other teams modernizing and thought that it would be straightforward because they were following an established playbook (a good playbook would raise awareness of this bottleneck). At best, only one of them will meet their commitment.

Avoiding the problem through better planning is ideal but not always possible or realistic. How do you deal with a bottleneck like this? When not managed well, it is left to the team responsible for the bottleneck—in this example the COBOL team—to fend for themselves. I've seen teams in this situation trying their best to help everyone, but in an impossible situation, everyone gets very stressed.

Leadership needs to set clear and explicit priorities at the bottleneck. Is modernization work a higher priority, or is ongoing feature work more important? If multiple modernization initiatives are in play, which one takes precedence? Everyone should understand that the bottleneck's roadmap directly reflects business priorities and is endorsed by leadership. The team working on the bottleneck should not be given stress or blame if other teams miss their deadlines. If such a scenario does happen, a post-mortem should occur with the involved parties to look for opportunities to prevent similar problems.

16.3.4 Balancing discovery, design, and delivery

Modernization involves different types of work. Understanding the different types of work helps teams assess how well they spend their time. A basic categorization is three tracks: discovery, design, and delivery. Discovery is about identifying modernization opportunities, design is about designing modernized architecture, and delivery is actually delivering modernization.

As figure 16.12 shows, discovery involves activities like stakeholder interviews and Wardley Mapping to identify business outcomes that architecture can contribute to. Design involves envisioning the future state, like the product taxonomy and the migration steps to get there. And delivery involves activities like building new capabilities and refactoring legacy systems. It's also where value is created and excitement is built as people see real, tangible progress.

All three types of work are valuable according to the context. But how do teams know what is optimal for their context? If delivery is where business and customer value is created, then too much discovery and design means less value is delivered. On the other hand, not enough discovery and design could result in delivering the wrong thing or encountering a lot of blockers that could have been avoided with a bit of upfront thinking, resulting in delivery taking longer and costing more.

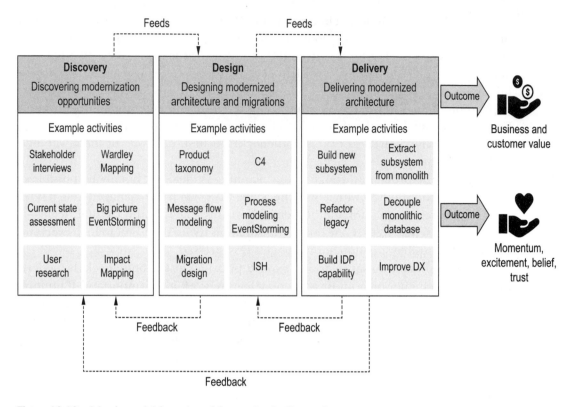

Figure 16.12   A basic model for categorizing modernization work

The sensible approach is for teams to continually reflect on how they are working and adapt according to their observations. Reflecting on the feedback loops is especially important. For example, if delivery does keep hitting avoidable roadblocks or priorities keep changing mid-delivery, are these insights feeding back into the design and discovery approaches, respectively, to avoid similar problems in the future?

Remember that roadmaps are hierarchical. For instance, a high-level roadmap might indicate that a certain initiative is currently being delivered, whereas a more granular roadmap for that same initiative could reveal that certain discovery work—such as EventStorming sessions—is still in progress. The higher-level roadmap emphasizes the overall status of each initiative, while the lower-level roadmap provides a more granular breakdown of activities within the initiative. So, a roadmap showing an initiative being delivered should not imply that only delivery activities are permitted.

REFLECTIVE QUESTIONS

While there is no flowchart for finding the optimal balance of discovery, design, and delivery, there are signs that indicate an imbalance. As an example, here are the types of questions a team can ask themselves periodically to surface meaningful insights:

- Have we delivered anything in the last three months that people outside the team would recognize as progress?
- Are people expressing concern at the lack of value being delivered?
- Are we designing parts of the architecture that won't be delivered for over a year? Could we instead design this later without any disadvantages?
- Are we constantly encountering issues during delivery, requiring us to stop and rethink the approach? Could they have been prevented with a little bit of upfront design?
- Are we changing direction regularly during delivery because new priorities have emerged? Would it have been possible to identify these up front with a bit more discovery?
- Is everything taking far longer than expected and costing significantly more than planned?
- Are people questioning our priorities because what we've delivered isn't the highest value opportunity?
- Are we constantly being blocked during delivery because we don't have sufficient resources or people to deliver the work? Would more discovery and design in advance help us to identify what we need earlier so we can have everything in place when we are ready to start delivery?
- Are we seeing misalignment between teams in terms of their priorities and their architecture choices? Would more discovery and design up front help to keep people moving in the right direction?
- Does our roadmap lack consistency—are we modernizing parts of the system ad-hoc rather than in a logical order?

Questions like these can be turned into regular surveys or used in retrospectives to adapt and improve the balance continually. The final section of this chapter provides some guidance and techniques for an evolutionary approach.

DECISION TIMEBOXES

Timeboxes are great for preventing modernization from getting stuck in analysis and not progressing. There is rarely 100% confidence in what to do next, which can lead to teams doing far too much discovery and design. When this goes on for too long, people start to lose interest and questions begin to be raised about modernization not going anywhere, which becomes an excuse for other work to creep back into teams' backlogs.

With timeboxes, you commit to making a decision by a certain date—for example, "We are going to make a decision about how to proceed after two months of discovery, which ends on July 16. We will never be 100% confident, but two months feels like the right balance of finding the right direction versus spending too long debating and risking a big drop in momentum."

Having a timebox encourages focus. Everybody knows they have limited time to share their feedback and raise concerns, but I advise that you ensure the timebox includes a period of reflection. This means people know the preferred option and have time to properly embrace the idea and raise any final concerns. So, with a two month timebox, you can use the first month to draft an initial proposal (or shortlist of options) and the second month to seek feedback and refine the proposal through a series of 1:1 sessions and group workshops.

16.3.5 *Balancing modernization and other work*

It would be great if teams could focus 100% on modernization work until everything is slick and modern and there is no more legacy. Realistically, that rarely happens, and teams are expected to do other work as well, like fixing bugs and continuing to add new features. This raises the important question of how to balance modernization work with those other types of work.

One of the biggest risks is falling back into familiar patterns and neglecting modernization. Building momentum is key, so at the beginning especially, there needs to be strong incentives and countermeasures. As discussed in the previous chapter, this is one of the primary purposes of an AMET. So, if modernization takes too much of a backseat, forming an AMET is worth considering.

In any case, having a compelling vision and clear commitment is essential. People need to understand the value of modernization, and teams need to feel empowered to say no to work that isn't as valuable as their modernization work. This is one of the important roles a well-crafted strategy can play. However, the message needs to be reinforced daily. Leaders need to continue emphasizing the importance of modernization and prioritizing it over other work.

One approach that I'm skeptical of is people's time being split across multiple teams. For example, a developer is expected to do modernization work with one team for three days a week and work on legacy with another team for two days a week. Maybe it can work, but I've never seen it work.

The common problems I observe are

- The context switching is disruptive for all parties.
- The developer usually gets pulled back into more legacy work, like when there are bugs and production issues.
- Modernization requires a lot of learning, which is hampered by only being with the team part-time and constantly context switching.
- People I've spoken to don't enjoy it.

I've heard the argument that splitting a developer between modernization and legacy work is necessary because they are one of the only people who understand the legacy, and the team needs them. This problem can be mitigated by identifying the problem as soon as possible and handing over as much knowledge as possible. The developer can then join modernization but be called back only in emergencies. Before committing to any decision, it's always vital to listen to the individuals involved and take on their opinions and concerns.

INDUSTRY EXAMPLE: USING THE COST OF CHANGE TO BALANCE LEGACY INVESTMENT AND PLATFORM EVOLUTION AT MOBILE.DE

> **NOTE** This industry example by David Gebhardt (CTO & CPO, mobile.de) and Christoph Springer (head of platform, mobile.de) demonstrates a great example of attaining buy-in for a continuous commitment to addressing legacy by articulating technical concepts in a language that all stakeholders understand—cost of change. This example also provides excellent insights into modernizing and evolving shared-service platforms at scale—in particular, how to evolve platform responsibilities as needs emerge rather than trying to predict everything upfront.

Back in 2017—when mobile.de was already over 20 years old and consisted of more than 400 technical artifacts—a group of engineers and product managers of mobile.de were asked to build a new global automotive platform using their deep experience and knowledge. Consequently, the mobile.de team suddenly became significantly smaller while the platform remained just as big and complex. The team was still expected to deliver on our ambitious product and business objectives, thus the focus was primarily on creating new value.

All of that is a natural development in such a situation but turned out to be unsustainable in the longer term. The first consequences became obvious after only one quarter, and we knew it was time to change our approach on platform health, especially around technical debt.

Our definition of technical debt

We believe that every platform has legacy.

Legacy describes systems and functions with a design contrary to architectural principles.

(Technical) debt is the part of legacy that is causing problems within our platform.

To illustrate the challenge, including for everyone outside of technology, we used the concept of *cost of change*. Cost of change in our case refers to the expenses (resources, time) incurred in implementing or executing a change or modification to a product, process, or system. The explanation we used was simple:

Delivery increases cost of change—Building new products or extending existing products increases complexity and therefore cost of change.

Excellence decreases cost of change—Focusing on removing technical debt, maintaining existing artifacts, and refactoring legacy decreases complexity and therefore cost of change.

With that simple model (see figure 16.13), it became clear for everyone: by focusing only on delivery and having less bandwidth at the same time, cost of change will eventually increase, meaning platform health will deteriorate and speed and ability to deliver will decrease, leading to tangible negative business impact.

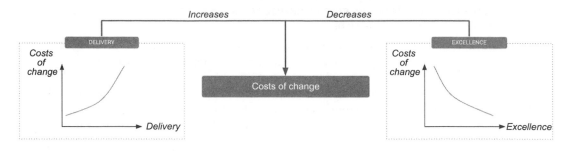

Figure 16.13   Maintaining a low cost of change by balancing delivery and excellence

With the cost of change in mind, we established a timeshare of 25% that teams allocate to functional excellence (removing technical debt, maintenance, and refactoring) and secured full buy-in from management.

To manage and prioritize, we established a process within our OKR framework to handle technical debt. The starting point is a technical debt inventory, where every item on the list is estimated roughly, and a goal is set for the given year for how much percent of the debt we want to repay. What items will be picked to meet that target depends on the priority of the respective items and also how the items are spread across teams and artifacts. We then gave focus and tracked progress through quarterly OKRs and OKR check-ins with the teams to understand progress and to help remove blockers. As a result of this process, we discovered two immediate consequences:

- With an again growing organization and product, we saw a lot of inter-team dependencies and also duplication across teams, affecting their flow, and we received requests for many foundational services that were currently scattered across teams (e.g., API for mobile.de consumer applications, picture services, and foundational handling of ads/listings).
- The concept of defining architectural principles of the platform to adhere to and subsequently tracking the inventory of technical debt and the progress of resolving it required more coordination and guidance and a clear mandate within the technology organization.

We deemed that introducing a coordinated way to establish and own shared services would help us reduce enterprise complexity, allowing teams to focus on their core missions and improve their time-to-market while reducing overall costs for the organization.

We started by bringing together individuals from different parts of the organization who individually took care of these kinds of services in their respective domain, and we transferred the ownership of those artifacts to the newly founded team whose mission was to holistically own the whole platform of shared services. We also decided that the team will be headed by a head of platform, with the clear mandate to drive technical decision-making and guidance (through architecture decision records and guidelines) as well as the coordination of the technical debt process.

At that moment, our Platform Team was born.

In the beginning, the team consisted of our most senior engineers/architects, with a focus on backend engineering. Today, the team also spans across mobile engineering, frontend engineering, and cloud and infrastructure. As part of the expansion, we established ownership and clarity and communicated a clear mandate, empowering them to fulfill their responsibilities.

Part of their responsibility is also to give guidance and consultation to our product teams who are responsible for business domains like *transactions* and *advertising*. Each of these teams has a defined technical lead role, a person who has the technical ownership of the team's applications and artifacts, as well as ensuring functional excellence and keeping it in balance with product and business objectives.

To ensure the platform best serves the needs of our product teams, platform engineers/architects are organized to support specific domains as shown in figure 16.14. They work closely with the technical leads of those domains and are included in crucial planning sessions for bigger or critical features. And further, they support those teams in building features that integrate with platform central services. Platform architects also collaborate with other functions (these are teams or departments that interact with multiple domains like marketing, SRE, and data).

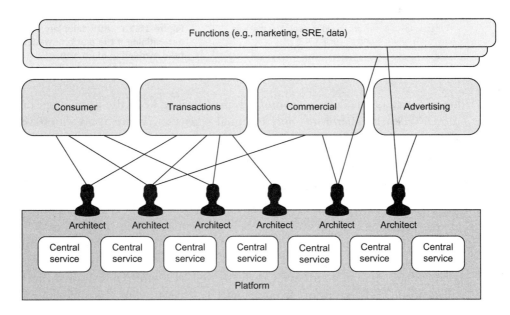

Figure 16.14 Platform architects worked closely with teams that used the platform.

As previously mentioned, the Platform Team owns central capabilities. Those are foundational for many of the services and products we offer. Due to the growth of our platform, processes had to be established on how to identify and review services that might become a central capability. In architectural review sessions, all our technical leads and platform engineers/architects get together to discuss new services, upcoming projects, or extensions of existing services. If one of those services gets identified as a candidate central service, it will be discussed and documented using the ADR format shown in figure 16.15, and the future ownership will be determined.

```
ADR <number>:<title>
<preamble text, artifact/service description>

Decision
<decision taken, reasoning>

Technical details
<artifact specific details>


Discarded alternatives
<Details of alternatives that were discussed>

Ownership
<Team that previously owned the artifact>

Status
<e.g., accepted>

Consequences
<What consequences are tied to the decision that was
taken, any future disadvantages, etc.>
```

Figure 16.15   ADR template for determining if the platform would take ownership of an artifact

One of the main challenges around this process is to keep the artifact-per-headcount ratio in balance. Therefore, only essential services that are used widely within the organization will be owned by the platform team, such as our central API and our ads/listings publishing service.

16.3.6 *Visualizing and communicating the journey*

Visualizing the modernization journey with roadmaps and other artifacts brings many benefits. Firstly, it's a great way to create alignment and bring people along. Everybody across the organization can see the work that is ongoing and planned, helping them to feel more connected, aligned, and prepared. As mentioned, it's also a good way to spot problems like dependencies early, as well as identify in advance the help that teams will need, like support from an AMET, learning and upskilling requirements, and hiring needs.

On the other hand, visualizing roadmaps carries significant risks. It can give a sense of a fixed timeline rather than an evolutionary journey, incentivizing the wrong behaviors. A lot will change in the course of two years or more. If a team commits to delivering by a certain date, any failure to do so may result in the team being negatively judged, even if they did the right thing by stopping and changing course. As a result, teams feel safer following a bad plan rather than taking a risk and changing course or even raising the problem. The roadmap isn't the problem; the culture and the incentives are. As a leader, you'll need to carefully consider what is appropriate for your organization and how you will work on the messaging.

There are different types of visuals to consider when visualizing a modernization journey. High-level, milestone-based roadmaps are good for providing an overview of what has been achieved and when major objectives will be achieved. These are usually organized into periods of months, quarters, or years. Conversely, fine-grained planning roadmaps serve a different purpose. They are used to help coordinate the work across multiple teams working toward shared goals and helping to identify and plan around dependencies.

I don't advocate for a specific roadmap template or format because it will vary according to the context, like the nature and shape of the work and the story you want to tell. In different scenarios, you will present your roadmap differently. You may want to organize swim lanes based on teams, domains, legacy systems, types of activity, or something else.

Another reason to embrace multiple roadmaps is for different architecture scopes (covered in chapter 6). A higher-level roadmap will show only the key details from lower-level roadmaps. For example, a scope 2 roadmap may show the various activities a group of teams will go through to modernize their services. But the equivalent scope 3 roadmap that covers other groups of teams as well might just show when the work each team is doing will be complete (omitting all of the steps that lead up to it). When I was at Salesforce, for example, each product group was in control of its own modernization roadmap and reported key highlights to the level above.

16.4 Continuously assessing and adapting

In a world of constant change, leaders need to be able to adapt their strategies and visions, sometimes incrementally and sometimes dramatically. This final section of the chapter looks at various ways to incorporate continuous change into the DNA of your modernization initiative and architecture operating model.

16.4.1 Metrics

Metrics are an obvious starting point to verify that modernization is progressing at an acceptable level. Slow progress, higher costs, or a mismatch between the value delivered compared to expected are examples of signs that could necessitate a change of course. In general, any of the metrics mentioned in this book may be good to track, including

- High-level business metrics like revenue and growth
- Product and portfolio north stars and north star inputs
- DORA metrics like deployment frequency and system stability
- Quality attributes like performance and scalability

Progress toward many of these metrics, like revenue and deployment frequency, can take a year or longer to become noticeable. People might not see any obvious progress and start to question the value of modernization. So, it's also good to identify relevant metrics that can help to show the progress of the modernization journey, including shorter-term feedback. Modernization metrics will depend on what is important to you, but here are some suggestions to get started:

- Number of subdomains that have been modernized
- Amount of traffic being routed to legacy versus modernized architecture
- Number of subdomains still persisting in the legacy database
- Number of teams that have begun modernization
- Number of tasks completed by users in legacy versus modernized UI

16.4.2 Pulse surveys

Regular surveys are an effective tool in understanding people's experiences and expectations of modernization. They can help to identify when things may have gone off course and detect problems early before they grow out of control. Pulse surveys are typically sent once per month to once per quarter and can cover any aspects of modernization that you feel are necessary.

The following are some example questions to get you started.

- How clear to you is the modernization vision?
- How strongly do you agree with the modernization strategy and roadmap?
- Are you seeing any benefits of modernization?
- Does your team's work feel connected to the bigger picture?
- Is your team spending enough time on modernization work?
- Do you have enough clarity about your team's roadmap?
- Does your team have all the support and resources needed to deliver modernization successfully?
- How well are the new principles being adopted on your team?
- Have you been able to change course when new insights have emerged?
- How much have unexpected dependencies blocked your team?
- Overall, how satisfied are you with your team's modernization progress?
- How useful do you find the modernization playbooks?
- What suggestions do you have for improving our approach to modernization?
- What do you think is working well with our approach to modernization?

16.4.3 Gatherings

Bringing groups of people together is a vital component of a successful modernization journey. It's an opportunity for ideas and insights to spread, and it's an opportunity for people to raise feedback, all of which helps everybody involved to continually assess and adjust the journey they are on.

MODERNIZATION ALL-HANDS SESSIONS

Modernization all-hands sessions are an opportunity to bring together everyone involved to keep people aligned on progress and show what's upcoming. You can run these sessions however you like. A format I've seen work well is to start by summarizing progress toward the big picture strategy, changes to the plan, and what's coming up next.

Then, have a space where teams and individuals share their work. I have found this to be incredibly beneficial at the start of modernization when teams that are not yet involved in modernization can see the real work being done and get excited about their opportunity to be involved in modernization.

I also find it highly beneficial to have an open Q&A session where anybody can post questions that will be answered live by modernization leaders. This can work well using digital tools where people are free to post anonymously, although I have seen problems with this approach where people post intentionally disruptive comments anonymously.

The frequency of modernization all-hands sessions is typically once every one to three months. I've heard some people say that once per month feels too frequent and a bit of a time waste, while on other occasions, quarterly or less seems insufficient, and people feel out of the loop. What's optimal will vary according to your unique context, so seeking out feedback and adapting where necessary is key.

RETROSPECTIVES

Another type of essential gathering is the retrospective. These are important moments where people can step away from their work, reflect on what is working, and discuss opportunities for improvement in a group setting. Everybody should be involved in some type of retrospective. Individual teams should have retrospectives at least once per month and so should modernization leadership teams.

I've also found that project-based retrospectives work well. This is where multiple teams collaborating toward a specific goal have retrospectives. I've seen this lead to huge improvements in collaboration between teams. At one organization, there were two stream-aligned teams and platform teams involved in delivering the first slice of modernization. The stream-aligned teams and platform teams had a rocky relationship, but well-designed and facilitated retrospectives brought them much closer together and improved the relationship immeasurably.

LARGE GROUP SESSIONS

When working with Dan Young and Mike Rozinsky in 2021, I began to see the value of larger group sessions, where 50 or more people attend virtual gatherings. The purpose of these meetings can be anything. One example is when we conducted interviews with many people from across the organization in different roles and then presented back the key themes that emerged and designed activities to allow the groups to explore certain topics. Another example was running workshops around the theme of developer experience to understand how different teams interpreted the concept and the help they needed.

Large group sessions are generally the hardest to design and facilitate, so if you're not an experienced workshop designer and facilitator, it's better to start smaller and safer or bring in an expert who can help. Chapter 3 covered this topic in more detail, along with links to additional resources.

COLLABORATIVE DISCOVERY, DESIGN, AND MODELING

As mentioned throughout the book, collaborative discovery and modeling techniques like EventStorming are excellent techniques for bringing groups together and helping them see the bigger picture. This can lead to all kinds of insights that help teams take their journey in a better direction, like reprioritizing work, improving the design, and discovering that something has already been built by another team. Therefore, encourage periodic EventStorming among related teams. Once or twice a year is not a huge ask and will easily pay for itself.

16.4.4 *Continuous feedback channels*

Conversation channels are an invaluable tool that allow teams to share knowledge and insights, which helps them to identify when they are not on the optimal path and get advice to help change course.

Channels can be created for a whole range of topics, including

- *Ideas and feedback*—This type of channel is for people to share feedback about what is or isn't working and ideas to improve modernization.
- *Success stories and lessons learned*—This type of channel is for teams to share what has worked and what hasn't so that other teams can incorporate the learnings into their own roadmap.
- *General Modernization questions and support*—This type of channel can surface common challenges teams are facing, which may indicate more fundamental, strategic problems.
- *Legacy systems*—This type of channel allows teams to raise requests for changes they require to legacy systems and get advice on what is possible and by when it could be completed.

16.4.5 *Spend time with people doing the work*

One piece of advice I would offer almost every technology leader, regardless of seniority, is to actually spend time with teams doing the work. Showing people that you are interested in and respect their work shows them that you are deeply committed to modernization and want to help them achieve it in the best way possible.

The reason I don't offer this advice to every modernization leader is that it has the potential to cause more harm than good if not carried out with care. At one organization, the CTO, who was based in another country, announced he would be visiting our office to introduce himself to the teams. He introduced himself by saying, "I have a reputation for shouting at people, but don't take it seriously. And if I don't shout at you, the CEO will shout at you louder." Unfortunately, this wasn't intended as a joke in the slightest. The CTO and CEO really were leaders who were renowned for shouting at people.

If you're genuinely interested in seeing how teams work and care about their well-being, then don't hesitate to spend time with them and show your support. If you're worried that your presence may be intimidating, then I recommend working with a coach who can help you work on this aspect of your leadership skills.

16.4.6 *Be prepared to make the difficult decision*

Continually assessing modernizing and looking for the need to pivot may result in uncovering major assumptions underpinning the architecture, strategy, or roadmap that no longer hold, requiring a big change of direction. Changing course may be expensive, or it may seem like the original decision was a mistake, or some other reason may cause fear of making the decision and continuing with the existing plan. It's also easy to be naive and assume a problem doesn't exist or will go away, but it's a risky strategy. I think it's better to be alert to potential problems and create an environment where your colleagues and teams feel encouraged to raise awareness to you.

Remember that you have already crafted a modernization strategy that attained buy-in from a variety of stakeholders. If you built a compelling narrative for the original plan, then there's a good chance you can build a compelling narrative for a difficult, but necessary, change in direction as well.

The sooner you identify the problem, the lesser the effect will be. Even if you aren't sure that a pivot is needed, it can be wise to let key stakeholders know about this risk that has appeared on the radar and that a change may be necessary in the near future. There's a risk it may alarm them unnecessarily if the problem never develops, but it could also build trust and make the problem feel shared.

You can help to address the problem by doing work up front—by making it clear that some assumptions may not hold, that pivots may be necessary from the start of the initiative, and by having an active and transparent risk management approach. Even more fundamentally, I recommend striving to continually build better relationships and trust with all the stakeholders and people involved in modernization. You'll have the greatest chance of dealing with whatever problems arise, including the most difficult ones.

Summary

- A good modernization strategy acts as a compelling vision that helps all stakeholders see the value of modernization and get excited about the journey.
- A good modernization roadmap allows people to see how concrete steps will be taken to achieve the strategy and how they can prepare to play their part.
- Strategies and roadmaps can be dangerous if not done well; they can become too fixed and rigid while lacking a strong purpose that connects initiatives to business outcomes.
- The most important aspect of strategy and roadmaps is to prepare for constant evolution.
- A *nail it then scale it* approach can help to deliver value early, de-risk a project, and lay the foundations for other teams to start modernizing.
- There doesn't need to be a single strategy and roadmap; different parts of the product taxonomy can define their own strategies and roadmap that connect back to the bigger picture.

- There is no perfect structure for a strategy deck, but it's generally a good idea to start with business objectives and product strategy and show modernization initiatives will contribute to them.

- A modernization roadmap doesn't need to be fully defined upfront; in fact, it's good to deliver a first slice within the first three to six months.

- Modernization Core Domain Charts and scorecards can be used to choose the first or next step in a modernization journey.

- Modernization involves different types of work like discovery, design, and delivery; an imbalance can lead to focusing on the wrong problem or encountering many blockers during delivery, which increase rework and costs and slow down modernization.

- Decision timeboxes are an effective tool for allowing for discovery and design without getting stuck and not delivering anything.

- Modernization will likely need to be carried out alongside other work, like new features and bug fixes, so it's important to use concepts like cost of change to avoid going too far in one direction.

- Metrics, pulse surveys, and various forms of gatherings are all crucial components of assessing progress of a modernization journey and identifying a need to evolve the strategy or roadmap.

17

Learning and upskilling

Technological advancements have been integral to human history, constantly transforming our lives and work. From the printing press to the internet, new technologies have disrupted existing systems and created opportunities for growth and progress. However, embracing these new technologies has often required a shift in mindset, as people have had to let go of old ways of thinking and adopt new ways of approaching problems. Following the invention of the printing press by Johannes Gutenberg in the 15th century, scribes and scholars were resistant to the idea of printing, as they were used to copying texts by hand. As the benefits of the printing press became more apparent, the mindset toward printing gradually changed, eventually revolutionizing the spread of information.

Keep this example in mind when thinking about modernization in your company. It is unlikely that everybody in your organization will simply transition overnight from your legacy systems and ways of working to modern technologies, patterns, and practices. They may even be skeptical, which history shows is normal. This means that to truly benefit from modernization, a significant investment in learning and upskilling is crucial financially and time-wise. This is where leadership plays a pivotal role in the success of modernization—creating the conditions where employees can properly get to grips with modern approaches, allowing your organization to fully exploit the potential.

The more ambitious your modernization, and the bigger the delta between the legacy world and the new modern world, the more investment in learning and upskilling will be necessary. It's crucial to consider these costs when planning and budgeting for modernization to avoid problems further down the line.

Learning and upskilling is more than looking at the upcoming modernization work and identifying the skills teams need to learn. For modern, high-performing organizations, learning and upskilling is a continuous process baked into the company's DNA. It ensures the business is always moving forward and adopting modern approaches rather than needing a big explicit modernization program every five years.

Leading organizations employ numerous techniques for learning and upskilling, including communities of practice, bytesize architecture sessions, and mentoring programs. These activities are built into regular working time and treated equally to other types of work. This chapter looks at some of the most common learning and upskilling approaches relevant to architecture modernization initiatives and more generally.

17.1 Planting seeds

Even when you explain the benefits of a new technology or practice perfectly, sometimes your managers or peers won't share your enthusiasm. It's frustrating because you're excited and feel this new concept could bring so much value to your organization if they made an effort to learn and apply it.

Most people find themselves in this position at some point in their careers. It's a question I'm asked often, and it's a question that is often raised at conferences and meetups: "How can I introduce this technique in my organization? How do I convince my boss and my colleagues to learn and adopt this technique?"

The reality is that introducing new approaches that are completely different from the current way of thinking will often be met with resistance. But that's not a reason to give up if you believe that there is a significant amount of potential. Instead, you can embrace the metaphor of planting and nuturing a seed. This metaphor is about being patient and persistent, seizing opportunities that present themselves, and gradually introducing new approaches.

17.1.1 Industry example: Planting the DDD seed at a French HR-tech unicorn

This industry example is an astonishing story of what can be achieved by planting a seed and patiently nurturing it. A small book club was the seed that gradually flourished into significant organizational changes and product development ethos.

NOTE This story is told by Krisztina Hirth, who joined PayFit as a staff architect in September 2022, bringing the necessary skills, energy, and passion to spread the DDD paradigm company-wide, evolving it from an engineering-driven initiative to a driver for product and organizational decisions.

PayFit is Europe's leading cloud-based solution for running payroll for small- and medium-sized companies. The company was founded in 2016, has offices in three European countries, became a French Unicorn in January 2022, and has close to 1,000 employees. The company motto, "To make work a source of fulfillment for everyone," speaks for itself. This is not only the vision of the product, but it is also mirrored by the core values at PayFit: care, passion, humility, and excellence. These values and their importance in the organization give some insights into the mindset of its employees and leaders.

The DDD journey was "officially" started at PayFit in 2021 (more than two years ago) by Damian Bursztyn, engineering director at PayFit, with a book club. The club was originally composed of engineers (mostly individual contributors and a few managers) and met biweekly. They discussed the concepts concerning their daily challenges at PayFit and looked for possibilities to apply what they learned.

Word of the book club started to spread, and the group started to grow partially organically and partially by inviting colleagues so that it became more diverse by having product, design, and domain experts as members. This allowed them to create and improve the common understanding of some domains and their boundaries. They defined and refined domains and terminology in domains like time planning and payments. The first seeds had been planted. Now, it was time to carefully and patiently nurture them.

The benefits of being patient soon became clear. Several features and refactoring initiatives began with collaborative modeling sessions, like EventStorming, as the first step. "It brought a lot of things to the table (including processes we never think about)," and "It was super useful to see the complexity and the different understandings of the team" are the types of comments received after these workshops.

As a side effect of our domain discovery workshops, evolving the understanding of our business domains brought improvement opportunities regarding our organization structure. This wasn't just a theoretical problem; there were improvement opportunities to act on:

- How teams were interacting
- High need for coordination and collaboration
- Slow product development
- Inefficient work

Additionally, PayFit was growing rapidly. The costs of dependencies and slow product development work were equally increasing and becoming untenable. The organization could see this and wanted to give teams more autonomy and empowerment and reduce dependencies. It became clear that a new way was necessary to organize teams:

aligned to the business outcomes and the domain rather than technological layers while leveraging platformization.

But this had to be done carefully. One crucial example was handling payroll data, which involves working with highly sensitive data. While it was time to find a way to empower teams, we also had to ensure a holistic approach to data governance, consistency, and decentralized decision-making.

Senior leadership gave the go-ahead for a series of domain discovery and modeling workshops to map out the company domains and rethink the organizational structure. Damian took the responsibility to get all this organized across the whole organization, and Krisztina became the facilitator of the workshops, both being aware of the potential impact this initiative would have.

One of the first workshops she ran was a deep dive into the company's core domain, *payroll.* As she spoke to different groups, everything seemed coupled to payroll, so this seemed like the essential starting point. The workshop's purpose was to gain alignment on the domain model, like what domain concepts are involved, how they relate, and where people see the boundaries.

Shortly before the first workshop, she started an unusual kind of domain discovery with Jean de Barochez (embedded architect in the payroll team). A *knowledge-crunching* session began with writing instead of stickies or diagrams. The topic was *pay period,* a core term "used by six people for seven different meanings" (a phrase Krisztina uses). The asynchronous exchange started on the documentation platform by asking everyone to add their definition and known usages for the term—a kind of RFC but to collect knowledge instead of suggesting one decision.

After some time, the gaps and misunderstandings became transparent. Having all the needs and interpretations in one place made it easy to realize that people were actually talking about different concepts. *Pay period* is the widely used, customer-focused term but is missing the concept of the payroll lifecycle—the period of time a payroll is referring to. Usually, this is one month, but some countries allow shorter periods too—for example, one week. This need was identified earlier as valuable, but it needed a name and a meaning to be able to implement it. Now, it had a name and a very clear description that could be used as the target vision for the deep-dive workshop.

The name *payroll period* is only slightly different from *pay period* as a name, but it leads to a completely different implementation. We continued to build up a mental model around this name, using the MindMap shown in figure 17.1, and after a short time, we ended up with a domain model ready to be implemented.

During the two-day workshop, a diverse, cross-functional group—including the product manager, design expert, and engineers—stormed, explored, and iterated on the *payroll period* domain model. They ran through the most important use cases to build a deeper shared understanding of the current functionality and proposed future changes. This helped them to explore the optimal architecture.

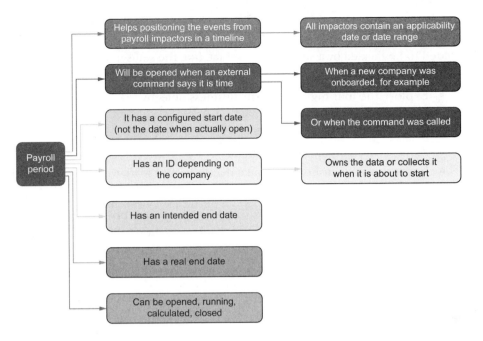

Figure 17.1   Payroll period MindMap

The artifacts from the workshops were

- A bounded context canvas documenting what belongs to *payroll*, what doesn't, its main responsibilities, and how it communicates with others.
- One draft of a canvas describing a new context called *payslips*, which was considered as an internal implementation detail of *payroll* until that moment (DDD started to do its magic: we started to divide and conquer based on business needs, not on technological heuristics).
- Four domain message flow diagrams describing the main use cases.
- The future design of *payroll* and its relationship with the *payroll period*, documented as the *payroll vision* to be shared with everyone impacted (and interested)—an RFC to share it throughout the engineering organization.
- The next step to make it happen—fast experimentation to validate the concept based on real production usage compared to planning and assuming things, which was the default.
- Key challenges, like rolling out a completely new architecture and design by migrating slowly from the old one. We knew the company couldn't afford to sit still while we rewrote the whole system, so had to be realistic.

I want to really emphasize that all of this happened because we focused on clarifying a single domain term. Naming is hard, and it is a key driver for all kinds of decisions, both business and technological.

After this first deep-dive into the heart of the product, a series of big picture discovery workshops were started for all payroll-related domains and other areas that needed to be tackled by a successful product, like the self-serve experience.

The purpose of the workshops was to

- Explore the four highest-priority business objectives
- Identify the relevant domains
- Define a shared language
- Explore team organization options
- Improve team autonomy to make decisions and work with fewer dependencies

I (Krisztina) designed and facilitated each workshop. Participants covered the whole spectrum of employees, from sales to customer support, product, design, and engineering experts, from multiple countries. Each workshop followed a similar structure:

- Describe the current situation (each topic owner added the most important resources to the Miro board before the workshop so that everyone could have read up, if necessary)
- Start a conversation about the daily work, about the problems and the needs, and put all this on the board
- Collect terms and their meanings so that the gaps and the misunderstandings become transparent.
- EventStorming on the most common use cases and identifying domain boundaries (this was the whole second half of each workshop)

Figure 17.2 shows one output from a workshop related to the domain concept of *Declarations* (you can see an interactive version on the book's Miro board: http://mng.bz/ PRO8). These are the different terms, activities, and topics regarding declarations that appear during work in different countries.

One piece of advice I would like to offer anyone interested in running these types of workshops is to focus on knowledge sharing and not just on the outputs. In our workshops, people heard about business needs and processes directly from those involved rather than a proxy. People loved getting this deeper understanding.

Although the agenda was the same for each workshop, the outcomes and next steps were completely different. For example, two topics were merged because we discovered they were both related to addressing the same needs. Another example was when a workshop uncovered three "black holes" (areas we didn't realize existed), which required three additional workshops. The third topic followed the initial plan to collect all the information, agree on the boundaries and pivotal events, and start filling the bounded context canvas. (This canvas will soon become the standard documentation for teams to talk about the domains they handle and start collaborations with other neighboring contexts.) The fourth topic was huge, including the whole self-serve experience and all the related domains. This initiative was already ongoing, so even before the discovery workshops were done, it was possible to create and use

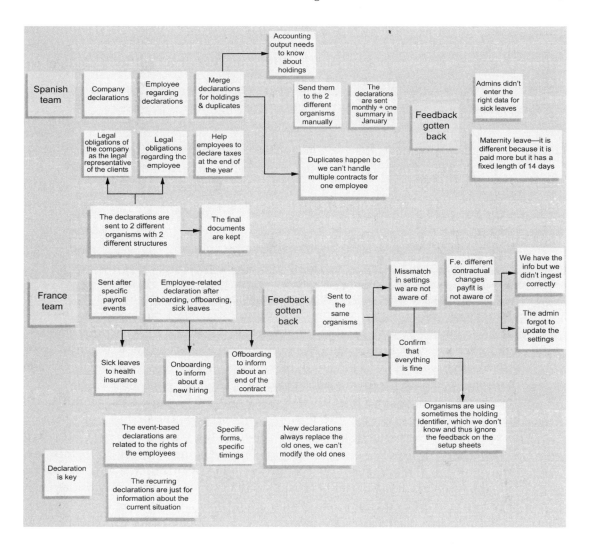

Figure 17.2 Notes taken during big picture domain discovery about declarations

the first message flow diagrams to challenge the boundaries and plan the iterative implementation.

There is so much more that I would love to share about our journey at PayFit, but for now, here are some of the quotes from some of our team:

- "We came to a satisfactory common definition of the declaration domain at the company level, and this let us make the right arbitrations to create a hybrid team with a diverse product/tech skill set, including a whole team of product builders."

- "This is a testimony to the efficient methodology behind DDD, and we are hopeful other significant results will come out of the discussions on other domains" —Ghita Benotmane, product France director after two rounds of big picture discovery workshops, expressed during a team review.

- "I was surprised by the high level of engagement and collaboration at a meeting where the attendees were supposed to take the ownership over more work!" —Francois-Xavier Paradis, product manager of declarations after a hand-over meeting necessary to move functionality to the right domain-owners.

- "Before the 'computes' and payslip generation were the same, but now they are different, and it has an impact on the UX. It's a great example of how DDD helps us to improve and to decouple the scope of teams because now we have two different concepts for what used to be one 'big thing,' and the payroll team has full autonomy to improve the UX related to payslip previews." —Clément Ricateau-Pasquino, engineer and DDD practitioner working hard on stability and reliability improvements.

All this started two years ago by planting a small seed, our DDD book club, and continuing to nurture it.

Nick: This story covers a lot of ground, starting with a developer book club and ending with domain discovery and modernization of almost the whole business involving people from every background. I asked Krisztina what advice she would offer to those who would like to go on a similar journey.

Krisztina: I often hear that DDD is hard and either impossible or not worth attempting. My experience at PayFit proved the opposite. The best tool that we have to gain control over complexity is DDD. Applying the paradigm is hard because it requires us to leave our comfort zones and silos: engineering doing engineering, product people thinking about the product evolution by themselves, and sales caring only about selling. These circles of activity that have traditionally been separated now need to talk to each other, translate what they do, and embrace being challenged.

If PayFit had been a start-up, it would have been much easier to start with DDD because of the small amount of legacy. But it would have also been less valuable because of the small amount of industry experience to draw from. We wouldn't know what the market needs from us. An eight-year-old, very successful product means eight years of experience—a huge asset allowing us to have better domain and boundary definitions.

As a result, the processes, the relationships, and nearly the whole system got redefined in the last couple of years. Opening the gates between the different roles, triumphing over inertia, changing the mindset of everyone involved—this is the hardest part, and this is what a real transformation means. But the key thing to keep in mind is that you don't need to do this all at once. You can start with a small seed like a book club or define a few key domain words and gradually introduce new ideas and ways of thinking at a pace that works for your organization. If you want to learn more about PayFit's journey, check out their blog: https://backstage.payfit.com/.

17.2 Upskilling for upcoming project needs

For many teams, learning and upskilling opportunities will be required as they start modernization. The level needed will vary according to the difference between their current technologies, patterns, and practices and what will be expected of them during modernization. The sooner you identify the upskilling needs of a team, the more time you have to get them up to speed so that modernization can start as smoothly and productively as possible.

However, many new skills take months to learn and can only truly be mastered by applying them to real work. As a result, whenever teams apply something new for the first time, even if they have had some training, patience and built-in opportunities for learning and experimentation are essential.

The first step in upskilling for an upcoming project is identifying the skills needed and working out where the team(s) currently stand concerning those skills. Then, for each upskilling need, a learning plan can be created. When deciding who and how to do this, involving the teams to some degree is important. One extreme is to give the teams full ownership of determining what upskilling they need. In some situations, this won't work well because teams don't know enough about what they don't know. They don't know what level of upskilling is needed. Therefore, they will need help from people with expertise in the new technologies and practices. This is where an AMET, new hire, or external help is required.

Taking a more global perspective for learning and upskilling topics is often healthy. They can be done in bulk, which can be more cost- and time-effective. For example, at one organization, the CTO and modernization leaders had agreed to adopt a serverless-first approach to their journey from on-prem to the cloud. So, they hired AWS serverless expert Yan Cui (https://theburningmonk.com/) to run training cohorts for the entire engineering organization.

The training created a lot of positive energy. People were learning together, even those who weren't yet involved in modernization. It helped them feel part of the journey and reassured them that they would be involved in the future. It also helped some people to grasp what was possible with the new technology. The head of IT, who had been skeptical before the training, began speaking very positively of serverless and cloud after he got to experience first-hand the process of building and deploying a serverless application to a live environment during the training. He was then much more responsive to helping teams address infrastructure and IT problems that arose.

Once learning needs have been identified, various approaches can be leveraged to help teams gain the required skills. I find people prefer different formats and teaching styles, so there is no one-size-fits-all. All of the following are worth considering:

- Books
- Public/private instructor-led training (in person or remote)
- Self-paced video training
- Embedding external experts/coaches within the team

- Building proof of concepts
- Attending relevant meetups and conferences

17.3   *Establishing a continuous learning environment*

Investing in learning and upskilling for upcoming project needs is important but is a long way short of achieving what is possible by investing in continuous learning and upskilling and embedding it into the fabric of the organization. In my experience, organizations that incentivize continuous learning and improvement are more innovative, more effective at building products, and better environments to work in.

In my first role as a junior software engineer, I had two perfect mentors. Learning was just part of the job. They introduced me to ideas like domain-driven design and all of Martin Fowler's work. They bought any book I wanted and bought me licenses to online video training (Tekpub was my preference back then). During working hours, we listened to tech podcasts, we discussed blog posts, and we experimented with new tools.

As .NET developers, we were using all kinds of open source frameworks like Castle Monorail. Back then, it was extremely rare for .NET developers to use anything but official Microsoft frameworks like ASP.NET. We always discussed different patterns for implementing code, and there was always space to explore different implementation approaches. As a result, I loved going to work every day, and the quality of my work was far greater than if I was just expected to deliver tickets.

When I moved to London and began working for 7digital in 2012, I was surrounded by colleagues who loved learning. The CTO, Rob Bowley, strongly incentivized learning and made space during working hours. In particular, everyone had two days per month to use for learning something. There were only two rules: you have to agree on the days with your team lead, and after, you need to write a short blog post sharing what you learned. I used to love my two days of innovation time each month. During 2012, I took every second available to me. I used my time to learn about things like Erlang and Hadoop.

We also had a couple of hours each week for the whole team to come together and discuss a certain topic. I remember at one point we were using the time to watch and discuss conference talks, and at other times we used them for code katas. Sometimes Rob or other leaders would invite experts to come and host sessions.

There would often be a book that people were reading, and it would become a topic in the office. It was exciting and infectious. But often, the books weren't just about programming. Books like *The Goal* and *The Lean Startup* touched on business, process, and culture. And as a result, software developers (including myself) felt encouraged to think about themselves as far more than programmers. We were expected to contribute in any way we wanted, from continuously improving our ways of working to getting more involved with product management and customers.

It's no coincidence that 7digital was a high-performing company where every team was deploying to production daily. It was the company where bugs raised during the daily standup would be resolved in production before lunch and where every developer deployed to production on their first day. Whenever I meet my former 7digital colleagues, we still agree it is one of the benchmarks of a high-performing organization.

In contrast to these experiences, I've worked for companies that had a poor attitude toward learning. At one company, I asked if I could attend a conference. The CTO said the company would pay half if I paid the other half. As a junior developer, I couldn't afford it. Then, the chief architect started openly mocking me because conferences were just places where nerds go to hang out. When I decided to leave shortly after, the CTO was exasperated. He explained to me that he was trying to turn the company around and improve how they build software, and he couldn't figure out why he was struggling to hire and retain good people.

For me, there is no doubt that making continuous learning part of an organization's DNA is one of the most important steps in becoming a high-performing organization. An architecture modernization journey is the perfect opportunity to become a learning organization because it requires a huge amount of learning and can lay foundations that last long after modernization.

17.3.1 *Communities of practice*

Communities of practice (CoPs) are a common and proven approach to enabling continuous learning and upskilling. A CoP is a group of people with similar skills, interests, or concerns. They meet regularly to improve in their relevant area of focus. A CoP can be formed around almost anything, such as a particular tool, practice, challenges an organization is facing, theme like modernization, or a particular aspect of modernization like dealing with legacy.

While CoPs appear to be very popular and seem like a simple idea, they don't always deliver the expected benefits for a variety of reasons, like people becoming disinterested or having insufficient time to organize and attend them. In her book, *Building Successful Communities of Practice* (http://mng.bz/K95O), Emily Webber provides four key pieces of advice for creating the conditions that set up a CoP for success:

- The ability to meet regularly
- The right community leadership
- Creating a "safe to learn" environment
- Getting support from your organization

I highly recommend reading Emily's book if you are new to the idea of communities of practice or have tried them before but didn't get the benefits you were hoping for or ran into problems.

17.3.2 *Regular small learning opportunities*

Incentives are a key part of creating a learning organization. People need to feel that leadership is incentivizing them to spend some of their time learning rather than just judging people based on how hard they appear to be working. Freeing up small chunks of time during working hours for people to come together and learn is a great way to show teams that you are genuinely committed to creating an environment where learning is incentivized.

Regular small learning sessions can be used in different ways. We've already seen some examples previously in the chapter, like book clubs, coding katas, presentations, watching videos together, and inviting external speakers. Another format popularized by Andrea Magnorsky is *Bytesize Architecture Sessions* (http://mng.bz/9QAr).

Bytesize architecture sessions are typically hour-long sessions for a group of people who work on the same or related parts of a system. The primary purpose is to spread knowledge and expertise among team members so that everybody has a deeper knowledge of the system they are working on and a greater collective understanding. The structure of a session can vary, but Andrea proposes the following as a default:

- *Goal*—The group decides on a part of the architecture to focus on.
- *Alone together*—Everyone spends 5 minutes alone drawing the chosen part of the architecture; when the timer ends, everybody reveals their drawing.
- *Consensus*—The group then discusses the various drawings and tries to reach a consensus by creating a single diagram together.
- The final version is stored somewhere.

Even if you don't use the bytesize architecture session format, there's still a lesson to be learned. Look around in your organization. Do you see people experimenting with new formats for sharing ideas and learning new skills? In a learning organization, people constantly seek new ways to learn and share knowledge. The environment encourages and rewards them, and it's a natural part of the job. When was the last time someone in your company invented a new format like this? Could you be doing more as a leader to incentivize this type of behavior?

INDUSTRY EXAMPLE: BYTESIZE ARCHITECTURE SESSIONS FOR INTERTEAM COLLABORATION

I developed the bytesize architecture sessions format because I wanted to help teams better understand the systems on which they were working. I wanted to empower everyone involved in building the system to get more involved in contributing to the architecture in a collaborative fashion.

> **NOTE**   This industry example was authored by Andrea Magnorsky, a software consultant with experience across various industries like TV broadcasting, automotive, games, and finance.

Bytesize sessions help create an environment where learning happens on a regular basis. Most teams are able to dedicate 45 to 60 minutes twice per month, so I built a workshop format around this timebox. After trying it, the idea seemed to work well, so I've continued to use the technique with different teams and in different organizations.

In every case, I have observed that teams improve their ability to

- Think about their systems
- Develop skills in systems modeling
- Learn how to model systems together, which improves team dynamics
- Increasingly have a homogeneous understanding of the system as more sessions happen

- See the value of having a shared mental model
- Have better tools to model potential solutions
- Learn to actively listen

Bytesize architecture sessions can be used for many purposes. I find them to be especially useful for exploring tech debt and getting new members of a team up to speed, but they can be used for more. For example, they are incredibly beneficial for inter-team collaboration.

When I was working with an organization in the broadcasting industry, three teams were involved in major improvements to the video streaming workflow. The three teams had to work in tandem due to dependencies between their work, as shown in figure 17.3. The first team triggered processes in the second team, and the second team kicked off processes in the third team. And the teams needed to be kept up to date on progress of other teams. For example, the first team needed to know when the processes in the third system were completed.

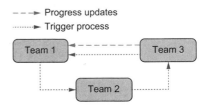

Figure 17.3 Dependencies between the three teams

Everyone involved knew about this level of dependence on each other, and we understood that it was likely we had relied on internals of services that we shouldn't have, but we didn't know where those inefficiencies were.

So, we organized a few bytesize architecture sessions with two programmers from each team and a tech lead who was knowledgeable in the area as a whole. The main objective was to think through what would be a simple and good architecture. To add to that, we had a good shared understanding of the product requirements, especially because the process we were exploring was well-established.

The first session was about modeling the system as it was that day. We used C4 context diagrams to draw what each person knew about these three teams working together. Remember that this part of a bytesize session, alone together, is done individually, where attendees work on their own. It is fair to say there was a lot learned during that session! For example, we learned concrete details about how the process in each of the teams worked, rather than the blurry assumptions each of us made. We also realized that the process that kicked everything off was used in slightly different ways by two different teams, which triggered two main areas of inquiry: Why are we consuming the same information from two different places? And how much extra work are we doing that we probably don't need to do?

Following the session, we captured some questions that needed to be answered for the next session. For example, we needed details about a part of the API of one of the services, and we also had some questions for people in teams that were not represented in the meeting.

The following session was about four weeks later (life happens; I would have preferred two weeks); the goal of the session was to model what the system should look like given the problem we had to address. While we were on the consensus section of the session, we realized that some aspects of the workflow as it is were a lot more complicated than needed to be, a common occurrence in bytesize sessions. For example, we found duplicated logic that was not giving us any wins. We also realized we could improve one of the system's inputs by removing some well-known but forgotten technical debt.

We explored the problem with duplicated logic and realized that the amount of work needed to fix it would be hard to negotiate, but we took notes, hoping to eventually address this problem. Then we proceeded to discuss the details of how the interaction between the three systems should look in an ideal world.

A few days later, one of the teams drafted an ADR for the contract about what would change and circulated it to the other two teams. There were some details that needed ironing out, and we set up an impromptu video call to deal with it. Thirty minutes later, all the details were in place!

At this point, everyone had all the context needed to solve the problem. And importantly, these bytesize sessions had improved relations between the teams, so they were perfectly set up to collaboratively address this interteam challenge in the optimal way.

In this particular example, all of the sessions were remote. I would like to emphasize that I have run bytesize sessions both remotely and in person, and the benefits are great in both. Sessions can also work in a hybrid format. I basically run them as though everyone is remote to ensure the session includes everyone. If you'd like to learn more about bytesize architecture sessions, or if you have any questions, feedback, or want to share some of your ideas, check out the website https://bytesizearchitecturesessions.com/.

17.3.3 *Mentoring*

Mentoring is a powerful tool for creating a continuous learning and upskilling culture. It provides big benefits for the mentee and the mentor. I'm grateful for the mentors I had as a junior and know firsthand how it can accelerate career development. I've also been a mentor and found it to be a rewarding experience that helped me improve my leadership skills. When I talk to friends and colleagues about mentoring, their experiences are very similar.

Mentoring happens naturally within teams composed of a mix of junior and senior engineers. Mentoring can also happen organically when someone reaches out and asks someone else to be their mentor. But in my experience, relying on mentoring to happen organically misses out on a lot of the potential. That's why I advocate for explicitly encouraging and incentivizing mentoring or even establishing an explicit mentoring program.

Mentoring programs can be set up and structured in various ways. In general, there needs to be a place for mentors and mentees to connect, a process for connecting them, and some structure to help them plan and conduct their sessions, especially the first introductory meeting.

It takes practice to become a good mentor, and some senior engineers may be reluctant to give it a try if they have no prior experience. So, a good mentoring program will provide support for first-time mentors by providing useful guidelines and connecting them with experienced mentors.

As with most learning and upskilling initiatives, it's essential that people are incentivized to take up the opportunity. If they are still expected to deliver the same amount of work with mentoring being stacked on top, mentoring will mostly likely be abandoned. In some organizations, mentoring is an explicit responsibility of senior engineers and is something that is discussed during their performance reviews with equal significance to the regular work they have accomplished.

17.3.4 Empowering influencers

Some people are highly respected by their peers. Their words and actions carry a lot of weight. These people are your influencers. They can play a crucial role in helping new concepts and practices become widely adopted in your organization. But they need support to do so.

One way to support influencers is to provide them with training so that they can teach others, aka "train the trainer." This could be in the form of public training courses, private coaching from an external expert, or opportunities to attend conferences relevant to the desired skills.

Then, influencers need to be given sufficient space and time to influence. They can do this in various ways like writing blog posts or documentation, creating videos, organizing internal workshops, and spending time with teams in a coaching role.

Whenever you are planning any modernization work, it's always a good idea to think about how you can involve influencers so that they can spread learning and insights. For example, the first slice of modernization may not involve a team that an influencer works in. Therefore, you may want to invite an influencer to join the team temporarily so that they can gain particular experience and then share it with others.

17.3.5 Blogging and public speaking

One behavior that can have a big impact on creating a culturing of continuous learning is sharing content publicly outside the organization. The most common examples are creating a company tech blog and supporting employees who want to speak at conferences on behalf of the organization.

Sharing content publicly has many positive internal benefits. On a personal level, it's motivating and rewarding for individuals to show their work off to a wider audience and get feedback. This inspires them to want to learn more and publish even better content. Then, these people become role models for other employees who see the value of creating public content. Even the content that is shared publicly can be useful knowledge to other parts of the organization. As a result of sharing content publicly, it's likely that sharing content internally will improve as well.

Sharing content publicly is also a great way to attract talent. It helps prospective employees to learn about what it's like to work in your organization and the type of people that work there. It also shows that the environment is conducive to learning and personal development.

17.3.6 Internal conferences

I'm a big fan of internal tech conferences. I find they create a real sense of excitement and community within an organization. They help to spread knowledge across a company and connect people who share similar interests. They are also another explicit sign that shows the organization cares about learning and upskilling and is willing to commit time and effort during working hours.

I've been invited to present at internal tech conferences, and there is some value in inviting external speakers, but the real magic is employees within an organization presenting to their peers. Topics can range from experiences working on real projects to talking about particular tools, technologies, and techniques, like a real conference. And obviously, this is extra beneficial when on an architecture modernization journey.

Internal tech conferences are usually held once or twice a year. They work well in person, remotely, or hybrid. It's hard to think of a reason why you wouldn't want to hold an internal tech conference. Although there can be a lot of logistics and preparation work involved.

> **NOTE** The book *Internal Tech Conferences* (https://leanpub.com/InternalTech Conferences) by Victoria Morgan-Smith and Matthew Skelton is an excellent starting point for organizations looking to run an internal tech conference. It provides guidance on planning and running an event along with real case studies.

17.4 Industry example: Learning-driven modernization at CloudSuite

Modernization doesn't always need a grand plan or a master strategy. Sometimes, it's better to start small and gradually build the foundations without thinking too far ahead. This was the approach taken by CloudSuite, an SaaS company offering an e-commerce platform where wholesalers and brand manufacturers can manage all their online channels (B2B, B2C, and B2X). In 2021, leadership sought to grow their customer base, with the ambitious goal of establishing themselves as an important player in the mid-market segment of e-commerce platform technology. Achieving this would also require scaling the organization, including the number of engineers, to develop new innovations. But leadership also knew that this wouldn't be easy.

At the time, CloudSuite had around 20 software engineers, effectively a single large team working in a shared monolith that had organically built up from the company's startup days, and a smaller frontend team. As a result, it was already taking too much time to develop new features, and it just wouldn't scale. A big improvement in sustainable velocity was needed to support the company's growth ambitions.

The company's first step toward architecture modernization was hiring Timber Kerkvliet. He joined CloudSuite as a senior software engineer with the remit of identifying where investment in modernization would best support the strategic objectives. It was apparent that the old architecture would need some modernization, but Timber didn't jump in on day one by starting to map out a fully defined future-state architecture using the latest patterns and technologies. Instead, Timber focused on building technical excellence first before making significant architectural changes: "What I've been focusing on from day one is improving day-to-day coding practices. How brilliant your ideas on being agile, continuously delivering in autonomous teams may be, you need technical excellence to get there. I wanted to reach a state where technical practices like test-first, pair programming, and merging often to trunk would be our standard. Then we would be in good shape to attempt more ambitious architecture modernization."

Timber offers some actionable advice for introducing new technical practices: "Simply telling your developers to work that way does not work. It takes time and effort to get there. And that really all starts with creating a learning culture. I experimented with different ways to foster the learning culture. What eventually really worked well for us was the Samman method by Emily Bache. It combines a more standalone short session (learning hour) with mob/ensemble sessions."

CloudSuite's modernization journey is a great example of tailoring a modernization journey to your organization's unique context. Rather than starting with big picture EventStorming and working down into the details, they chose a different path; they made decisions based on what would best motivate the team as a way to build a collaborative environment and increase engagement: "What is kind of atypical to our story is that the biggest changes really started at the tactical level. The strategic aspect was always in mind, with early discussions on subdomains and what is core. However, the strategic discussions and decisions were really driven from the tactical changes. Developers got excited and got started with the tactical (software design and modeling) aspect of DDD first, leading to a need for a ubiquitous language, which led to collaborative modeling, more vertical alignment, and eventually organizing teams around our identified subdomains."

But did a bottom-up approach to identifying domains and subdomains lead to the desired results? "Our bottom-up approach worked well. We identified two core domains, discovery and ordering, that represent phases in the e-commerce user journey" (see figure 17.4).

The discovery phase encompasses the time from when a user arrives on a web page until they develop an intention to purchase. The ordering phase begins with capturing customers' purchase intentions and guides them toward the point of order creation.

Breaking a journey or process into steps is one heuristic for identifying subdomains, but it's not always the correct approach. Timber and his colleagues were careful before committing to these boundaries: "We were confident that these subdomains were optimal because they have a

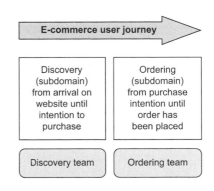

Figure 17.4 CloudSuite's subdomains identified with a bottom-up modernization approach

minimal connection to each other. The coupling is low because the latter part of the journey (ordering) doesn't require in-depth knowledge of how a customer reached that stage."

Timber and his colleagues also encountered a common modernization challenge leading to a crucial learning moment: "In the beginning, CloudSuite mostly thought of the change as a technical one. Fortunately, we quickly came to the conclusion that this was far too narrow. I had created a module in the legacy using TDD and DDD patterns. But the teams weren't comfortable just being handed over the module that was drastically different to other parts of the system. I realized that for new ideas to be accepted, everybody needs to feel comfortable with the direction; they need to be involved in the decisions and feel safe raising their concerns."

One modernization challenge that is hard to avoid is a messy migration phase. CloudSuite wanted to apply the inverse Conway maneuver (organizing teams based on the target architecture), but they couldn't ignore the constraints of the current system: "The inverse Conway maneuver does not work if you cannot change your system. We did the transition in phases. In the first phase, we reorganized our teams, but they were still aligned to the old architecture" (see figure 17.5). They addressed the difficulties by being realistic about the management and compromises needed during the transitional phase: "We expected, and planned for, more intense collaboration between the teams because they were sharing technical artifacts. For instance, our backend API extended across team boundaries. Separating it physically demands considerable effort, and modifications to this API are currently minimal. As a result, our priority is to concentrate on collaboration and modularization within this component first."

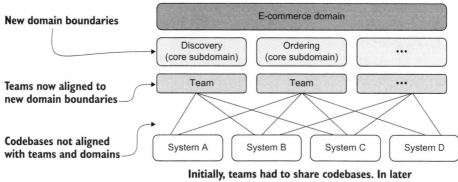

Initially, teams had to share codebases. In later steps, the codebases were aligned to subdomains.

Figure 17.5   In phase 1 of the inverse Conway maneuver, teams were reorganized first.

If there is one thing that can make or break a modernization journey, it is trust—trust from senior leadership to teams doing the work and vice versa. Timber explains: "For us, modernization was about trying lots of new things on a technical and organizational level. We didn't know what was going to be effective so we had to keep trying and experimenting to see what worked. As the architect, I was responsible for facilitating the process, helping and supporting teams from high-level workshops to hands-on coding. We were always looking to improve every aspect of our architecture. This experimental mindset was necessary to make the barrier of starting as low as possible and to reach the point where everyone was on board with the new directions. However, one of the most crucial aspects of this was the support we had from senior leadership. They were encouraging us to experiment and continuously improve and this gave us the confidence to try things like Mob Programming, which have made a huge improvement to how we work. Without the support of leadership, we would never have had the time and space to properly give this a try."

Summary

- Architecture modernization involves a tremendous amount of learning and upskilling about technologies, patterns, and practices.
- Understanding the benefits of modern approaches and learning to exploit their full potential takes time and requires patience and investment.
- Learning and upskilling are often essential for immediate project needs, but it is much more important to make learning and upskilling an ingrained behavior treated with equal importance to what is considered real work.
- Even when you are passionate and can see the value of an approach, your peers and superiors may not yet share your optimism, so it's sometimes necessary to be patient.
- A good analogy for patiently and gradually introducing a new skill approach into your organization is the analogy of planting a seed.
- Starting small, with activities like a book club for a group of enthusiasts, can gradually grow into a big idea that is adopted by the whole organization, so patience and persistence are worthwhile.
- To ensure a modernization project gets off to a good start and stays on track, teams need the opportunity to learn the new tools and techniques they'll be applying.
- Even when teams have had some training, it's not until they have applied them to real projects that they become fully proficient, so any plans should be built around this constraint.
- There are many learning formats that can be used for short-term upskilling, like books, training courses, and hiring coaches; what's best will depend on the preferences of the individuals involved, so they should be consulted first.

- An environment where people continuously learn and upskill leads to better-performing teams and more motivated employees.
- Teams should be incentivized to learn and upskill during working hours.
- Communities of practice, mentoring, blogging and public speaking, and internal tech conferences are all valuable practices that help to learn and upskill an organization during architecture modernization and beyond.

index